I0715307

A NIMBLE ARC

A Nimble Arc

Visual Arts of Africa and Its Diasporas

A series edited by Kellie Jones and Steven Nelson

James Van Der Zee and Photography

Emilie Boone

DUKE UNIVERSITY PRESS

Durham and London

2023

© 2023 DUKE UNIVERSITY PRESS
All rights reserved

Printed in Canada
on acid-free paper ∞

Project Editor: Lisa Lawley
Designed by A. Mattson Gallagher

Typeset in Warnock Pro, Source Sans 3,
and Ogg by Copperline Book Services

COVER ART

James Van Der Zee, *Self Portrait,*
G. G. G. Photo Studio, 2077 Seventh
Avenue, 1937–1943.

4¹⁵⁄₁₆ × 7¼ in. (12.5 × 18.4 cm). © James Van
Der Zee Archive, The Metropolitan Museum
of Art, New York. Source: James Van Der
Zee Archive, The Metropolitan Museum of
Art, New York.

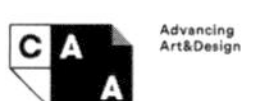

PUBLICATION OF THIS BOOK HAS BEEN
AIDED BY A GRANT FROM THE
WYETH FOUNDATION FOR AMERICAN ART
PUBLICATION FUND OF CAA.

PUBLICATION IS MADE POSSIBLE IN PART
BY A GIFT FROM ELIZABETH WARNOCK
TO THE DEPARTMENT OF ART HISTORY AT
NORTHWESTERN UNIVERSITY.

PUBLICATION OF THIS BOOK IS
SUPPORTED BY DUKE UNIVERSITY PRESS'S
SCHOLARS OF COLOR FIRST BOOK FUND.

Library of Congress Cataloging-in-
Publication Data

Names: Boone, Emilie, author.
Title: A nimble arc : James Van Der
Zee and photography / Emilie Boone.
Other titles: James Van Der Zee and
photography | Visual arts of Africa and
its diasporas.
Description: Durham : Duke
University Press, 2023. | Series: The
visual arts of africa and its diasporas |
Includes bibliographical references
and index.

Identifiers: LCCN 2022056029 (print)
LCCN 2022056030 (ebook)
ISBN 9781478024903 (paperback)
ISBN 9781478020189 (hardcover)
ISBN 9781478027164 (ebook)

Subjects: LCSH: Van Der Zee, James,
1886–1983. | Photography, Artistic. |
Portrait photography. | Harlem
Renaissance. | African American
photographers—United States—
Biography. | Portrait photographers—
United States—Biography. | BISAC:
PHOTOGRAPHY / Individual
Photographers / General | SOCIAL
SCIENCE / Ethnic Studies / American /
African American & Black Studies

Classification: LCC TR140.V37
B667 2023 (print) | LCC TR140.V37
(ebook) | DDC 770.89/96073—dc23/
eng/20230119

LC record available at
https://lccn.loc.gov/2022056029
LC ebook record available at
https://lccn.loc.gov/2022056030

*To Felicie Leonise Lundy
and Dorothy Leona Chesnutt*

Contents

Because of the nature of his studio practice, James Van Der Zee rarely titled his photographs; he did, however, occasionally inscribe titles on negatives. While many Van Der Zee works have commonly used titles (for example, *Beau of the Ball*), these are often descriptive or have been applied posthumously by scholars or by Donna Van Der Zee, the artist's widow. She was most responsible for the stewardship of his legacy and estate before the establishment of the James Van Der Zee Archive at The Metropolitan Museum of Art in 2021. In this book, all titles, including descriptive titles, are italicized.

Acknowledgments

Scholarship always begins with relationships. Individuals at the following institutions have shaped the contributions found within this book. Thanks to Amherst College, Washington University in St. Louis, McGill University, Northwestern University, Williams College, Howard University, the Metropolitan Museum of Art, Emory University, the Archives of American Art, Alice Yard, the Center for Creative Photography, the Schomburg Center for Research in Black Culture, the Studio Museum in Harlem, and the Smithsonian's National Portrait Gallery. The Terra Foundation for American Art Summer Residency in Giverny, France, served as a major turning point in the project and my larger sense of value as an academic. Many thanks to the Center for Photography at Woodstock Artist-in-Residence Fellowship for reminding me that the contemporary art world was not so distant from Van Der Zee. The City University of New York (CUNY) returned me to the place where both my parents were educated. To CUNY New York City College of Technology, thank you for bringing me back to the very same halls my paternal grandmother navigated as a college student later in life and for launching me on my next steps where my maternal grandmother traversed.

This book has benefited greatly from subvention publishing awards from the Photography Network, Professional Staff Congress–City University of New York (PSC–CUNY) Research Award Program, Mellon Emerging

Faculty Leadership Fellowship, Northwestern University Warnock Publication Fund, and the College Art Association Wyeth Foundation for American Art Publication Grant. Gratitude for assistance in acquiring images goes to multiple individuals and institutions, with particular thanks to the Metropolitan Museum of Art and the I. P. Stanback Museum and Planetarium of South Carolina State University.

This project became all the more complete because of the insightful Duke University Press anonymous peer reviewers, along with those who engaged with and offered thoughtful critiques of earlier chapter ideas, sections, and drafts. Many thanks to Paisid Aramphongphan, Anthony Barboza, the departed Camille Billops, Rodger Birt, Elizabeth Block, Alison Boyd, the departed SJ Brooks, Emily Burns, Tina Campt, Zirwat Chowdhury, Peter Cohen, Rhea Combs, Sherman De Jesus, Natanya Duncan, Marta Effinger-Crichlow, Brynn Hatton, Melanee Harvey, Eleanor Hughes, Richard Hunt, George Larkins, Angela Miller, Amy Mooney, John Peffer, Regenia Perry, Brian Piper, Meredith Reiss, the amazing Karan Rinaldo, Ann Shumard, Ellen Tilton-Cantrell, Tashima Thomas, Robin Veder, Bobby Walsh, Sylvia Yount, and colleagues from the New York City Area American Art History Reading Group and CUNY's Faculty Fellowship Publication Program.

Individuals at different stages of this life in art history have made the book possible. Nicola Courtright validated, stoked, and encouraged my research interests during my very first ventures into art history. Rowland Abiodun nurtured my early ambitions to formally study the visual and life-giving contours of the African diaspora. The recently departed Margaret Vendryes was a mentor for close to twenty years; I will always recall her laughter and bold presence. Angela Miller, Alicia Walker, and Elizabeth Childs each gave me welcome in St Louis. In Montreal, Charmaine Nelson offered a front seat to viewing what is possible in this world. My doctoral adviser, Krista Thompson, showed me how to create a new world. Also in Chicago, dissertation committee members Huey Copeland and Hannah Feldman, along with Jesús Escobar, helped shepherd me through to the other side. Ken Wissoker saw the early merits of this book and has continued to serve as a generous editor alongside his dedicated colleagues at Duke University Press, including project editor Lisa Lawley. Special thanks to Charles Waddell Chesnutt for offering a familial model of excellence. Recognition is also due to steadfast supporters Andrea Achi, Barbara Becker, Jutta Brettschneider, Maurice Gattis, Ellen Handy, the departed Marilyn Houlberg, Reginald Jackson, Sheika Luc, Jeff Rosenheim, Donna Van Der

Zee, Vanessa Villaverde, and Deborah Willis, who each contributed to this book and to my life of formalized curiosity.

Writing and thinking with others have been central to this project's advancement. Shireen Lewis, Kia Melchor Quick Hall, Nadine Mattis, and Jacqueline Mattis have all been at the helm of communities of writers who come together, break bread, and move their ideas on paper forward. Spirited individuals to whom I have been accountable for my writing include Marielle Barrow, Elizabeth Benjamin, Javiela Evangelista, Faye Gleisser, and Christina Olivares. Thank you for partnering with me at different stages of the writing process, and, most important, thank you for your sustaining camaraderie.

Utmost gratitude is given to Team Jack and Tobias: Bret Alan Boone, Marie Yolande Boone Lundi, Richard Lundi Boone, and Eze Obinna Nwachukwu. Your invaluable support and encouragement are golden. Onward. The next adventure awaits.

To Pivot Lightly

Adding the Vernacular to Art History's Sight Line

A Return to *Family Portrait*

IN 1926 JAMES AUGUSTUS JOSEPH VAN DER ZEE (1886–1983) took a portrait of enduring consequence (figure I.1). A Black woman, formally dressed, sits in a chair, flanked on one side by a tall man in a suit. On the other side, another woman stands, wearing a plaid dress. A plain backdrop and a side table decorated with flowers center the figures. Based on its composition alone, *Family Portrait* can be described as a handsome image, one that fits neatly within Van Der Zee's larger oeuvre of photographs from his Harlem studio business. Yet, through its reproduction in print, the image has been asked to do more than its sitters, Mattie, Estelle, and David Osterhout, could have ever imagined.

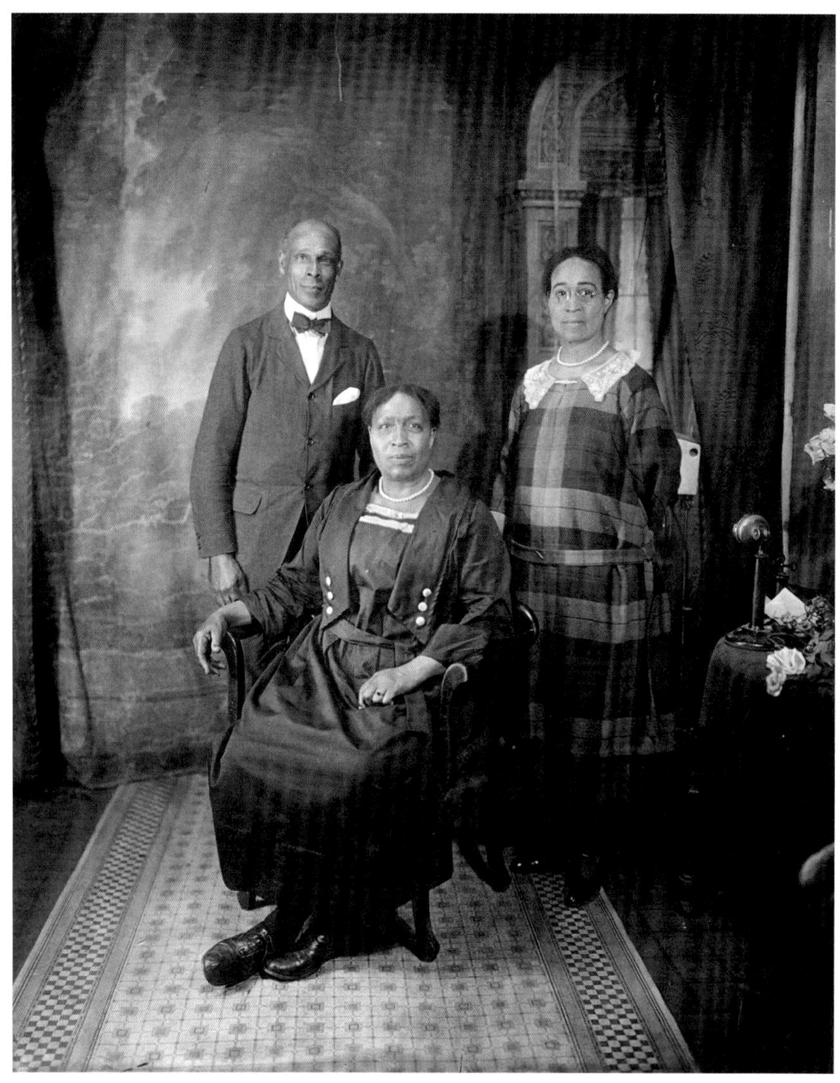

James Van Der Zee, members of the Osterhout family,
Van Der Zee's maternal aunts (possibly Mattie and Estelle)
and uncle, David, often referred to as *Family Portrait*,
1926. This image was included in *Camera Lucida*, Roland
Barthes's consequential book on photography.

10 × 8 in. (25.4 × 20.3 cm). © James Van Der Zee Archive,
The Metropolitan Museum of Art, New York. Source:
The Metropolitan Museum of Art, New York.

For many art historians, *Family Portrait* has made a lasting impression through its inclusion in Roland Barthes's 1981 book *Camera Lucida*.[1] By way of autobiographical reflections and personal reactions, Barthes writes Van Der Zee into a larger meditation that explores what photographs do. In highlighting his own personal biases and fixations, he attends to his concept of the studium and punctum through the Van Der Zee photograph. Numerous scholars have returned to Barthes's discussion of *Family Portrait* to lament and critique his reductive reading of the photograph's Black figures and to offer more generous analyses grounded within art historical methods. Such correctives have kept the portrait in art historians' visual bank of iconic photographs in ways that determine its significance based on, for example, its cultural relevance to the Harlem Renaissance.[2] Yet when neatly slotted within a designated artistic movement, Van Der Zee often becomes pigeonholed within a circumscribed moment and place as opposed to being understood as a Black artist with a broad temporal, material, and spatial reach. *Family Portrait* and other Van Der Zee photographs can be understood through a more comprehensive approach. Given that individual Van Der Zee photographs—like *Family Portrait* or the even more celebrated 1932 *Couple Wearing Raccoon Coats* (figure I.2)—are typically given art historical interpretations centered on the Harlem Renaissance movement and all its defining themes, how might a vernacular turn that examines the larger scope of Van Der Zee's work reinvigorate the very ways that his photographs are understood and valued?

Van Der Zee and his work have repeatedly been framed through the conventional methods of an art history of photography, approaches that persistently structure approaches to thinking about photographs by established photographers. It is common, for example, for scholars to situate an artist within a movement defined by a discrete time period and set of themes, drawing out the exceptional nature of their aesthetic contributions and showing the artist to be exemplary among their peers. While Van Der Zee's engagement with photography spans 1900–1983, such methods frame him as a distinct and important photographer in the approximately fifteen-year Harlem Renaissance era.[3] As a result, his status as the most prominent Black studio photographer within the canon of photography transforms his everyday images from something socially curative and familiar to something exceptional.[4] His photographs are regularly discussed in art history classrooms and frequently appear within academic publications as representative of the Harlem Renaissance era's New Negro subject, even though, remarkably, Van Der Zee had no direct contact with any of the artistic movements of Harlem during his more than fifty years of operating a studio.[5]

Long cared for within the permanent collection of the Metropolitan Museum of Art, the Whitney Museum of American Art, and the Museum of Modern Art (MoMA), among others, Van Der Zee's photographs garner a distinguished status.[6] Yet existing approaches to Van Der Zee's work leave out defining aspects of photography as a medium. The iconic and singular value attached to his photographs has worked to the detriment of scholarship on his broader contributions, obscuring the range of functions carried out by Van Der Zee's photographs: as interlocutors with the work of peer photographers, as reproductions circulated in newspaper features, as modifications of photographs originating in other studios, and as images repurposed as enlarged exhibition photomurals.

Arguably, Van Der Zee's photographs exist at the crossroads of art and vernacular photographic practice. His photographs are Black quotidian images, but his position within scholarship as a known, celebrated Harlem Renaissance photographer abides by art history's framing. Vernacular photographs, like those made by Van Der Zee, include commercial studio portraits, wedding photographs, pet portraits, news and advertising images, travel albums, school portraits, identification photographs, snapshots, and "pop photographica" such as the photo-backed mirror illustrated in figure I.3.[7] Custom-made fans, blotters, thermometers, and "Negro Art Advertising Company" photo calendars were also among the products offered at Van Der Zee's 2077 Seventh Avenue studio location.[8] These are the photographs of the everyday that operate at the level of the quotidian, "the photographs that preoccupy the home and heart but rarely the museum or the academy."[9] While the history of photography most often begins with the biographical details of named photographers, considerations of vernacular photographs commonly start elsewhere. Interpretations depend heavily on the images' historically specific social uses and viewing conventions, their physical and tactile nature, and the networks enabling their circulation. Scholarship that attends to such details of everyday photographs may highlight material that is too mundane or uncomfortably ambiguous or that may even seem to contradict art history's traditional mores.

Yet, at moments, Van Der Zee's engagement with photography requires an approach that pivots among the kinds of questions art history wants to ask and those that vernacular photography elicits. With such movement in mind, this book remaps the broader importance of Van Der Zee's photographs, tracing the arc of his work chronologically to il-

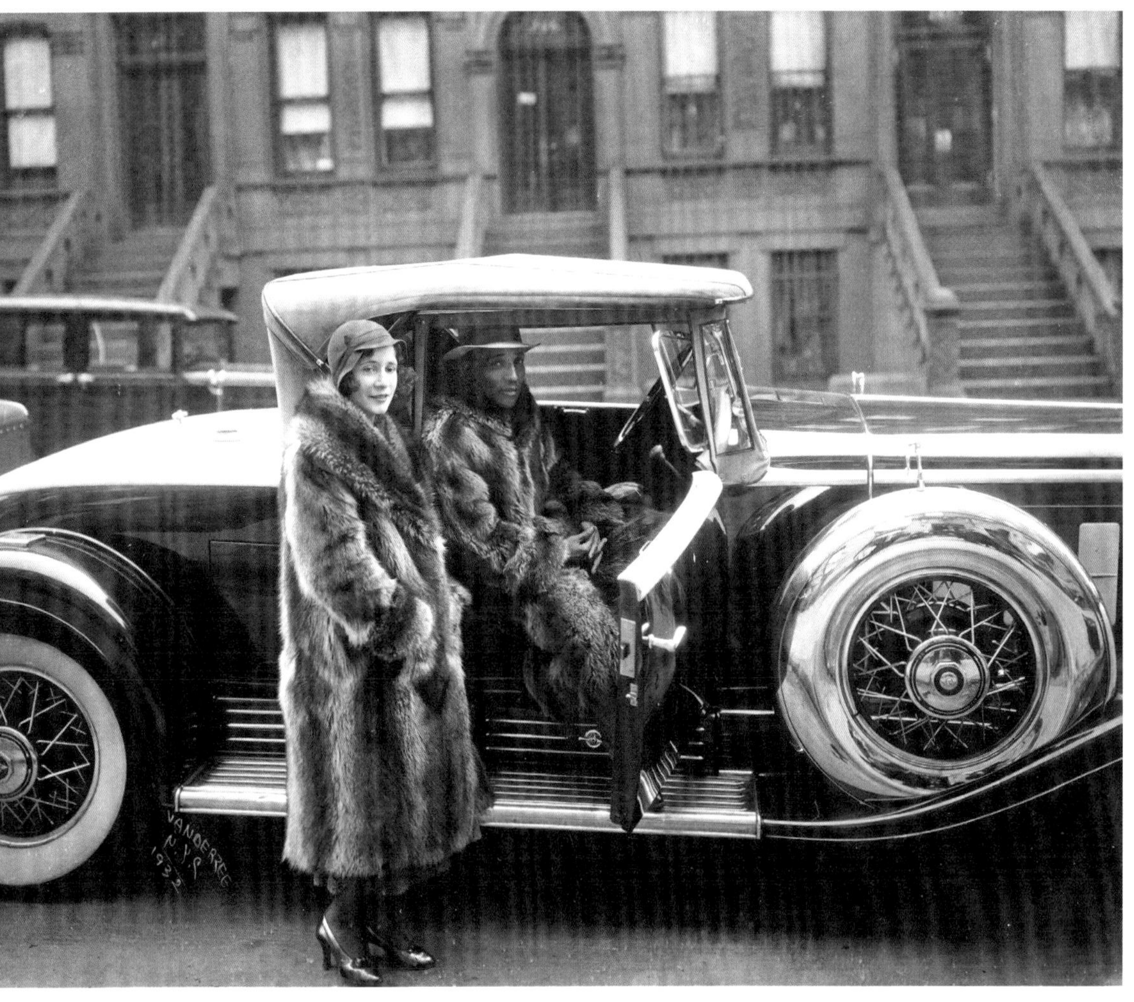

FIGURE I.2

James Van Der Zee, *Couple Wearing Raccoon Coats, Harlem*, 1932. Many scholars have commented on the elegance, confidence, and success that the image suggests, even in the midst of the Great Depression.

7½ × 9⁵⁄₁₆ in. (19 × 23.7 cm). © James Van Der Zee Archive, The Metropolitan Museum of Art, New York. Source: Museum of Modern Art, NewYork.

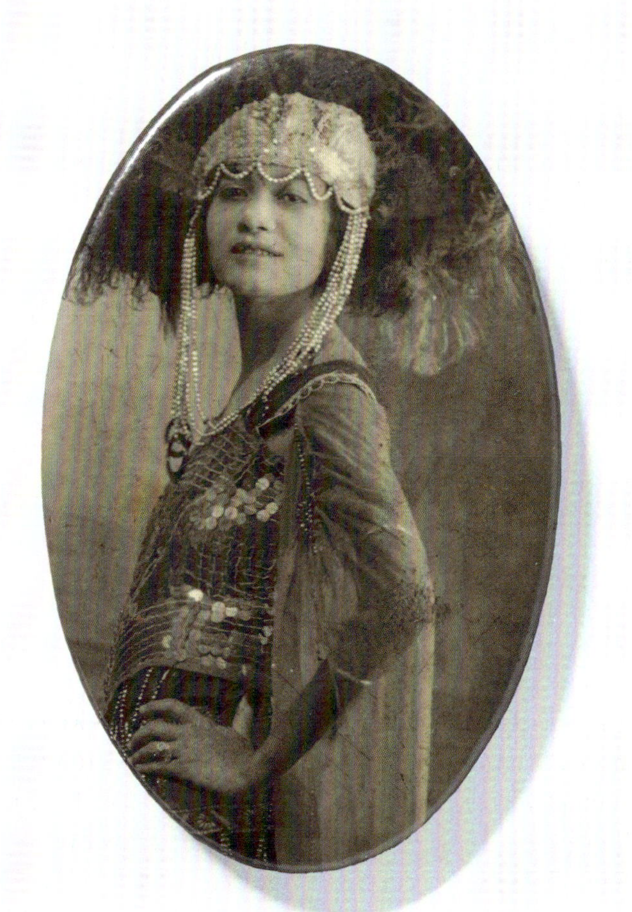

luminate how the multifaceted uses and registers of photography reveal the quotidian as a central idiom of African diasporic photographic practice. These insights are possible only through recognizing Van Der Zee as an artist whose work takes on a new level of complexity and significance when vernacular attributes are considered. This book aims to change the terms of Van Der Zee's participation in art history by engaging in a vernacular turn; thereby, the shape of the art history of photography changes for other photographers too.[10]

Aside from this book's main contribution to the history of photography, this study adds to African diasporic art history by recentering the quotidian. Although current scholarship in this subfield of art history tends to focus on the studio practices of contemporary artists, this book, in part, harks back to a longer arc of African diasporic art history in which the utility of popular objects dominated the historiography.[11] And while scholars in this area privilege the global dimension of the Black experience, this often manifests through international exhibitions, artists who travel abroad, and movements or collectives of creative practitioners. In contrast, this study refocuses the international component of the African diaspora in two of the chapters through the circulation and exchange of quotidian images through unassuming channels including the newspaper, the post office, and the movement and reproduction of photographic images. In addition, this book assumes that the African diaspora is an intrinsic part of Van Der Zee's world of Harlem, since the Black experience there draws from various populations of African descent, not only those born in the United States. Against the assumption that Van Der Zee catered strictly to a middle-class clientele, it takes seriously the photographer's description of his clients as being "the high class, the middle class, [and] the poorer class," people who "all looked good on Sundays," the most popular day for studio portraits.[12] Most important, this book builds on the belief that while Black image makers operate in contexts in which their visibility and invisibility within dominant structures of meaning and value endlessly fluctuate, there has always been a rich tradition of visuality among Black viewers, creatives, and patrons, for whom a Black tradition of the visual is centrally located in the quotidian. As scholars of African American studies may term this space as part of a Black interiority, this book is indebted to a commitment to understanding the ordinary as part of the extraordinary, a space that reflects the richness of Black quotidian life.[13]

A Nimble Approach

In describing photographs, the word *nimble* is often linked with speed. People speak of "catching" something in motion—whether troops or an astronomical happening—in describing a nimble photographer's praise-worthy skill in capturing a scene. The word also fittingly connotes decisions that Van Der Zee made about his photographs: the nimble practices carried out by the artist.[14] The photographer's quickness in responding to changes in his clients' needs is notable, as is the sage wisdom evident in the act of keeping an excellent archive for the purpose of delayed returns. At other times, the images themselves can be regarded as entities committed to their persistent presence in front of viewers, and the images—through their rich "social lives" and shifts in material form—can also be described as nimble.[15]

Yet I primarily use the word *nimble* to specifically describe the ease with which one must transition between art history and vernacular photography—or, stated differently, approaches to both fine art photography and vernacular photography—when considering Van Der Zee's work. The changing contexts of Van Der Zee's photographs require that the reader be nimble in an effort to make sense of Van Der Zee's images, their temporal reach, their material history, and their limits and possibilities within and against current scholarship on the photographer. Photographs are interpreted and used across so many registers: as evidence, art forms, narratives of identity, and political provocations. However, it is uncommon for the images created by one photographer, and one studio-based practice, to do so many things over a span of more than half a century. The work includes gelatin-silver prints (many hand-colored), "real photo" postcards, panoramic representations, and copy photographs, plus large-format glass plate and sheet film negatives, and small- and medium-format roll film negatives housed within Van Der Zee's archive, as well as those found in various contexts such as the visual economy of studios within a one-mile radius, the layout of newspaper pages, and the immersive gallery displays of the Metropolitan Museum of Art. This turn to a selection of images that highlight aspects of the material practice of photography shifts the focus of inquiry from questions of representation to questions of materiality.[16]

Through this shift a natural kinship becomes evident. This study is built on the relationship between Van Der Zee's mindful decisions in his engagement with the medium of photography and those instances—as in the case of reproductions—where his photographs were outside of his jurisdiction. It illustrates the malleability of photography, a medium that is inherently mobile and unfixed in ways that parallel the African diaspora. Van Der Zee's photographs are analogous to diasporic identities in that they "are constantly producing and reproducing themselves anew, through transformation and difference."[17] While the term *diaspora* both spatially and temporally signals the way subject positions are shaped by movement, distance, and time, the term also speaks to the very means through which photographs signify.[18]

A nimble approach captures these shifts and changes in materiality and purpose, which at times are intentional and at other times are a consequence of context. There has always been a tension between photography's commercial characteristics and the value of a photographer's biography and aesthetic intentions. Any narrative of photography is a moving target and a hybrid affair.[19] However, this discordance is not created by Van Der Zee or his images but by the discourses applied to his work. To extend a practice of agility toward Van Der Zee's photographs over the course of eight decades is to propose a revised framework for his full body of work and, by extension, for the photographic practices of the African diaspora more broadly.

This approach parallels other scholarly projects that are forthright about navigating difference. A 2019 publication on African photography, *Ambivalent: Photography and Visibility in African History*, edited by Patricia Hayes and Gary Minkley, aims to simultaneously hold binary positions that are perhaps irreconcilable. For the editors, recognizing the seen and the unseen worlds captured by photography illustrates its many paradoxes along the planes of the conscious and the unconscious.[20] These positions not only exist but also coexist in ways that cannot necessarily be disentangled. Tanya Sheehan in "On Display: The Art of African American Photography" similarly highlights the inherent duality of photography in the context of the art world's relationship to Black photographers and the possibilities of the vernacular. In parallel ways Tobias Wofford compellingly describes two competing art historical models within African diasporic art history. On the one hand, artworks from the diaspora are often read as stable cultural signs with little agency given to its image makers or the fluidity of meaning in artistic practice. The other method does the complete opposite, focusing instead on the malleability of meaning as derived from the artist and the artist's position in relationship to the experience of, for example, migration. He goes on to write, "Certainly, many art historians and cultural analysts employ a mixture of these methodologies in the same texts. The tension between the two strategies may be more indicative of broader art-historical problems as we attempt to answer questions of identity and difference in art and art making."[21]

A Nimble Arc aligns with these methods in that it brings to light how Van Der Zee benefits from incongruent approaches. However, rather than framing this difference as a conundrum, this book attempts to elicit such nimble movement between art history and the quotidian, not as a problem, constraint, or plane of contention. There is no need to reconcile differences or dichotomous frameworks of address, but instead we can see each approach as part of a constellation, as curator and scholar Okwui Enwezor may elegantly describe it, or as an occasion for opacity, to borrow a similarly generative concept from writer and philosopher Édouard Glissant.[22] As cultural geographer Katherine McKittrick insists, "The contradiction and ambivalence, that feeling and expression and thick representation of unresolved uneasiness, is where black aesthetics live."[23] To really see Van Der Zee is to find him within the space of both art history and the vernacular.

Concurrently, this study acknowledges and recognizes that *vernacular* is an imperfect and elastic term, one that has caused much debate surrounding its efficacy and suitability. Implied in the word's meaning is a sense of being less than, separate from, or on the margins of a dominant system of value. When one starts with such a premise, the problem caused by the use of the word makes sense. But the term *vernacular* also puts pressure on the very structures of meaning that have relegated the vernacular to a separate category. The term self-referentially draws attention to a problem. Why not continue to use the word in order to recognize the baggage of hierarchy implicit within the term? In addition to employing the word as an acknowledgment of difference, I also insist that other aspects of what the word connotes, for the purposes of this book, completely supersede any ambivalence caused by the term's pejorative implications. For many scholars, as photo historian Catherine Zuromskis succinctly explains, to study vernacular photography is ultimately to "focus on the ways that photographs are used, the codes of practice that surround them, and their clusters of meanings within quotidian contexts" and to place "valuable emphasis on the practice of everyday life and the way that photography has become a vital part of that practice since its very invention."[24]

An emphasis on the everyday practices of photography is paramount to this study. While considering the limitations of *vernacular*, I insist on its utility within the context of Van Der Zee's work while choosing, through each chapter's focus, to amend its scope of meaning to highlight the Black quotidian.

I use the word *vernacular* to signal to a discourse outside of an art history of photography. I reclaim the word for use, especially when talking about the Black quotidian. The approach I hope to model is about making a new path that is not strenuously constructed but joyfully illuminated by swiftly moving within and between two main frameworks, engaging with their utility, revealing the futility of their stakes, their shortcomings, and their possibilities. Doing so illustrates a way to navigate and move forward with Van Der Zee and his work as guiding beacons.

Through this project's intentional pivots between art history and the vernacular, a fuller range of Van Der Zee's work can be considered. This range expands our understanding of the roles that Van Der Zee and his clients in Harlem—as well as others outside of the neighborhood—asked photography to play at various points in the twentieth century. This book's chapters switch back and forth between Van Der Zee's intentional engagement with his craft of photography and examples of external factors that took over and determined the fate of Van Der Zee's photographs. A consideration of Van Der Zee and his photographs sits neatly within an art historical narrative only when one turns a blind eye to the photographs' multivalent social uses. At the same time, focusing only on a photograph's social uses would mean missing out on a more holistic view of Van Der Zee's work and the terms of its aesthetic value.

Expanding Art History's Sight Line

For the writer and critic Hilton Als, the study of art history begins with a rudimentary understanding of the present's link to the past and proceeds to offer an increasingly intricate framework for coming to terms with a wide range of images. In his personal essay "The First Step of Becoming an Art Historian," he considers what the transformation from a general reader of images to a skilled, learned viewer and interpreter of the visual world entails. While no step-by-step guide transpires within the short six-page essay, Als instead illustrates his musings most forcefully through everyday images, one of which is a vernacular photograph of his mother. Through reflections on this photograph, Als succinctly provides what is arguably one of the most astute explanations of what scholarship about images is tasked to accomplish, and one through which this book finds its purpose. Accordingly, "to see, one must possess a language which directs the eyes to what is being perceived."[25] Although Als implies that art history provides this enchanted language, the more useful direction comes from critically examining where exactly art history has set its sight line and then looking more expansively for a clearer view beyond the field's own hierarchies and biases.

By taking a sidelong glance, this book allows Van Der Zee and his contributions to photography to be perceived more fully through the contexts of their production, modification, and reproduction.[26] Shifting the site of meaning away from the singular artist allows for an approach that more readily incorporates collaborations among producer, viewer, and object, as African diaspora scholars Leigh Raiford and Heike Raphael-Hernandez insist.[27] The distinctness of Van Der Zee's work—and, even more crucial, the distinctness of Van Der Zee's position within art history—allows for this important reframing to take place. The specificity of Van Der Zee's position within art history deserves a close look. To step back and view the current landscape of scholarship on Black artists and the production of art by those from the African diaspora is to peer into a completely different space than, for example, what art historian Darby English had in mind in his 2007 publication critiquing the shortcomings of existing scholarship on Black artists. English's *How to See a Work of Art in Total Darkness* addresses a lack of nuance outside of recurring narratives of uplift and African American advancement that tend to define Black artists while eliding many of the complexities implicit in any creative endeavor.[28] This is a phenomenon that literary scholar Kevin Quashie may regard as the narrative impulse to privilege a public assertion of progress and resistance instead of the intricacy of Black interior life.[29] Arguably, English's book would not be produced today, close to two decades later. The historicity of the text is both a relief and an important reminder of the field's past limitations and its current state.

Nonetheless, orienting Van Der Zee within the conversation that English advances is still relevant: not because Van Der Zee is an African American artist, but because he is not a contemporary one. New methodologies in the field are strongly concentrated within the contemporary art sphere, while artists from earlier moments, like Van Der Zee, are often understood within the recurring conversations English so adamantly critiques. Numerous exceptions do exist.[30] Yet in African American art's focus on contemporary art, the field misses out on a major advantage of studying older works: the longevity of their makers' careers. This study on Van Der Zee leverages an asset that can serve as the driving force behind revised discourses of Black artistic cultural production. This resource is time, and the extensive duration of insight it provides. The exceptionalism of Van Der Zee's long career has not been lost on scholars. Biographer Jim Haskins compellingly captures this point: "[Van Der Zee] has seen photography advance from a primitive process to a highly developed science and a true art form. . . . He could remember when color photography was impossible, when a picture was spoiled if the subject moved, when things that are invisible to the naked eye were also invisible to the camera's eye.

He has taken up photography at a time when the photograph and the camera were rare items and lived to see a time when visual images are perhaps the chief means of communication in the modern world."[31]

Artists whose practices unfold over a lifetime offer art history the benefit of their long engagement with the medium of their choice and the multiplicity of ways that their images function in the world. Not only did Van Der Zee's career significantly overlap with photography's relatively short history, but he diligently produced work as photography shifted from a tool of documentation to an artistic form. His engagement with photography traverses both technological advancements and major changes in its discourse over the years. More specifically, the time between his first photograph, in 1900, and his last, in 1983, overlaps with nearly half of the medium's history, from photography's invention in 1839 to the present moment. Indeed, a history of photography could be told through Van Der Zee.[32] Taking such a perspective gives new resonance to a statement by the photography scholar Joanna Sassoon: "Through its life, the photograph, as both image and object, can potentially move across several spaces, including the sites of production, use, reproduction and preservation, and along with each change in ownership and context, new meanings are acquired."[33] While Van Der Zee's career was incredibly lengthy, his photographs have persisted even longer.

And they persist, in part, because of the artistic quality of Van Der Zee's vision as a photographer. Turn to a comparison of multiple photographs of the same Harlem resident taken at different studios, only one of which is by Van Der Zee. More specifically, three black-and-white photographs depict this same man, in varied compositions (figures I.4, I.5, and I.6). The 1925 photograph *Barefoot Prophet*, by Van Der Zee, captures the nearly seven-foot-tall Elder Clayhorn Martin seated and dressed in a dark suit while barefoot, as was his usual appearance when preaching; he was one of the orators known on the bustling streets of Harlem.[34] As was common in Van Der Zee's aesthetic style and photographic output, the image includes a posed subject with carefully selected props.

There is an elegant aesthetic quality to Van Der Zee's photograph; as in so many of his portraits from this period, in figure I.4 Van Der Zee incorporates a carefully arranged setting evocative of Victorian mores. From the hazy painted domestic backdrop of a wall, an ornate column, and pulled-back curtains revealing a pastoral scene, to the throne-like chair the figure seems to claim, to the small additions to the side table on which he rests his elbow to support his head, deep in thought, this photograph

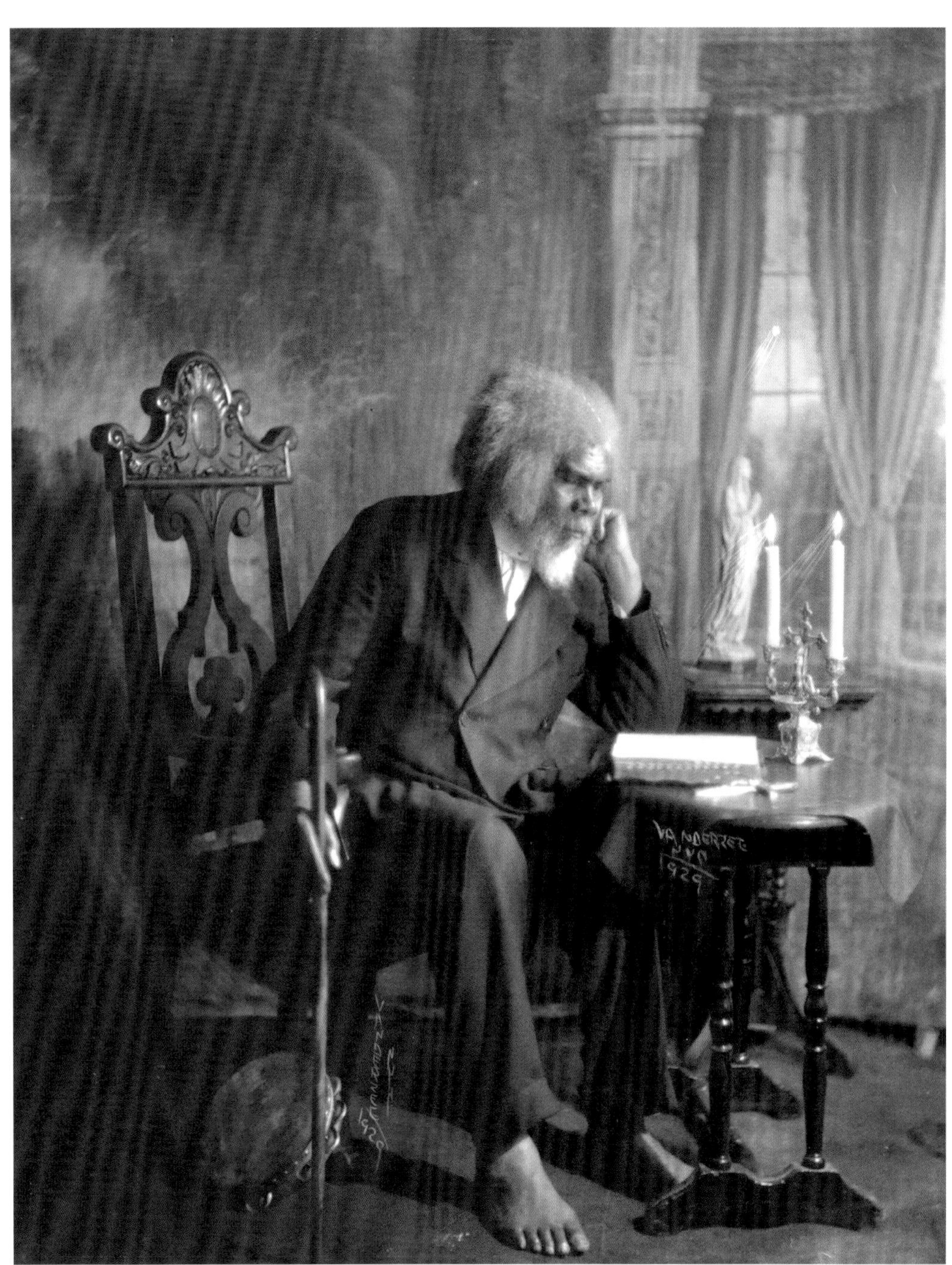
VAN DER ZEE
NYC
1929

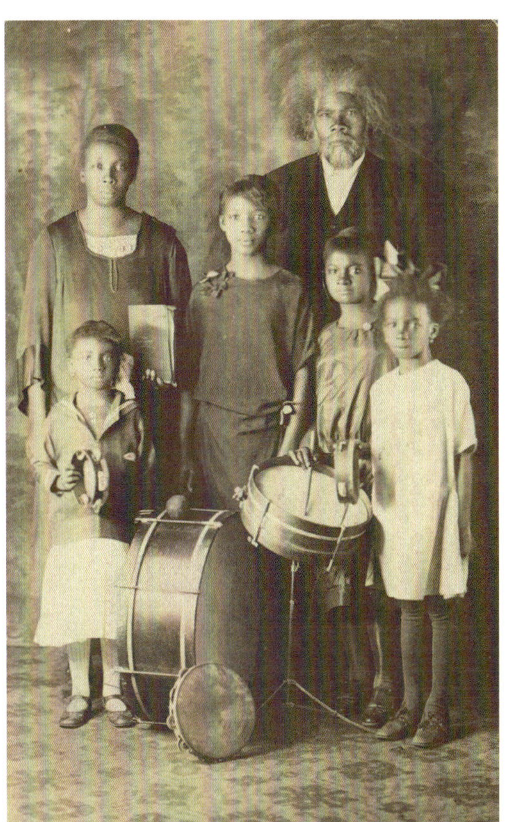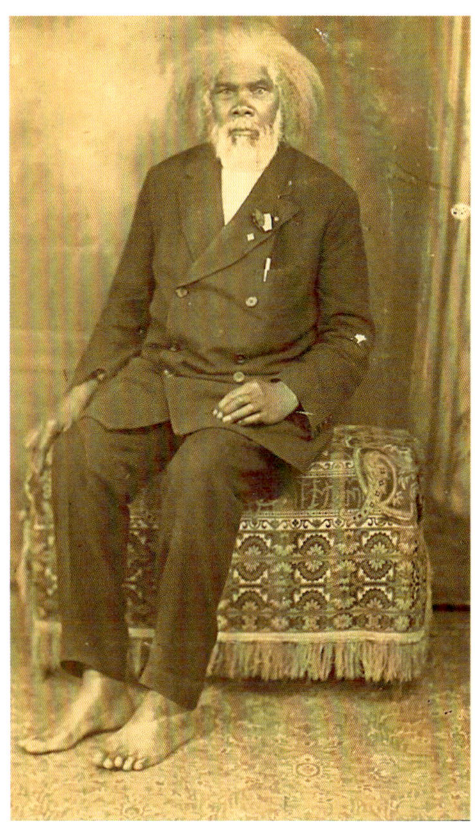

FIGURE I.4 (opposite)

James Van Der Zee, *Barefoot Prophet*, 1929.

9½ × 7⅜ in. (24.1 × 18.8 cm). © James Van Der Zee Archive, The Metropolitan Museum of Art, New York. Source: James Van Der Zee Archive, The Metropolitan Museum of Art, New York.

FIGURE I.5 (above, left)

Unidentified photographer, *Barefoot Prophet with Woman and Children*, ca. 1930.

5 15/16 × 3⅞ in. (15 × 9.9 cm). Source: Robert Langmuir Photography Collection, Emory University Archives, Atlanta.

FIGURE I.6 (above, right)

Unidentified photographer, *Barefoot Prophet*, ca. 1930.

conveys the utmost sense of respectable style and sensibility. As a portrait conjuring the character of the figure, it is made complete with the walking staff and tambourine, two objects that were dear to the Barefoot Prophet. In addition, Van Der Zee's handwork adorns the photograph's surface through the added enhancements of light rays emanating from the two lit candles.

Undeniably, the composition of figure I.4, carefully posed and situated within the space, along with the natural and compelling countenance of the sitter, sets this portrait apart from two other undated photographs of the Barefoot Prophet. In the first of these (figure I.5), the Barefoot Prophet is accompanied by four children (two of whom hold tambourines), a woman, a drum set, and a larger tambourine, which is identical to the one in Van Der Zee's photograph. The second (figure I.6) bears no date and is from an unidentified source. Its composition is simple and direct and lacks the pictorial impact of Van Der Zee's version. Despite the abundance of props and figures involved, figure I.5 lacks the lighting quality, sharp focus, and contented expression on the Barefoot Prophet's face in figure I.4. Given the busy scene and the positioning of the figures, figure I.5 depicts the group as stiff and awkward. In comparison, in figure I.4 Van Der Zee combines features from the other two photographs (the bare feet and the tambourine) with his skillful composition and technical mastery.

Photographs like *Barefoot Prophet, 1925* illustrate, in true art historical fashion, Van Der Zee's signature style and aesthetic as distinct from and superior to his peers. When scholars write about Van Der Zee, they frame his merit through certain aesthetic aspects of his images. Art historian Victoria A. T. Sancho has written about the tactile surface of his photographs and the way his employment of combination printing carried him beyond the use of props.[35] Performance studies scholar José Esteban Muñoz continues by analyzing the narrative impulse in Van Der Zee's combination printings, in which images are superimposed in his portraits as a way to draw out a story line.[36] Art historian Mary Schmidt Campbell comments on the stillness and quiet assurance that Van Der Zee's images evoke, while art historian Deborah J. Johnson notes that "more than any other photographer, his works carry the mark of the craftsman and artist who turned to photography primarily because of the speed and efficiency with which it facilitated art."[37] Art historian Miriam Thaggert insists that his photographs arrest time so that the subjects are caught in an anachronistic moment of "New Negro-ness," a period of great artistic originality.[38] Van Der Zee is continuously praised for his creativity and innovation.[39]

However, defining Van Der Zee's significance through his aesthetic exceptionalism has overshadowed the diversity of his photographs' forms and the kinds of relationships, transformations, and modifications that cast them anew. Too often, the terms of Van Der Zee's significance have simultaneously buoyed the high regard for and popularity of Van Der Zee's distinctive photography and prevented the full range of his output from being considered. To trouble narratives of Van Der Zee is to see outside of what is familiar and known.

The Black Quotidian and States of the Mundane

The question of even considering Van Der Zee's work as vernacular may arise. Unlike many photographers whose work is identified as vernacular, Van Der Zee is named as the creator of his works, a distinguishing characteristic of a fine artist. In contrast, the anonymous makers of many photographs comparable to the ones Van Der Zee produced are lost to history. In addition, Van Der Zee is known as a portraitist of artistic intent, a practitioner of a genre that fits neatly within art history as one of the discipline's representational touchstones. Only a few scholars have used the term *vernacular* to describe his work; the phrase *vernacular artist*, used on at least one occasion, highlights the ambiguities that always arise when trying to define a term.[40] Nonetheless, the term *vernacular artist* contradicts the vernacular's assumed distance from fine art forms.[41]

Sources on Van Der Zee and his self-referential status as an artist offer inconsistent accounts. For example, figure I.7 shows a 1940 Van Der Zee photograph capturing a display of his portfolio prints for sale, all of which have the words "Van Der Zee, artist" located in the lower right-hand corner (figure I.7).[42] In contrast, during a 1980 interview, Van Der Zee admitted, "I really don't consider myself an 'artist' now as far as that's a concern." Then he stated that all of his family engaged in artistic work, so he just "followed in line and continued doing what the rest were doing," implying that he did indeed consider his image making as part of a creative endeavor, even though he might have had some ambivalence toward using the term *artist*.[43]

Yet unlike the term *art/ist*, the word *vernacular* is more strictly tied to a historical era and to a niche audience. While the word *art* is omnipresent, *vernacular* is not. Although it aims to serve as an umbrella term for utilitarian, domestic, and popular photographs, *vernacular* as a word

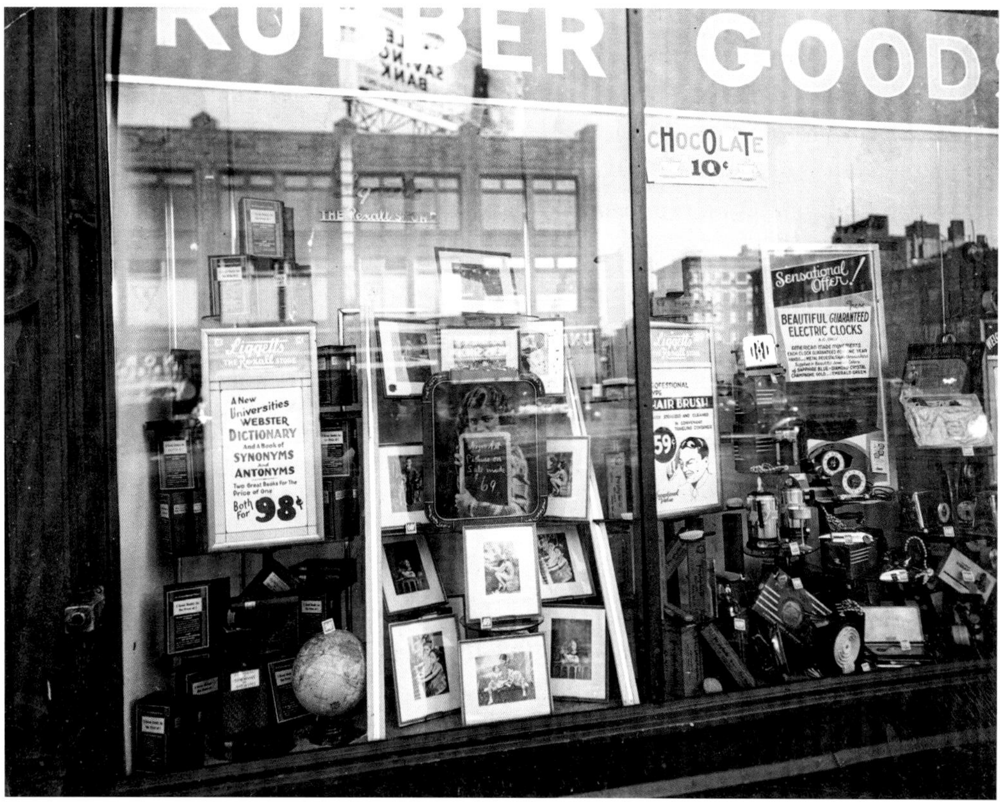

FIGURE I.7

James Van Der Zee, *Liggett's Drugstore Window
with Van Der Zee Photo Display*, ca. 1940.

8 × 10 in. (20.3 × 25.4 cm). © James Van Der Zee Archive,
The Metropolitan Museum of Art, New York. Source:
Michael Rosenfeld Gallery, New York.

does not have an expansive reach.[44] As applied to describe architecture starting in the 1940s, the term *vernacular* would not have been applied to Van Der Zee's photographs within his lifetime. The vernacular as a site of serious photographic discourse starts around 2000, nearly two decades following Van Der Zee's passing.[45] The exact definition and application of the term *vernacular* have remained consistently debated for decades now. Some scholars apply the word and all its implications wholeheartedly, some use it tentatively and sparingly, and others aim to remove the term from their vocabulary. For example, the diversity of perspectives found in the

2020 publication *Imagining Everyday Life: Engagements with Vernacular Photography* represents a microcosm of the kinds of conversation that exist and arguably will continue to take place about photographs that are considered vernacular.[46]

What remains consistent among the varying definitions of *vernacular photography* is a commonness or everyday nature, the fact that the images do not always fit within art historical narratives, and their prevalence at the core not only of photographic production but of the visual culture of the modern era more broadly.[47] Yet there is nothing mundane about Van Der Zee's photographs or, for that matter, any vernacular photographs of Black sitters. Within the context of the Black quotidian, the everyday and its visual culture always incorporate the extraordinary because Black life is contingent on extraordinary historical circumstances of subjection and precarity that operate in pervasive ways, named and unnamed, seen and unseeable. This is how conventional portraits become radical evocations of Black everyday life.[48] Van Der Zee's photographs—and Black portraits in general—have been interpreted as radical, given the history of Black representation in which images of progress, uplift, and respectability have fought against dominant representations of Blacks as inferior.

Photographs by Black artists become a counternarrative within this context, and the visual ambitions of Black photography studios, in particular, served at the forefront of what can be described as a war over the representation of the Black subject.[49] In similar ways, vernacular photographs in general can be understood as defiant, in that vernacular photographs intrinsically defy convention.[50] They are the ultimate renegade images, sidestepping art history's conventions just as the radicality of Black subjects within studio photography took shape through their own refusal of the way things were for Black individuals.

However, a small pause is in order here. Quashie has warned about the consequences of privileging resistance as central to Black life. He writes, "Part of what hinders our capacity to see [character qualities such as vulnerability and interiority] is a general concept of blackness that privileges public expressiveness and resistance. More specifically, black culture is mostly overidentified with an idea of expressiveness that is geared toward a social audience and that has political aim; such expressiveness is the essence of black resistance."[51] He provocatively asks, "Simply, what else beyond resistance can we say about the shape and meaning of black culture and subjectivity?"[52] While he outlines a theory of Black quietness through a range of Black cultural expression, this book aims to spotlight aspects of Black quotidian life that come into view specifically through Van Der Zee's photographs. Aligned with Quashie, I move away from a paradigm of understanding Blackness through resistance or as a counternarrative to Black subjection. Instead, this book insists that the shape and meaning of Blackness exist in the mundane fabric of everyday life—a sense of interiority and dimensionality most forcefully expressed through vernacular Black photography.

Therefore, another kind of refusal modeled throughout this book is a turn away from the iconicity of Van Der Zee's prototypical Harlem Renaissance photographs toward the noniconicity of the Black quotidian. This book's objective relies on a range of Van Der Zee's photographs, and not only those that can easily be read as clear indications of a higher moral or cultural good.[53] The Black quotidian encompasses all of Van Der Zee's photographs and their multiple ambivalences. Just as "vernacular photographs refuse to be organized or analyzed according to the paradigms that have guided traditional historical studies of photography" so, too, do I choose to deny the validation of Van Der Zee's photographs through only one configuration of meaning.[54]

A Nimble Arc departs from traditional art historical models of a monograph as a "scholarly treatise devoted to the sustained examination of a single clearly identified subject."[55] Its main claim is not grounded within an exhaustive study of Van Der Zee's oeuvre and the choices he made as an artist but instead in a focus on key chronological moments that remap the significance of his photographs and the way they operate in the world. Important developments in Van Der Zee's career are missing from this study, such as his foundational early years in Lenox, Massachusetts, and Phoebus, Virginia. Instead, it aims to contribute to a conversation that is more urgently needed when reimagining what future studies of Black photographers can look like by letting the complexity of African diasporic photographic practices—their creators, viewers, networks, and enablers and, too, the causes for their erasure—redefine the significance of a photographer's work.

But, simultaneously, the particular quotidian turns taken through this book are possible only because art history validated James Van Der Zee in the first place. As one approach hinges on the other, the only way to do Van Der Zee and his work justice is to selectively do both. While this book advocates for a more comprehensive view of Van Der Zee, it would be remiss not to recognize the numerous monographic exhibition books on Van Der Zee that have made a certain advantageous visibility of his work and cultural cachet possible. It is through art history that Van Der Zee has gained visibility as a photographer of exceptional aesthetic facility.[56]

In fact, he may be considered *hypervisible*, especially to those familiar with photography.[57] This term describes the phenomenon of being always seen or referenced through the circulation of particular photographs; in the case of Van Der Zee, through his representation within major museum collections, and the sustained return to his photographs within scholarship. The term also captures how Van Der Zee's photographs are, at times, consumed in ways that are characterized by a kind of excess, to the point that the mention of his name leads to visual associations, often with photographs that are not even of his own making. Van Der Zee becomes so overly associated with the Harlem Renaissance that he comes to mind with any black-and-white photograph featuring Black subjects of the jazz era. These factors have simultaneously buoyed the high regard for and popularity of Van Der Zee's photography and also the assessment of photographs that look like Van Der Zee's, while preventing the full range of his images from being considered.

To be clear, the iconic nature of Van Der Zee's photographs is to be celebrated, especially since there are visual economies within the broader African diaspora for which few iconic photographs exist. The artist Albert Chong makes this pressingly apparent in his question "I wonder, where are the great photographs of the Caribbean, the iconic pictures that have become part of the visual memory of the people?"[58] Within African American visual culture, iconic photographs exist along an extended chronological curve, with a number of Van Der Zee's photographs, such as *Family Portrait* and *Couple Wearing Raccoon Coats*, among them. Nonetheless, for a selection of his work to be hypervisible is for other works not to be seen at all.

This book recognizes and is indebted to such scholarly framing and contributions. The privilege of working on a canonical photographer means attending to not only the prevailing circumstances of the work itself but also an assortment of publications, exhibitions, and mainstream recognition. This is the call-and-response structure that canonical artists can build.[59] Van Der Zee offers the rare example of a Black photographer whose recognition is secure within the art history of photography. For sure, arguments can be made about the extent to which Van Der Zee has failed to be fully celebrated, but there is no doubting that he has a place, albeit belated, within the canon of the art history of American photography. Notably, in no way was Van Der Zee written into the early history of the medium through collecting efforts, journal articles, or important publications such as Beaumont Newhall's *The History of Photography from 1839 to the Present Day*.[60] Regardless of exactly when Van Der Zee emerged, among Black photographers practicing in the mid-twentieth century he has gained a level of visibility within the photography world comparable only to Roy DeCarava, Gordon Parks, Malick Sidibé, and Seydou Keïta.

As opposed to making space for Van Der Zee to be seen and recognized, it is time to set new discourses for how to critically attend to his photographs.[61] Therefore, this book offers one possibility among new histories of photography. Yet creating such histories requires more than shifting approaches. In a certain sense, writing such a history necessitates engaging with the past in order to reimagine a new way forward.[62] It is impossible to unhinge Van Der Zee from the art historical version of him found in various books, articles, and exhibitions on his work, nor does this book aim to do so. In fact, such materials essentially buttress this book's focus and make its ensuing argument possible. To imagine something anew requires that something was imagined in the first place. Similarly, to pivot, one must have something to push against. This book recognizes, and is indebted to, what art history has done for Van Der Zee.

At a time when there are frequent calls to decolonize art history, this book respects that call while arguing that instead of rewriting the art historical narrative, it may be more useful, for this book at least, to recognize the foundational ways art historical methods have gotten Van Der Zee's reputation to where it is today and build on that, by taking a vernacular turn for the purpose of rebalancing and expanding how his significance—and the importance of his photographs—is determined.[63]

Chapters along the Arc

The light box on which the glass plate negative is placed brings the image to life (figure I.8). The material of glass has a different weight and texture from the pages composing Barthes's 1981 edition of *Camera Lucida*. *Family Portrait* still depicts three figures. Also, within this context, Barthes's musing on photography falls to the wayside as a framework. *Family Portrait* can now be positioned side by side with another glass plate from Van Der Zee's studio. Both images are from a set of photographs that Van Der Zee took in his Harlem studio while in the company of his family members, presumably during their visit from his hometown of Lenox, Massachusetts. Within the second glass plate negative, an identical background

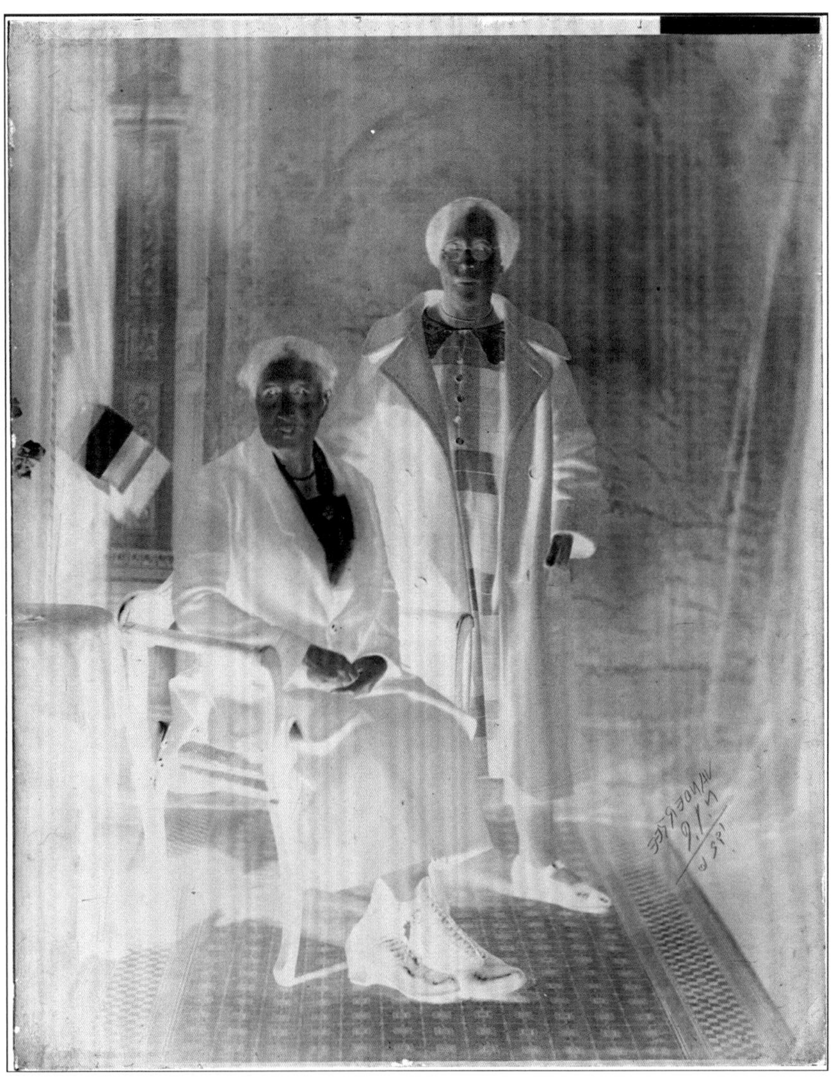

FIGURE I.8

James Van Der Zee, glass plate negative picturing two
of Van Der Zee's maternal (Osterhout) aunts, 1926.

10 × 8 in. (25.4 × 20.3 cm). © James Van Der Zee Archive,
The Metropolitan Museum of Art, New York. Source: James Van
Der Zee Archive, The Metropolitan Museum of Art, New York.

frames two female figures from the Osterhout side of his family, while the man does not appear in this version. One sits; the other stands. As we peer into the details, light and dark tones are deceptive, as everything gets flipped once the image is processed; white becomes black, and vice versa. Positioning also is flipped, offering an alternate viewing experience of looking. Such a reframing parallels the interpretive shifts this book encourages of its readers.

For example, with few exceptions, scholars have long positioned Van Der Zee as a singular phenomenon. This individual status is reified in ways that obscure the intersocial operations of the artist and his neighborhood. Decentralizing the singular artist narrative common to art history can open up a productive space for other photographers, a space in which Van Der Zee becomes one among many, to the benefit of his photographs' significance. In the first chapter, I contend that Van Der Zee's photographs were able to function to the extent that they did specifically because Van Der Zee was not the lone photographer in Harlem. This chapter brings attention to the surprisingly large number of photography studios within a very small geographic area. Evidently, Van Der Zee had to shape and modify his business according to the circumstances of the neighborhood, and it was within this context that Van Der Zee was able to establish and differentiate himself. In addition, instead of thinking of Van Der Zee's work as a collaboration between the sitter and the photographer standing behind the camera, a larger field and network of often hidden considerations come into view in which the multiplicity of photographers and their images becomes key.

The following chapter focuses on images made by Van Der Zee during the summer of 1924, when he served as the official photographer for Marcus Garvey, the Pan-African leader of the Universal Negro Improvement Association (UNIA). It considers the format, arrangement, and circulation of Van Der Zee's UNIA images in international print media in order to illustrate the impact of the photographs' translation into print and thereby the impact of their mass reproduction. In addition, although Van Der Zee took the photographs, editorial decisions made on behalf of UNIA were not necessarily in Van Der Zee's purview as the commissioned photographer. Also, an image by an unidentified photographer upends the larger themes of veracity and authority through a crucial case of mail fraud, which demonstrates the larger context of Garvey's employment of Van Der Zee's photographs.[64] Therefore, this chapter is very much about how UNIA's print media used Van Der Zee's photographs, as opposed to solely what Van Der Zee intentionally crafted as a photographer with an in-depth photographic practice. The chapter shows how reproductions of Van Der Zee's photographs, adapted for Garvey's newspaper, were strategically used to reach a global diasporic audience outside of Harlem during the 1920s. A different kind of photographic vision is animated specifically through Van Der Zee's photographs' reproduction in print, one in which a photographer's lack of control over how his photographs are viewed enables new ways of thinking beyond the photographic image's accrual of value through the intentional choices made by Van Der Zee alone. The images' social uses, material form, reproduction, and circulation illustrate a different understanding of Van Der Zee's photographs.

I then trouble the importance of authorship by highlighting Van Der Zee's practice of reproducing and modifying images. The third chapter reframes Van Der Zee's talent, and the elements of his work that are considered notable, by examining the application of his talent to other people's work. It continues to move chronologically into the decades following the Harlem Renaissance era by considering Van Der Zee's resourceful strategy of cultivating a clientele both locally and internationally through his enlargement and retouching services. The labor of photography, as opposed to its genius, is considered. Initiating one of the predominant forms of engagement with his photographic practice during this later period of the 1940s and 1950s, Van Der Zee invited his clientele to bring or send him their photographs made by other proprietors for the purpose of reprinting, resizing, or adding enhancements to the surface. He also advertised this service through ads placed in different print media, which led to his receipt of various new clients through mail arriving from places as far away as Europe, Latin America, Africa, and the Caribbean. Often mentioned as an afterthought to his career, when considered at all in scholarship, the body of work examined in this chapter illustrates the full scope of the changing forms and functions that thread throughout Van Der Zee's long career. By enlarging his clients' photographs and enhancing their surface, Van Der Zee adapted his engagement with photography to serve the needs of his clients in ways that can redefine how we value Van Der Zee's relationship to the medium.

The following chapter considers the rediscovery of Van Der Zee's photographs in the late 1960s and the implications of their display in the Metropolitan Museum of Art's 1969 *"Harlem on My Mind": Cultural Capital of Black America 1900–1968* exhibition, a highly criticized show in which Van Der Zee's photographs were featured. He gained the title of the leading singular contributor with more than fifty enlarged and reproduced images in the show. Many scholars have addressed the show through the lens of the Metropolitan Museum of Art's missteps in excluding the voices and works of Black artists and the resulting repercussions from those urgently calling for reform. When addressed in relation to Van Der Zee, the show is regarded as the moment that spearheaded his photographs' discovery for a larger audience and the emergence of his recognition. Instead of setting its sights on what happens to Van Der Zee and his career following the exhibit, this chapter asks the reader to return to the show. It centers the recollections of two people, Deborah Willis and Dawoud Bey, who visited the show individually as young adults, as a starting point for reimagining how to interpret the context of Van Der Zee's validation as a photographer. The chapter frames the potential moment of encounter between a mural-sized Van Der Zee photograph and a viewer who had never seen these kinds of photographs before as a generative site. By reclaiming the power of Van Der Zee's images outside of an art world context, this chapter offers a way to read the *Harlem on My Mind* show as an occasion of defiance on the part of the images' persistent presence through their enlargement and reproduction. Doing so highlights the possibility of an impactful experience for viewers, for whom photography's meaning is always open to interpretations outside of a museum's missteps and faltered framing. In many ways, this last chapter is the culminating example of how pivoting between the spaces of the vernacular and art history, and thus attending to different kinds of viewing practices, gives Van Der Zee's images dynamic opportunities for meaning and interpretation.

A Nimble Arc and its chapters focus on the relational and material dimensions of Van Der Zee's photographs across the twentieth century, from his early years in Harlem to the moment of the *Harlem on My Mind* exhibit. In doing so, the book offers insight into the changing role of photography as art, the very hierarchies that define art, and the terms through which an artist becomes an icon. I have described my approach as nimble, moving comfortably back and forth between art history and the vernacular to reexamine Van Der Zee and his work most fully. The coda explores yet another kind of nimble movement, this time through a rewinding motion back in time to circa 1994 to witness an occasion of multivalence. Such multiplicity inspired this book and can more broadly encourage other studies in photography and African American visual culture. It does so not necessarily to propose new approaches, but to consider old ones in different arrangements of address. I engage three interconnected examples constituting this period: the essay collection *Picturing Us: African American*

Identity in Photography, edited by Deborah Willis; *Van Der Zee, Photographer, 1886–1983*, a major exhibition of Van Der Zee's work at the National Portrait Gallery; and Lorna Simpson's homage to Van Der Zee's practice and legacy through *9 Props*. I aim to illustrate that often what is needed to expand studies on African American photography is already in the historiography. To nimbly rewind is to explore and refine which groupings of ideas are worth reengaging in tandem. The coda offers but one example by turning back in time to circa 1994. Doing so highlights the kinds of diverse evidentiary materials that can create compelling constellations of ideas for redirecting scholarship.

For the study of photography of the African diaspora in particular, such flexibility is necessary. Indeed, photography's distinct attributes include its unmanageability, given its scale and growing ubiquity; its very mobility, which makes it slippery; and its endless plasticity and capacity to become unfixed.[65] By following a nimble arc, Van Der Zee serves as an important anchor, a tether through which photography's multivalences can be further explored.[66] This reframing requires—to borrow a phrase—an act of wrestling with the image, given the unresolved tensions that always arise specifically with Van Der Zee's work.[67] Yet, unlike that metaphor, which implies a laborious task of will and strength, this book encourages a lightening of one's feet and a sense of possibility.

1

"More, Many More"

Van Der Zee's World of Harlem Renaissance
Studio Photographers

TO TAKE A BIRD'S-EYE VIEW OF HARLEM during the early twentieth century would be to peer into a small but mighty subsection of Manhattan, bustling with the cultural and social activities known to Harlem's streets, its civic centers, its churches, and—most significantly—its many photography studios. If one were to create an aerial map of Manhattan with lights showing where studios were located during the 1920s and 1930s, the grid of Harlem would consistently be illuminated. Such a map would provide convincing visual evidence of the widespread presence of Harlem photography studios (map 1.1). And the movement of lights—one light turning on as another turned off—would illustrate the transient nature of photography studios in Harlem. The world of Harlem studios might be still and present for a moment and then be altered by the closing of one studio or the establishment of another. It was within this dynamic environment—in which

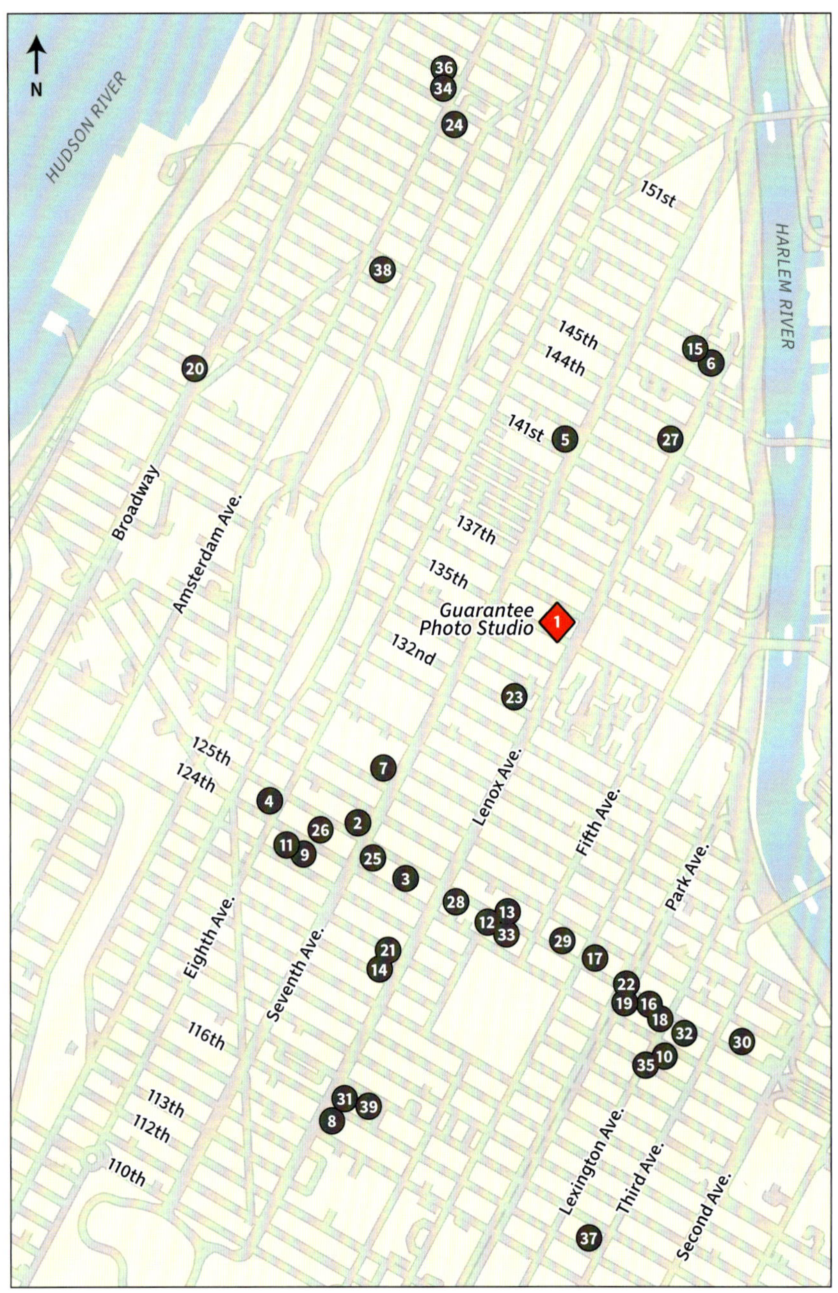

MAP 1.1

Photography studio map of Harlem. With the exception of Van Der Zee's studio in red, each numbered dot on the map indicates a photography studio found in *Phillips' Business Directory of New York City*, 1919–1920 or 1929–1932.

Map designed by George R. Larkins.

the studios were ever changing but ever present—that James Van Der Zee came to be a photographer sought out by people in Harlem.

Van Der Zee developed as an image maker among, beside, and because of other photographers. Little is known of these other image makers today; many of their archives do not survive, or they have received less attention than Van Der Zee. It is nevertheless crucial to acknowledge and reconstruct this professional sphere of Harlem studio photographers to understand Van Der Zee's work and significance. As opposed to excelling as a singular talent, Van Der Zee thrived through social structures built to advance photography in Harlem. The writer and activist Angela Davis first modeled this relational approach to Van Der Zee in a 1983 essay, in which she insisted, "Although mainstream photography scholarship treats Van Der Zee as an exception—that is, if he is acknowledged at all—there must be more, many more."[1] Just as scholarship often interrupts the obvious by calling into question foundational assumptions taken for granted, this chapter aims to rebuild a new common sense around Van Der Zee's early years.[2] By reframing Van Der Zee as one among "more, many more," I place him within a dynamic world of photography in Harlem filled with other ambitious photographers who were also intent on capturing aspects of the Black quotidian.

Long known as "the pre-eminent studio photographer of African-American life" in interwar Harlem, Van Der Zee is also acclaimed as "the photographer of choice for Harlem's most distinguished residents," who represents "Harlem's most significant photographic biographer."[3] These kinds of accounts begin early in the historiography on Van Der Zee and reappear in more recent examples, including both academic texts and museum exhibitions.[4] The persistent tokenism of Van Der Zee emerges in scholarship following the 1969 *Harlem on My Mind* exhibition and has continued for decades in spite of scholars' efforts to widen the scope of the field beyond a few well-known and celebrated names. Even back in 1983, curator Valencia Hollins Coar's show *A Century of Black Photographers, 1840–1960*, "demonstrated that there was much more to African American photography than Van Der Zee, DeCarava, and Parks, and that the history of photography, as [Beaumont] Newhall had conceived it, needed to be rewritten."[5] Nonetheless, the reverence that led to Van Der Zee's nomenclature as dean of African American photography in the years following 1969 continues to overdetermine contemporary approaches to the photographer's work. For example, such proclamations often muddle any distinction between Van Der Zee's recognition during his day and Van Der

Zee's standing assessed retrospectively, decades after his career. While this chapter is not interested in reaffirming or disproving the truth value of these statements, it does aim to point out the implications of such grand gestures. Crowning Van Der Zee the most prominent or the best photographer of the Harlem Renaissance subtly implies that a comparison has in fact taken place; of course, one cannot be a photographer of choice if there's only one photographer.

However, who are these other photographers, and who serves as the arbiter of their ultimate significance? And what would it mean to reframe the visual relationship so that the works of Van Der Zee and his Harlem peers are regarded as dynamic images that often have subtle, nuanced, and varying differences, as opposed to Van Der Zee's images being leaps and bounds above the generic rest? This shift—from a focus on the individual to a focus on many—parallels Tina Campt's approach to thinking of portraits as dynamic and complex entities when differences are recognized. She writes, "When we think about the seriality of . . . photographs as not simply hollow replication of a particular photographic genre . . . we begin to understand these images as part of more complex processes of cultural articulation, improvisation, and reiteration."[6] Seeing Van Der Zee's practice outside of singularity allows his work to provide a glimpse into the social realm that Black quotidian life affords. Van Der Zee became the photographer he became because of the everyday significance of photography within Black life.

Without other studio photographers, and without the clientele in whom both Van Der Zee and his peers found their purpose, his body of work would not exist in its current robust and varied form. Such a relational approach to Van Der Zee also resonates with the terms central to diaspora: scholar Anna Arabindan-Kesson suggests that diaspora "foregrounds the dialogic nature of Black artistic practice and the multiple affiliations of Black diasporic artists."[7] Diaspora enables us to see the visual relationships, networks, and overlaps of Van Der Zee with his peers. At the same time, it is important to distinguish this domain from any romanticized sense of solidarity or an idyllic close community among photographers: with the exception of Eddie Elcha, there is no evidence that Van Der Zee had close relationships or exchanged ideas with any of his peer photographers.[8]

In addition, there is a lack of photographic evidence, a predicament that has long been at odds with art history's focus on the visual. Perhaps, at times, art history privileges the visual to its detriment. While James Smalls writes that "art history—a field which is supposed to be based on the analysis of visual information—suffers in the area of African American art due to an incredible lack or inaccessibility to high quality visual reproduction of artwork," there are ways to resolve this dilemma.[9] Rather than privileging robust collections of images, the relationality this chapter highlights how and why people of African descent cross paths and exercise a deep engagement with the visual, in this case, through and because of photography. It does so by putting stock in lists of addresses, print advertisements, and other materials referencing the mere existence of other photographers, in lieu of extant and extensive photographic examples. Compellingly, when other photographers are considered and seen in this relational world, Van Der Zee at moments gets lost in the crowd, illustrating what it means to be part of something larger than just one. Such a shift is cause for wonder and curiosity as Van Der Zee becomes intrinsically linked to a Black creative space animated by numerous image makers and not necessarily by their archives of high-quality works.

Van Der Zee's detailed biography offers an entry point into this world filled with the partially known archives and lives of peer photographers. Born in 1886 in the New England town of Lenox, Massachusetts, Van Der Zee first came to photography in 1900 after winning a mail-order kit comprising a small box camera, a few glass plates, and an assortment of chemicals.[10] While his first attempts at developing film in a makeshift darkroom in his bedroom closet produced insufficient results, he continued to develop his interest with the purchase of a 4×5-inch Klieg box camera from a company on Chambers Street in Manhattan, the borough in which he would later establish his photography studio business.[11] On moving to New York City years later, he turned first to his skills in music for employment while continuing to take pictures.

In 1911 Van Der Zee's engagement with photography shifted from a personal practice to a more professionalized experience. Van Der Zee started as a photography assistant in a department-store portrait concession at the Hahne & Company Department Store in Newark, New Jersey. He first worked as a darkroom technician and then as the person responsible for posing the clients.[12] In less than twelve months, Van Der Zee was invited by his sister, Jennie Louise Van Der Zee, to join her and her husband at their recently opened Harlem establishment for music and art, called the Touissant Conservatory of Art and Music, at 253 West 134th Street. Known as Madame E. Touissant Welcome, Van Der Zee's sister referred to herself in advertisements as "the foremost female artist of the race," given her own pursuits as a filmmaker, visual artist, and school director.[13] At her establishment Van Der Zee worked in his first, unofficial Harlem studio, housed on the second floor above the school.

Van Der Zee went on to consecutively run four studios centrally located in Harlem. The first, the Guarantee Photo Studio, at 109 West 135th Street, opened in 1916 or 1917, next door to the West 135th Street branch of the New York Public Library and across the street from a barbershop, possibly one among the numerous hair grooming establishments clients frequented before entering the studio's front door.[14] In one photograph of the studio's exterior, a well-dressed woman stands next to the studio's open door, visually welcoming potential and returning clients (figure 1.1). In 1930, Van Der Zee and his second wife, Gaynella Greenlee, moved the studio to a former Chrysler automobile showroom for up to thirty cars at 2065 Seventh Avenue, a location that afforded them the space to serve as a polling site during elections and compose large group photographs such as *Children in Front of a Christmas Tree at Van Der Zee's G. G. G. Photo Studio* (figure 1.2).[15] In 1937 the business moved a few doors down, to 2077 Seventh Avenue, and finally, in 1941, to 272 Lenox Avenue.[16] The Van Der Zees would remain at this location until evicted in 1969. During the earlier years, the sidewalk near the Lenox studio served as a loading point for buses to and from Picatinny Air Force Base in New Jersey, while the studio's busy window display enticed passersby (figure 1.3).[17] Van Der Zee often sat outside the studio, giving out samples to promote his photographic talent among those walking by.[18]

Rethinking Van Der Zee's World of Photography

One sunny day in 1932, a couple sought out Van Der Zee to take their portrait on the street outside his studio. The now-celebrated *Couple Wearing Raccoon Coats* depicts a shiny, imposing Cadillac parked in the middle of a Harlem street with a row of brownstones in the background (see figure I.2 in the introduction). The car door is wide open, and a man sits inside the automobile with his hands clasped in his lap. The light-colored rim of his hat echoes the large fender flares. A woman stands outside the car wearing a luxurious, full-length fur coat that matches her partner's. This sense of partnership and connection is key to understanding the photograph.

In describing this photograph, art historian Richard Powell writes, "As can be seen from Van Der Zee's well-known *Couple wearing raccoon coats with a Cadillac taken on West 127th Street Harlem New York (1932)*, it was important even in the depths of the Depression for 'commoners' and 'high society' alike to maintain Harlem's image as a 'Black mecca' and a symbol of material wealth and glamour in order to advance community, culture and 'the race' in general."[19] For Powell, Van Der Zee captures progress pictured through visual markers of class and attainment. Numerous scholars focus on the elegance, confidence, and success that the photograph suggests; art historian Rebecca VanDiver augments such interpretations by considering the photograph in terms of vehicular and social mobility.[20] Her reading opens up space to consider what the technology of automobiles offers to the modern Black man and woman. While nuances and differences exist in how scholars choose to attend to this photograph, their interpretations of the image often illustrate larger concepts about Black advancement, modernity, and the New Negro. These key ideas of the Harlem Renaissance determine the terms through which the photograph is understood. This kind of approach frames Van Der Zee's work within its larger cultural milieu. Yet an anecdotal insight offers the possibility of a different approach to this iconic image.

The details of the photograph's production can be found in the writing of art historian Regenia Perry, the earliest scholar to publish widely on Van Der Zee. She writes, "[In] one of Van Der Zee's most popular images, this handsome couple posed on a Harlem street graced by beautiful brownstones. Thought to be 'hoofers,' the term for dancers of the time, the couple drew Van Der Zee out of his studio requesting they be photographed with the brand new car."[21] Why the couple coaxed Van Der Zee in particular out of his studio will never be known. What is clear is that this image epitomizing New Negro attributes also illustrates something else: even before the couple was intentionally positioned, either by themselves or by Van Der Zee, they needed to make an important decision. They had to decide who would take the photograph—or, more specifically, which photography studio they would patronize. They intentionally selected Van Der Zee.

For Van Der Zee to succeed as a studio photographer, his work needed to be enticing for his clientele. What drew people into his studio went beyond the attributes that W. E. B. Du Bois celebrated in his support of Black photographers. In the frequently referenced 1923 issue of *Crisis*, Du Bois pointedly asks, "Why are there not more colored photographers?"[22] The question is followed by Du Bois's insistence that Black photographers, as photographers of color, had the potential skill and eye to capture the beauty of African American skin, in contrast to the "botched skin" of Black sitters captured in the photographs of white photographers. It is possible to re-

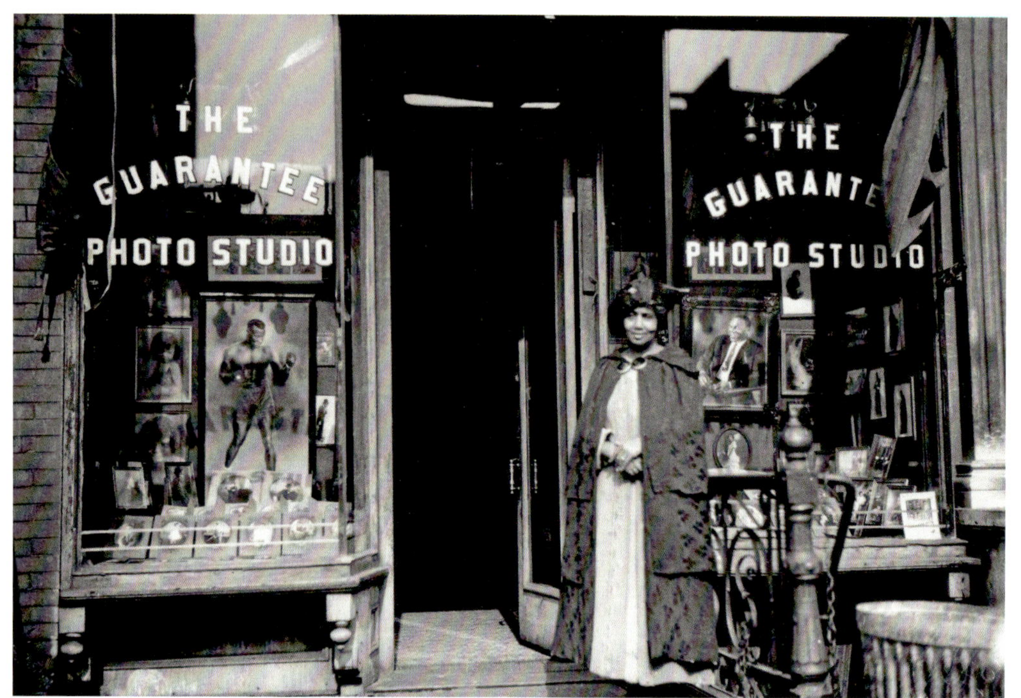
THE
GUARANTEE
PHOTO STUDIO
THE
GUARANTE
PHOTO STUDIO

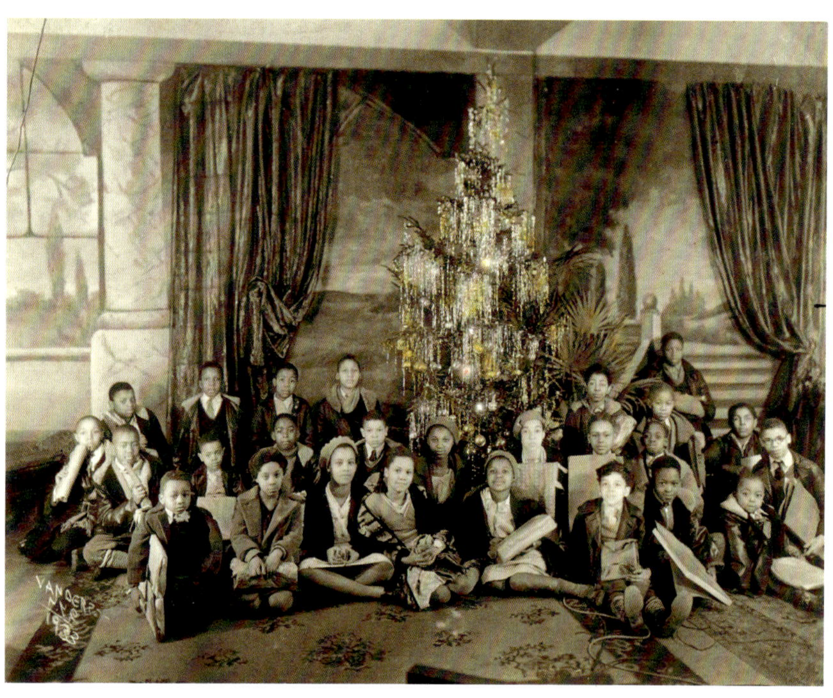

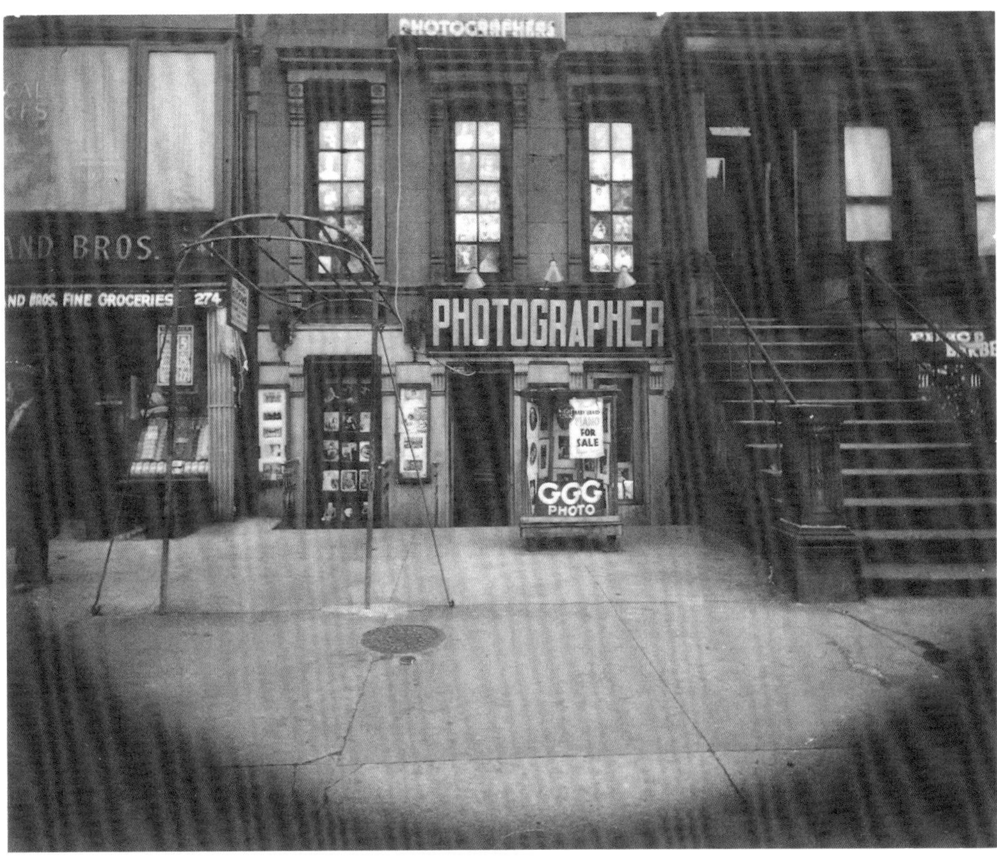

FIGURE 1.1 (opposite, top)

James Van Der Zee, *Guarantee Photo Studio,* ca. 1920.

6⅝ × 9⅞ in. (16.9 × 25.1 cm). © James Van Der Zee Archive, The Metropolitan Museum of Art, New York. Source: James Van Der Zee Archive, The Metropolitan Museum of Art, New York.

FIGURE 1.2 (opposite, bottom)

James Van Der Zee, *Children in Front of a Christmas Tree at Van Der Zee's G. G. G. Photo Studio,* 1933.

8 × 10 in. (20.3 × 25.4 cm). © James Van Der Zee Archive, The Metropolitan Museum of Art, New York. Source: Smithsonian American Art Museum, Washington, DC.

FIGURE 1.3 (above)

James Van Der Zee, *Van Der Zee Studio and Residence at 272 Lenox Avenue (now Malcolm X Boulevard),* 1940s.

Approx. 8 × 10 in. (20.3 × 25.4 cm). © James Van Der Zee Archive, The Metropolitan Museum of Art, New York. Source: Howard Greenberg Gallery, New York.

frame Du Bois's question. The query shifts from "Who can effectively represent me?" to "Among the many, whom do I want to choose today from the queue of skillful practitioners?" This subtle shift allows for a different project for engaging photography, one that is based on abundance and availability as opposed to scarcity and lack. Framing Van Der Zee as the only one—through the kind of selectivity and exceptionalism that drives art history—puts him on a deserved pedestal. But by rupturing this framework and suggesting a relational and network-based approach, we can shift attention from how his talent and distinctiveness set him apart from others to how the presence of other photography studios became intrinsic to his becoming. If most photographs are characteristically vernacular because of their ubiquity and commonness, what would it mean to reframe photography studios in Harlem as plentiful too?

Finding Van Der Zee's peers poses many challenges and limitations that necessitate shifting the terms on which comparative work among photographers can unfold. Contextualizing Van Der Zee's peer photographers becomes a moving target given the range of incomplete, misleading, or even missing information. For instance, Van Der Zee himself implies that there were not many other photographers in his vicinity. In interviews given in the 1960s, he names only photographers Walter Baker and Eddie Elcha as his Harlem peers.[23] Public records offer partial information since many photographers may have lacked an official or long-standing business, as was the case for Van Der Zee himself when he worked as a photographer in his sister's school before opening his own studio.

There is a pattern of inconsistency and a scarcity of records when it comes to determining the actual number of Harlem studios. Myrtle Evangeline Pollard, writing in 1936, reports seven African American photography studios in Harlem in a table of statistics titled "Economic Survey of Negro Business in Harlem 1928."[24] Harlem's photography studios were never acknowledged within the pages of *Survey Graphic* despite the publication's consideration of other networks of business, religious, and cultural endeavors. Contemporaneous publications on photography studios, which might have recognized the presence of studios in Harlem, also overlook the neighborhood; sources such as *Studio Light*, a trade publication by Kodak featuring studio photographers from around the country—including those in Lower Manhattan—omit any indication of a photography studio scene in Harlem.[25] A similar oversight can be found within the pages of New York newspapers that catered to a general daily readership, such as the *Evening World*. Occasional pithy articles in the newspaper focus on making the most of a visit to a photography studio, and endless advertisements assert the quality of a particular Lower Manhattan photography studio.[26] Harlem, though, is never mentioned. When Harlem photographers do appear in the mainstream print media, the reporting is incidental. In one example, a studio photographer in Harlem becomes visible to the paper's readership when a fire in a three-story business building leads to the quick departure of the photographer, who operated a studio on the top floor.[27] Of the secondary sources, Deborah Willis-Thomas's 1985 *Black Photographers, 1840–1940: An Illustrated Bio-Bibliography* features six other Harlem-based studio photographers overlapping with Van Der Zee's time in the neighborhood.[28] Photo historian Rodger Birt, in a 1989 publication, accounts for four prominent Black studio photographers working in Harlem's business district by the end of World War I, Van Der Zee included.[29]

In addition, the archives of Van Der Zee's peer photographers are often nonexistent, and even if archives exist at all, their holdings are most often very limited. Comparatively, the disparity in numbers between locatable photographs by Van Der Zee and those by his peers is substantial. For example, fewer than two hundred photographs identified as being by James Latimer Allen (1907–1977), another Harlem photographer, survive today, as opposed to Van Der Zee's tens of thousands.[30] Van Der Zee amassed between thirty thousand and fifty thousand prints, sheet film negatives, and glass plate negatives varying in size from 2 × 2 inches to 11 × 14 inches.[31] In the case of many other studio photographers, not even one image can be found.

Yet a significant number of Harlem studio photographers did exist. Their numbers come into view through evidence that leaves little room for any kind of extensive and illuminating visual comparisons. Instead, indirect clues suggest the existence of an active photography scene. For example, Van Der Zee's mention of Kodak salespeople visiting his and other studios in the neighborhood indicates, at the very least, a market base in the area.[32] In addition, Van Der Zee's comment about professionals who went around and did retouching for the various photographers in the area supports the claim that a significant number of studios created a dynamic domain of photography.[33] Within an archival file, a glimpse of Van Der Zee's peers emerges in text that did not survive the editorial process for a 1993 museum publication. An unpublished draft of one of the exhibition catalog entries states, "His wedding portraits have a unique delicacy and beauty. The photographer was so successful in photographing these rituals he became admired by other photographers in the area."[34] Some of these other photographers may have become visible through popular magazines geared toward Black audiences. In the case of Black print media (including *Crisis*) details—such as the accolades earned by individual Black photographers, the kind of clients they catered to, and the spaces they occupied— were central to how many of the narratives of studio photographers were articulated.[35] Such print sources often produce photographs, although their print quality is poor, making it hard to seriously consider the merits of the featured photographer's craft.

Noteworthy evidentiary exceptions do exist. Turn to a collection of scrapbooks by Black performer and model Maurice Hunter spanning 1920 to 1962. Hunter was known to have "transformed modeling into an art form" and vocation through his appearance in print advertisements for retail products including gin, cigarettes, and luggage. In addition, Hunter strategically used attention from the press as a platform for publicizing his versatile and expansive services as a model.[36] The scrapbooks of this "man of 1,000 faces" include photographs by Harlem photographers James Latimer Allen and Morgan and Marvin Smith along with drawings, pictures, letters, and magazine articles, all relating to his career as a model.[37] Also among the various photographs are a significant set of portraits by Van Der Zee. In one portrait by Van Der Zee, the outline of a Black male body appears in relief near a draped scenic backdrop, one of the many props found in Van Der Zee's early twentieth-century studio (figure 1.4). The man's face, his bent leg, and a raised tight fist are partially depicted in silhouette, while the other half of his body, its curvature and depth, is illuminated by backlighting. Although he is merely in silhouette, the man appears naked, a physical state that is an anomaly to those familiar with Van Der Zee's larger oeuvre and dissimilar to the more modest work by other photographers included in the scrapbook. This evocative formal style is not the only attribute of note for this 8 × 10-inch photograph from Harlem in 1925.[38] Within the scrapbook the portrait exists among a series of images by other photographers and alongside different printed versions by Van Der Zee, an arrangement curated contemporaneously by Hunter as opposed to belatedly by curators decades later.

Van Der Zee's photographs in Hunter's scrapbook share pages with images by James Latimer Allen.[39] When positioned side by side with Van Der Zee's, Allen's photographs enhance our understanding of Van Der Zee's aesthetic style and his photographs in relation to the diverse photographic styles of his peers (see figures 1.5 and 1.6). Allen's portraits are dramatized solely through a focus on Hunter's face and its expressions. True to Allen's general style, as described by photo historian Camara Dia

Holloway, the portraits in the Hunter album "adopted the austere modern portrait format, which presented the subject in a shallow space against a neutral backdrop." Holloway continues, "This portrait mode eschewed the use of props to convey information about the sitter."[40] Allen captured a closely cropped portrait of Hunter in sharp lighting with a plain white background, whereas Van Der Zee's photographs of the man create a scene through soft lighting, a detailed background, props, and carefully selected attire. Each photograph's composition also signifies differing eras, styles, and photography studio traditions. The scrapbook prompts its viewers to think about Van Der Zee in relationship to various studios and their diverse styles of representation, in turn emphasizing the highly tailored options available to early twentieth-century subjects. While Hunter was known to embody various kinds of characters as part of his entrepreneurial ambitions as a model and performer, the allure of expressing the multivalences of identity was not limited to professionals alone.[41] Everyday people similarly turned to photography studios to occupy different versions of themselves. Therefore, the multiplicity of photography studios amplified and encouraged their ability to stage different identities before the camera, just as it had afforded the same to Hunter. Nonetheless, such ideal comparative examples are few and far between, given the limited number of collections available.

Insisting on a world of photography beyond the finite number of stylistic comparisons that are possible between the surviving examples requires a different approach. In the absence of numerous high-quality photographs, it is necessary to amplify the significance of something as simple as a list of Harlem addresses. Otherwise, foregrounding only compelling images would tell a different and arguably biased narrative driven by visual data. Despite the absence of generous archives of photographs, sketching the contours of a robust world of photography opens up different possibilities of meaning. The volume of Van Der Zee's various peers comes into view, not through actual photographic collections, but through mere mentions of their location and existence through a compilation of various sources. Primary documents make clear that numerous studios could be found within walking distance of each of Van Der Zee's studio locations. This becomes evident, for example, in *Phillips' Business Directory of New York City*, a yellow pages–like publication printed every few years during the early twentieth century that listed business names and their addresses, organized alphabetically by business type.[42] This directory captures Harlem-based studios that do not appear in Black newsprint ads, articles, or other

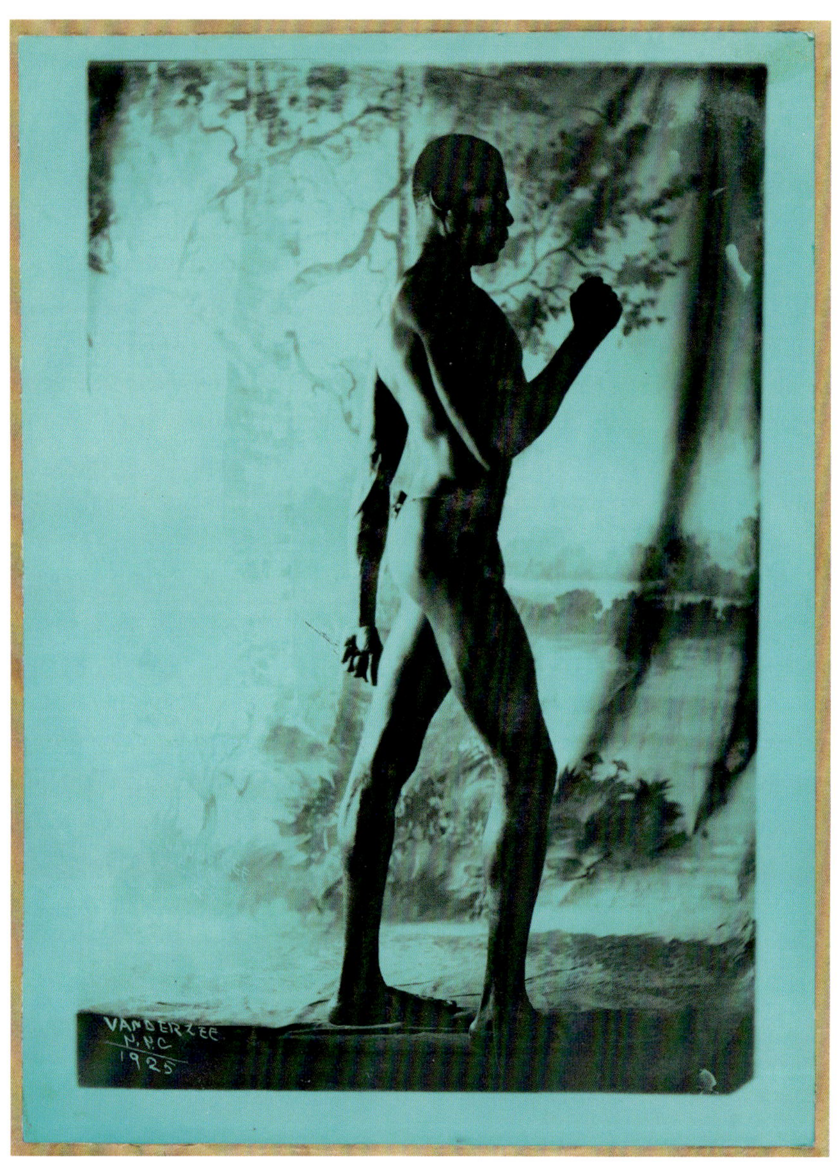

FIGURE 1.4

James Van Der Zee, *Maurice Hunter* (from Hunter's scrapbook), 1925. Hunter, a performer and model, appeared frequently in print advertisements for retail products such as gin, cigarettes, and luggage.

10 × 7½ in. (25.4 × 19.1 cm) on 15½ × 11 in. (39.3 × 27.9 cm) scrapbook page. © James Van Der Zee Archive, The Metropolitan Museum of Art, New York. Source: Photographs and Prints Division, Schomburg Center for Research in Black Culture, New York Public Library.

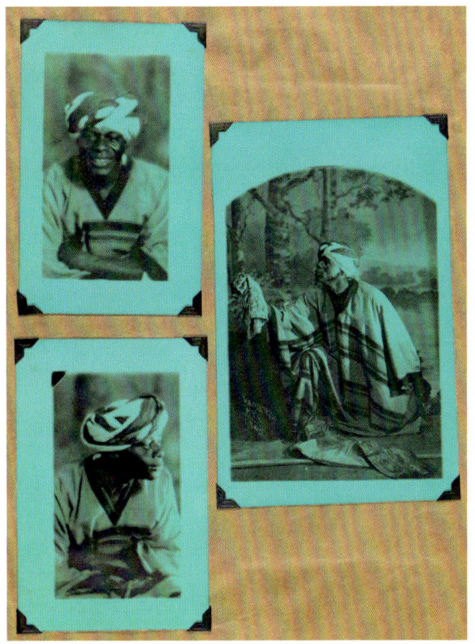

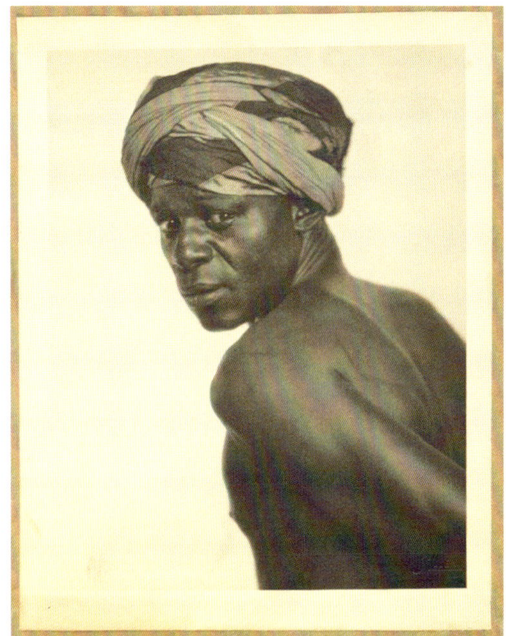

FIGURE 1.5

James Van Der Zee, *Maurice Hunter* (three portraits from Hunter's scrapbook), 1928.

6 × 4 in. (15.2 × 10.1 cm), 6 × 4 in. (15.2 × 10.1 cm), and 8 × 5 in. (20.3 × 12.7 cm) on 15½ × 11 in. (39.3 × 27.9 cm) scrapbook page. © James Van Der Zee Archive, The Metropolitan Museum of Art, New York. Source: Photographs and Prints Division, Schomburg Center for Research in Black Culture, New York Public Library.

FIGURE 1.6

James Latimer Allen, *Maurice Hunter* (from Hunter's scrapbook), 1928.

10 × 7¾ in. (25.4 × 19.7 cm) on 15½ × 11 in. (39.3 × 27.9 cm) scrapbook page. Source: Photographs and Prints Division, Schomburg Center for Research in Black Culture, New York Public Library.

sources. More important, the directory provides the most succinct evidence of the ephemeral nature of the studio photography business in the area. For example, twenty-five studios from the 1919–1920 New York directory fall within, or close to, the early twentieth-century boundaries of Harlem.[43] In the 1929–1932 business directory, under the category of photographers, seventeen studio locations in Harlem are listed.[44] As in the earlier directory, only two of the businesses share the same address. Of the twenty-five studios listed in 1919–1920 and the seventeen studios listed years later in the 1929–1932 directory, only five appear on both lists.[45]

This substantial shift suggests the constant changes taking place within the world of photography studios in Harlem, a trend that may have continued as the unstable period of the Great Depression stretched from 1929 to the late 1930s.

Van Der Zee's name does not appear on either list, despite his long-standing presence in the area. Such an oversight begs the question of what other studios were not listed and how race might have factored into their exclusion. To trust that various Harlem studios existed, to a certain extent, one must close one's eyes and depend on common sense, on an inconsistent compilation of evidence, and on educated assumptions. For example, Van Der Zee's omission from the mainstream business directory, in light of his very existence, hints at a robust and dynamic environment that defies any single method of documentation—an environment, too, in which most of the photographers are assumed to be Black, yet one in which the presence of white studio photographers is hard to qualify and quantify. Presumably, studio photography businesses were accounted for along racial lines, as some directories most likely excluded Black businesses, while Black reporting paid attention only to Black proprietors. This segregation, which complicates any efforts to capture a more nuanced understanding of photography in Harlem, most likely prevailed even though Black- and white-run studios operated in close proximity.[46] Definitive information about the photographers, and likewise about many of the photographs, has been lost to history and is thereby overlooked within the existing narratives about Van Der Zee's Harlem.

Scholars have often regarded Van Der Zee as operating with little to no attention to the larger world of art and photography. Echoing widespread sentiments, curator Ben Lifson writes that Van Der Zee "work[ed] intuitively, without a thought for the larger world of art or for his place in the history of his chosen medium."[47] Van Der Zee himself reinforces this general opinion with statements that illustrate his lack of knowledge about photographers such as Edward Steichen and Alfred Stieglitz; he also had never heard of the early twentieth-century Photo-Secession movement or read a copy of the well-known journal of pictorialism, *Camera Work*.[48] Both scholars and the photographer himself have reinforced a history of photography ordered by canonical figures as opposed to a Harlem-based narrative, despite a rich context in which photographs by local photographers were plentiful. In addition to the paper trail left by multiple photography studios, it also seems a matter of common sense that there would have been many studios and that their presence would have impacted Van Der

Zee's studio, for reasons that include the simple fact that studios needed to vie for clientele.

How and why this network existed and thrived reveals the relevant and quotidian context of Van Der Zee's photographs. Centering Black spaces and local photographers does more than highlight the role of photography within Black life. Doing so changes the structural ways that comparisons are made and values predicated. The terms of a photographer's relevance are no longer determined by the key art historical themes and by comparison to well-known photographers of the same period or subject matter. What existed in and because of the density of Black individuals in Harlem takes precedence here in setting the terms of photography.

In many ways, the studios generated events other than the taking of photos. These events include the mundane circumstances of individuals appraising Van Der Zee's window displays, walking into the studio, and later divulging their experiences at the studio to an attentive friend. The existence of multiple studios within a mile radius offered potential clients a choice of different kinds of visual representation and a range of photo-related events that informed day-to-day life, essentially because the neighborhood was full of studios. Just walking by a studio had the potential to serve as a "significant catalyst of events," one filled with a series of decisions based on preference, longing, practical logistics, and the availability of time.[49] The studio became a "theater of desire," to use Alan Trachtenberg's phrase, not only because of the staging that took place in front of the camera but because of the series of decisions that led to entering a photo studio in the first place.[50] Walking down the street toward one's selected studio serves as part of the performance photography asks its subjects to enact. Choice may have bolstered the attachment clients had to the photographs produced at Van Der Zee's studio, not only because he approached the practice with care, but also because they had judiciously chosen him. This ability to select a photographer among many offered a little bit of freedom in the face of the precarity intrinsic to early twentieth-century Black life.

Links among Harlem Studio Photographers

The photographer Eddie Elcha lived on 135th Street while Van Der Zee occupied his 109 West 135th Street studio.[51] Of all the local photographers, Elcha provides the most substantive view of what friendship and collaboration between Van Der Zee and other Harlem photographers might have entailed. In one candid shot, the two men—both originally from Massachusetts—are dressed in suits, smiling and leaning their heads on each other (figure 1.7). Such an intimate photograph departs from the formalities of the studio and illustrates how Van Der Zee's engagement with photography was about building relationships, many of which were filled with kindness and care. Elcha's social exchange with Van Der Zee also entailed painting Van Der Zee's backdrops, along with borrowing his camera.[52]

Just like Van Der Zee, Elcha (1885–1939) made his living as a studio photographer. However, Elcha had the experience of running a studio outside of Harlem. When his business of "Portraits of Refinement" with partner J. Montanya failed at the 230 West 135th Street location in Harlem, Elcha independently opened a studio in Midtown. Progress Studio was housed in the Navex building at 220–24 West 46th Street, a location that also served as home to a Black dance company, an African American music publisher, and the headquarters of a jazz orchestra. In addition to this midtown location's appeal to an African American clientele, he catered to the theater community to the extent that he became a known portraitist among a range of white performers.[53] Presumably, various vaudeville and theater actors, such as the Corbitt Twins of the Corbitt and Conway Revue, made the trip to his studio specifically to sit before Elcha's camera (figure 1.8). The resulting portrait captures a glamorous and enhanced style reflecting the theatrical vocation of the photograph's subjects. Aside from his careful and intentional lighting and posing, Elcha very skillfully added enhancements to the women's eyes to amplify their allure. Elcha also became known for his painted sceneries for Black stage productions, which led to his immersion in Harlem's theater scene. Indicative of Elcha's close ties to the stage, one photograph of Elcha's depicts the interior of the popular Harlem nightclub Connie's Inn, an arresting photograph depicting the intimate and thrilling mood of being an audience member completely enraptured by the performance onstage (figure 1.9). Aside from theater-related assignments, Elcha served as the staff photographer for the *Pittsburgh Courier*'s New York office, a role that may have facilitated his photographs' appearance in the *Saturday Evening Post*, the *Philadelphia Evening Post*, and the *New York Morning Telegraph*. In addition, the *Amsterdam News* and the *Crusader*, two popular Black periodicals, published Elcha's photographs with his signature legible. Elcha clearly had a greater national reach through journalistic work and arguably a more niche New York client base than Van Der Zee, indicative of his status as

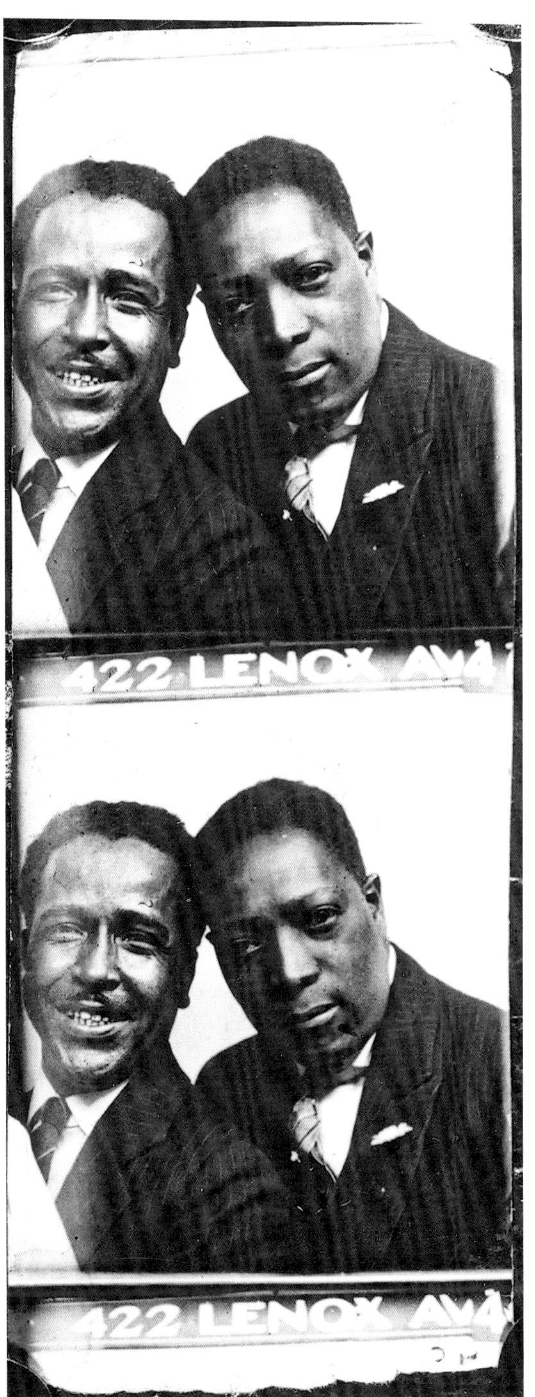

FIGURE 1.7

Photobooth portrait of Eddie Elcha (*left*) and James Van Der Zee (*right*), 1930s. Like Van Der Zee, Elcha made his living as a studio photographer.

4 × 1½ in. (10.1 × 3.8 cm). Source: Collection of Anthony Barboza.

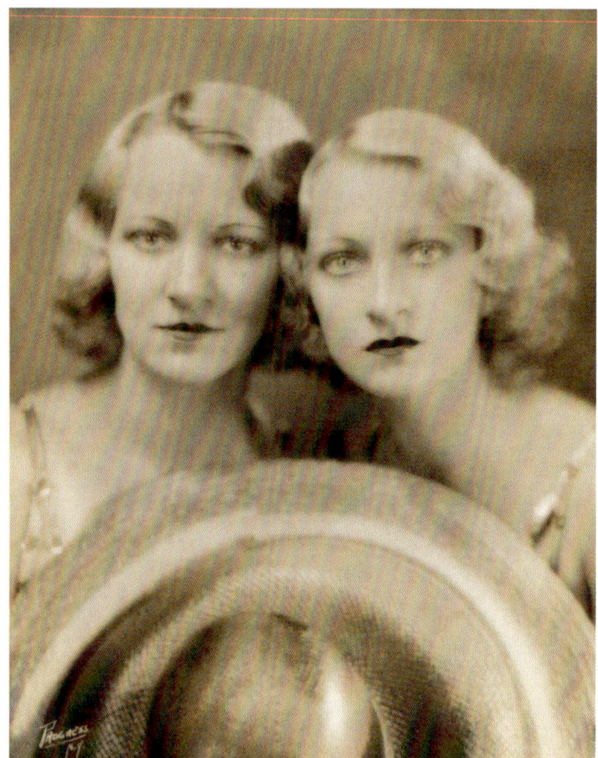

a highly skilled photographer sought after and respected by the clients of his day.

To turn again to evidence from the early twentieth century, additional local photographers found themselves as celebrated, respected, and recognized talents. The work of Black photographers was often exhibited within the public sphere, beyond the window displays created by each studio in order to attract clients. For example, James Latimer Allen's local presence in Harlem extended beyond his studio, as evident in "An Exhibition of Portraits by James L. Allen (A Group of New Portraits)" from April 20 to May 4, 1930, held at Hobby Horse, a popular Harlem bookstore at 205 West 135th Street whose social gatherings were chronicled in Black newspapers.[54] More impressive was his association with the Harmon Foundation, a major patron at the time of Black artists working in all media. For example, Allen earned honorable mention for the Harmon Award in 1927 and won the Commission on Race Relations Prize for Photographic Work in 1930, the first time that photography was officially

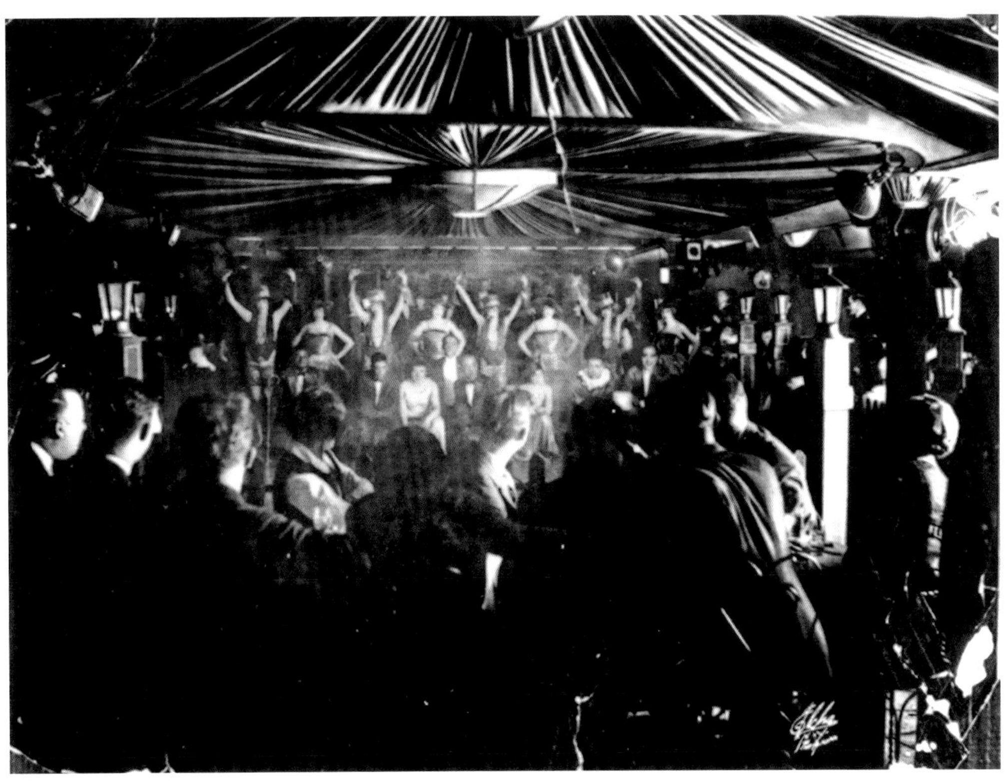

FIGURE 1.9

Eddie Elcha, *Interior of Connie's Inn*, 1930s.

8 × 10 in. (20.3 × 25.4 cm). Source: Collection of Anthony Barboza.

recognized as an art form by the foundation.[55] In addition, the move of Allen's studio from 121st Street to 2138 Seventh Avenue, as reported in a 1932 *New York Amsterdam News* issue, frames Allen as an acclaimed and talented photographer for the newspaper's readership.[56] While the prices of Van Der Zee's and Allen's services were relatively similar, public recognition and exhibition opportunities were not as abundant for Van Der Zee as they were for Allen.[57] A portfolio set appearing at a retail business called Liggett's Drugstore offers the only evidence of a formal display of Van Der Zee's photographs outside of his studio (see figure I.7 in the introduction). Aside from exhibit opportunities, their client base differed significantly. In comparing the two, Holloway insists that although both photographers developed a healthy roster of clientele, it was to Allen that the cultural elite of Harlem turned.[58]

As opposed to numerous accolades for Van Der Zee's peer photographer mentioned in published outlets, few examples of Van Der Zee's treatment in popular media of the day can be found, and one example focuses more on Van Der Zee's suite of services as opposed to the kind of prestige consistently conferred on Allen.[59] The description of Van Der Zee is partially reproduced here to illustrate the lens through which Van Der Zee may have come into view for many of his contemporary peer photographers and clientele. Within the 1932 article, Van Der Zee appears as follows:

> This high-class photographic business is under the direction of Mrs. G. G. Greenleaf [*sic*], who has been at the head of it for many years. Mr. J. Van Der Zee is the photographer and artist. He is a recognized expert with the camera, at posing at developing and in every other respect that enters into the photographic art. The GGG Photo Studio has built up a splendid population for its service in the finest for high class portraiture work. While a fine, well-equipped studio is maintained, a specialty is made of taking the pictures desired in the homes of the subject. The studio does considerable commercial work, but its chief specialty is distinctive photography.

Proclaimed as an artist and expert, Van Der Zee is hailed for his portrait work, domestic on-site shots, and commercial abilities. However, the range of offerings does not stop there. His engagement in photography goes beyond this diverse selection. The quote continues, "The GGG Photo Studio also teaches modern photography at very low charges. Harlem advertisers also have occasion to avail themselves of the services of this expert concern, many realizing the value of photographs in advertising. This concern [*sic*] specialty is copying and enlarging old and faded photos, Mr. Van Der Zee has spent 35 years in this line of work and is truly an artist of more than ordinary ability."[60] With the addition of teaching, advertising, and copying and enlargement services rounding out the list, the article portrays Van Der Zee as extraordinarily skillful in all things photographic. His services can appeal to every kind of client, from the individual who wants to leave the studio with a noteworthy photograph to someone who wishes to depart with a whole new set of skills in order to make their own photographs. The life cycle of studio photography and its offerings for sitters come to life in this tightly packed paragraph highlighting Van Der Zee's breadth and depth of photographic practice.

Notably, the blurb leads with Greenlee as the head of it all, a rare recognition of a woman's role in the management of a photography studio. Naming the studio G. G. G. only served to reinforce the central role Gaynella Greenlee played in the studio's management and success. To reinsert Greenlee more forcefully back into Van Der Zee's engagement with photography is to be receptive to the various ways that she helped Van Der Zee to develop his business acumen. By taking on the lion's share of the clerical duties, she also helped Van Der Zee to focus on cultivating his clients and craft. The photography studio did not move forward without the work of a woman, dutifully introduced within this 1932 article even before the first mention of Van Der Zee. To let this sense of teamwork and of a diversity of photographic practices lead in descriptions of the studio is to rethink the very ways that his photographs are produced and valued.

Allen's positioning through markers valued within art history offers a powerful and revealing comparison to Van Der Zee's standing as a photographer. In Allen's case, his success is evident through the praise and recognition of his photographs within a larger public sphere, much of which extends beyond Harlem. A range of institutions of art located both near and far also buoyed his career. Exhibition opportunities throughout the United States and abroad—including at the Harmon Foundation (1929, 1931, 1933, 1934–1935), the National Gallery of Art (1933), and the Rotterdam Salon in London (1929–1930)—positioned Allen as a studio photographer with ties to the larger art world. In addition, he had a presence, albeit small, in published materials appealing to a diverse readership, including a mention in *Art Digest* (1933) and *Thumbnail Sketches of Exhibiting Artists*, a 1936 publication resulting from the Texas Centennial Exposition.[61] Unlike Allen, to advance his career Van Der Zee needed to depend on his own diverse engagements with photography enabled through his own business acumen, Greenlee, and relationships like the one he had with Elcha, as opposed to a number of exhibition opportunities and support from key figures of the Harlem Renaissance era.

A photographer's education and training also illustrate the layered and dynamic social networks and intersections that defined the world of photography for Van Der Zee and his peers. Although he is most often regarded as self-taught, Van Der Zee's path to developing his craft in photography within a professional setting included exposure to the medium through his sister's business and a short stint working at the Hahne &

Company Department Store as a photography assistant.[62] Nonetheless, Van Der Zee's brief and ad hoc exposure is very different from the more formal training his peers completed. For example, the large New York City studio Stone Van Presser and Co., most likely more prestigious than the department-store portrait stand at which Van Der Zee began his career, trained Allen as an apprentice.[63] Allen also spent considerable time learning the methods of Irvin Berkey, the noted Czechoslovakian artist-photographer.[64] Given this comparatively professional elite training, it is perhaps unsurprising that this Harlem-born studio photographer was best known for his close-cropped, pictorialist portraits of an elite clientele from the 1920s and 1930s.

Allen's subjects included individuals, such as W. E. B. Du Bois, A'Lelia Walker, and Carl Van Vechten, along with others who were from "Harlem, downtown, and prominent visitors to the city."[65] Many of Van Der Zee's subjects were just as well known. They include Marcus Garvey, Florence Mills, Countee Cullen, Jack Johnson, Harry Wills, "Kid" Chocolate, Ferdinand Q. Morton, Sam Langford, Bill (Bojangles) Robinson, Hazel Scott, Adam Clayton Powell Sr., Father Divine, Daddy Grace, and A'Lelia Walker.[66] However, the existing images, the sole article quoted at length above, and 1960s interviews with Van Der Zee mark this history, in contrast to the significant amount of historical examples from the early twentieth century, like exhibition listings and newspaper articles, for Allen and other peer photographers.

Reconstructing Van Der Zee's practice during the Harlem Renaissance predominantly depends on the very existence of his images. His rich archive of high-quality photographs has enabled and amplified his status within art history, whereas the kinds of text-based materials that exist for Van Der Zee's peers during the early twentieth century are often not available for him. Readers during the early twentieth century would have been able to learn about other Black photographers through how they were framed in the press. For example, one newspaper notes how Thos. H. Green's photographic practice reaches back to his years at the studio of A. F. Bradley on Fifth Avenue; after five years as head printer there, he moved on to work at the studio of Kazanjian, referred to as "One of the Finest Portrait Artists of New York." He worked with Kazanjian for five years before establishing his own business.[67] These years working for other studios, combined with his degree from the School of Arts and Science, provided Green with a rich educational background that aligned with that of many of his peer studio photographers. Other Harlem-based peers active in the early twentieth century were also noted for their educational achievements and aspirations. In 1923 William E. Bartholomew, from Grenada, West Indies, and his former classmates from the New York Institute of Photography announced the opening of a studio on April 15 of that year. Referred to as the "New Photo Art Studio opening in the vicinity by well-known men of the district," the newsworthy announcement aligns photography with Black men identified by their various educational accolades.[68] Yet existing photographs by Green and Bartholomew are extremely limited.

In contrast, Van Der Zee's lack of advanced education and extensive training or apprenticeships separated him from his peer photographers, such as Green, Bartholomew, and Allen. Van Der Zee needed to leverage his skills and experiences, rather than drawing on any exterior accolades that could reinforce his regard in the neighborhood. Such a difference between Van Der Zee and his peers begs the question: What exactly was Van Der Zee's standing among his peer photographers? Knowing where a photographer was trained does a few things. It indicates the seriousness of the individual at his vocation and craft of choice. It also potentially aligns the individual with a particular style common to a teacher or school. Mostly, it offers a cultural and social cachet, a kind of coveted currency that found an eager audience within the pages of the newsprint of the day.

However, Van Der Zee departed from this model. He had other assets, such as an inviting and impressive parlor room, enhanced by its central location in Harlem. His photographs speak to his popularity among clients, many of whom—whether well-known or unnamed—even returned for multiple sittings. While Van Der Zee lacked a sense of pedigree in obtaining professional training, other characteristics, in essence, spoke for Van Der Zee. As much as running a commercial photography studio came down to selling oneself, Van Der Zee was able to stay not only afloat but very popular through his photography studio. Based on historical published directories alone, Van Der Zee's studio would inevitably be overlooked by prospective clientele. Along similar lines, if Van Der Zee's educational attainment or exhibition history served as an indication of his importance, again, he and his studio would remain marginalized. But these things did not seem to hinder his popularity during the early twentieth century. Instead, his photographs speak to the care he took with his clients on a day-to-day basis just as the stunning photographs within his archive have persuaded scholars of his talent and significance. Nonetheless, existing materials from the early twentieth century highlight different attributes of note.

Some of Van Der Zee's peer photographers thrived because of their robust networks and social links. They were not only highly trained but also very forthcoming in their role as educators and proprietors. Consider Walter Baker, an individual whose engagement with photography extended beyond his position as photographer to his role as an active self-promoter and exhibitor. During his Harlem-based career, the Louisville, Kentucky, native started a photography school for Black photographers, under his own name, located in the same building as his studio (figure 1.10). His school was likely one of two advertised schools in Harlem dedicated to teaching the medium at the time, the other one being the Cyrus School of Photography at 461 Lenox Avenue.[69] A festive June 1920 graduation party planned in honor of the Walter Baker School of Photography's recent graduates suggests the integral ways in which the world of Harlem photography overlapped with the local community. Aside from social gatherings, photography provided business opportunities, as evident in an advertisement expounding the following reason for joining Baker's "Home of Correct Photography": "Why hunt jobs when business opportunities are looking you in the face. Join our School of Photography. Learn to make pictures. Come and make Money."[70] No longer solely a tool for visualizing Black upward mobility and middle-class mores, the practice of photography also became a means to economic stability.[71]

This link between photography as a visual practice and photography as a vocation for achieving a certain social standing is evident in both Van Der Zee's biography and the ways Baker's school characterized photography as a profession. The duality highlights how photography became integral in the burgeoning economy of Harlem in the early decades of the twentieth century. In considering the language used in the advertisement for Baker's school, a particular understanding of the medium's role in Van Der Zee's neighborhood emerges. According to the advertisement, the Walter Baker School of Photography, at 463 Lenox Avenue, opened its fall session with a picture show and dance at the Manhattan Casino. This November 10, 1920, evening marked over twenty years of the studio's operation.[72] Baker founded the school with the stated intention of placing "a colored photographer in every town of 5,000 or more colored people in the country."[73] After completing three to four months of study, students could immediately benefit from their enrollment in the Colored Photographers' Association, an organization designed to assist emerging photographers with locating and establishing a studio.[74]

In addition to offering a path toward upward mobility within Harlem, the benefits of photography studios extended beyond the neighborhood. Baker, for example, promoted the creation of a network of photographers

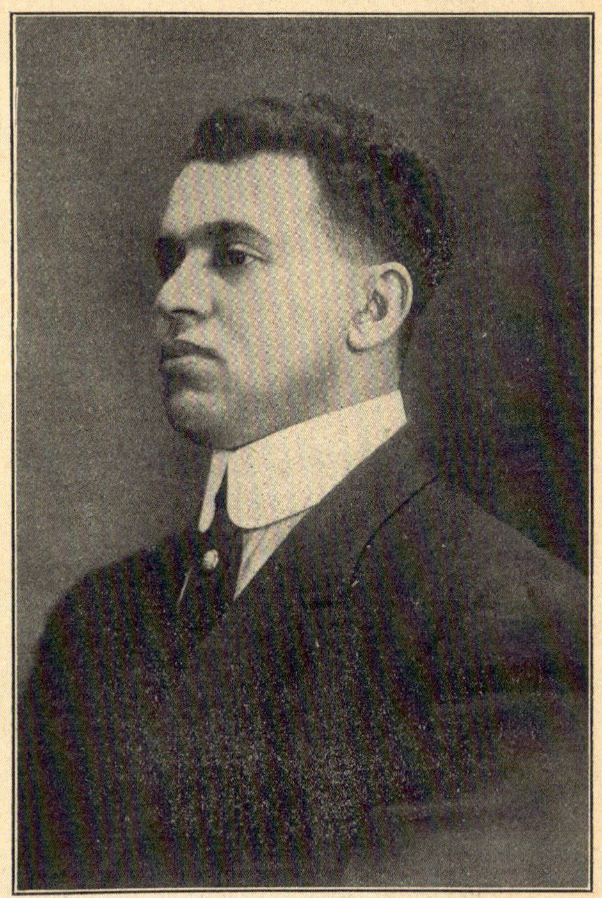

FIGURE 1.10

Advertisement for Walter Baker's School of Photography, *Crusader*, October 1920.

Source: Manuscripts, Archives and Rare Books Division, Schomburg Center for Research in Black Culture, New York Public Library.

whose reach stretched across the United States. With advertisements for his school appearing alongside noteworthy information about the Black community throughout the country and abroad, his interest in expanding Black influence far and wide through his selected vocation of photography reflects a parallel desire to spread out geographically by using photography as a ticket to economic stability and respect. This desire is evident through the advertisements' language, particularly when the expected outcome of the school is couched in the rhetoric of supporting a family.

One representative advertisement proclaims that the recent graduates are "all single men out to make a name of themselves and a supply of coin for the love-nest before taking on family responsibilities."[75] Here the vocational implications of photography during the early twentieth century take center stage. The life that photography could provide for its professionals, and men in particular, is paramount. Although the archive reflects the presence of female photographers in Harlem, these individuals remain invisible in Baker's description, thereby reinforcing a male-dominated gender dynamic that departs from both the description of Van Der Zee's studio and its female namesake. Simultaneously, despite evidence pointing to a range of sexual orientations and living arrangements among lovers, friends, or strangers in Harlem, Baker's advertisement advances a traditional configuration of what family could be during the early twentieth century.

Nonetheless, the school's intentions point to an environment filled with businesses using photography to generate Black establishments. Aligned with Booker T. Washington's rhetoric focused on skilled labor as a path to Black advancement, graduates such as those featured in the class of May 1921 could set up a photography studio at a selected location where they had "practically no competition."[76] From Tampa to Detroit to Savannah, recent graduates would, as the newspaper states, "carry on," "take up," or "give [their] photographic attention" to a new place. The Harlem-based school served as a launching place for Black photographers to learn the skills vital for a successful studio, such as the finishing work occupying four male students and, evidently, one female student in figure 1.11. Just as impactful, the students realized new business opportunities as part of the economic and social landscape enabled by the rich culture of photography studios. Their work shaped the everyday lives of these photographers, not only by giving them a vocation but also by shaping and directing their position in the world. The practice of photography became a practice of life. The graduates of the school checkered the United States just as they took up space within the commercial areas of Harlem, reframing the role

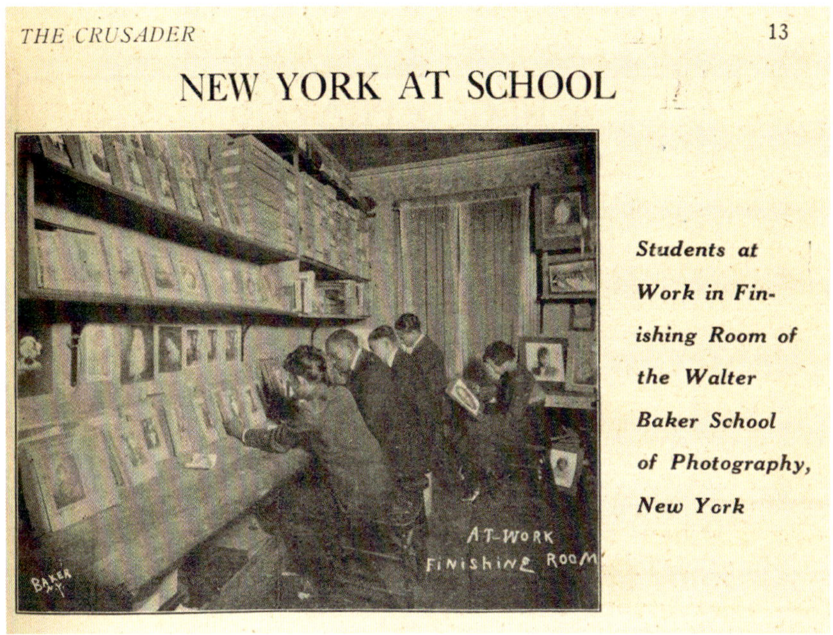

FIGURE 1.11

"New York at School," advertisement for the Walter Baker School of Photography in Harlem, *Crusader*, May 1920. The training offered in such schools provided respected skills and a path to economic advancement within the Black community.

Source: Manuscripts, Archives and Rare Books Division, Schomburg Center for Research in Black Culture, New York Public Library.

of photography as not just the production of printed images but the catalyst behind one's life purpose.

Van Der Zee was part of increasing the number of trained photographers, albeit to a much lesser degree than Baker. Van Der Zee taught photography to private students, including one named Walter Morace. According to Van Der Zee, "One of the best photographers in Jamaica was one of my students, fellow by the name of Walter Morace. And they all speak of him and say, 'Oh, he's the best photographer in Jamaica.' And I have gotten pictures from him . . . and I must say they do look very much like pictures I've taken myself."[77] Records relating to the work of a Walter Morace from Jamaica, Queens, or from the island of Jamaica are thus far unlocatable.[78] That said, Van Der Zee's commentary about the similarity between the work of Morace and his own reflects a self-awareness of the overlap among the photographs produced by local studios. Just as Angela Davis suggested, there must have been many, many more Van Der Zees. That Morace worked with Van Der Zee and followed his style creates a kind of genealogy of photographers based on the power of reproducing photographic portraits that repeated the poses, styles, and aesthetics of others. For Morace to produce photographs that looked like those taken by Van Der Zee himself pushes against the concept of Van Der Zee as an individual, distinct photographer and instead creates a configuration where repeated images, forms, and styles were looked on with pride as being part of a larger constellation of imagery.

While the photographs abided by the conventions of portraiture, they also speak to the heart of a different kind of repetition, one that depends on a community of photographers and their output. Van Der Zee's commentary about Morace's work not only allows for a realistic consideration of Davis's statement quoted at this chapter's beginning but also reveals a kind of kinship that took place, not between subject and photographer, but through the stylistic similarities between one photographer and the next. This configuration of repetition and significance centers a kind of engagement that is often obscured when the focus remains on the individuality of the artist or the subject and what his or her representation reveals about their characteristics. Instead, similarities are privileged and valued, rather than the photographs' distinctness. As opposed to significance being forged in and through difference, on another level it is also sameness and multiplicity that can reframe Van Der Zee's photography. As Stuart Hall reminds us, "The boundaries of difference are continually repositioned in relation to different points of reference."[79] Considering Van Der Zee's peers offers different points of reference that reframe Van Der Zee's status. Many art historians have implied Van Der Zee's difference through his exceptionalism, with limited regard for what he is exceptional and distinct from. His presence and skill alone conjure his distinctiveness. However, Van Der Zee can be repositioned in relationship to his peers, so that the boundaries of difference are no longer determined by Van Der Zee's status as the preeminent photographer of his era. To understand Van Der Zee's photographs requires a consideration of the photography world that enabled and buoyed his business success and the production of his photographs.

In fact, there were not "many, many more" Van Der Zees, not when Davis made her statement within the context of 1983; by then, his historiography had made him great. But if we read her quote as a call to return to the Harlem Renaissance, before all the books were penned, before his archive was rediscovered, before scholars proclaimed his distinctiveness, Van Der Zee was one among many photographers who seemed to be prominent, successful, and special, depending on what material one uses to determine their worth. In this sense, this study fails at doing what art historical monographs traditionally do. But through this failure, its significance becomes clearer. Indeed, to early twentieth-century audiences, there was also only one James Latimer Allen, one Walter Baker, one Thos. H. Green, and so on. It can be surmised that each photographer had their cheering section within Harlem, that everyday people with very practical photographic needs each had their preferences and that their preferences counted for a lot, more than what scholars writing years later, and prioritizing only the visual, have determined as truth. So, yes, in many ways, there were many Van Der Zees, but they all went by different names and had different audiences determining their value and their significance. This, arguably, is a more realistic understanding of what Van Der Zee's world of photography during the Harlem Renaissance entailed—a network of early twentieth-century image makers, patrons, and viewers who set the stage in ways that were constantly shifting and reforming, depending on whom you turned to or what newspaper you had access to. The voice of authority resided in whomever one chose to listen to—an important influence, of course, being one's own experience with walking into a local studio and posing before a talented photographer's camera.

The Space and Place of Harlem's Photography Studios

So what might have influenced clients to patronize, often repeatedly, one photographer as opposed to another? Of course, the style and quality of the photographers' images ranked high. Additional factors also offer nuanced insight into how photography functioned in Van Der Zee's Harlem during the early twentieth century. For example, often the location of a studio made photography an integral part of everyday life and of neighborhood happenings. Harlem drew photographers, and certain areas within the neighborhood proved beneficial for photography studio owners. For example, one of Van Der Zee's peer photographers—William E. Woodard of the Woodard Photo Studio—was drawn specifically to the location of Harlem. After beginning his career in Chicago, he eventually moved his studio, which he advertised as "Photos of Style and Dignity," to Harlem around 1934.[80] In a 1936 interview, Woodard explained his reasons for the move: New York had a larger population than Chicago and therefore offered more opportunity for his studio's growth. Like Van Der Zee's, Woodard's studio was located on the popular thoroughfare of Seventh Avenue, yet his clients were said to come from all over the city, preferring his services over the row of photography studios located downtown at Fourteenth Street. He often photographed large groups and auditorium settings, including the theatrical sets from the Commerce Center of City College, and his photographs frequented the pages of Black periodicals.[81] By moving to Harlem in 1934 and proclaiming such success in the Harlem community within just two years, Woodard followed a path that illustrates important aspects of Harlem's photography scene at the time. Longevity in the neighborhood was not essential to a photographer's success in establishing himself among a range of clients. The vast number of people in Harlem and the need for their likeness to be fixed in time drove various photographers to settle in Harlem, which served as a central location for Black photography.

Soon after entering the field of photography, Jamaican-born Winifred Hall Allen worked as an apprentice to Woodard and was said to have taken over his business once Woodard moved back to Chicago.[82] Before doing so, she operated her own studio on Seventh Avenue, around the corner from the Lido Recreational Center at 160 West 146th Street, a location that drew crowds and therefore probably foot traffic for the studio.[83] Renamed Winifred Hall Photo Studio, the business offered a full range of services, from staged portraits to photo-machine booths that gave six pictures for a dime. As an active photographer, Allen also entertained house calls and covered events such as birthday parties, weddings, and club celebrations. Like Van Der Zee—and presumably many photographers in Harlem—studio portrait photography was where she really excelled. For example, in a portrait of a seated man wearing a suit, the debonair pose, the eye-level perspective, and the backdrop featuring an open window offer a striking balance of formality and fantasy (figure 1.12). Allen also taught at the Mwalimu School, founded by Manet Harrison Fowler and relocated in June 1928 to Harlem, which emphasized African culture and language.[84] Along with Allen, the esteemed roster of musicians, artists, and intellectuals who taught at the Mwalimu School included the composer Hall Johnson and the historian Carter G. Woodson. Photographers, who were undeniably a part of the cultural scene that made Harlem distinct, permeated all aspects of the neighborhood's cultural life.

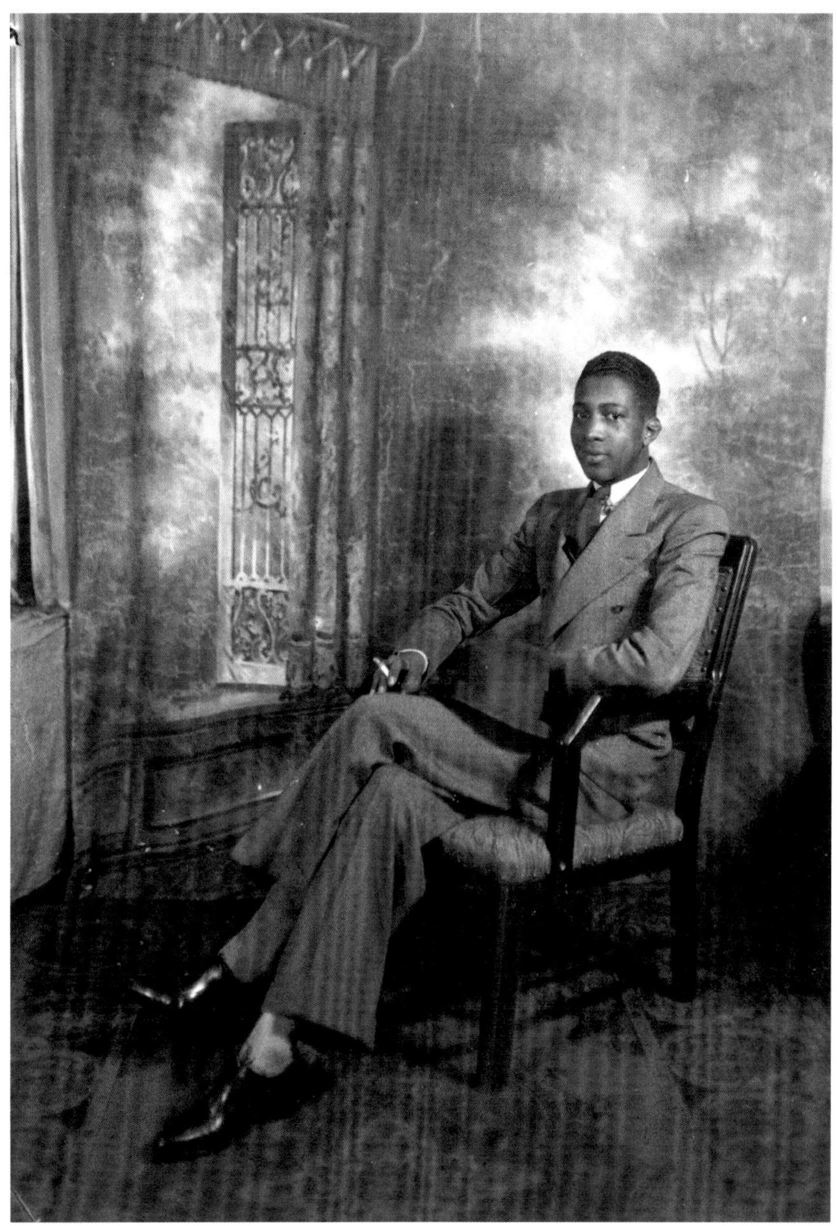

FIGURE 1.12

Winifred Hall Allen, *Portrait of a Man*, 1920s. Jamaican-born Allen operated a studio in Harlem and also made house calls to photograph events such as birthday parties, weddings, and club celebrations.

Courtesy Jeanne Moutoussamy-Ashe.

A studio's location often influenced the clients who walked into the business. Consider the Vernon and King Photo Studio on West 135th Street, which was located near the YWCA, a place so highly trafficked that the front-desk guestbook became a valuable tool for tracking new arrivals to the city. As described by a woman who worked as the membership secretary at the YWCA around 1927, "There was a guestbook on the counter of the YWCA where everyone signed up and you checked it every few days to see who was in town and the *Amsterdam News* and *The New York Age*, the two newspapers, checked it for their list of people visiting the city."[85] As with Van Der Zee's close proximity to the library, now known as the New York Public Library's Schomburg Center for Research in Black Culture, the Vernon and King Photo Studio's location likely impacted its engagement with a Harlem clientele.

Two photographers in particular were able to prolifically capture an audience of entertainers owing to their highly advantageous location. Twin brothers Marvin and Morgan Smith, from Nicholasville, Kentucky, opened their first studio in 1939 at 141 West 125th Street in Harlem. The studio's location on the second floor of the building next to the Apollo Theater served as a huge draw, which aided in their business's successful role as the Apollo's official photographers.[86] The brothers lamented their second-floor location, since it reflected the practice of white owners not renting ground-level property to Blacks, a predicament that Van Der Zee seems to have avoided, given the first-floor location of all four of his studios.[87] However, in spite of this shortcoming, the brothers thrived within the field, later occupying two adjoining ateliers on West 125th Street, with a sign stating "M. Smith Photo Studio—Portraits of Quality."[88]

Many Black photographers called their studios "ateliers" to point to their intentional molding of the studio into a space for creating images that would have artistic cultural significance. Upon entering Van Der Zee's business at 2065 Seventh Avenue, visitors encountered a parlor room, as though they were stepping into a well-manicured and tasteful domestic space (figure 1.13). Complete with framed photographs on the wall, the studio started the photographic experience of self-fashioning even before one stood in front of the camera. This space both evoked the commercial parlor room of nineteenth-century photography studios and created a sense of domestic home life that reflected many of the residences Van Der Zee captured for his clients.[89] "Not quite public but not private," parlor rooms like Van Der Zee's also anticipated a long tradition of what can be termed a *migrant aesthetic*, the practice in homes of Blacks who migrated from

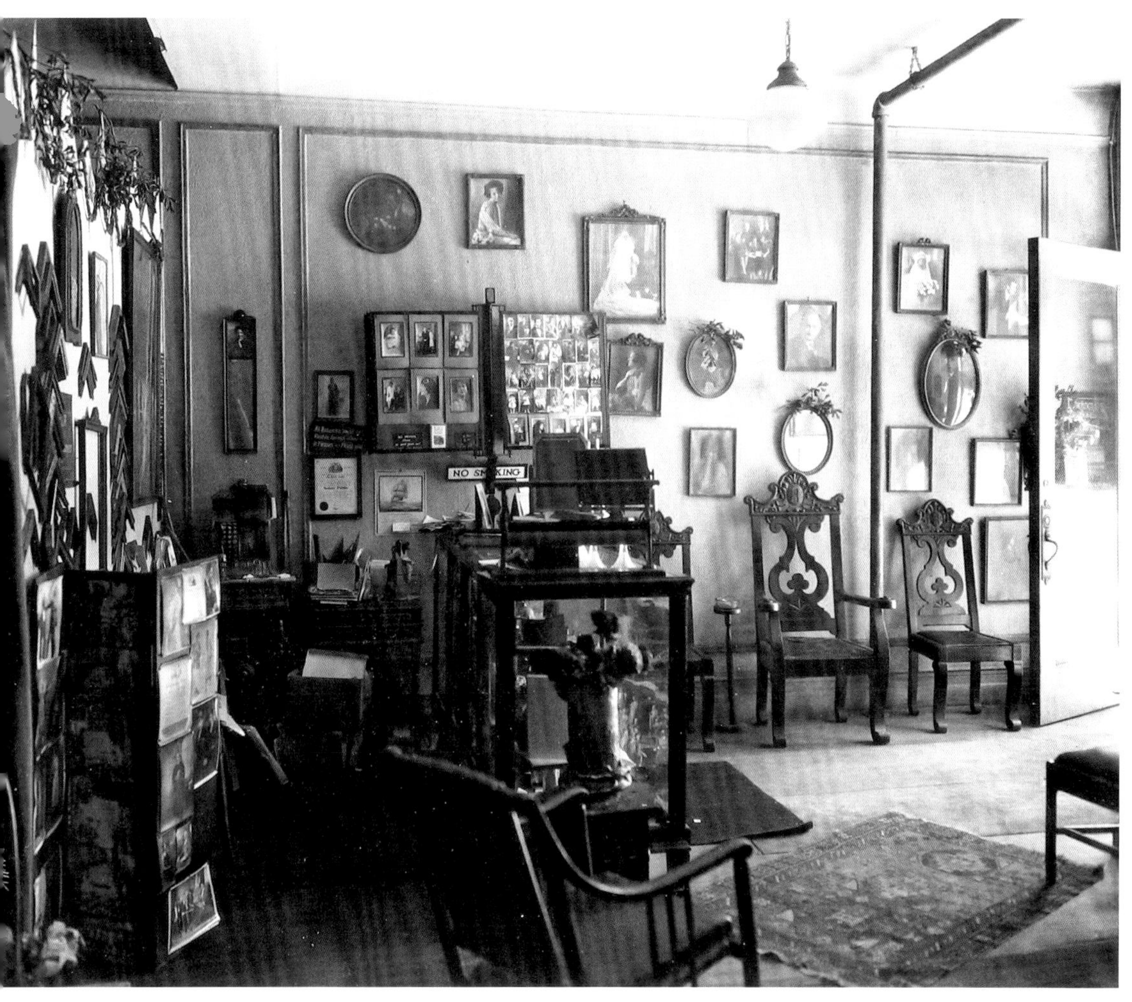

FIGURE 1.13

James Van Der Zee, *Van Der Zee Studio Interior at 2065 Seventh Avenue* (now Adam Clayton Powell Jr. Boulevard), 1930. The parlor room created a sense of domestic home life for Van Der Zee's clients.

Approx. 8 × 10 in. (20.3 × 25.4 cm). © James Van Der Zee Archive, The Metropolitan Museum of Art, New York. Source: Howard Greenberg Gallery, New York.

the Caribbean of having highly curated and decorated front rooms.[90] As entry points and signifying spaces, these rooms set an important tone for those who entered.

Descriptions of studio spaces during the Harlem Renaissance era became newsworthy. An article introducing the photographer C. B. Campbell—originally from Shannon, North Carolina—highlighted the alterations and remodeling of his 2312 Seventh Avenue studio.[91] Such changes included the shift from restricted quarters to "a large reception room, stock, enlarged work, operating and dressing rooms," which occupied the entire floor.[92] Campbell's business—devoted to portraits and commercial, newspaper, and theatrical work—benefited from the help of his wife, Ethel Campbell, and a young newspaper photographer, Edward Lewis. Similar to the way that Greenlee played a central role in the studio's operation—by, for example, taking photographs in Van Der Zee's temporary absence—Campbell's studio became an enterprise with many people involved.[93] Another of Van Der Zee's peers, Thos. H. Green, incorporated a photograph depicting his studio's parlor room for the purpose of advertising his studio to the *Crusader* newspaper's readership (figure 1.14).[94] Complete with a baby grand piano and walls tastefully covered with framed photographs, along with curtains, the room conveys a kind of domesticity that is as formal and elegant as Van Der Zee's studio's anteroom.

Of course, within the spaces of the photography studio, photographs were taken. According to the historian Myrtle Evangeline Pollard, writing in the 1930s, photographers in Harlem ran studios on Seventh Avenue for fifteen or twenty years, having learned of "the Black man's love of play, parades, and pictures."[95] Such a statement confirms the existence of longstanding photographers within the neighborhood and draws attention to their Black clientele and the occasions for which a photographer was needed. In addition, Pollard makes a distinction between white and Black photographers. According to Pollard, Woodard (and Black portraitists in general) gained a favored position among studio photographers because of his "added service of home sittings, commercial work and a peculiar understanding of eccentric vanities."[96] Along these lines, photographs—including Van Der Zee's numerous images of Black home interiors—may have reflected photographic subject matter that was limited, within Harlem, to Black photographers and their Black clientele.

Such assumptions can be extended to other genres, such as Van Der Zee's various mortuary photographs. For such intimate and emotionally driven photographs, Black clients most likely sought out Black photogra-

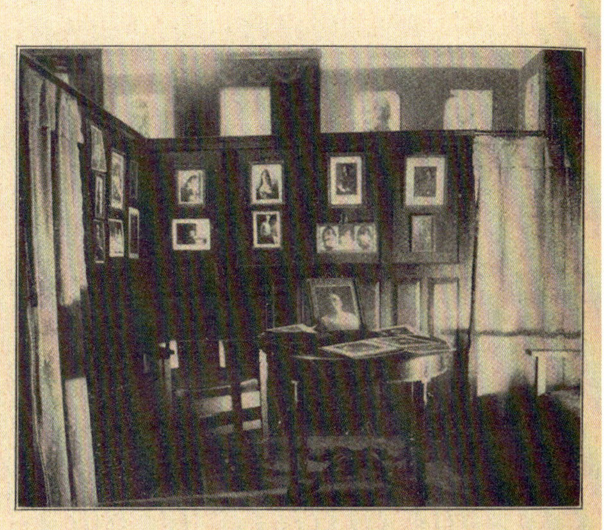

FIGURE 1.14

Thos. H. Green's studio parlor room, *Crusader*,
February 1921.

Source: Manuscripts, Archives and Rare Books Division,
Schomburg Center for Research in Black Culture,
New York Public Library.

phers. While Black clients did patronize white photographers, the ability
to choose a Black photographer illustrates the various options and possibilities for Blacks to not only choose how they wanted to be visually
represented but also purposefully select who would be responsible for ac-
tualizing their wishes.

Within such a niche environment, there were overlaps in subject matter among the photographers of Harlem. For example, along with Van Der
Zee and James Latimer Allen, a peer photographer by the name of R. E.
Mercer contributed to the numerous photographic representations of the
first Black millionaire, the New York–based Madame C. J. Walker and her
daughter, A'Lelia Walker.[97] Mercer worked in three of New York's leading
photographic studios in the 1920s, and as for many of Van Der Zee's peers,
his work was featured in the photographic exhibit catalog produced by the
Harmon Foundation in 1928.[98] Although they shared the Walker empire as
clients, Mercer's and Van Der Zee's engagement took different forms. Mercer

traveled outside Harlem with his client (as 1924 photographs that he took at the Walker's Villa Lewaro mansion in Irvington, New York, demonstrate), whereas Van Der Zee rarely did after establishing his business in Harlem.

One of the few Van Der Zee examples from a location outside of Harlem is a playfully posed photograph of three women lying next to each other at a New Jersey beach. This was most likely a scene Van Der Zee came upon, as opposed to clients he traveled with on assignment. It remains unclear to what extent most of Van Der Zee's peers had a reach outside New York. However, details about Mercer's presence in Irvington highlight the mobility of Harlem's world of studios, while reinforcing the centrality of the neighborhood within Van Der Zee's practice. This is one of the attributes that make Van Der Zee distinct: his strong link to Harlem, something scholar Leigh Raiford described in stating that "for Van Der Zee, Harlem was the world."[99] Of course, as much as Van Der Zee was a mainstay in Harlem, his images traversed places, times, and contexts that Van Der Zee himself could never have predicted. Elsewhere in this book, different occasions when Van Der Zee's photographs transcended their status as mere personal keepsakes are addressed. However, to return to Raiford's phrase for now, Van Der Zee's world in early twentieth-century Harlem was a world in which the practice of photography across studios, as opposed to one eminent photographer, was king.

Centering the Black Quotidian

Approaching Van Der Zee's world of photography through the lens of many has implications beyond Harlem. It offers an occasion to reconsider a popular paradigm of race and representation. Within much of the scholarship on Black vernacular photography—and on documentary and photojournalism—the structure of meaning and analysis is often tethered to a long-considered dialectical relationship, one that Frantz Fanon so succinctly articulates in his book *Black Skin, White Masks*. For Fanon, the fact of Blackness is inextricably linked to dominant narratives of whiteness. Fanon illustrates this phenomenon by using the example of Black Antilleans and their relationship to language. He writes, "All colonized people . . . position themselves in relation to the civilizing language: i.e., the metropolitan culture."[100] While Fanon equates the dominant culture with that of the French, other writers look elsewhere to center the dependent relationship between Black and white. Canonical theories such as Du Bois's double consciousness present a twinning of Black and white as inescapable. Du Bois's realization of being defined as other in relationship to whiteness first manifested through anecdotal life experiences, as described in *The Souls of Black Folk*. For him nationality is also key as he writes about the dilemma of being both Negro and American. In the case of Van Der Zee, the twinning to whiteness often becomes evident when scholars, for example, compare and contrast his work and engagement with Harlem to that of white photographers, as opposed to turning to one of Van Der Zee's Black Harlem peer photographers. Van Der Zee is most often compared to white photographers who did not own studios in Harlem and whose livelihood did not depend on a portraiture business. To Miriam Thaggert, like many scholars before her, Van Der Zee defines a particular time period along with photographers such as Aaron Siskind and Carl Van Vechten. In her words, the three photographers "are central to visual definitions of the Harlem Renaissance."[101] She continues, "Van Der Zee in the 1920s and 1930s, and Siskind, in the 1930s and 1940s, portray the black body in ways that counter traditional representations of blackness."[102] While some scholars focus on the representational possibilities of Blackness, others linger on the limitations of the work of white photographers, who were merely visiting and failed to ever fully access Harlem.

The late art historian Maurice Berger illustrates this point in his scholarship on the Photo League's "Harlem Document" project. He situates the league photographer Aaron Siskind in relationship to Black photographers of Harlem in ways that have relevance and applicability beyond the Harlem Document. In giving substantial attention to the role of photography for and by African Americans in his article "Man in the Mirror: Harlem Document, Race, and the Photo League," Berger writes, "With the exception of Carter, who was African American and lived in Harlem, the project team was exclusively white and predominantly Jewish. The history of black self-representation that it ignored or did not know—particularly the long-standing use of photographs, taken by and for African Americans, to educate, motivate, and empower—was august and consequential. Work by these photographers rendered aspects of the Harlem Document and its methodology nearly obsolete by the time of its completion."[103] With one foot intimately in the larger and more dominant narrative of the history of photography, Berger as a scholar was ideally positioned to make these kinds of critiques. But such critiques, although effective in highlighting the common erasure of Black photographers and their contributions, again build from a comparative paradigm between Black and white. Alternatively, understanding Van Der Zee in relationship to whiteness repeatedly manifests in interpretations of Van Der Zee's dignified photographs as a counternarrative to the more degrading and racist representations of Blackness circulating throughout the dominant culture.

However, is there a way to center Black experiences and bring certain truths into view by foregrounding Blackness but not through this tethered relationship to dominant systems of meaning and value that seems so unavoidable and inherent?[104] Might these relational distinctions lose their prominence when we presume and center the Black quotidian? Assuming a world in which Van Der Zee's work is understood through the other photographers who operate studios around his has the potential to shift the nature of scholarly discussions. The materials to which we turn for comparison become more localized. Ironically, looking at the work produced closest to Van Der Zee broadens the scope through which his photographs are understood. When we compare him to those photographers who served a similar purpose for Harlem residents and visitors—instead of comparing him to photographers like Siskind based on their fame and subject matter (Harlem)—the stakes of Black quotidian life disrupt common narratives.

Instead of considering how Van Der Zee's photographs illustrate a visuality of uplift against the backdrop of Black denigration, what happens when we consider the experience of Black clients visiting his and other Harlem studios? Did they get dressed that morning consumed with the terms that usually render Van Der Zee's photographs as historically significant representations of Black pride and progress? Were they thinking, it is time to stand before the camera so that I can represent my Blackness in light of how whiteness has rendered me less than human and invisible? Or did they get dressed that morning pondering, for the umpteenth time, which outfit to wear that day? Did they slide their arm through their shirt or dress with the anticipation of eventually sharing their photograph with their mother, their uncle, or their cousin? Answering these questions is not feasible, nor is there a response that can account for every client. However, it may be wagered that these kinds of questions lead to a more layered and complex understanding of photography in the lives of Van Der Zee's clients, one that can be ordered by big proclamations of Black advancement just as significantly as by the small gestures of everyday, mundane Black experiences. Recognizing the choice in thinking differently about Van Der Zee's photographs offers additional approaches to the dichotomous relationship that pervasively orders our racialized lives.

Doing so reframes the cultural logic of Blackness as not dependent on its role as counter to white but centered on other examples within a Black sphere. This sphere is Harlem's dynamic world of photography, a part of the Black vernacular practices of photography built and engaged through the lens of everyday living, as opposed to the larger implications of how Black progress is visually represented in the face of consistent abjection. This all, of course, describes a relational practice of photography that comes into view—but not through the kinds of shadow archives theorist Allan Sekula has privileged and numerous authors have taken up to consider photography's dialectical relationship as one among opposites or drastic differences. The archive of interest no longer must be based on a hierarchy in which racial difference is implicit. This archive no longer has to be, as Sekula writes, an "all-inclusive archive necessarily contain[ing] both the traces of the visible bodies of heroes, leaders, moral exemplars, celebrities, and those of the poor, the diseased, the insane, the criminal, the nonwhite, the female and other embodiments of the unworthy."[105] Instead, there are benefits to privileging a kind of archive that thrives on nuanced similarities, repetitions with slight differences among a group of photographs made in one place predominantly by Black photographers. Because there were so many studios, sitters and photographers alike developed a visual literacy that enabled them to determine their preferred aesthetic style and, in turn, the photography studio they chose to visit. The subjects featured in *Couple Wearing Raccoon Coats* patronized Van Der Zee, possibly not because they wanted to represent an idealized example of modern Black subjects of means and mobility, but because they liked the way Van Der Zee welcomed them into his studio. They may have appreciated how his style and skill as a photographer resonated with their desire to memorialize their likeness; he may have successfully stood apart from the other studios down the street.

Photography and its production served as a part of Harlem's everyday landscape. Aside from the actual act of having one's likeness captured in the studio, the impact of passing not one, not two, but maybe three of these proprietors on a walk to the local grocery store would have positioned photography as an embedded feature of everyday life. While photographs within the home gave Black families an opportunity to become—as bell hooks describes—"keeper(s) of the walls" as well as curators who arranged photographs to illustrate relationships and genealogies, a similar paradigm was taking place through photography's literal presence throughout the streets of Harlem.[106] And these were not just any streets but the very streets on which history was often made through the processions of groups celebrating, commemorating, or resisting. Not just one studio but many created a center of Black visual culture in Harlem through the medium of photography and the contours of the Black quotidian. So, too, did this environment significantly impact Van Der Zee's life in photography.

2

The Newspaper and Ubiquity

1924 Photographs as Moving Objects of the African Diaspora

Animating a Different Kind of Photographic Vision

JAMES VAN DER ZEE'S PHOTOGRAPHS are moving objects.[1] His photographs—once developed, dried, paid for, then taken by the owners—found their destiny elsewhere. Whether enclosed in envelopes addressed to family members out west, centered and mounted on living room walls in the Caribbean, or reproduced in calendars advertising local Harlem businesses, his photographs were transformed into moving objects simply by what happened to them, in action and even in thought, after leaving the studio.[2] The ways a photograph moves impact the kinds of imagining it can elicit. This chapter frames Van Der Zee's photographs as images that function in circulated and printed media, given Marcus Garvey's commissioning of Van Der Zee during the summer of 1924.[3]

Van Der Zee served an important role as a commercial photographer, carrying out Garvey's whims and serving this client's desire for visual ubiquity through print, just as Van Der Zee inhabited the role of an artist through his work as a photographer. Photography enabled Van Der Zee to do both. He served as a self-proclaimed and recognized artist as he simultaneously labored in unromanticized ways as a photographer running a business. In this chapter the context in which his photographs were viewed and engaged takes precedence over the photographer's skillful hand. Instead of focusing on Van Der Zee as a celebrated image maker worthy of art history's honorary pedestal, this chapter amplifies his photographs' significance once they leave the studio and are no longer narrowly tethered to Van Der Zee solely as his visual creation.

The means and channels through which people can see and engage with images are central to understanding iconic images of African diasporic art history. This concept is most evident in how the trope of the ship signifies. According to cultural studies scholar Paul Gilroy, beyond its straightforward function, a ship carries a significant amount of conceptual heft as a symbol and as an image. To Gilroy, ships "immediately focus attention on the middle passage, on the various projects for redemptive return to an African homeland, on the circulation of ideas and activities, as well as the movement of key cultural and political artefacts." Of these key artifacts, Gilroy's references include books, gramophone records, and choirs. Along the same lines as books, Gilroy could easily have included newspapers, like the *Negro World*, the print media that served as a physical vehicle for the circulation of Van Der Zee's photographs.[4] Ships represent a means for connection across the diaspora, just as newspapers were "mobile elements" that joined *Negro World* viewers and readers from across the Atlantic.[5] While the ship has functioned as the prototypical icon of the Black diaspora and Black Atlantic, in many ways *Negro World* can advance understandings of photography's role within this transnational context. Stated differently, just as the physical mobility enabled by the ship was fundamental to thinking about diaspora, so too are the possibilities of viewership created by the newspaper's ability to be folded, to be tucked within suitcases, and to embark on journeys that crisscross the globe.

This chapter prioritizes print media as the dominant mobile unit of the diaspora, within an unfolding narrative filled with photographic images and their important role in advancing and at times—in the case of mail fraud—impeding Garvey's hopes for UNIA. Photographs. Postcards. Reproductions in print. These are the cultural units that enabled Garvey's vision to spread. If the ubiquity of images is central to vernacular photographs, this chapter highlights the avenues through which Van Der Zee's photographs became ubiquitous, thereby shifting the rarified framework of art history's more common way of attending to Van Der Zee's photographs toward a more intricate and expansive redress.

In the summer of 1924, as a departure from his focus on indoor studio portraits, Van Der Zee became the official photographer for the international leader Marcus Garvey and his organization, the Universal Negro Improvement Association (UNIA).[6] Some of the best known of the many resulting photographs were printed from a series of negatives showing Garvey seated in an open-top car as part of a Harlem parade procession. In one iteration of *Marcus Garvey in a UNIA Parade*, Garvey sits among his entourage (figure 2.1). The driver looks to his left. Another man sits to Garvey's right in the paused vehicle.[7] A third man, wearing a striped necktie, stands against the car with a hand grazing the fender. The inferred busyness of the parade in the background offsets Garvey's regal comportment in his extravagant plumed hat and bedecked military attire. His crew don suits, academic regalia, and military uniforms.

The range of characters depicted, the direct and central view of Garvey within the parade setting, and the urban street background make this a particularly remarkable photograph among the many Van Der Zee took as part of his commission. However, the most compelling aspects of *Marcus Garvey in a UNIA Parade* exist outside of what appears within the photograph's four corners. Viewers in the early twentieth century would have seen a version in newsprint, a format nearly absent from existing scholarship on Van Der Zee.[8] The image is included in one of the three photograph series of the 1924 UNIA convention featured in the *Negro World* newspaper. They appeared on three Saturdays in 1924: August 9, August 16, and August 30.[9]

Scholars have turned to *Marcus Garvey in a UNIA Parade* and closely related prints from Van Der Zee's larger oeuvre to illustrate aspects of the African diaspora during the 1920s. For example, photo historian Deborah Willis features the photograph as a way to describe UNIA and its international and domestic reach.[10] Gilroy includes the image in a discussion of the early twentieth-century transnational nature of Harlem.[11] In addition, the African American studies scholar Leigh Raiford attends to the image as a touchstone for her argument on the photographic practice of diaspora.[12] For Raiford, the phrase *photographic practice of diaspora* captures her intention of interrogating how photography articulates

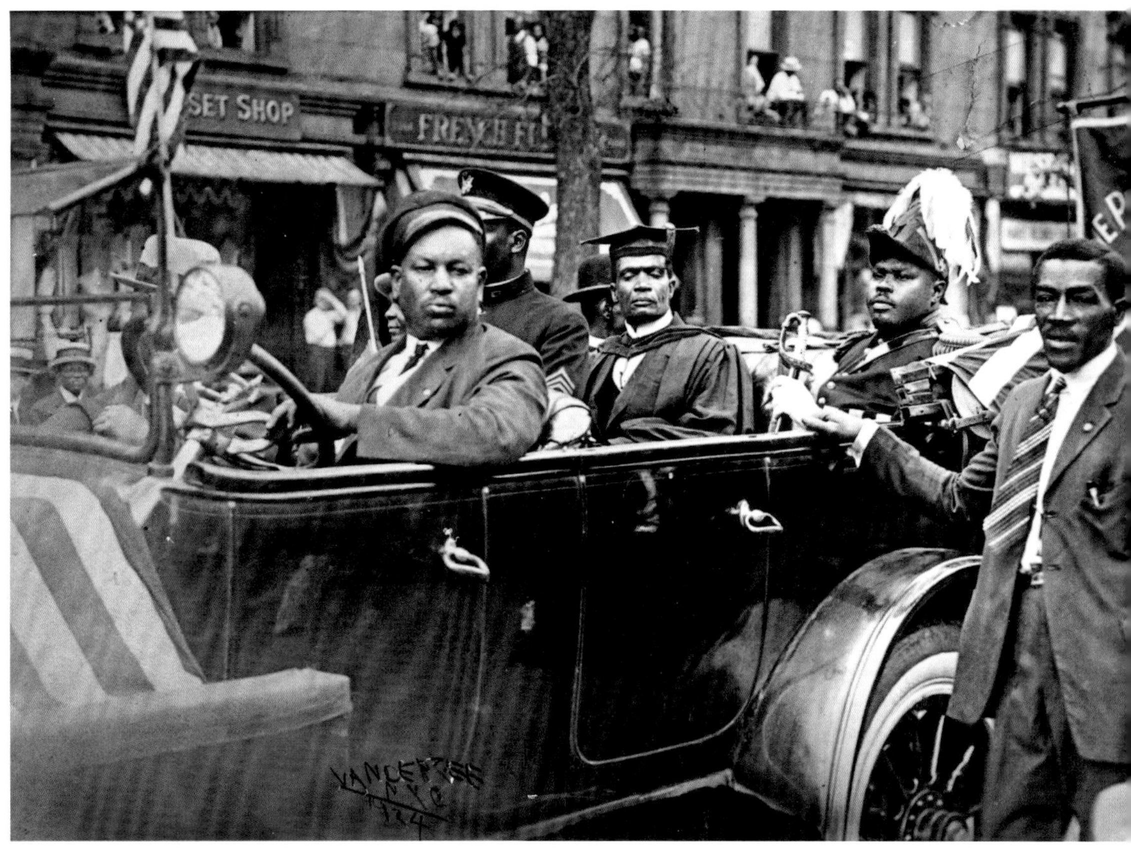

FIGURE 2.1

James Van Der Zee, *Marcus Garvey in a UNIA Parade*,
1924. Van Der Zee served as official photographer for
Garvey and the Universal Negro Improvement Association.

6⁷⁄₁₆ × 9⁷⁄₁₆ in. (16.4 × 24 cm). Source: The Metropolitan Museum
of Art, New York.

transnational Black connections.[13] As an amendment to Brent Hayes Edwards's idea of the practice of *diaspora*, a term that, for Edwards, captures the links—albeit often skewed, uneven, or constitutively based on difference—among populations of African descent, Raiford's photographic practice of diaspora similarly aims to signal the way subject positions are shaped by the fact of spatial reach and movement.[14] She does so through highlighting the composition of the photograph as indicative of diaspora, since Garvey as a Jamaican Pan-Africanist is triumphantly taking up space and carrying out his mission on the streets of Harlem. Here diaspora becomes something that can be seen and understood through the historical relevance of the depicted subject and the way they are visually represented.

Both the medium of photography and diaspora intrinsically depend on channels and networks, and the link between them is paramount here. By turning to Stuart Hall's scholarship, the art historian Kobena Mercer reminds readers of how concepts of the diaspora have a lot in common with how photographs operate.[15] Aligned with Gilroy's articulation of Black diasporic formation as a phenomenon that reveals culture as something that becomes disarticulated out of one context and rearticulated into others, Hall offers the following powerful assertion: "There is no such unitary thing as 'photography.' Photography is a convenient way of referencing the diversity of practices, institutions and historical conjunctures in which the photographic text is produced, circulated, and deployed."[16] Photography and diaspora become parallel concepts, each defined by their ability to move, shift, change, and transform through time.

Nonetheless, in existing conversations on diaspora and on Van Der Zee's photograph of Garvey, limited consideration is given to what happens to this photograph or its larger set, or to the visually specific ways in which it traveled and reached audiences of the day—all important aspects of how photography enables Van Der Zee's images to have resonances and iterations that transcend what may have been intended. To fill this gap in how Van Der Zee's work has been framed, this chapter insists that the newspaper medium in which the UNIA photographs appear and the photographs' arrangement and reproduction animate a different kind of photographic vision—one that expands the possibilities of Van Der Zee's images and their global circulation as moving objects.

Details of Marcus Garvey Commission

Although UNIA was headquartered in Harlem as of 1916, its goals were an extension of aspirations developed from Garvey's early experiences in Jamaica. After employment in the printing industry and leading a printers' strike at the young age of twenty in British colonial Jamaica, Garvey began his commitment to improving the lives of individuals of African descent through organized efforts that included the dissemination of his message of Black empowerment via a number of means, such as textual and visual printed materials.

In July 1914 Garvey founded the Universal Negro Improvement Association and African Communities League in Jamaica with his first wife, Amy Ashwood.[17] Initially, Garvey confined his emerging movement to Jamaica. With time, and with encouragement from the African American civil rights leader Booker T. Washington, Garvey planned a fundraising lecture tour throughout the United States for the end of 1915. The two leaders had begun to correspond in 1914 about Garvey's desire to raise funds for UNIA's industrial farm and institute.[18] However, the trip was postponed to 1916 following Washington's unexpected death. Garvey arrived in New York on March 23 of that year. He wasted no time in moving toward his lecturing goal. With a job at a printing press and housing temporarily secured, he started saving money for the tour. Initially, Garvey intended for Jamaica to serve as the main location of his endeavors, and he conceived of this trip to fit within his plan for advancing the movement. After a tour that took him to thirty-eight states over the course of a year, he returned to Harlem, a location that was increasingly, according to the historian Tony Martin, a "microcosm of the Black world."[19] There he set up a temporary base.[20]

While in Harlem, Garvey frequently spoke as a soapbox and stepladder orator, a common practice on the streets of the neighborhood for a range of commentators. In addition to making his voice heard to passersby, Garvey started to form alliances with some of Harlem's activists, including the West Indian radical Hubert Harrison; he also began to cultivate a following through the weekly meetings he held every Sunday at Lafayette Hall. Harlem soon turned from serving as a temporary site to being integral to the movement's existence as an international force. No longer an auxiliary to the Jamaican headquarters, UNIA was incorporated under New York laws on July 2, 1918. A month or two later, Garvey created the *Negro World*, his organization's newspaper, to increase the influence and visibility of UNIA. Martin sheds light on the beginnings of this publication in Harlem, explaining that "the earliest issues [of the *Negro World*] were distributed free by being pushed under peoples' [*sic*] doors in the early hours."[21]

From these initial beginnings, UNIA developed into an extremely powerful organization; its flagship newspaper was distributed worldwide. Garvey became a singular leader with a significant following in over 1,100 branches across the United States, Africa, the Caribbean, and Latin America.[22] By 1919, three years after Garvey's arrival in Harlem, he was recog-

nized by followers all over the globe. Through the organization he aimed
to embody the aspirations to self-determination, justice, and freedom from
institutional and colonial racism held by millions of individuals of African
descent. By the mid-1920s, seven hundred UNIA branches operated in the
United States alone, many of which were located in the South. Internationally, active branches existed throughout Africa and in every corner of the
African diaspora, including the Spanish- and French-speaking Caribbean
and South and Central America.[23] The *Negro World*'s coverage of UNIA's
annual conventions reflected many of Garvey's goals. These events began
in 1920 but were canceled in 1923; when the convention was revived in
1924, Van Der Zee was involved. In a June 14, 1924, *Negro World* advertisement with a design similar to a broadside poster, the convention's purpose and agenda come into view. The event was billed as the occasion for
the "formation of Negro Political Union to Protect Rights of Race."[24] The
topics for discussion were divided into eleven categories, including industrial, commercial, social, religious, and political concerns. Despite high
aspirations, UNIA and Garvey's ability to lead followers weakened over a
very short period of time.

Between the second annual convention in August 1921 and the third
in August 1922, UNIA's political influence and economic stability declined.[25]
Subsequently, a "Garvey Must Go Campaign," which derided Garvey as an
overly bombastic fraud, gained the support of many of his internal oppo-
nents within UNIA. By the 1924 convention, a number of the organization's
top leaders had left after major conflicts, in one extreme case leading to
manslaughter. Concurrently, the US government was building a case against
Garvey, piece by piece. Federal officials considered Garvey a major threat
for several reasons; for example, many of his speeches that included statements about the treatment of Blacks in the country were considered in-
flammatory by the government. In isolation, each example might not have
alarmed government officials. Yet, given the frequency of Garvey's rousing
statements and the massive audiences to whom he spoke, government officials grew apprehensive.[26]

Within the Black community, opinions about Garvey remained mixed
as people took sides. Respected individuals remained loyal to Garvey,
thereby bolstering his standing and access to individuals and communities
who might have ignored his presence otherwise. For example, John Edward Bruce committed the final years of a long and respected career of ad-
vocating for Black advancement to being a major defender and supporter

of Garvey and UNIA. Aside from regularly publishing in the *Negro World*, Bruce had a network of influential people across the globe, which aided in the development of UNIA's presence throughout the continent of Africa. From a local standpoint, Bruce leveraged his community standing among fraternal and professional organizations for Garvey's benefit. For example, along with Arthur Schomburg, Bruce encouraged the Prince Hall Masons to serve as major supporters of UNIA during the early 1920s.[27]

At the same time, many influential political figures of the early twentieth century deplored Garvey's agenda. During the 1920s the *Chicago Defender* "had led a pack of Negro papers in shrilly denouncing Garvey as a menace and disgrace to the Black race."[28] Individuals made sharp slanders; Hubert Harrison, the former editor of the *Negro World*, mocked the focus of Garvey's "intensive propaganda" on "sensationalism, self-glorification, and African liberation—although [Garvey] knew nothing of Africa."[29] Comments poking fun at Garvey's somewhat extravagant style—illustrated by signature hats with an array of colorful feathers—only encouraged the ostracizing of Garvey, beyond his political ideas and motivations for change. Such disparaging monikers that focused on Garvey's appearance highlight the centrality of the visual in eliciting meaning. Garvey understood the power of images and employed his own culture of the visual accordingly through Van Der Zee's photographs.

In the spring of 1924, Garvey requested that Van Der Zee serve as his official photographer, a role that distinguished him from other photographers who captured Garvey's likeness. Van Der Zee captured Garvey and his full participation in Harlem during the August 1924 convention. Because the government would eventually indict and deport Garvey on charges related to mail fraud, 1924 was Garvey's last year as a free man in the United States.[30] This was also a time of continuing and consistent unrest related to Garvey's conviction. Against this backdrop the August convention was extremely significant—a swan song of sorts. According to the Garvey historian Robert Hill, the 1924 convention was "the largest and the best documented of Garvey's meetings, to which James Van Der Zee's photographs give eloquent visual testimony."[31]

However, Van Der Zee's photographs did more than offer an exceptional witness to Garvey's project. They offered proof of Van Der Zee's reach. A nimble read holds both the photography's intentional composition and the other side of things together. Just as "photography exceeds human intentionality," the uses of his photographs, once they left the highly controlled space of his photography studio, likewise intersected with a larger and often unplanned platform of meaning.[32] If vernacular photographs, as art historian Brian Wallis writes, are defined more by their destination than their origin, what exactly were Van Der Zee's photographs destined for?[33]

Although the exact terms of Van Der Zee's agreement are unknown, he seems to have concentrated on the parade and the convention proceedings in Liberty Hall. He also produced in-studio portraits of Garveyite families. In one example, the male figure of the family proudly appears dressed in his military-like UNIA uniform (figure 2.2). As opposed to being positioned in a way that would elicit a sense of close relationship among the figures, the male figure stands slightly apart from the other two figures, allowing the full grandeur of his outfit to become a focal point of the photograph. The 1924 convention schedule included featured speakers from all over the world and a host of very visible events, including parades, plays, and evening balls. For example, as the finale to all the UNIA conventions, a processional parade took place down Seventh Avenue, not far from Van Der Zee's studio at 109 West 135th Street. In addition to the aforementioned images in the *Negro World*, Van Der Zee reproduced and distributed copies as scene postcards, individual portrait photographs, and even a calendar.[34] Like the man in the Garveyite family portrait, individuals wanted to visually memorialize this moment.

On the heels of the convention's conclusion, Van Der Zee was bombarded with inquiries and orders from UNIA members around the world.[35] Van Der Zee may have produced, for example, the photo postcard of UNIA's Black Star Line steamship, the *Yarmouth* (circa 1920), in response to or in anticipation of such increased business (figure 2.3). The international circulation of and demand for Van Der Zee's photographs are demonstrated by the portraits of Prince Kojo Tovalou-Houénou of Benin, a featured speaker at the 1924 convention, who requested fifteen hundred copies from the local photographer.[36] In one portrait Van Der Zee's popular props of a telephone, stack of books, and simple backdrop frame the seated prince, while another is a close-up of the prince's face and torso.[37] However, as opposed to prints with uncertain destinations like the *Yarmouth* postcard and the Prince Tovalou-Houénou portrait, Van Der Zee's multiple photographs in the *Negro World* had an audience of anyone, anywhere in the world, who opened and viewed the newspaper pages. The ubiquity of photographic multiples enables Van Der Zee's presence in the world. Focusing on reproduction illustrates what a vernacular turn to Van Der Zee can offer.

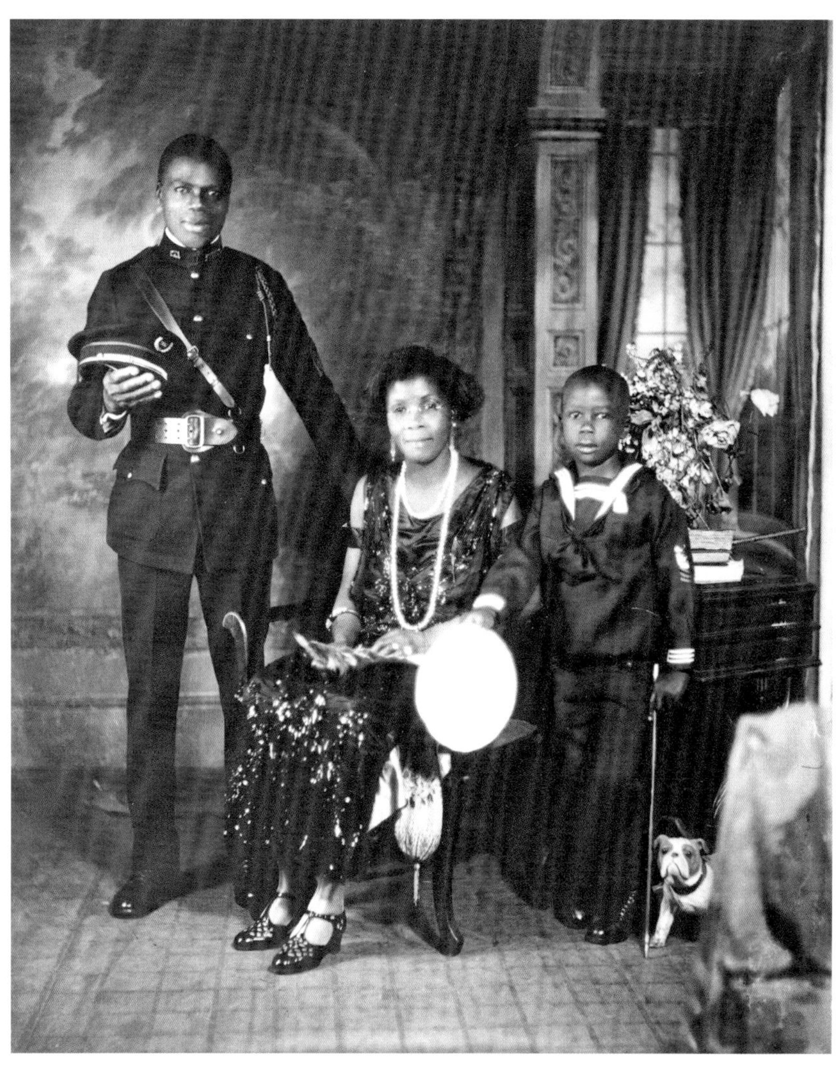

FIGURE 2.2

James Van Der Zee, *A Member of Garvey's African Legion with His Family*, 1924.

9½ in × 7¾ in (24.1 × 19.6 cm). © James Van Der Zee Archive, The Metropolitan Museum of Art, New York. Source: Museum of Contemporary Photography, Columbia College, Chicago.

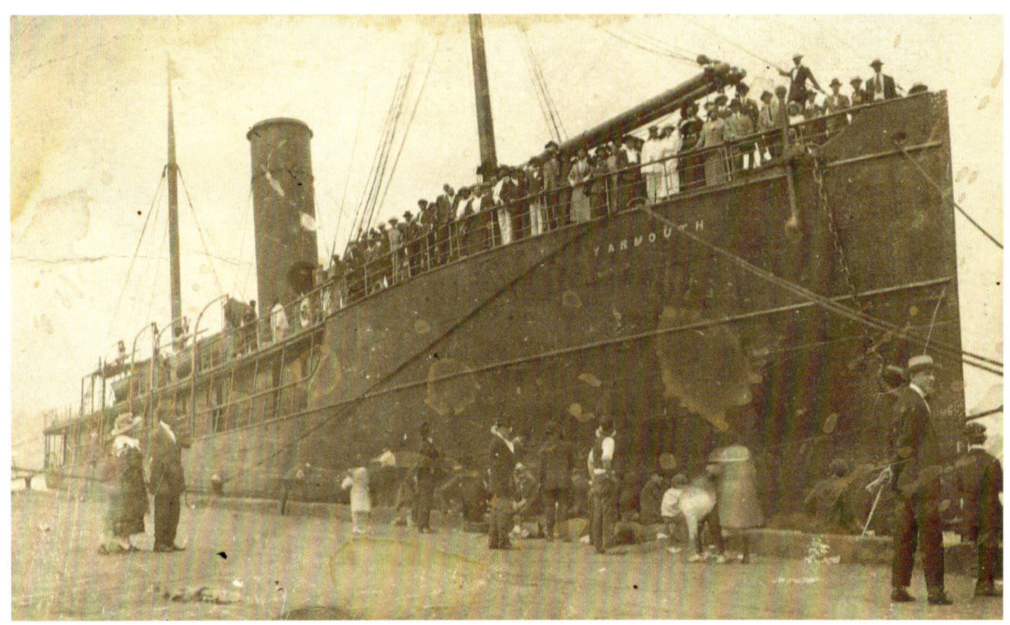

FIGURE 2.3

James Van Der Zee, SS *Yarmouth* (a Black Star Line passenger ship), ca. 1920.

3¼ × 5⁷⁄₁₆ in. (8.3 × 13.8 cm). © James Van Der Zee Archive, The Metropolitan Museum of Art, New York. Source: James Van Der Zee Archive, The Metropolitan Museum of Art, New York.

The Power of the Newspaper through Its Reach

Described by Black studies scholar Theodore Vincent as the "greatest single power in the negro race" in 1926, the Black press had a distribution and readership that reached unprecedented levels during World War I and continued through the height of the Great Depression.[38] The *Negro World* (1918–1933) counted among various print media outlets vying for engaged readers through a range of means. Images played a central role in their appeal. For example, in a holiday subscription circular from 1925 (figure 2.4), the *Crisis*—the magazine of the National Association for the Advancement of Colored People (NAACP), edited by W. E. B. Du Bois—conveys holiday cheer and its gift potential through a pair of Winold Reiss's festive Afro-influenced illustrations, insisting, "In 1926 we plan a banner year. There will be beautiful covers and our usual selection of exclusive pictures from

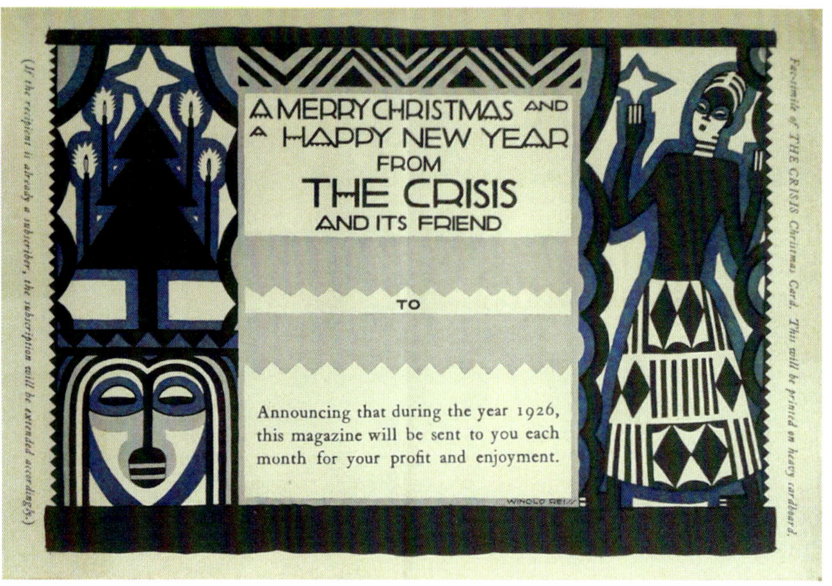

FIGURE 2.4

Facsimile of *Crisis* Christmas card, 1925.

Source: Carl Van Vechten Papers, Manuscripts and Archives Division, New York Public Library, and *Crisis* magazine.

all over the world together with a new arrangement of typography. We shall especially stress and explain the problems of the colored world. . . . We are in direct and continued communication with all parts of Africa, with Europe, all Asia, the West Indies and South America."[39] Images were enough of a selling point for early twentieth-century audiences that the *Crisis* boasted that they would appear in upcoming editions. Halftone printing made the high-quality reproduction of images possible. Photographs, in particular, had become an expected part of newspapers by 1900.[40]

Van Der Zee's images of Garvey in the *Negro World* achieved a particularly high level of visibility. Although the *Negro World* aligned with other Black newspapers—such as the NAACP's *Crisis*, the Black cultural journal *Opportunity*, the Harlem-based *Amsterdam News*, and the news and opinion journal the *New York Age*—in their intention to impact Black audiences, the *Negro World* reached a distinctly large international audience.[41] The *Negro World* became the first Black paper with a circulation of over two hundred thousand within both domestic and international spheres during the early 1920s, which cemented the periodical's prevailing role.[42] That a Black organization achieved such exposure reflects the success of UNIA's networks of distribution and its solid link to broader African diasporic audiences. By extension, a noteworthy number of readers outside of the United States would have had access to Van Der Zee's photographs at the time of the 1924 convention.

Facing the Larger African Diaspora

Marcus Garvey's Pan-African world during 1924 was very much grounded in Van Der Zee's Harlem. In an era that is often remembered through W. E. B. Du Bois's talented tenth and Alain LeRoy Locke's New Negro rhetoric, Garvey offered an alternative philosophy that spoke to the people of Harlem and, arguably, by extension, the larger African diaspora.[43] By this time, Harlem's dominant population was composed of the descendants of enslaved Americans from the Great Migration, recent immigrants from the Caribbean islands and Africa, and a constant stream of people from all parts of the country and the globe visiting and experiencing the acclaimed Black mecca. To walk down the streets of Harlem was to walk through a place where UNIA's imprint was palpable, whether or not one recognized it as such. On street corners, orators added to the defining bustle and urban life of Harlem's streets, while places run by UNIA—including two grocery stores, a millinery shop, a bakery, and the organization's headquarters at 56 West 135th Street, one block away from Van Der Zee's studio—ensured that the visual and material manifestations of Garvey's vision and his paradigmatic presence were prevalent.

Under Garvey's direction, the *Negro World* identified Harlem as an archetypal location of Black advancement. A one-page illustrated advertisement from the Saturday, July 8, 1922, edition of the *Negro World* is telling. Readers are given a descriptive tour of select UNIA businesses in Harlem, all of which were "recent ventures" established in 1922. The reporters exult, "We visited Grocery Store No. 1, 47 West 135th Street and found Mr. E. Wright, the manager and his assistant Mary Crawford serving a stream of morning customers." The article continues, highlighting places such as UNIA's Universal Grocery and Market and the Universal Restaurant.[44]

Image and text are paired to build a powerful narrative about the Bee Hive Printing Plant, which published the *Negro World* newspaper and other UNIA materials. The article's words are completed with a portrait of Lyllian Galloway, the plant manager, along with five separate graphic illustrations of printing presses arranged across the page. The depictions of machines can be likened to character studies. Presenting the machines in profile or in three-quarter view, these portraits capture a full range of knobs, jutting extensions, wheels, and towering flat boards. Said to print "the bulk of colored Harlem's job printing and magazine making," the two-floor plant represented in these illustrations exposed readers of the diaspora to these important machines that labored in ways analogous to the busy worker "bees" populating the Harlem UNIA establishments.[45] This was just the kind of exemplary microcosm Garvey wanted to see multiplied throughout the Black world. Through local entities like the Bee Hive Printing Plant, Garvey advocated for the self-empowerment and self-sufficiency of the Black race within Harlem and beyond.

As scholars Brent Hayes Edwards, Theresa Leininger-Miller, Krista Thompson, and others have shown, the New Negro movement was grounded within a domestic sphere as much as it unfolded within a more global platform.[46] Edwards's reflections on Locke draw out this point even though a considerable portion of the historiography on the New Negro emphasizes US-bound themes. He writes, "The cosmopolite Howard University philosophy professor Alain Locke claimed in the introduction to his 1925 anthology *The New Negro* that his title was partly an allusion to the Negro's 'new internationalism,' which represented one of the few 'constructive channels' for Black cultural institution building beyond the 'cramped horizons' of postwar U.S. racism and segregation."[47] Harlem, in many ways, served as the nucleus of this outward-facing New Negro discourse.

This compelling notion filled Black print media of the day. Locke made this clear by praising newspapers as a constructive channel through which a new way of thinking could take shape and enlarge its reach. According to Locke, the pulse of this advancement had begun to beat in Harlem in the form of a new internationalism that aimed to recapture contact with people of African descent. This aspiration, according to Locke, could in the future possibly lead to the greatest rehabilitation of the New Negro.[48] However, as the writer, activist, and editor of the *Negro World* Hubert Harrison explained, the goals of the New Negro went beyond recapturing contact with the larger African diaspora. He wrote in his 1919 article "Our Larger Duty" that any attempts at solving Western world problems must be integrated or "linked up" with robust efforts being made elsewhere. Creating a substantial linkage and reaching toward a unified front are central to a dynamic formulation of the New Negro during the early twentieth century.[49] While images played a role in formulating the New Negro, the driving force was not in the image alone. The everyday nature of the vernacular, which moves images from being worth seeing to being seen, changes everything.

Why Multiple Photographs Matter

In spite of the visibility of reproductions, the reception of Van Der Zee's photographs cannot be determined. Local accounts are no longer extant. With the exception of a recollection published in 1938 by the British photographer Cecil Beaton, few primary documents survive concerning how Van Der Zee's photographs were received by his contemporary viewers.[50] This void aligns with examples of well-known subjects from the period. Like the available accounts of the reception of photographs of the author and orator Booker T. Washington by Black viewers, records of the reception of images of Garvey are scarce. However, in considering Washington's representation, art historian Michael Bieze insists that the prevalence of Washington's image among the Black populace demonstrates their engagement and his importance. He writes, "The best evidence of his legendary status within this group is found in his ever-present images and letters. One finds many references to his image tacked to the walls of tar paper shacks, propped in black store windows, filling the papers of calendars, and plastered on walls produced for speaking engagements. Washington's image for this audience did not depend upon high art refinement but rather ubiquitous presence."[51] As vernacular photographs comprise the bulk of photographic production, their ubiquity is their strength.[52] It affords the opportunity for images to become part and parcel of everyday life.

The circulation of images, for Garvey, aligns with this strategy of ubiquity, which is also parallel to the way that Van Der Zee placed advertisements in newspapers to increase his exposure to potential clients (figure 2.5).[53] Visually, reusing the same props and backdrop over and over could also serve as a way of being present in many places for Van Der Zee's photographs. Although portraiture is often regarded as an honorific genre historically reserved for the gentry, at its core is the attribute of repeated visual conventions. Images circulate as immaterialities, meaning through conventions, patterns, and content.[54] For example, in the case of Van Der Zee's portraits, the same landscape backdrop, the same desk, or the same rug is repeated over and over again. However, the most effective strategy for his photographs being many places at once manifested beyond the doors of his studio.

During the 1924 UNIA convention, the *Negro World* newspaper enabled the most significant circulation of Van Der Zee's photographs of UNIA. The newspaper did so through a surprising number of images, which is a clear departure from the paper's more frequent text-heavy block layout with a limited number of illustrations, such as page 2 of the March 25, 1922, *Negro World* issue (figure 2.6). The page is filled with various articles, with one photograph of UNIA members at a meeting in Gary, Indiana, at the very top, along with two advertisement images at the very bottom of the page. The top photograph was taken by William E. Woodard, one of Van Der Zee's peers who had formerly run a studio in New York. Similar layouts of articles and a small number of photographs by both identified and unidentified photographers repeat throughout the *Negro World.* Examples include a page from March 31, 1923, with a photograph of a Black Cross Nurse, and the front page of the August 23, 1924, issue, featuring a photograph of one of the UNIA ships, named the *General G. W. Goethals.* Although photographs were common within the periodical's pages, the number was consistently kept to a maximum of two or three per page.

In other Black periodicals, such as the *Amsterdam News* and the *New York Age*, it was common for entire pages to lack any images. When one or two photographs do appear, portraits are the most prevalent type of representation. If multiple images appear on one page, each image is often affiliated with a different news story. In turn, readers envision an event through a singular visual moment. For example, a front page of the *New York Age*, published right around the time of the UNIA convention, includes two portrait photographs, unrelated to UNIA, near the bolded headline "Legion Head Repudiates Garvey," which refers to the demise of his leadership among the organization's administration (figure 2.7).[55] Both linked to more mundane news stories: the first portrait captures the former treasurer of Tuskegee Institute, while the second depicts a nominee for assemblyman. In contrast, a conventional portrait would not have been able to complement the drama of the Garvey-related headlines. Whereas a portrait in the *New York Age* simply enhances a singular narrative, the *Negro World*'s arrangement of photographs animates the 1924 convention through multiple—and therefore more compelling—views. Within this context, the three series of Van Der Zee's photographs construct an especially distinctive arrangement, not necessarily because of where the photographer focused his lens or how he mindfully developed the film, but because of what happens out-

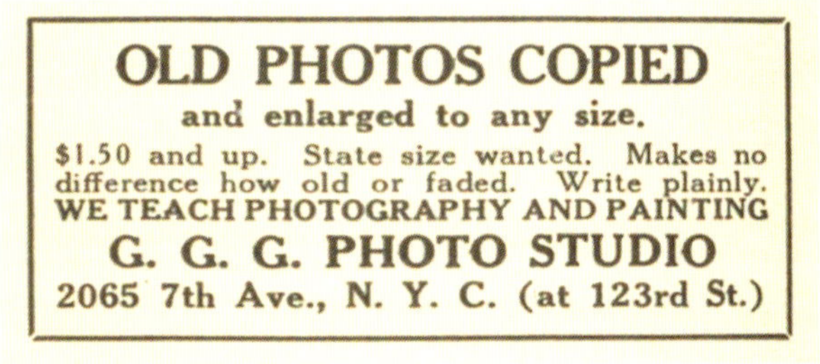

FIGURE 2.5

Advertisement for G. G. G. Photo Studio, *Crisis*, February 1934.

Source: Manuscripts, Archives and Rare Books Division, Schomburg Center for Research in Black Culture, New York Public Library.

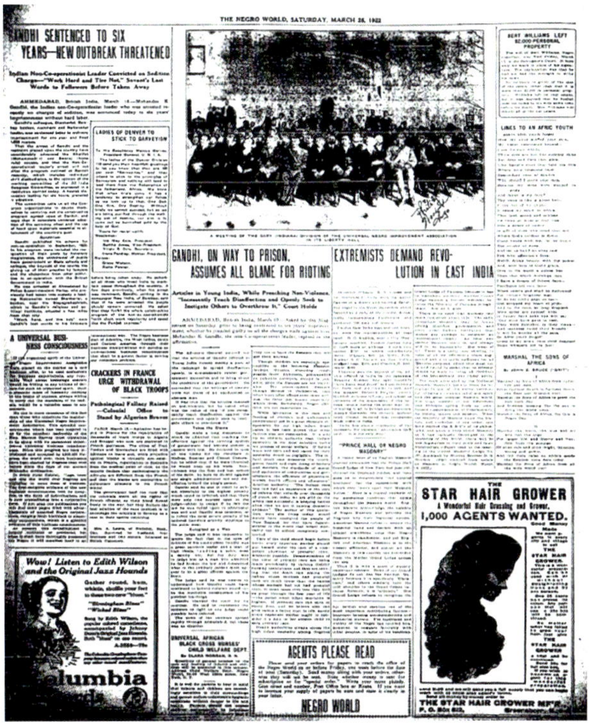

FIGURE 2.6

A page from Marcus and Amy Ashwood Garvey's *Negro World*, March 25, 1922, featuring photography by William E. Woodard.

Source: Research and Reference Division, Schomburg Center for Research in Black Culture, New York Public Library.

side of his discretion. Not only are the meanings of photographs unfixed, but their jurisdiction under a sole creator also remains unstable.

Reading the Reproduced Photographic Images

Rather than viewing Van Der Zee's photographs on the mantlepiece of a home or in a museum exhibit, early twentieth-century viewers with access to the *Negro World* would have seen the first series of Van Der Zee pho-

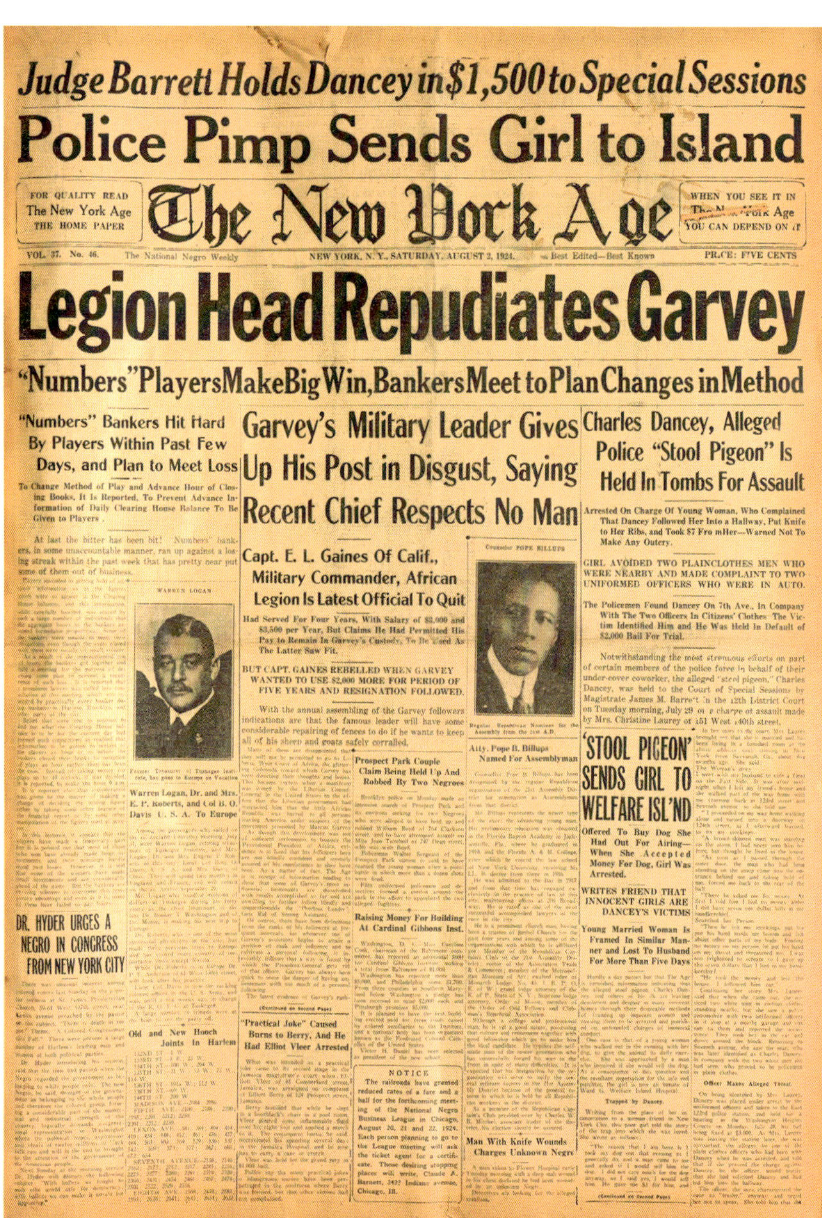

Judge Barrett Holds Dancey in $1,500 to Special Sessions

Police Pimp Sends Girl to Island

FOR QUALITY READ
The New York Age
THE HOME PAPER

The New York Age

WHEN YOU SEE IT IN
The New York Age
YOU CAN DEPEND ON IT

VOL. 37. No. 46. The National Negro Weekly — NEW YORK, N. Y., SATURDAY, AUGUST 2, 1924. — Best Edited—Best Known — PRICE: FIVE CENTS

Legion Head Repudiates Garvey

"Numbers" Players Make Big Win, Bankers Meet to Plan Changes in Method

"Numbers" Bankers Hit Hard By Players Within Past Few Days, and Plan to Meet Loss

To Change Method of Play and Advance Hour of Closing Books, It Is Reported, To Prevent Advance Information of Daily Clearing House Balance To Be Given to Players

Garvey's Military Leader Gives Up His Post in Disgust, Saying Recent Chief Respects No Man

Capt. E. L. Gaines Of Calif., Military Commander, African Legion Is Latest Official To Quit

Had Served For Four Years, With Salary of $2,000 and $3,500 per Year, But Claims He Had Permitted His Pay to Remain In Garvey's Custody, To Be Used As The Latter Saw Fit.

BUT CAPT. GAINES REBELLED WHEN GARVEY WANTED TO USE $2,000 MORE FOR PERIOD OF FIVE YEARS AND RESIGNATION FOLLOWED.

Charles Dancey, Alleged Police "Stool Pigeon" Is Held In Tombs For Assault

Arrested On Charge Of Young Woman, Who Complained That Dancey Followed Her Into a Hallway, Put Knife to Her Ribs, and Took $7 From Her—Warned Not To Make Any Outcry.

GIRL AVOIDED TWO PLAINCLOTHES MEN WHO WERE NEARBY AND MADE COMPLAINT TO TWO UNIFORMED OFFICERS WHO WERE IN AUTO.

The Policemen Found Dancey On 7th Ave, In Company With The Two Officers In Citizens' Clothes. The Victim Identified Him and He Was Held In Default of $2,000 Bail For Trial.

'STOOL PIGEON' SENDS GIRL TO WELFARE ISL'ND

Offered To Buy Dog She Had Out For Airing—When She Accepted Money For Dog, Girl Was Arrested.

WRITES FRIEND THAT INNOCENT GIRLS ARE DANCEY'S VICTIMS

Young Married Woman Is Framed In Similar Manner and Lost To Husband For More Than Five Days

DR. HYDER URGES A NEGRO IN CONGRESS FROM NEW YORK CITY

FIGURE 2.7

Front page of *New York Age* (August 2, 1924) with the headline "Legion Head Repudiates Garvey."

Source: Research and Reference Division, Schomburg Center for Research in Black Culture, New York Public Library.

tographs in five rows of three under the heading "Some Striking Scenes in Convention Parade" (figure 2.8). Mostly dated and signed, they depict crowds on Harlem streets from different perspectives. Some are evocative of an aerial shot, as when Van Der Zee positioned his camera above a crowd, while others capture the Harlem landscape and a compact sea of people advancing down the neighborhood's wide streets. The second series, from August 16, 1924, is also laid out on a single page (figure 2.9) and includes a version of *Marcus Garvey in a UNIA Parade*, the photograph discussed at the onset of this chapter. The *Negro World* page includes thirteen photographs, many of which are signed; this time, they are arranged with a central column of five, framed by angled images, under the heading "Photographic Views of Great Convention Parade." The photographs are laid out in such a way that they suggest a dynamic movement outward from the central image to the edges of the page. The third series is from Saturday, August 30, the last day of the convention. This series includes eight photographs arranged on a single page in two columns under the heading "Drawing Room Scenes at Third Royal Court Reception of Universal Negro Improvement Association to House of Delegates."[56] Each photograph captures an indoor scene of the convention, presumably events taking place inside Liberty Hall and other locations of UNIA gatherings.

The convention spoke directly to the generalized New Negro ideal along with the more specific goals laid out by UNIA. Garvey and his organization insisted on constructing a nation-state in Africa, promoting exchange between business enterprises in all-Black communities, and consolidating the political forces of Black subjects throughout the world. The strategies employed by the organization were vast. For example, UNIA aimed to address these three goals through a massive back-to-Africa plan, which would be financed through the purchase of stocks by UNIA members, among other means. The organization bought ships and anticipated the purchase of additional ships to transport Black travelers, facilitate transnational business relationships, and serve as examples of the organization's advancement.[57] Similarly, the annual conventions in Harlem—and the pictures of these events—served as important strategies for advancing the movement's specific aims through photography.

The three photograph series from the August 1924 convention establish a particular visual representation of the New Negro as a Black populace pridefully inhabiting their space. For example, although clear views of individuals are peppered throughout the fifteen photographs featured in the August 9, 1924, edition, overall these pictures highlight Black spaces

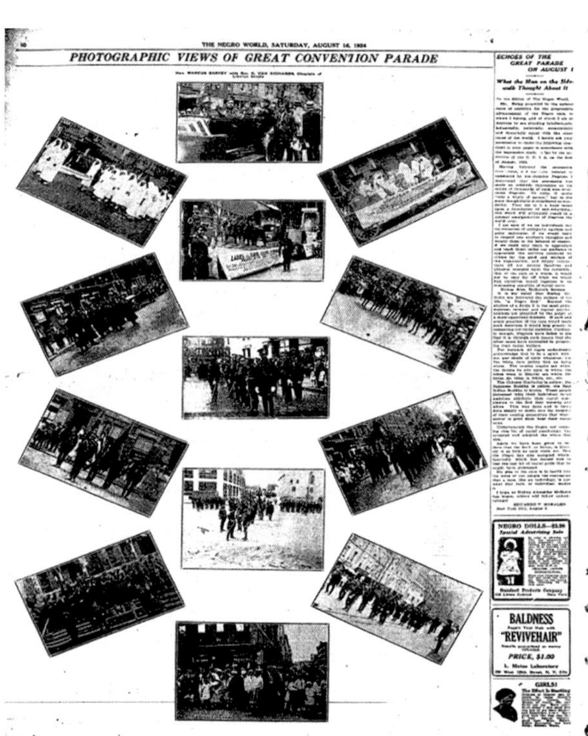

FIGURE 2.8

Page from the Garveys' *Negro World* (August 9, 1924) with Van Der Zee photographs from the UNIA Convention.

Source: Research and Reference Division, Schomburg Center for Research in Black Culture, New York Public Library.

FIGURE 2.9

Page from the Garveys' *Negro World* (August 16, 1924) with Van Der Zee photographs from the UNIA Convention, including a version of *Marcus Garvey in a UNIA Parade*.

Source: Research and Reference Division, Schomburg Center for Research in Black Culture, New York Public Library.

(figure 2.8). They chiefly capture spectacular crowds of well-dressed Black people within a cityscape. Additionally, store facades, residential buildings, and vehicles included in the parade processions (such as a boat on wheels) become legible. These details of a flourishing community of Black people capture the look of the era through their photographic representation.

The photographs reproduced in the *Negro World* all have certain aesthetic attributes in common that convey this sensibility. The more than thirty images collected on four newspaper pages from 1924 diverged from the highly detailed 5 × 7-inch and 8 × 10-inch gelatin-silver photographs familiar to Van Der Zee's Harlem-based clientele.[58] In the newspaper format, the convention's images lack the clarity, crispness, and tonal range of Van Der Zee's printed photographs. The images are small, creating an engagement similar to peering into the receding details found in urban photographs of the nineteenth century. These attributes point to provocative new questions, especially in light of the fact that the material transformation of Van Der Zee's photographs into newsprint was central to the photographs' power and significance. How might the reproduction and arrangement of such images impact the viewer's ocular experience? How might the characteristics inherent to these reproduced photographs be advantageous in ways that offer new approaches to considering how Van Der Zee's images functioned as they were translated and shifted from one material form to another?

In Van Der Zee's case, his photographs evoke a palpable kind of energy and specific presence. Motion, whether choreographed or natural, is captured throughout Van Der Zee's images of groups of Black figures in action. This sense of vitality is enhanced through the range of perspectival views offered in Van Der Zee's photographs dominating the center of the page. For example, fifteen images are arranged in a grid on one page of the August 9, 1924, issue of the *Negro World* (figure 2.8). Each picture has the same rectangular shape, with a long horizontal view. Each provides a window onto a crowded scene. In some, viewers are afforded a slightly elevated position as they look down and across to what is happening on the street below. In others, it appears as though Van Der Zee is standing at the front on the sidelines, with a clear and unobstructed view of the groups of UNIA members holding signs. Through a few examples, Van Der Zee offers a third perspective. In one photograph, there exist close-up figures in what otherwise would have been a clear sight line to the street's happenings. Viewers catch the close profile of a fellow observer; his upper body takes up one-fourth of the photograph. This man's features are hard to discern. His presence is the only thing recognizable, as are the basic outlines of what appears to be a festive parade. Despite the variations among the different perspectives, they all have one thing in common. The photographs strategically capture the population of Harlem in its full magnificence; the neighborhood is a backdrop. Van Der Zee's photographic vision offers a portrait of a city completely animated by the UNIA presence and leadership and—most of all—a manifestation of Black advancement through a sense of unity afforded by the medium of photography.

Indeed, unity became a major goal for the convention. On the front page of the July 12, 1924, *Negro World*, under the headline "Big Gathering of Negroes Will Be History-Making," Garvey describes the impending convention while highlighting the parade on the streets of Harlem. He continues to address his *Negro World* readers by sharing specific details as to where the celebrations in Harlem will take place and when people should assemble. All of this planning supported Garvey's larger goal. He aimed to "let us all unite to put the program over, and make 1924 the most brilliant and successful year in the history of the great Universal Negro Improvement Association."[59]

Van Der Zee's photographs and their circulation in the 1920s were part of a visual discourse in which unity became an asset that urgently needed to be witnessed. At a talk held at Liberty Hall days before the convention's start on August 1, the second assistant president general, William L. Sherrill, spoke to a capacity crowd of loyal UNIA members: "This convention . . . is one that the world will be watching, and in the hands of this convention will rest the destiny of the race."[60] More so than at any previous convention or UNIA gathering, the stakes of being viewed as united and understood as strong were articulated both textually, through statements such as Sherrill's, and visually, through Van Der Zee's compelling content and the editor's careful arrangement of his photographs.

In turn, Van Der Zee's photographs instructed viewers to witness. Important aspects of Black life are captured through photography, which can help construct a compelling narrative. As the subheadings on August 9, 1924, read, "Parade Biggest in History of Negroes Is Witnessed by Two Hundred Thousand People—Populace Is Carried Away with Enthusiasm at Success of Movement and Its Wonderful Demonstration—Harlem Home of 200,000 Negroes, Culls Out a Holiday—Marcus Garvey Cheered by Dense Throngs That Line Route of March." The photographs directed viewers as to what they were seeing, and the reasons for this perspective, beyond the display of unity, were made clear in the *Negro World*. According to the newspaper, the parade was "symbolic of an organization that has a purpose—the purpose of showing to the world that the Negro is capable of doing big things in an orderly and systematic way. No longer were the spectators a morbidly curious crowd who looked and scoffed but people who gazed with admiration at the wonderful demonstration staged by an organization which but a few short years ago was laughed at and jeered."[61] The spectators' response is emblematic of the kind of unity Garvey desired. Not only were his followers important in their presence, but so, too, was the audience's reaction. Van Der Zee's photographs served as an important visual conduit through which UNIA's unity could be seen. The circulation of these images through the particular material form of newsprint is key to understanding this visual sense of unity and its ability to galvanize connections. Once released into the world, the photographs literally move through different registers of meaning through their reproduction and arrangement in print.

More specifically, the halftone reproductions of Van Der Zee's photographs within the *Negro World*'s pages reinforce a sense of unity when considering how variations of skin complexion within the Black community often serve as a divisive subject, or at the very least a topic of interest pertaining to photographers. For example, in 1923 W. E. B. Du Bois called for Black photographers to tap into their talent to properly capture the skin complexions of Blacks.[62] In addition, James Latimer Allen, one of Van Der Zee's Harlem peers, was described in a newspaper article as specializing "in studying the color of skin of various Negro subjects and . . . adept in getting the proper background to match the skin texture."[63] This topic of skin, apart from photography, is also evident within Garvey's writings. Addressing the tendency for Black newspapers to carry ads for skin bleaching, Garvey asserts:

> There were many degrading exhortations to the race to change its black complexion as an entrant to society. There were pictures of two women, one black and the other very bright and under the picture of the black woman appeared these words: "Lighten your black skin" indicating perfection to be reached by bleaching white like the light woman. . . . These advertisements could also be found in any of the negro papers published all over the country influencing the poor, unthinking masses to be dissatisfied with their race and color, and to aspire to look white so as to be in society. . . . The "Negro World" has rendered a wonderful service to Negro journalism in the United

States. It has gradually changed the tone and make-up of some of the papers.[64]

The extent to which the *Negro World* "changed the tone and make-up" of Black journalism across the United States is hard to gauge. However, Garvey's newspaper certainly did depart from the content of many of the Black newspapers given its almost exclusive inclusion of dark-skinned individuals of African descent, thereby illustrating alternate ideals of racial beauty. However, Garvey's stance went to extremes.

For example, unlike organizations such as the NAACP that favored reforming national marriage codes, Garvey and UNIA supported anti-miscegenation laws in order, as Garvey insisted, to "save the negro race from extinction through miscegenation." Garvey forcefully expressed his distaste for interracial marriage and sexual relations, practices that, according to Garvey, tainted the "racial purity of both the Negro and white races." His disparaging attack on the NAACP as a "Miscegenationist's organization" illustrates a complex web of intraracial factions, which may have inadvertently impacted the readers who saw Van Der Zee's photographs on newspaper pages.[65] Unlike the two photographs appearing in the ad for skin-bleaching products, everyone in Van Der Zee's photographs appears to have the same dark skin, even though in actuality differences existed from one individual to the next. This is one of the invariable effects of reproducing photographs in newspapers at a smaller size with diminished picture quality. The process of reproduction itself reformulates the viewer's visual experience. Thus the material form of Van Der Zee's reproduced photographs in newspapers worked to Garvey's advantage in his quest to create a unified following.

In this case, this unification happened visually, and possibly unintentionally, through the shared tone of one skin complexion in print and its ubiquitous presence through the photographs' arrangement and halftone reproduction. Poor reproductions of photographs advantageously buoyed a certain representation of what Blackness was supposed to be.[66] Of course, a translation of images from one space to another can never be perfect. Something is always left out, while something else is generated. In what other ways does the translation of a Van Der Zee photograph from a gelatin-silver print to a newspaper reproduction drive the signifying chain forward?[67]

Although this book attends to the vernacular, Van Der Zee most often approached photography as an art. A deep dive into his practice and his archive reveals an artist who relentlessly tinkered with fine-tuning his abilities. His persistent, meticulous way of engaging with photography over the course of decades created a heightened relationship to the medium built on innovation and creativity. According to art historian Regenia Perry, as a photographer, Van Der Zee held a belief in idealism that shaped both his engagement with clients and his photographic practice. On the majority of his portraits, his perfected retouching technique is evident not only through the visibility of his handiwork but also through the intentional absence of flaws. To him, photography was a tool for banishing imperfections.[68] As art historian Mary Schmidt Campbell describes, "His studio portraits are identifiable by a few carefully composed sets, which were meant to represent an orderly bourgeois life. . . . And if, by chance, a sleeve was frayed or a button missing, Van Der Zee conveniently hand-painted and corrected the detail. In fact, he touched up imperfections, straightened teeth, sketched a few extra pieces of jewelry, smoothed out skin color—whatever was necessary to make his clients fit the New Negro mold."[69] Van Der Zee commonly limited himself to only three portrait sittings a day, and his intense work on the surface of the photographs parallels the care and time he took to pose his clients before the camera.[70]

As a departure from the intentional arrangement Van Der Zee practiced in his studio with his portrait clients, positioned among furniture props and atmospheric backdrops, in the *Negro World* newspaper Van Der Zee's photographs were mindfully positioned by the editorial team. This movement from the intentionality practiced in the studio to something that is outside of Van Der Zee's control is important. Through an art historical lens, the studio represents a place to engage artistic genius and autonomy. It is a place where the specific conditions under which individual artists actually worked and labored are often ignored. It is a place where Van Der Zee put his stamp on his genius. What happens to the status of the artist when his work leaves the studio, and when its introduction to the public is determined by an editorial team? Scholarship has aimed to show certain aspects of Van Der Zee's practice while overlooking the nature of what running a commercial photography studio business entailed. Van Der Zee's complete autonomy over his images is as fictive as art history's construction of the studio as an elevated space for genius—where one conceptualizes a sacred place meant only for creation.[71]

Instead, the layout of newspaper pages became a noteworthy terrain for meaning and interpretation. Describing the nuances of early twentieth-century discrimination, the journalist William Pickens, in his 1916 book *The*

New Negro: His Political, Civil and Mental Status, and Related Essays, turns to a newspaper editorial about Booker T. Washington. He writes that "Washington was given an inch on the last page, and the Negro purse-snatcher was given the whole of the front page."[72] In this case, it is as though the Old Negro paradigm comes to life on the printed sheet through the layout and organization of text. These attributes of design mattered to readers during the New Negro era.

In many ways, the translation of Van Der Zee's pictures into newspaper images is of utmost importance because the arrangements themselves advanced Garvey's goals while illustrating how the ordering of photographs informed their interpretation. Return to the series of fifteen photographs arranged on one page of the August 9, 1924, *Negro World* (figure 2.8). At first glance, it is easy to assume that the photographs are meant to be understood as a narrative that temporally unfolds from one image to the next, from left to right and top to bottom. But the fifteen views are not quite sequential. The arrangement of the photographs seemingly captures more of an aesthetic effect of varying perspectives than an entire temporal sequence of happenings. For example, the Black Cross Nurses are captured in a number of different photographs, which are not arranged one after the other. Instead of encountering three successive views of the Black Cross Nurses, the viewer's eyes proceed from the Black Cross Nurses, to a float, to a group of men in uniform.

The vitality of the New Negro is conveyed through the organization and presentation of photographs (in figure 2.9 as well as figure 2.8) on the pages of the *Negro World*. The composition, in addition to the order of the photographs, becomes especially important when one compares a printing decision made by Van Der Zee to the images' very different layout in the pages of the *Negro World*. In Van Der Zee's print, he includes two images, one above the other, in an 8 × 10-inch print (figure 2.10). In contrast to the previous example, these two photographs—given Van Der Zee's printing arrangement and clues found within the two photographs—are indeed part of a sequential narrative.[73]

In one photograph the UNIA members salute, and in the second Garvey reciprocates by saluting the officers. However, the arrangement on the August 16, 1924, *Negro World* page (figure 2.9) does not repeat this sequence. Instead, between the two photographs is a third, depicting uniformed members lining a very wide intersection in Harlem, which appears to be a completely different location from the organization's headquarters. Visually, it provides a striking arrangement; it allows for alternative

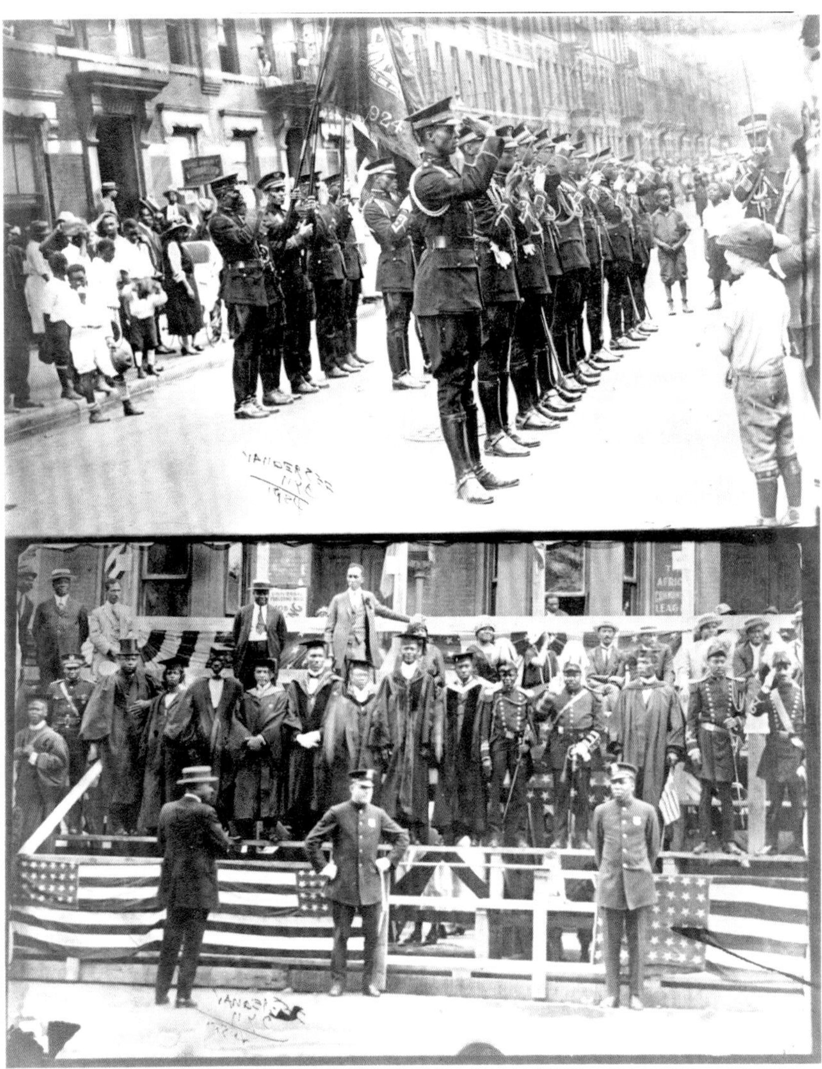

FIGURE 2.10

James Van Der Zee, *Marcus Garvey and the Garvey Militia, Harlem*, 1924, plate VII from the portfolio *James Van Der Zee: Eighteen Photographs*, 1974.

Two negatives printed on one sheet: 9¾ × 7¾ in. (24.7 × 19.6 cm). © James Van Der Zee Archive, The Metropolitan Museum of Art, New York. Source: Prints and Photographs Division, Library of Congress, Washington, DC.

views to shape the viewers' perspective. The middle photograph is taken at a slightly aerial perspective, whereas the other two photographs represent a street-level view. By mixing up the photographs, the arrangement creates more of an engaging multidirectional narrative—a story of potential moments of lively contact, connection, and experience—rather than a documentation of the parade's development from beginning to end. The strategic use of photography in this case provokes a desired narrative through alterations.

More specifically, the nonsequenced nature of the arrangement conveys the fullness and busyness of the streets of Harlem. It is a montage, organized and mobilized to evoke a sense of activity. The images perform as a group to show a highly populated neighborhood filled with people who are there to celebrate UNIA, its presence, and the possibilities for the future. Viewers see not one scene or view but an overwhelming composite of many—all in a newspaper that contemporary readers could hold in their hands as they scanned such an image-heavy page within an otherwise text-based edition. These viewers, accustomed to reading articles from top to bottom, would have been likely to also scan the images this way, a habit reinforced by the newspaper's layout. In doing so, they would take in a narrative of abundance, excitement, and pride.

The heightened sense of accountability felt by the UNIA leaders echoed the care with which the photographs needed to be organized. Sherrill conveyed this in an address to an audience of members by insisting that "in the hands of this convention will rest the destiny of a race. The Universal Negro Improvement Association has reached a point now where it has to be very careful of every and each step it takes."[74] The newspaper staff selected and arranged Van Der Zee's photographs in print with the same care and intentionality as they executed numerous aspects of the convention. Although the "destiny of the race" did not depend on Van Der Zee's featured photographs, the keen sense of responsibility and commitment surrounding this particular convention led to a level of precision that extended to every detail—from the vast parades to Van Der Zee's reproduced and circulated images.

Once the photographs left Van Der Zee's studio, they served a very particular purpose in the pages of the *Negro World*—one that went beyond what Van Der Zee most likely ever imagined or intended. To recognize the lack of control one has over images once they are released into the world is to better articulate the nature of photography; these photographs are forever linked to Van Der Zee through their original making,

   CHAPTER 2

but they are emboldened by the material world, in which their meanings manifest anew.

When Ephemera Become an International Threat

Such minutiae about the pages of print media from 1924 are far from inconsequential. In that moment the newspaper pages of the *Negro World* represented something so powerful that they became a threatening entity to government agencies around the world. People sensed the *Negro World*'s potential to effectively impact the diaspora already years before Van Der Zee's commissioned photographs. A May 9, 1919, letter from an American consulate in the South American country of British Guiana (present-day Guyana) signaled concern; the nervous consul, G. E. Chamberlin, noted in reference to Garvey's *Negro World* that the inspector general of police had called the consulate to "enquire as to whether any actions have been taken in the United States to investigate the nature of these publications, stating that they were becoming alarmed as to what might result from an unrestricted circulation in the colony of these papers on account of the nature of some of their articles."[75] Urgent letters from officials in various locations throughout the world, including Mexico, British Honduras (Belize), and the United States, echoed this anxiety-ridden statement.[76] Colonial governments, such as those in Togoland (Togo) and Dahomey (Benin), went a step further, enforcing more extreme measures. After banning the *Negro World*, these countries deemed it a felony for any man or woman to be seen with a copy of the newspaper.[77] Other reports note propagandist circulars inserted into the *Negro World*.[78] A number of sources evince that Garvey and UNIA regularly distributed printed portraits of Garvey and other UNIA officials to supporters through events and mail order.[79]

In one instance the circulation of apprehensive letters started a chain reaction. J. Edgar Hoover, then the leader of the Federal Bureau of Investigation, sent a memorandum to Special Agent Ridgely after being prompted by a distressed letter about Garvey's impending visit to the Panama Canal. The governor of the Panama Canal Zone, who did not want Garvey to exacerbate the state of near rebellion among the country's West Indian workers, included a clipping with his letter as supporting evidence. In the memo Hoover wrote, "Unfortunately, however, he has not as yet violated any federal law," which limited action at that stage in time. However, Hoover foresaw that Garvey's shipping company would be fodder for building a case around fraudulence.[80]

This came to bear in Garvey's eventual 1923 trial and conviction for mail fraud based, surprisingly, on issues surrounding one single photograph. Nonetheless, as a precursor to Garvey's conviction, Hoover's letter insinuates the kinds of strategies proposed by the US government in order to end Garvey's reign. More important, it establishes the *Negro World* as not merely a newspaper but a powerful platform opposed by authorities seeking to maintain the status quo and venerated by individuals open to radical change.

The photograph, published by UNIA, that led to Garvey's conviction is of a Black Star Line ship labeled the *Phyllis Wheatley*. The steamship extends across the photograph's whole horizon, in line with its massive reach across the water. The sky above the lengthy ship and the water below lack much detail. Hints of waves become evident in what appear to be lines stretching across the still water. The perspective makes it feel as though viewers are seeing the ship from the deck of another ship at sea as opposed to from land, almost as though they are on board one of the other UNIA ships. Absent any visible signs of people, the ship is presented as one big unit. Each dollar collected by UNIA for the benefit of the ship was meant to contribute to this oceanic entity of epic size—a testament to Garvey's grand vision and arguably to an even larger point. As Wilford H. Smith reminded a UNIA audience in April 1921, "We came in the ships of the white man. We came as slaves. We are going to return freemen, and in ships of our own."[81] Although a clear departure from images of slave ships, of which no photographs exist, later photographs of Black Star Line ships nonetheless enabled the reimagining of the ship's symbolic importance in ways that resonate with Smith's words.[82]

The sense of empathy and horror encouraged by the famous eighteenth- and nineteenth-century engravings of the slave ship as a means toward the abolition of slavery is significantly different from, to use Cheryl Finley's phrase, Garvey's "dreams of ships" evoked in the photograph of the *Phyllis Wheatley*.[83] As an extension of a "general sense of longing for seafaring in the public mind at this time," Garvey's images of ships elicit imaginings of hope and new beginnings in an ancestral homeland for Black viewers.[84] In contrast, the historical engraving of the slave ship offers an aerial and interior view of how individual slave bodies were painstakingly arranged in a very tight space. More akin to an architectural drawing, lithographs offer a kind of cartographical guide to where each body was laid, labeling

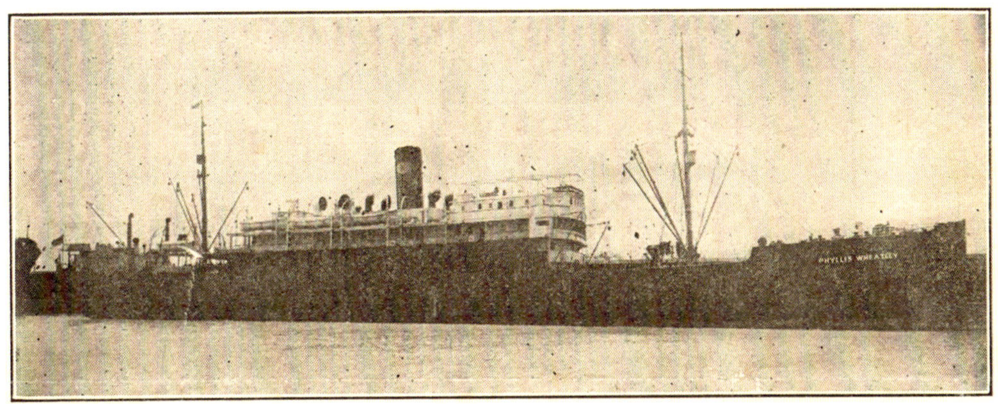

FIGURE 2.11

Unidentified photographer, *Black Star Line Passenger Ship*, 1921.

Source: Smithsonian National Museum of African American History and Culture, Washington, DC.

the locations of the storage rooms. The shape of the ship is one of the most confirming details that shows the viewer that this is indeed a ship. Missing any depiction of sea or sky or depth, the slave ship becomes a crude representation meant to didactically show the extent to which slaves were dehumanized as mere cargo.

In contrast, Garvey's photographs of ships operate suggestively. Within the *Phyllis Wheatley* photograph in particular, the ship's bow, pointed right, visually shows the direction of its motion. Similarly, the letters that appear to be added to the photograph's surface are not positioned in the center of the ship. Instead, they are on the far right of the ship and tilt slightly upward in support of the ship's forward-moving direction. The letters state the ship's name: *Phyllis Wheatley*. Aside from the text's position, the artificial, but sharp, written-in nature of the name contrasts with the reproduced and unfocused photograph. Adding text to label the ship with its name represented it as UNIA's property. The *Phyllis Wheatley* was said to be the largest among UNIA's fleet.[85] With this very large ship came very big dreams of a luxurious fleet to transport members elsewhere. Complete with electric lights, fans, music rooms, and other modern conveniences, the ship would serve not only literally as a vehicle of movement but also

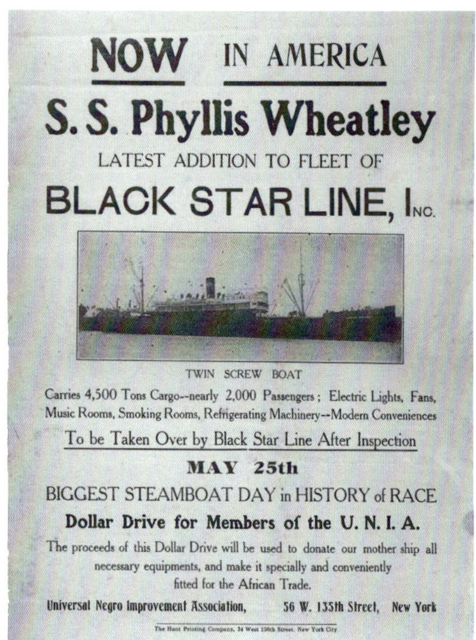

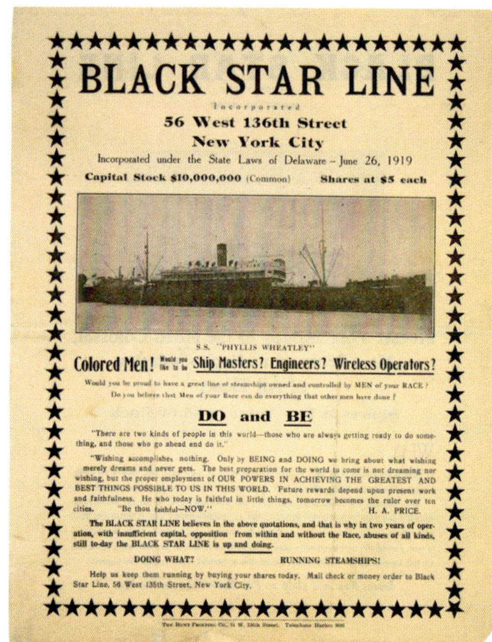

FIGURE 2.12

A 1921 UNIA fundraising circular, "Latest Addition to Fleet," with a photograph of the Black Star Line passenger ship SS *Orion* misattributed as SS *Phyllis Wheatley*, evidence that led to Garvey's conviction on federal mail fraud charges.

Source: Swann Auction Galleries, New York.

FIGURE 2.13

Another UNIA circular from 1921, "Do and Be," aimed at potential investors in the Black Star Line, also referred to SS *Orion* as the *Phyllis Wheatley*.

Source: Swann Auction Galleries, New York.

figuratively as a move toward modern and more comfortable experiences of Black transatlantic mobility.

Significantly for the case built against Garvey, the ship appeared on circulars distributed in 1921 to UNIA's mailing list (figures 2.12 and 2.13). In both publications, the *Phyllis Wheatley* photograph is featured in the very center, drawing attention directly to the image itself. In the first circular, the ship is announced as the "Latest Addition to Fleet of Black Star Line." Underneath the photograph, readers are given details about the ship's capacity, such as the number of tons and passengers it can carry. Attributes mentioned above, such as electric lights and fans, described as "Modern Conveniences," are listed as well. The photograph visualizes UNIA's engagement with being modern through the advanced amenities implied with the ship's very existence as the property of the organization.

Visual aspects of the photograph become increasingly important in light of details about their origins.[86] In an attempt to learn more about the photograph, a government agent by the name of Amos contacted Standard Engraving, the company that had printed the circulars, on February 25, 1921. According to the bureau report, a UNIA representative requested that Standard Engraving do "plate and art work" to the plate used for printing the circular containing the *Phyllis Wheatley* photograph.[87] More specifically, the UNIA representative requested that the name *Phyllis Wheatley* "be painted on the picture in his possession, and also asked that the Black Star line flag be likewise painted thereon, which was done."[88] The representation of the flag apparently was never actualized in the existing examples, but the name was intentionally added per UNIA's request. Also, through the bureau's investigation, it became evident that the photograph did not really depict the *Phyllis Wheatley* but instead misled viewers into believing it was the ship Garvey claimed it to be.[89] In actuality, it is an image of another ship, the SS *Orion*, and UNIA originally received the photograph of the SS *Orion* from the shipbroker.

For UNIA, it was worth the trouble of repurposing the SS *Orion* photograph from the shipbroker, including it in the original plate designed by the engraving company, and then pursuing the added step of requesting visual manipulations of the photograph. These efforts may have been inspired by the implied truth value of photography, although the photo, in reality, was not a true representation at all. The photograph became central to the government's case against Garvey. The importance of the falsified name on the photograph is illustrated through a series of questions asked by the government not about the text appearing on the circular but about the photograph itself. In Federal Bureau of Investigation records, questions were asked about how the name *Phyllis Wheatley* got on the picture and whether the Black Star Line had any authority to publish a picture.[90] There was also interest in where the photograph originated and what steamship it truly represented. All of these details were revealed in interviews and documents collected by the bureau for the purpose of finding Garvey guilty of breaking the law.

The appearance of this image in circulars played a significant role in Garvey's prosecution. It represented a steamship property—and, by extension, the possibility of economic advancement—that neither Garvey nor UNIA actually owned. Therefore, UNIA was accused of making false claims to its members and of using the US postal system to circulate these fraudulent claims. Garvey was found guilty of "sending promotional circulars through the mail with the intent to defraud their recipients by selling stock in what had become a worthless corporation."[91] As succinctly stated by Robert Hill, "In view of the government, publication of a picture of the ship, advertisements of its sailing to Africa, and bookings of passengers and freight for its voyages [were] evidence of fraudulent intent on the part of Garvey and his co-defenders."[92]

The charges represented the conclusion of years of surveillance by the Federal Bureau of Investigation, which included an undercover Black informant, referred to as "800," who used his role within UNIA's structure and high level of access to Garvey to the government's advantage. The government's main goal was to find Garvey guilty of violating a federal law. In keeping tabs on his and UNIA's activities, the government monitored the organization's printed and circulated materials.[93] The height of these surveillance activities took place from the fall of 1918 to the fall of 1921, several years before Van Der Zee became Garvey's official photographer. However, legal actions against Garvey continued throughout Van Der Zee's 1924 tenure with UNIA. Garvey's first grand-jury indictment, in February 1922, was followed by his conviction in June 1923 and the subsequent affirmation of judgment by the US Circuit Court of Appeals for the Second Circuit in February 1925.[94]

At one point during the case, Garvey faced eight counts of postal mail fraud. None of them could be proven in court with the support of evidence, with the exception of one count in which the *Phyllis Wheatley* circular became central. The prosecutor introduced an empty envelope addressed to Benny Dancy, claiming that a letter promoting the purchase of stock (i.e., the *Phyllis Wheatley* circular) had been mailed inside the envelope.[95] The use of the postal system was illustrated by the postmark of the College Station Post Office in Harlem on the envelope, along with Dancy's mailing address.[96] During the trial Dancy testified that although he had supplied the empty envelope to the government agents, he could not remember its specific contents given the numerous letters and circulars he received.[97] Nonetheless, the prosecutor introduced printed circulars that he believed had been mailed in this envelope, as well as in other envelopes, at the time. Surprisingly, the printed circulars held up in court as valid pieces of evidence against Garvey.[98] Even more shocking, based on this weak evidence, Garvey was prosecuted, found guilty, and eventually deported for misusing the mail for fraudulent purposes. It all hinged on the photographic representation of a ship. Here the alterations to the photograph that afforded UNIA a visual manifestation of their hopes and dreams simultaneously led to their downfall.

Given this devastating outcome, a keen awareness of and attentiveness to photography on the part of Garvey and UNIA should come as no surprise. The detrimental consequences of the *Phyllis Wheatley* photograph must have heightened Garvey's and UNIA's careful production, selection, and reproduction of photographs found within UNIA print media, including later issues of the *Negro World*. At moments, this concern became extreme. Garvey's paranoia and careful consideration of reproduced images in the *Negro World* continued for years after his 1924 commissioning of Van Der Zee. In a Western Union telegram sent to his then wife, Garvey advised her to consult a white lawyer and bring action against the *Baltimore Afro-American* newspaper over a photograph.[99] The image featured Amy Jacques Garvey but was captioned with the name of his former wife, Amy Ashwood Garvey.

In his publishing of Van Der Zee, Garvey likely had an amplified sense of what photographs could do and of the inherent vulnerability of the *Negro World*. Through Van Der Zee's photographic vision, UNIA could regain the appearance of progress and stability and inspire representations of Garvey's returning reign after the cancellation of the August 1923 convention. In addition to the year 1924 being an opportune time to commission Van Der Zee, Garvey may have chosen the photographer for other reasons, as revealed in a Van Der Zee photograph of another ship, Black Star Line's steamship *Yarmouth*, circa 1920 (figure 2.3). This image of the ship was important given its relevance to the *Phyllis Wheatley* image. Instead of being co-opted for the government's malicious intentions, this photograph might have contributed to the larger history of why Garvey selected Van Der Zee and his specific photographic vision, especially in light of the *Phyllis Wheatley* photograph.

Although the *Yarmouth* is partially included in Van Der Zee's frame, this incomplete view takes up the majority of the photograph. Its eminence and expansiveness are conveyed through its fragmentation. Viewers are privy to what appears to be the bow of the ship. People gather near the ship's bow for reasons that become apparent if we recall one of the most important aspects of the *Phyllis Wheatley* photograph—the ship's labeled name. In Van Der Zee's composition, people are concentrated both above and below the ship's name, which can be read clearly on its bow. The people on the ship's deck are most important to this interpretation. They stand, lined up near the boat's railing, facing the camera. They are waiting for a photograph to be taken of them aboard a ship—clearly marked as the *Yarmouth*. Either standing or seated on the dock, the majority of the people look toward the people on the ship as opposed to Van Der Zee's camera. The onlookers enhance the drama.

This photograph therefore reenacts—with key differences—the *Phyllis Wheatley* photograph in order to visually rewrite a past misstep in Garvey's visual narrative. The ship is the main focus, while the people peering up at it further enhance the ship's importance. As in the *Phyllis Wheatley* photograph, the text of the ship's name is slightly angled diagonally and upward. Van Der Zee could have chosen a less oblique angle from which to photograph the ship. He could have done so and still prominently shown the *Yarmouth*'s name. Yet he positioned his camera to capture the steamship angled up for the visual effect of doing so. Through the visual framing decisions made by Van Der Zee, the importance of the ship's name becomes evident.

Decisions made after the photograph's taking are also relevant. First of all, Van Der Zee's signature is accompanied by the initials NYC, thereby locating the photograph in a particular place. As in the circular with the *Phyllis Wheatley* picture, place factors into the viewer's understanding of the photograph. Second, the paper on which one version of the image appears suggests its potential circulation. A photo postcard of this photograph from the early twentieth century, now housed in the James Van Der Zee Archive at the Metropolitan Museum of Art, may have been sold at UNIA meetings. As an indication of UNIA's power and support, this photograph conveys a particular message more effectively than the *Phyllis Wheatley* photograph and other images of UNIA ships.

Van Der Zee's photographic vision was not his only asset. It is arguable that Garvey chose Van Der Zee because doing so enabled an appealing level of control—on Garvey's part—over the images produced by the photographer. Van Der Zee kept negatives within his archive and printed photographs on request.[100] Yet if Van Der Zee technically owned the negatives, Garvey and UNIA members, as clients, presumably had access to their reproduction. In turn, this arrangement allowed for control over the distribution of images. In contrast, other photographs of Garvey had different provenances, such as a 1922 photograph of Garvey in a parade

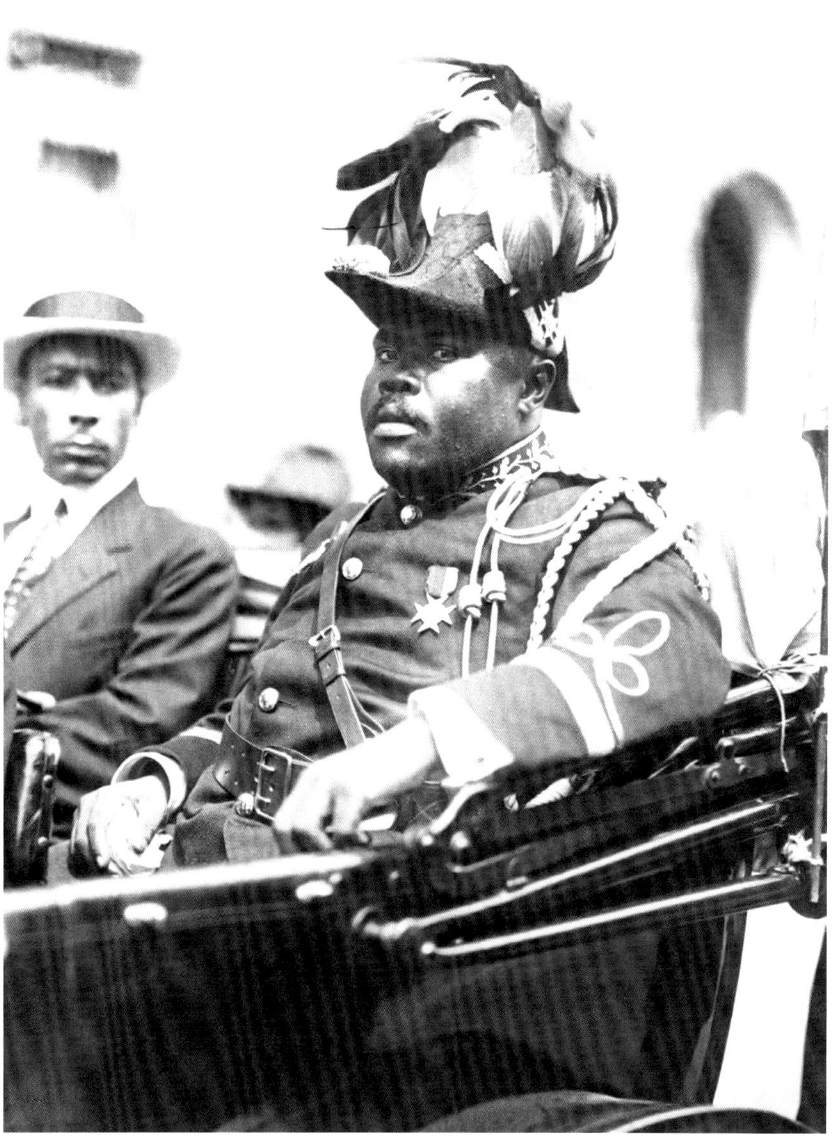

Press photograph of Marcus Garvey during the inaugural parade of UNIA's third annual International Convention of the Negro Peoples of the World, August 2, 1922.

Source: *New York Daily News* archive.

(figure 2.14). An unidentified *Daily News* photographer took the picture. It appeared in the *Daily News*, then was reproduced in the *Literary Digest.* The official credit is given as Pacific and Atlantic Photographs.[101] Just for this one photograph alone, there are three entities outside UNIA that have some say in the photograph's circulation and reproduction. In addition, these three entities are relatively less invested in their images than was Van Der Zee, an individual neighborhood photographer who lived within walking distance of the organization's headquarters and whose work appeared in the *Negro World.* As Raiford argues, control over the movement also meant control over an image's production.[102]

In choosing Van Der Zee, Garvey simultaneously streamlined his engagement with photography and localized it to Harlem. This move toward supporting local Harlem businesses is evident in other ways. For example, Garvey switched from using two different white-owned printing presses in Lower Manhattan for the *Phyllis Wheatley* circular and the Christmas 1921 newspaper issue to using his own Harlem-based Bee Hive Printing Plant.[103] As Judith Stein's *The World of Marcus Garvey: Race and Class in Modern Society* makes evident, for Garvey, Black business enterprises were key.[104] To him, they replaced Black education as the critical strategy for Black advancement. Accordingly, Garvey was impressed with the "active part played by Negro men and women in the commercial and industrial life of the nation."[105] Therefore, Garvey may have selected Van Der Zee in part owing to his role as a successful Black businessman with ties to other Black businesses. Think back, for example, to Van Der Zee's involvement with his sister Madame E. Touissant Welcome's conservatory and his collaboration with fellow Harlem photographer Eddie Elcha. Despite Van Der Zee's lack of engagement with the particular tenets of UNIA, the very core of Garvey's aspirations were, on some level, what Van Der Zee had already achieved.[106] His business acumen as the proprietor of a photography business laid the groundwork for all the eventual photographs of Garvey that were taken in his studio, reproduced, and circulated. In many ways, the quotidian demands of running a successful commercial enterprise led to the creation of these photographs as much as Van Der Zee's exceptional talent and skill as a photographer committed to making art. A vernacular turn to Van Der Zee brings the greater impact of his photographic production—along with the stakes of photographs as moving, reproduced, and modified objects—into view.

What a Hand-Colored Photograph Reveals

It is not simply Van Der Zee's images that contribute to an understanding of photography's role during this particular moment in time. It is also the terms central to their circulation as moving objects. Yet Van Der Zee's reproduced photographs have their limitations. Images reproduced in the *Negro World* cannot capture the same sense of detail gained through a limited number of hand-signed photographs, nor can they have the same cultural cachet or aura for those who acquired these special photographs. Mass-produced print media images serve a different role than individually printed and hand-altered photographs. Although both types of photographs are vernacular, they register for viewers in different ways. In the case of the newspaper images, the photographic image serves as a component of an object, while in other cases, the photograph is a signature object.[107] For example, the contrast between Van Der Zee's newspaper reproductions and an original print of the Black Cross Nurses, by an unidentified photographer, is noteworthy (figure 2.15). In the approximately 7 × 10-inch albumen print, the women, dressed in white, are tightly grouped in seats along the image's horizon line. This is a 1921 group portrait of the Black Cross Nurses taken on a cobblestone street in upper Harlem.[108] In the foreground, empty space further focuses the viewer's attention on the photograph's top half. A UNIA flag appears above the group of women and in the center of the buildings. The flag makes this photograph distinct and relevant for comparison: the flag's bold red, black, and green stripes are hand-painted on the photograph's surface. These colors were accepted as the colors of Black unity during the 1920 convention: red represents struggle, black stands for the race, and green reflects the natural wealth of Africa.[109] These identifiable colors became central to Garvey's construction of group identity. The tricolors of UNIA graced a number of the organization's materials, including the flag, the uniform, and the backdrop of theatrical productions.[110]

Commentary on the colorfulness of the 1924 parade and convention became a trend in numerous articles featured in the *Negro World*. One description offers insight. In a section titled "Graphic Description of Parade," which precedes another section called "a colorful scene," Harlem is described as being "en fete. Festooned with flags, it represents a gala appearance. Every vehicle carries the emblem of Negro aspiration, the Red, the Black and the Green, the colors of the Provisional Republic of Africa."[111] Lacking color, Van Der Zee's photographs in the *Negro World* needed an-

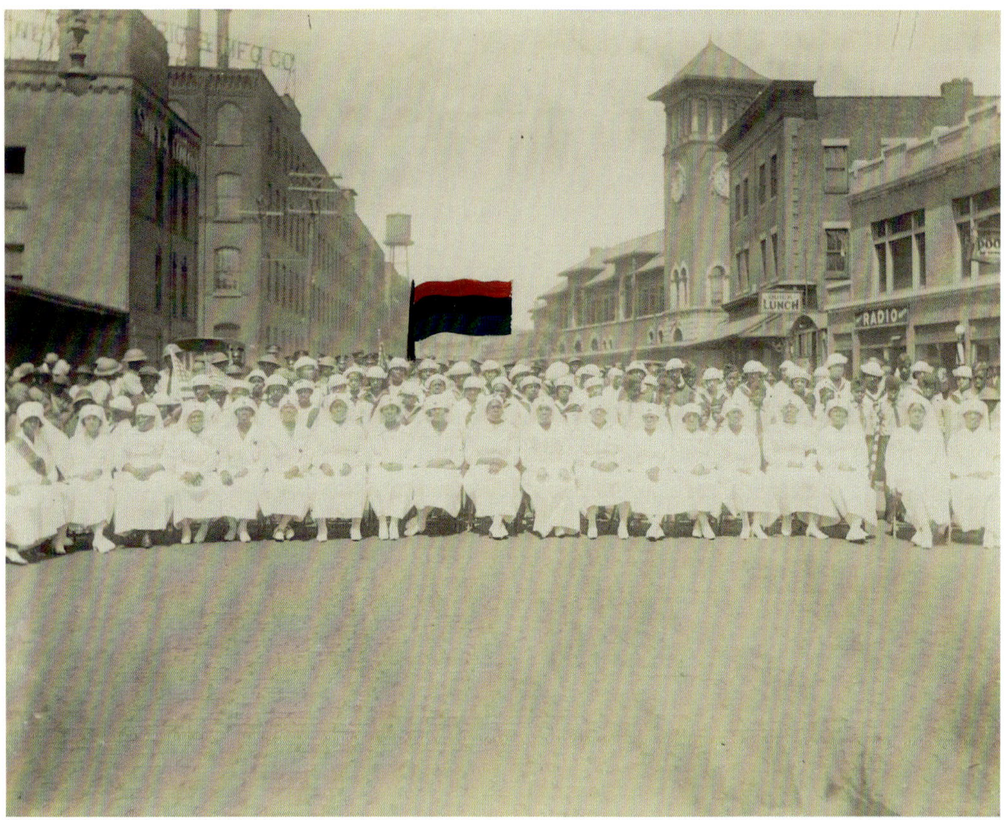

FIGURE 2.15

Unidentified photographer, *UNIA Black Cross Nurses*, ca. 1921.

7⅛ × 9¾ in. (18.1 × 24.7 cm). Source: Swann Auction Galleries, New York.

other means to convey a message in the black, white, and tonal grays inherent to mass-reproduced print media.

In comparison, the painted flag in this photograph of Black Cross Nurses turns the image into an object that can be commodified given its uniqueness, a valuation familiar to art history. The photograph becomes one precious thing to acquire. This kind of reasoning drove sales for the organization, as is evident in how a reprinted photograph of Garvey was described and advertised. A *Negro World* advertisement in the April 12, 1924, issue reads, "A Large Size Picture of Marcus Garvey for Framing and Hanging in the Home, with His Autograph Signature, the Only Official Pic-

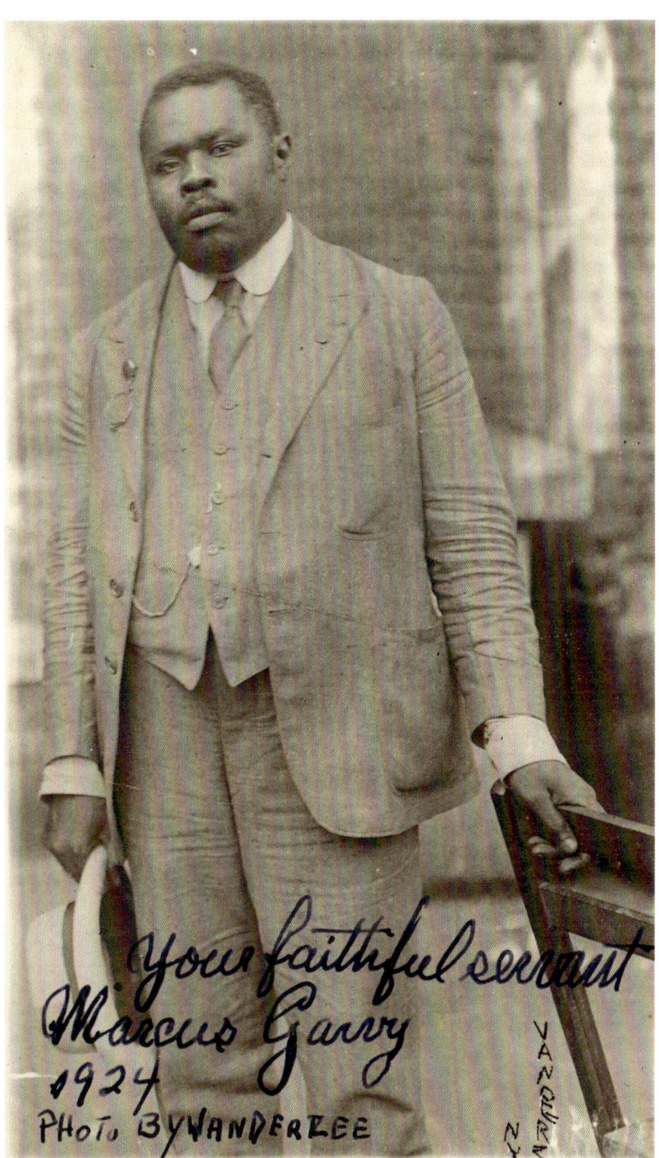

FIGURE 2.16

James Van Der Zee, *Marcus Garvey*, 1924, possibly the kind of signed photograph sold to supporters.

5 × 2¹⁵⁄₁₆ in. (12.7 × 7.4 cm). © James Van Der Zee Archive, The Metropolitan Museum of Art, New York. Source: National Portrait Gallery, Smithsonian Institution, Washington, DC.

ture in Circulation with Copyright" (for a possible example, see figure 2.16). Such a photograph gains significance through its ability to transform from just an image into a prized object that bears the mark of Garvey.

Reproducing Van Der Zee's street-scene photographs in newsprint functioned very differently. Although they neither depict colorful hues nor convey the same sense of distinction as an individual photograph, they nonetheless allow for certain visual possibilities. For one thing, without color, Van Der Zee's photographs did something just as identifiable for UNIA. They used the presence of UNIA members en masse on the urban streets of Harlem to create a recognizable image that could unite and mobilize readers as easily as the tricolored emblem of UNIA. Instead of a signature or a hand-painted flag, the location and the animated sense of what was taking place on the street—the presence of UNIA as a group with a strong visual identity—became the driving force behind these photographs' significance.

In addition, by circulating through the *Negro World*, Van Der Zee's photographs acquired their own sense of Black visibility, not based on their singularity or scarcity but on their arrangement, repetition, and abundance. If, as Sherrill proclaimed, the convention "is one that the world will be watching," Van Der Zee's images reinforced the New Negro's presence through mass viewing and global circulation, in contrast to the rarified viewing experience of a hand-signed or colored photograph.[112] Focusing on what Van Der Zee's photographic vision in print offered to Garvey and to viewers throughout the diaspora thus serves as a part of a broader look at what a vernacular turn to Van Der Zee can reveal.

3

A Reframing of Value

Van Der Zee's Restoration Work of the 1940s
and Beyond

WITHIN THE PHOTOGRAPH a family is stiffly posed: the hands of the standing figures hang slack along their sides while the hands of the seated are set formally on their laps. This portrait is not a photograph by James Van Der Zee, at least not as traditionally understood within art history (figure 3.1). The background is too flat and too plain, the figures too rigid and somber to be included among Van Der Zee's elegantly posed subjects. The chairs within the photograph are far too ordinary to take up any of the limited and valuable space. The two men stand shoulder to shoulder with a woman in the middle and visually appear to press against the photograph's tight borders. This and other photographs like it are not an index of the person, couple, or group who opened the front door of Van Der Zee's studio, stepped inside, and eventually found themselves well lit and intentionally positioned before the camera's lens. Nor did Van Der Zee position his

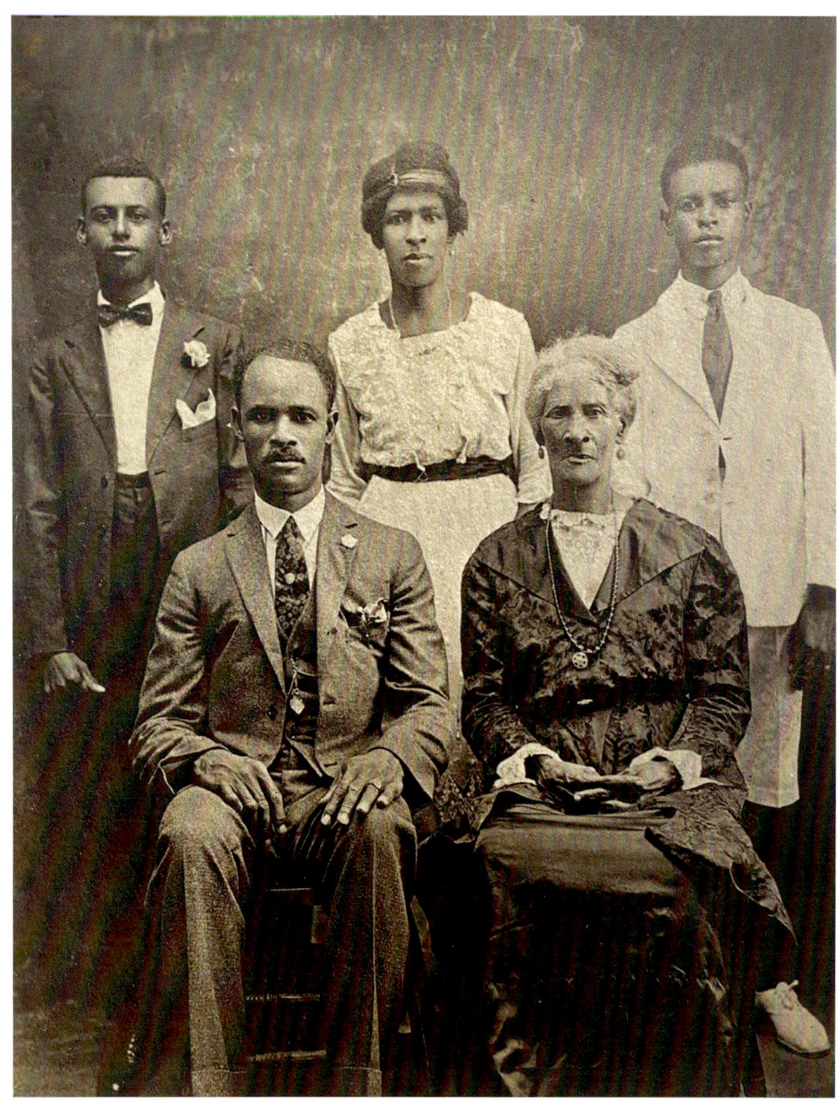

James Van Der Zee, copy photograph of a family group (original photographer and date unknown), likely reproduced 1930s–1960s.

$9\frac{5}{8} \times 7\frac{5}{8}$ in. (24.5 × 19.4 cm). © James Van Der Zee Archive, The Metropolitan Museum of Art, New York. Source: James Van Der Zee Archive, The Metropolitan Museum of Art, New York.

camera in front of the sitters, open the lens shutter, take the photograph, and then diligently develop the film and print the image in his studio's darkroom. Found in his archive, along with other photographs that depart from Van Der Zee's signature aesthetic style, these kinds of photographs trouble many of the concepts that establish Van Der Zee's position within the art history of photography while simultaneously allowing vernacular practices of photography to come into view. Photography, a most flexible and resourceful medium, can accommodate desires for modification: in this case, those of the owners of the photographic images on which Van Der Zee worked.

Starting in the 1940s, Van Der Zee directed a significant portion of his energy to the photograph restoration, copying, and enlargement services offered through his studio.[1] As demand for more traditional studio portraits steadily decreased, these services dominated his business until the studio's eventual closure in the late 1960s. In essence, these services meant that he worked on photographs taken by other photographers, a process that commonly began with taking a picture of a picture. As one guidebook to this type of work explains, "It is not practical, except in a very few instances, to do the restoration work upon, or to, the original old photograph. This is usually copied photographically and the re-touching or restoring is done upon a copy print."[2] The text highlights the rhetorical implications of the language used when, in actuality, a separate and distinct photograph is created. The guide insists that "the term 'photo-restoration' is a misnomer, as the process does not involve restoring the damaged or faded photograph to its original or new condition. Rather it involves making a copy of that photograph and creating, or re-creating, a new picture while removing blemishes and faults by photographic means by artwork and retouching."[3] This chapter explores photographic prints that Van Der Zee's clients hired him to enhance. However, details about what was done on each image, why the original was left behind in the archive, and where the image came from unfortunately are lost to time. Of all the orphaned images left in Van Der Zee's photographic archives, these are the most ambiguous.[4] The only certainty is that this photograph made its way to Van Der Zee, and Van Der Zee was charged with completing a task according to the client's directions. Such photographs reframe the context of knowledge that most commonly prepares viewers to engage with the photographs Van Der Zee took within his Harlem studio. Because they take away the information that typically makes a Van Der Zee photograph a Van Der Zee, these photographs within the archive are among the most fascinating. They reveal alternate modes of Van Der Zee's photographic practice that remain unfamiliar to canonical histories of photography, because they trouble the purity of a photograph's pedigree.

By turning to Van Der Zee's practice of copying and modifying photographs, this chapter illustrates how such a practice brings different configurations of meaning to photographs of the Black quotidian. It reframes themes common to African diasporic art history such as migration, repetition, and global circulation by highlighting histories of representations, and their attending cultural and material conduits, that often go uninterrogated.[5] During the later years of Van Der Zee's practice, his indirect impact, discerning hand, and skill reached farther and wider than previously imagined. He collaborated not with a sitter but with a faraway client and a photograph by another photographer that was already in existence. In addition, instead of bracketing these photographs as an afterthought to his career, this chapter reframes Van Der Zee's copy and restoration practice as having more in common with his widely cherished work than previously realized. Likewise, this chapter questions, in cultural studies scholar Lily Cho's words, the panache of auteurship wielded by the photographer in order to unpack the limitations of Van Der Zee's iconicity and the hierarchies of values on which art history commonly depends.[6] Last, this section of the book explores how the practice of recopying and modification brings into view the importance of multiplicity, delay, and trust—notions, this chapter insists, that are relevant to how Black quotidian social links are maintained through vernacular photographic practices.

A Departure from Traditional Portraiture

In March 1943 Gaynella Greenlee and James Van Der Zee moved to Van Der Zee's last studio, in a building they owned at 272 Lenox Avenue. This twelve-room brownstone allowed the couple to continue renting rooms to short-term boarders. The studio included a display room, a posing chamber, and a darkroom. The specific location of this studio and the country's entry into World War II improved Van Der Zee's business. The loading point for buses going from Harlem to the Picatinny Air Force Base in New Jersey was right in front of the studio, and so many soldiers had their photographs taken there—just as clients had during World War I.[7]

In previous studios, the window display served as a meager invitation to enter the studio. With the 272 Lenox Avenue studio, the outside became more critical and central. The elaborate display in the form of a jutting case, perpendicular to the studio, solicited the attention of passersby. Photographs covered the case from top to bottom, in contrast to the relatively sparse window arrangements of Van Der Zee's past studios. Because of Van Der Zee's waning business, this studio more than the others needed to leverage and showcase his prolific production through an overly busy window display. Unlike in the past, the business could not depend solely on a frequent flow of clients commissioning Van Der Zee for the striking and involved portraits of years earlier.

A 1935 photograph of a woman by Van Der Zee serves as an exemplar of the celebrated skillful work and careful composition for which the photographer is best known (figure 3.2). A smiling woman dressed in a floor-length dress sits at a baby grand piano as one arm clutches a white cat and the other touches the instrument's keys. The photographer's hand is very present. The woman's outfit and shoes are enhanced with color, applied by hand to the photograph's surface. Similarly, a hand-colored bracelet and nail polish complement the hand-colored tiara worn by the woman. Skillfully applied rouge also brings color to her lips and cheeks. And before all of this enhancement work even began, the woman in the photograph would have selected the final image from among various proofs.

Through photographs like this portrait, Van Der Zee generates a visual culture that offers a much-needed respite from and counternarrative to derogatory images of Black life. Within scholarly texts, his photographs are valued for their ability to show a version of Black life that is proud, aspirational, and morally attuned to lives of note and value. They also gain significance when his photographs are interpreted as expanding narratives of Blackness—as is the case with *Beau of the Ball*, whose subject, as scholars maintain, is on their way to one of Harlem's costume or drag balls (figure 3.3).[8] For a range of subjects, by "cutting a figure," as art historian Richard Powell would describe it, Van Der Zee's arresting portraits illustrate an expressive cultural strategy through the subject's posing in front of the camera. Such displays of the body become an avenue to attend to "the process (and politics) of portraiture, identifying its performative aspects, and revealing the whys and hows of modern and composite human design."[9] However, just as Van Der Zee's ability to appeal to his clientele through such highly stylized and compositionally rich portraiture declined, so, too, did scholars' interest in his later work.

Instead, scholars lament how tastes were changing and how Van Der Zee's signature style did not resonate with or draw clients as it had in the

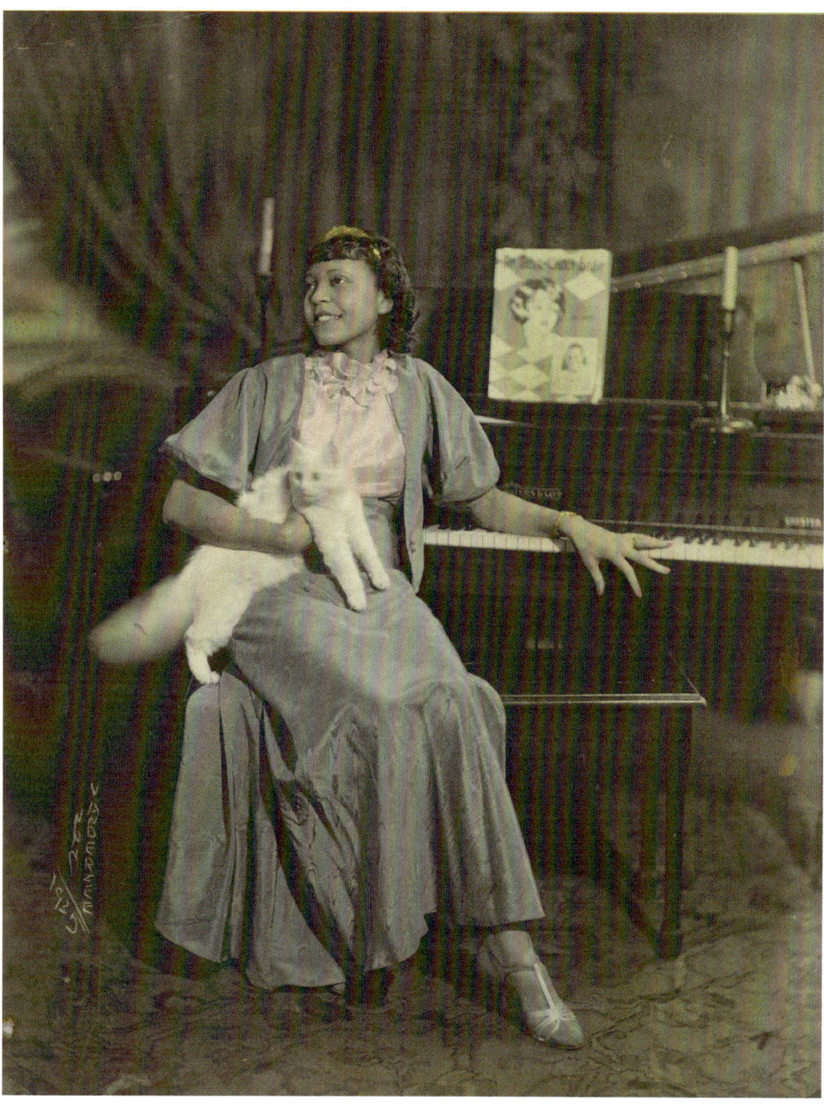

FIGURE 3.2 (above)

James Van Der Zee, *Woman with Cat at Piano*, 1935.

9⅝ × 7½ in. (24.5 × 19.1 cm). © James Van Der Zee Archive, The Metropolitan Museum of Art, New York. Source: James Van Der Zee Archive, The Metropolitan Museum of Art, New York.

FIGURE 3.3 (opposite)

James Van Der Zee, *Beau of the Ball*, 1926. As mentioned in existing scholarship, the subject is assumed to be on their way to a costume or drag ball.

9¾ × 7⅜ in. (24.8 × 18.8 cm). © James Van Der Zee Archive, The Metropolitan Museum of Art, New York. Source: James Van Der Zee Archive, The Metropolitan Museum of Art, New York.

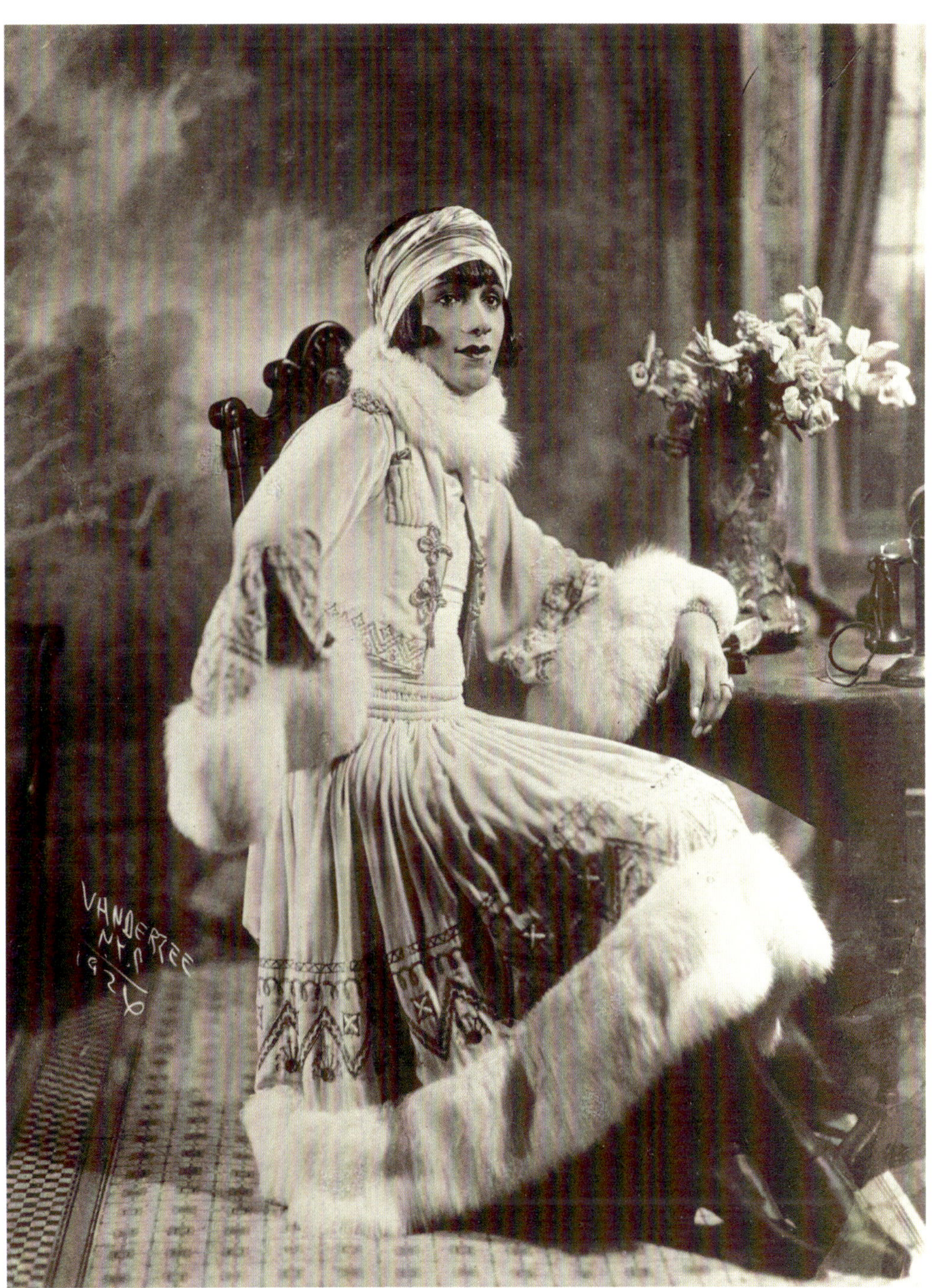

VANDERZEE
N.Y.C
1926

past, consistently describing the last decades of Van Der Zee's business with a sense of defeat. For example, art historian Cheryl Finley interprets one of the advertisements for Van Der Zee's photograph modification services as hinting at the photographer's own sense of loss as his world was changing.[10] Art historian Margaret Olin writes, "By the 1940s…Van Der Zee's success waned, but he continued to seek business where he could, eventually simply restoring old photographs by mail order, before he ran out of angles and gave up in the 1960s after a long career."[11] Her tone echoes that of earlier scholarship on Van Der Zee, such as an exhibition catalog from 1979, in which the author, Stephen Perloff, used similar terms—such as "business dropped off" and "he came to rely on"—to forlornly describe Van Der Zee's mail-order services.[12]

Although Van Der Zee's advertisements for these services are used as evidence of his fall, a closer look at a few examples reveals nothing more than information about his business practices and clientele. An ad for Van Der Zee's services from 1937–1942, before his move to Lenox Avenue, proclaims, "Old Photographs Are Priceless" (figure 3.4). The ad offers pertinent information as to how his recopying services were presented to the public. More specifically, its language provides revealing clues about Van Der Zee's general printing practices. He offered plain black-and-white prints or those finished in colors or sepia brown. The sizes ranged from 3 × 5 inches to 20 × 24 inches The "artist finish" cost approximately twice as much as the plain black-and-white print. A price increase from $3.50 to $7.75 for an 8 × 10 that was artistically finished instead of plain black-and-white helps to gauge the monetary value of the labor beyond the basic printing.

In other advertisements Van Der Zee made big promises about his photograph enlargement services. For example, advertisements claiming to "Bring Old Photos Back to Life!" appeared in printed materials, such as the *New York Age.* He also began to court clients from abroad in the late 1940s and into the 1950s through magazines such as *Sacred Heart Magazine: The Messenger*, published by the Catholic Church.[13] Lacking any images, the text of the ad reads, "Bring Old Photographs 'Back to Life;' We enlarge, frame, and copy old or faded photographs. Send for price list. Please print name plainly, following by G. G. G. Photo Studio, 272 Lenox Avenue, New York New York." In some versions, the sentence "Please print name plainly" is followed by the directive to "mention this magazine." These magazines found a readership throughout the world, and according to the scholar Rodger Birt, the resulting letters to Van Der Zee from Europe, Af-

OLD PHOTOGRAPHS ARE PRICELESS!

Sometimes they can never be replaced at any cost. But we can save them, Recopy and Enlarge them for the Home, School, Church, Lodge Room, etc. From a watch picture to an Oil Painting. Tell your friends, they will appreciate knowing where to have this work done.

Call or send by insured mail the picture with money order for the size you want. Beautiful artist finished in colors, Black, and White or Sepia Brown.

SIZE	ARTIST FINISH	PLAIN BLACK AND WHITE
3" x 5"	$ 5.75	$1.50
5" x 7"	7.75	2.50
8" x 10"	7.75	3.50
11" x 14"	10.75	4.75
16" x 20"	12.75	6.75
20" x 24"	15.75	7.75

CA. 8-4070   EST. OVER 35 YEARS

G. G. G. Photo Studio

2077 SEVENTH AVENUE

NEW YORK, N. Y.

FIGURE 3.4

"Old Photographs Are Priceless," advertising circular for G. G. G. Photo Studio and its photo restoration, copying, and enlargement services, ca. 1942.

Source: Willis-Braithwaite, *VanDerZee, Photographer, 1886–1983*, 54.

rica, South America, and the Caribbean demonstrate the demand for his services and the effectiveness of such advertisements in reaching an audience outside of Harlem.[14]

Another example—featured in the February 1934 issue of *Crisis* and therefore preceding the decades that are the focus of this chapter—includes the following text: "We copy and Enlarge any Old or Faded Photograph to look like New." Given *Crisis*'s appeal and readership among a broad domestic audience, we can assume that many of Van Der Zee's clients answered this ad from locations outside of Harlem, thereby expanding his clientele domestically. However, other aspects of the ad appealed specifically to local audiences. The same ad includes the text "We teach Photography and Painting" in bold letters. That Van Der Zee offered such services through his studio would have reassured readers, both within and outside of Harlem, that Van Der Zee was highly skilled as an artist. The modification services—which could have been viewed as rote activities of copying and enlarging—were elevated to an art form by association. If the enlargements were carried out by a person who could also teach painting, then the valued skills needed for painting would also benefit his enlargement, recopying, and modification services. The potential in photography for creating copies provided another opportunity for Van Der Zee to apply his range of both technical and artistic skills in ways that often blur the lines between art and the vernacular.

However, as much as Van Der Zee may have been able to drum up business by advertising his artistic talent, the photographs modified by Van Der Zee reveal a huge departure, not only from Van Der Zee's aesthetic, but from the usual conceptualizations of an artist. By doing so, they also trouble ideas of authorship. Without information about their origin or an understanding of their development, these photographs do not fit into the common narrative of Van Der Zee as a distinguished photographer; nor is it easy to create a separate narrative for them, given the extent to which they are marked by difference and numerous unknowns. The photographs within the archive that were sent to his business for modification are wildly different from each other and easily identifiable as outside of Van Der Zee's oeuvre. A turn to two photographs illustrates this point (figures 3.5 and 3.6). In the first, two women wearing 1960s patterned dresses are captured trying to elegantly navigate a strange fishnet drape that continues onto the floor on which they stand. In turn, the second photograph goes back in time, possibly preceding the era when Van Der Zee even knew how to operate a camera. In it, a woman of small stature but grand disposition stands wearing a long dress that dates her to the mid- to late nineteenth century. She looks directly at the camera and gracefully rests one hand on the back of an oversized chair. The backdrop includes plain drapes, and the lighting, concentrated on the upper portion of the photograph, allows curved shadows to form underneath her dress and the chair. These photographs may seem more different than similar. Yet they illuminate a kind of disjointed intersection where the common denominator is Van Der Zee and his ability to appeal to a range of clients through the promise of improving existing photographs. As a result, through Van Der Zee, their disparate time periods and content recede into the background while their affinity as images that persisted through modification and multiplicity comes into view.

Leveraging Past Experiences in Photography

In mid-career, Van Der Zee continued to make small identification photographs, which measured no more than 3 × 3 inches. In addition to his modification services, this became a lucrative business patronized by taxicab drivers, security guards, and small tradespeople among other sitters in need of ID photos.[15] Individually, the photographs depict female and male sitters strictly conforming to a conventional ID portrait style. Looking straight into the camera, with the same proportion of head, neck, and shoulders shown, each individual lacks the formality and detail of Van Der Zee's most celebrated formal portraits. These portraits also became another way for Van Der Zee to advertise his restoration, recopying, and enhancement business, given the stamps found on the backside of various examples (figures 3.7 and 3.8). Using one genre of photography to advertise another genre of photography reflects the strategies Van Der Zee used to increase his volume of work. While Van Der Zee insisted that his volume of business decreased only slightly during the Great Depression, it is worth contemplating whether this was also the case during the years in which there was an uptick in his restoration, recopying, and enlargement services.[16] What if Van Der Zee's value was based on the volume of photographs he produced, as opposed to the kinds of representations he fashioned? How does this shift in approach reframe Van Der Zee through aspects of his practice that are usually overlooked in art history?

If attention is shifted to Van Der Zee's production volume, the long development of his modification skill comes to light. No longer just an activity he turned to in order to keep his business afloat, his modification services can be framed as Van Der Zee leveraging and fine-tuning a skill set he already had. Take, for example, a photograph made outside, of a nurse in front of a garden bush, in 1934. The 8 × 10-inch print is the result of Van Der Zee's enlargement and enhancement work (figure 3.9). Van Der Zee placed the photograph, once enlarged, in matting that featured his business label prominently on the back. In comparison to a similar but smaller image found within a photo album (figure 3.10), the framed image is much larger, and the tonal range has been altered to improve the woman's appearance. More specifically, in the original photograph, whose corners were carefully slipped underneath their black mounts, the woman's white dress is overexposed to the extent that the folds and creases of the fabric are lost. Selected from among different versions of the woman

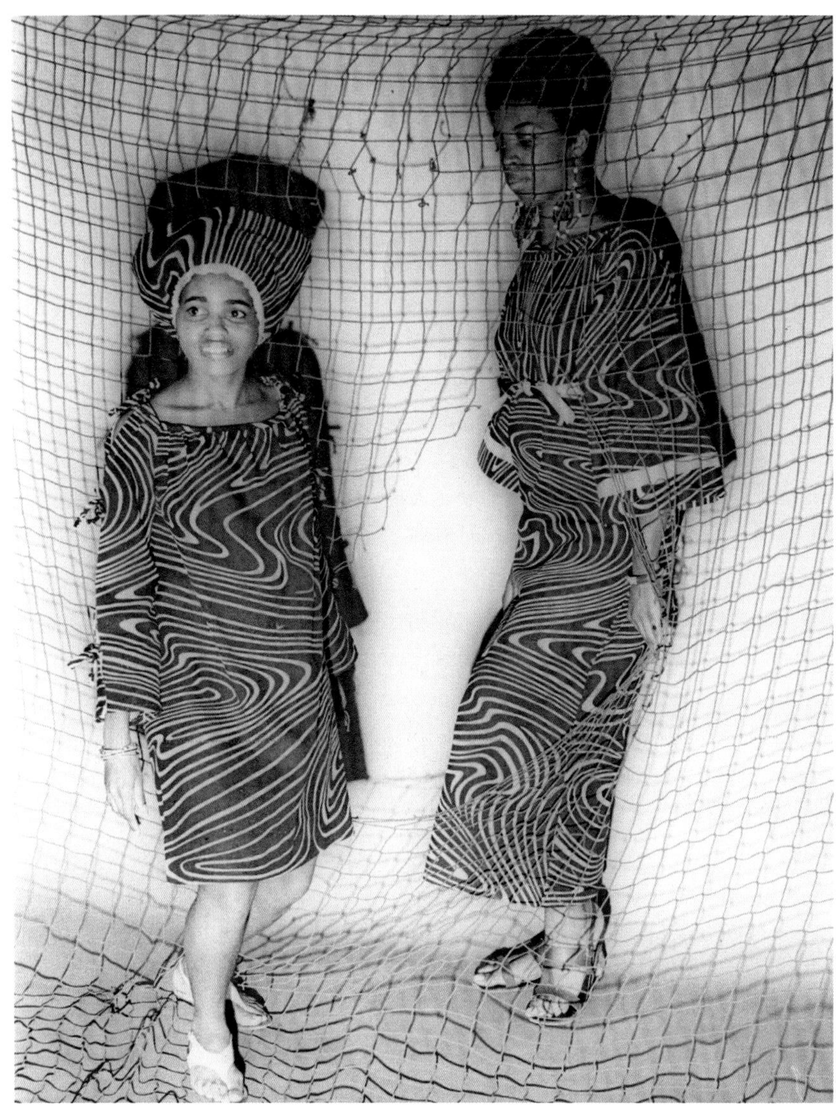

FIGURE 3.5 (above)

Unidentified photographer, *Studio Portrait of Fashion Models with Netting*, 1960s. The photograph was likely sent to Van Der Zee's studio to be copied.

9½ × 7⅜ in. (24.1 × 18.7 cm). © James Van Der Zee Archive, The Metropolitan Museum of Art, New York. Source: James Van Der Zee Archive, The Metropolitan Museum of Art, New York.

FIGURE 3.6 (opposite)

James Van Der Zee, copy photograph of a woman standing by a chair (original photographer and date unknown), likely reproduced 1930s–1960s.

9¾ × 7¾ in. (24.7 × 19.7 cm). © James Van Der Zee Archive, The Metropolitan Museum of Art, New York. Source: James Van Der Zee Archive, The Metropolitan Museum of Art, New York.

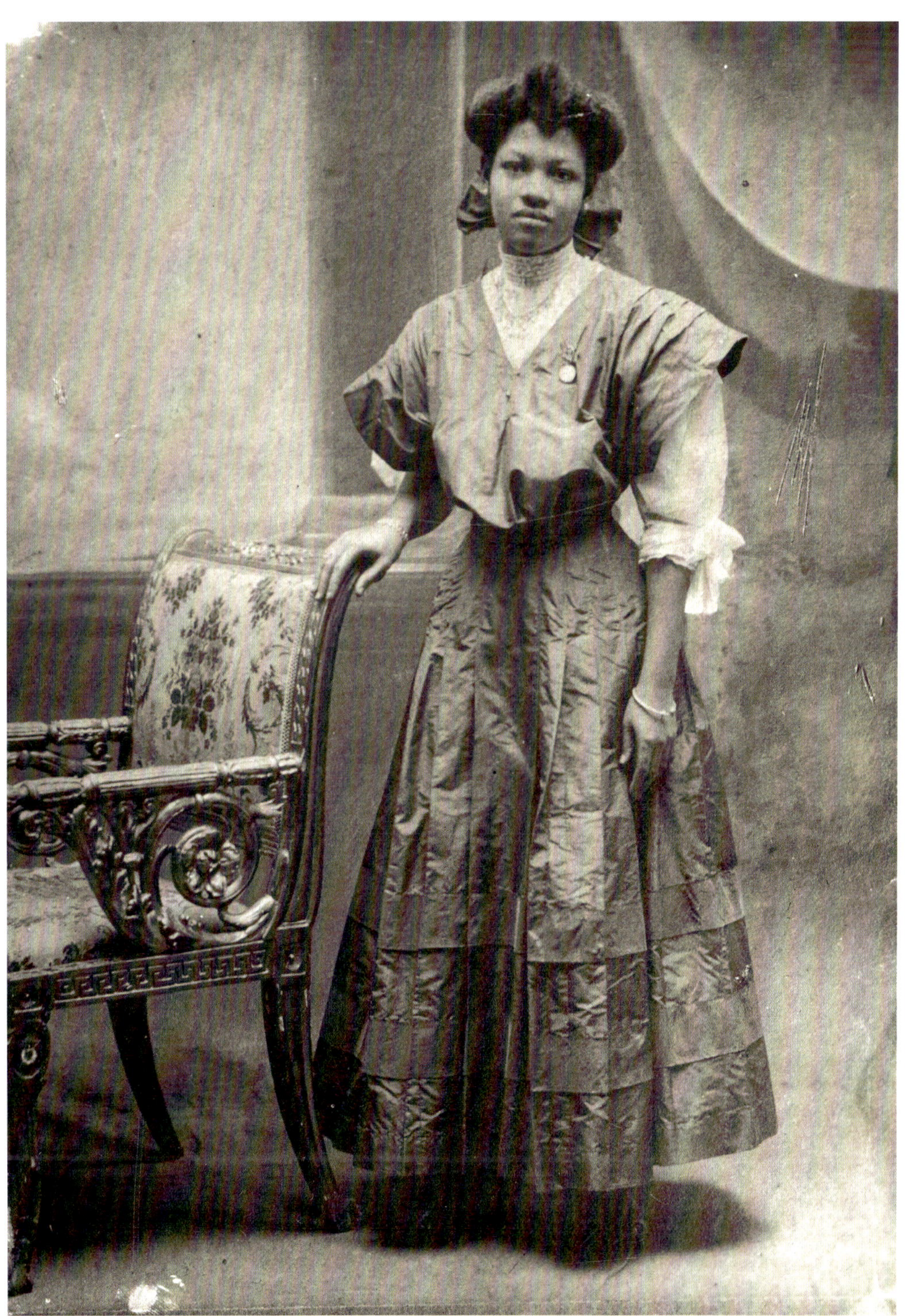

James Van Der Zee, *Woman with Hat*, 1950s.

$3\frac{3}{16} \times 2\frac{1}{8}$ in. (8.1 × 5.4 cm). © James Van Der Zee Archive, The Metropolitan Museum of Art, New York. Source: James Van Der Zee Archive, The Metropolitan Museum of Art, New York.

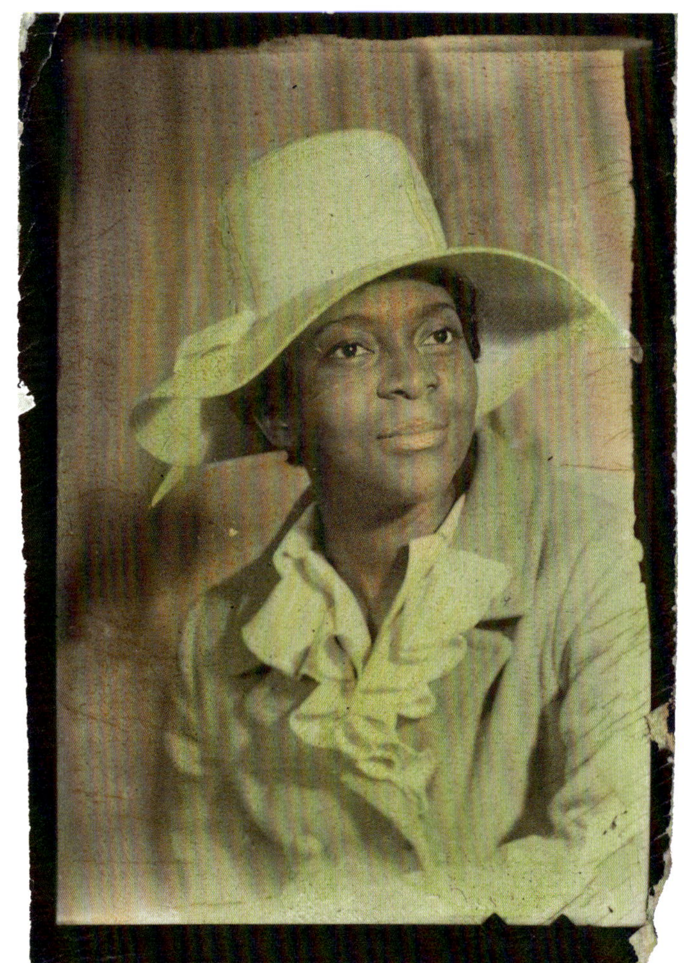

James Van Der Zee, verso of a photograph with G. G. G. Photo Studio stamp: "Bring Old Photos Back to Life!," 1950s.

Sheet: $3\frac{3}{8} \times 2\frac{5}{16}$ in. (8.5 × 5.9 cm). © James Van Der Zee Archive, The Metropolitan Museum of Art, New York. Source: James Van Der Zee Archive, The Metropolitan Museum of Art, New York.

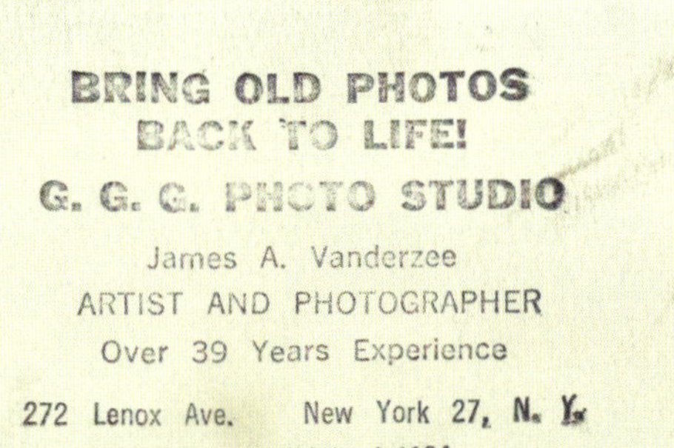

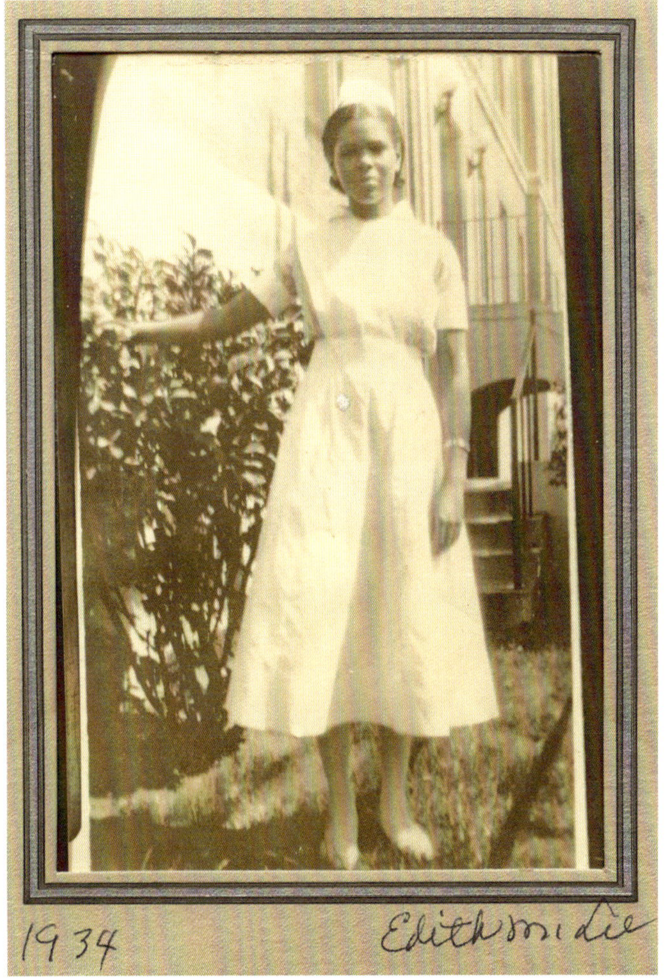

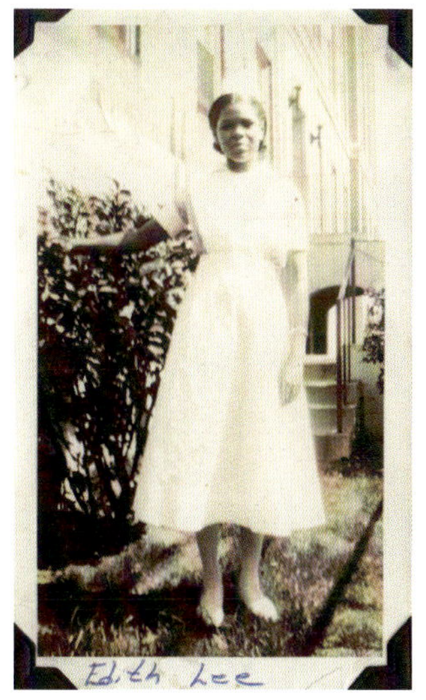

FIGURE 3.9

James Van Der Zee, enlarged and enhanced copy photograph of a nurse, identified as Edith M. Lee, 1934.

6¾ × 4¾ in. visible in 6¾ × 9¼ in. studio mount (17.1 × 24.8 cm). © James Van Der Zee Archive, The Metropolitan Museum of Art, New York. Source: Collection of the author.

FIGURE 3.10

Unidentified photographer, original photograph of nurse Edith Lee, ca. 1934.

4½ × 2½ in. (11.43 × 6.35 cm). Source: Collection of the author.

captured in her nursing uniform, this particular photograph was enlarged and enhanced through Van Der Zee's studio. This photograph, and presumably many more, preceded the 1940s, thus predating the period that usually marks the start of the photographer's dependence on this aspect of his craft to support his business.

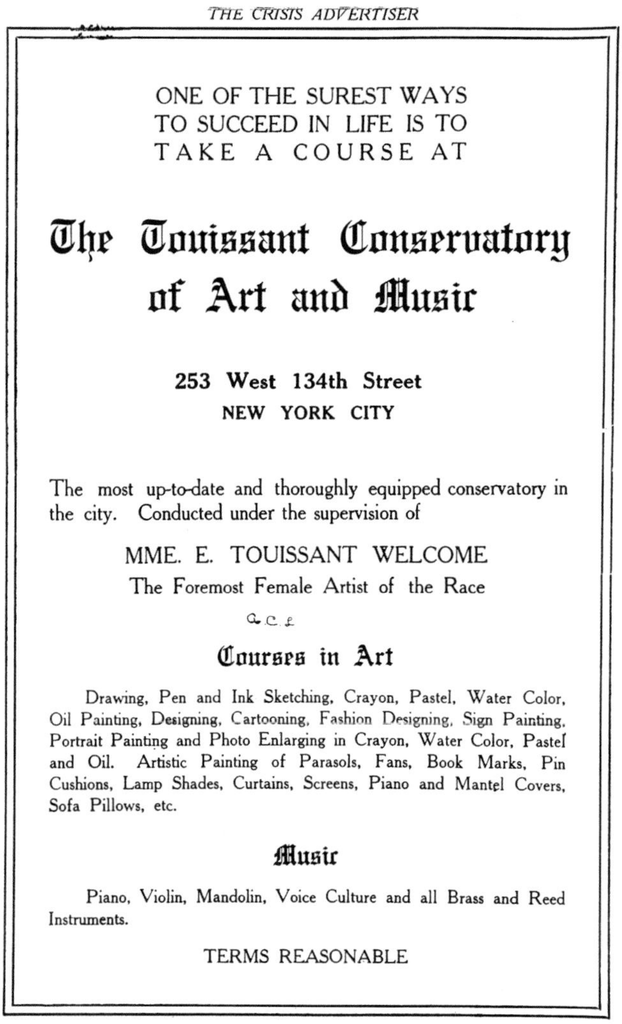

ONE OF THE SUREST WAYS
TO SUCCEED IN LIFE IS TO
TAKE A COURSE AT

The Touissant Conservatory
of Art and Music

253 West 134th Street
NEW YORK CITY

The most up-to-date and thoroughly equipped conservatory in
the city. Conducted under the supervision of

MME. E. TOUISSANT WELCOME
The Foremost Female Artist of the Race

Courses in Art

Drawing, Pen and Ink Sketching, Crayon, Pastel, Water Color,
Oil Painting, Designing, Cartooning, Fashion Designing, Sign Painting,
Portrait Painting and Photo Enlarging in Crayon, Water Color, Pastel
and Oil. Artistic Painting of Parasols, Fans, Book Marks, Pin
Cushions, Lamp Shades, Curtains, Screens, Piano and Mantel Covers,
Sofa Pillows, etc.

Music

Piano, Violin, Mandolin, Voice Culture and all Brass and Reed
Instruments.

TERMS REASONABLE

FIGURE 3.11

Advertisement for the
Touissant Conservatory of
Art and Music, *Crisis*,
November 1910.

Source: Manuscripts, Archives and
Rare Books Division, Schomburg
Center for Research in Black
Culture, New York Public Library.

In fact, the services described had a long precedent that is evident
before Van Der Zee ran his own studio and before he even had the chance
to depend on the kinds of photographic services discussed in this chapter.
In 1911 Van Der Zee was invited by his sister, Jennie Touissant Welcome,
to join her and her husband, Ernest Touissant Welcome, at their recently
opened Harlem establishment for music and art. It was there that Van Der
Zee worked in his first unofficial Harlem studio, which was housed on
the second floor, above the couple's school, known as the Touissant Conservatory of Art and Music, at 253 West 134th Street. In a 1910 advertisement found in the *Crisis* magazine, Van Der Zee's sister was prominently

named as proprietor of the conservatory (figure 3.11). As listed in the ad, "Mme. E. Touissant Welcome[,] the Foremost Female Artist of the Race," offered music classes in more than six instruments along with over twenty art classes, many of which were listed by name within the ad, strategically placed for the best exposure on the interior cover page of the magazine's first issue and in subsequent issues.[17]

The advertisement marked the beginning of a very long career for Van Der Zee, one that included enlargement work from the beginning. Although Van Der Zee is not mentioned in the ad, his presence at the school the following year may be inferred through the listing of one particular class. A class in "Portrait Painting and Photo Enlarging in Crayon" is the only mention of photography. The portrait crayon practice has been described, by a nineteenth-century author writing for the journal *The Art Amateur*, as a kind of "solar print." It is when a photograph is "faintly printed and enlarged to life-size from the portrait to be copied. The man who makes the solar print . . . mount[s] it on a stretcher and thus . . . the artist finds ready prepared for him the foundation of the picture for which he will . . . have gone over certain parts of it with a crayon tint, and worked up the details with a little point work by the aid of a few sittings from the original."[18] Since Van Der Zee most likely offered such photographic services to his sister's clients, this early experience at the Touissant school reveals his dominant practice during the 1940s and later as contingent on a number of photographic skills that he developed and marketed starting in the early twentieth century. Compellingly, Van Der Zee insisted on using the phrase *making a photograph* instead of *taking a photograph*.[19] This subtle shift in language reinforces the centrality of not only shooting an image but working on an image.

In the existing scholarship on Van Der Zee, there is evidence of his commitment to working on images in order to figure out and experiment with the craft and labor photography demanded. Photography posed technical problems that Van Der Zee found answers to, often through the trial and error that came with his high volume of work. In describing a portfolio of portraits by Van Der Zee, art historian Regenia Perry writes, "The . . . portraits posed challenging problems in the handling of figures in outdoor light, as well as in composition, depth and detail, which Van Der Zee solved skillfully long before the advent of the light meter."[20] As additional evidence of Van Der Zee's skillful engagement with the craft of photography, Perry explains that "he preferred flash powder even after the introduction of the flash bulb, and maintained that it was more effective because it provided as bright a degree of illumination as desired and also could be used to shoot outdoor pictures at night."[21]

The most important aspect of Van Der Zee's practice was the camera itself, which almost never appeared as the subject matter in any of his photographs from this early period.[22] Van Der Zee most often used an 8 × 10 camera with glass plates in addition to 5 × 7-inch and 4 × 5-inch large-format box cameras.[23] As Van Der Zee explained, the advantage of using these large-format cameras was that he could always do a lot of retouching if necessary.[24] Hence, this technology allowed Van Der Zee to continue an engagement with enlargements and other enhancements that had started earlier in his career. Changing the lens on the camera also worked toward different purposes, as some lenses provided more roundness and softness with less detail.[25]

When one approaches his later work as a continuation of work he did earlier in his career, the disparate photographs found in his archive originating from other photographers' studios have more in common with the rest of his oeuvre than previously understood. They all required similar skills of working on the photograph's surface. In addition, this highly tuned skill offered an opportunity for Van Der Zee to flex his stylistic dexterities. Each modification he intentionally made in turn informed the viewer's aesthetic experience with the photograph. Cho theorizes the darkroom in ways that illuminate Van Der Zee's practice. She contends, "Despite the job title, the darkroom technician's work is never merely technical, not simply an automated process of churning out contact sheets and printing images through a prescribed formula. Like the photographer, the darkroom technician must master an array of equipment and substances. The enlarger. The printer. The chemicals and the paper. And the norm references or indexes. It matters where and in what context a photography technician learns their craft; like photography itself, photographic development processes are not neutral."[26] Like the photographs developed by the darkroom technicians in Cho's scholarship, the work Van Der Zee did on behalf of his clients was not neutral, generic, or mechanical. Each example offers an occasion to reconsider how Van Der Zee's creative endeavors took place while using an enlarger, making additions to the material surfaces of photographs, or rephotographing an aged keepsake, as opposed to him skillfully instructing posed subjects from behind his studio camera. The mechanisms of Black visibility and subjectivity extend beyond what the camera lens captures to reveal the inner workings of Van Der Zee's creative expression.

Shifts in Photographic Practice

A look to how this time period is often framed within the art history of photography further illustrates the nuances that a vernacular turn brings into view. The rise of the personal camera during this time factors greatly into Van Der Zee's dependency on his modification services. Yet the correlation might go beyond Van Der Zee's need for a different kind of business. The increase in modification services may speak to a new value placed on photographs more generally. What prompted the owners of a portrait of a couple to send it to Van Der Zee's studio for work (figure 3.12)? More important, was the desire for enlargement, retouching, and recopying of photographs a result of a growing interest in photographs manifested through the surging interest in personal cameras and snapshots?

As the domestic ownership of cameras increased, photographs taken at home became more widespread, in contrast to the formalized process of visiting a studio. Indeed, by the 1950s, family cameras and snapshots were extremely prevalent nationally. A 1950s article titled "Photographic Business in the U.S.A., 1950–1953" states, "An estimate of the number of snapshots made during 1950 is 1,500 million. Thirty million of the families in the United States (about 70 per cent of the nation's families) own at least one camera. Twelve million of these families have cameras with flash attachments."[27] The popularity of cameras and the industry that supported their sale and the sale of attachments such as a flash resulted in a corollary increase in image production. While cameras became more ubiquitous, the formal studio portraits did not. However, Van Der Zee increased his modification services to fill the gap where his portrait practice left off. His modification services, in some ways, may have worked in tandem with the rise of personal cameras, as individuals formed new relationships with photographic images. However, certain practices have come into view more than others.

Indeed, the world of Harlem studio photographs described in chapter 1 changed drastically. Alternative kinds of photographic practices took shape. Although it remains hard to pinpoint actual numbers, it can be surmised that, instead of opening photography studios, portraitists had a different kind of presence in Harlem, potentially as itinerant photographers. Given that the lower overhead costs would have relieved the burden of paying rent, the rise of such a photographic practice is likely. Visual evidence of itinerant photographers appears in a 1935–1936 photograph by Russell

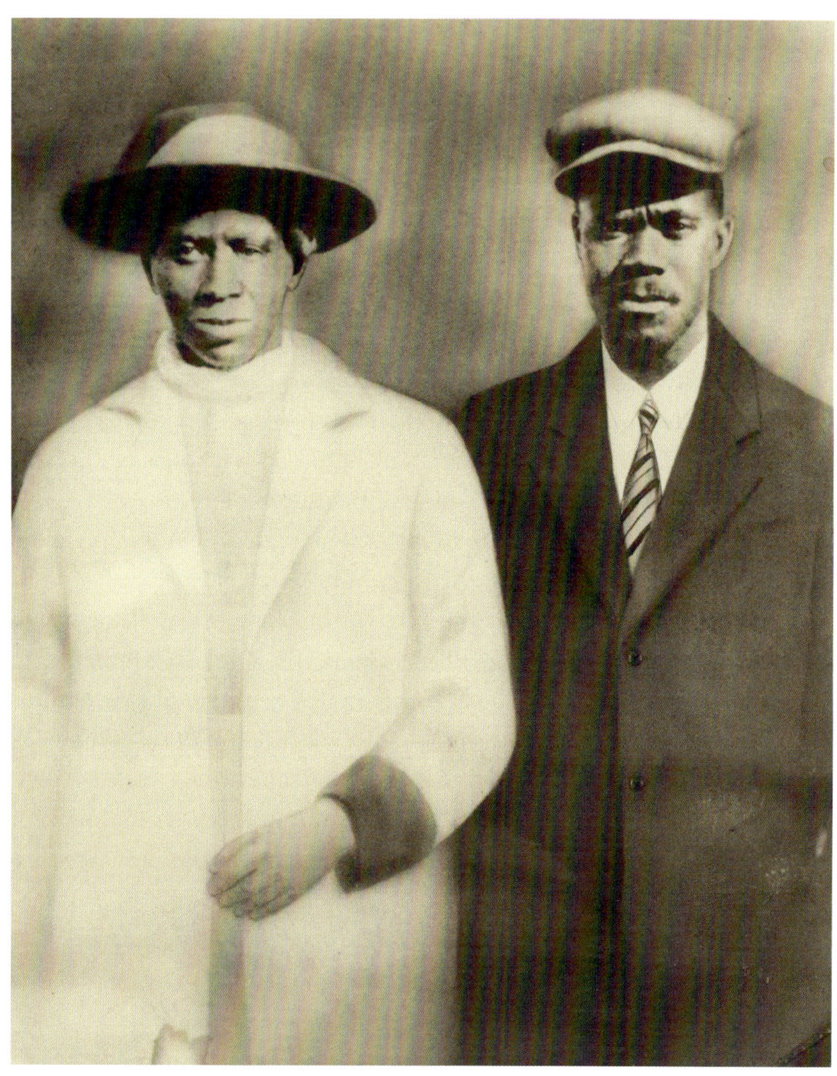

James Van Der Zee, copy photograph of a man and a woman (original photographer and date unknown), likely reproduced 1930s–1960s.

© James Van Der Zee Archive, The Metropolitan Museum of Art, New York. Source: James Van Der Zee Archive, The Metropolitan Museum of Art, New York.

Lee titled *Street Photographer, New York*, taken at the height of the Great Depression (figure 3.13). The photograph depicts a Black photographer peering into the viewfinder of a camera mounted to a light, portable tripod. Attached to the camera are sample photographs, carefully arranged to display the photographer's skill. In contrast to Van Der Zee's elaborate window displays, the visual presence of Black photographers here is a lot more modest. As a reflection of the times, the itinerant street photographer still responds to the photographic needs of the neighborhood but in ways that seem more transient and unstable than the rhetoric of stability and establishment that defined an earlier time.

A painting on a similar theme by Jacob Lawrence echoes such sentiments while inadvertently illustrating the growing need for access to these kinds of portraits (figure 3.14). In contrast to the lone young Black man who stands before the itinerant photographer in Lee's photographs, there are three individuals in Jacob Lawrence's painting *The Photographer* (1942). The respectable family unit of a mother, father, and child has been moved from the studio space to the street. They stand, dressed in what appears to be their Sunday best, on a busy and hectic corner to have their likeness recorded within an environment with little similarity to the calm and domestic interior of Van Der Zee's studio. The historical moment depicted in both Lee's photograph and Lawrence's painting was one in which Van Der Zee's own engagement with the medium shifted to accommodate changes in the demand for images. Van Der Zee's modification services count among these subtle shifts. Both examples point to the continued importance of photography and representation to Black families, despite the decline in patronizing a more traditional studio.

In contrast with an era in which the portrait photographer ruled, the years following the beginning of the Depression are most often explored through different kinds of photographs, those that were journalistic and documentary in nature. In turn, Harlem became, as photo historian Sara Blair explains, "a site that afforded charged visual opportunities, spectacles, evidence, found objects, and decisive moments—moments that were recorded with unprecedented regularity by men (and some women) armed with cameras, eager to shoot."[28] Aligned with Russell Lee, who captured the itinerant Black photographer through his camera, those from outside Harlem regularly came to the neighborhood to take documentary photographs that differed decidedly from Van Der Zee's studio portraits. The New York Photo League's 1932–1940 Harlem Document project, through which many of Aaron Siskind's photographs of the neighborhood would

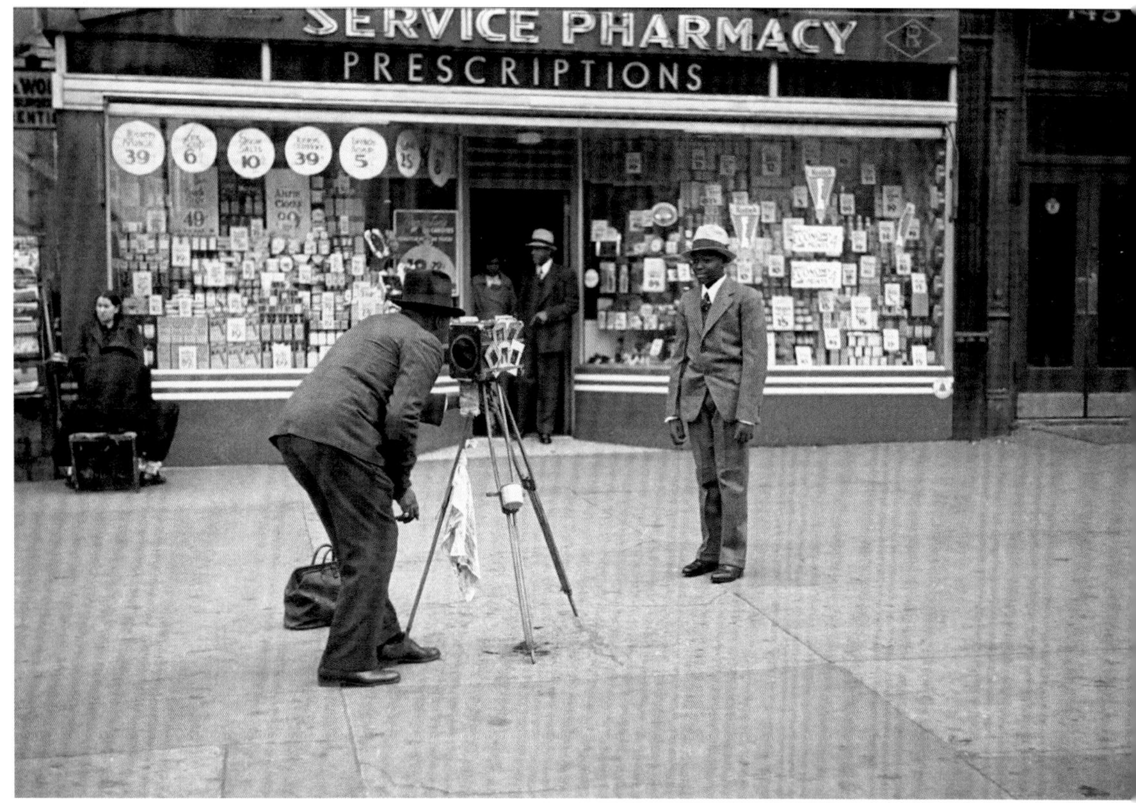

become known, accounts for one instance.[29] As photo historian and cura-tor Mia Fineman insists, there existed a renewed confidence in documen-tary truth, which was met by an audience wanting to consume images and narrative through journalistic reporting.[30] For example, the subject matter and media outlet of Gordon Parks's celebrated 1948 *Life* magazine photo essay documenting one Harlem gang leader fit neatly within this narra-tive.[31] While Parks remained an anomaly as a Black photographer within journalism at that time, the visual representation he produced garnered an audience eager for this type of reportage. His photographs became iconic and representative of an era, in contrast to the everyday depictions cap-tured in studio portraiture, which obscured the complex social and cultural changes that defined African American life during the decades leading up to and including the civil rights era. Van Der Zee's modification services did not align with common understandings of this historical movement, nor the kinds of stories that readers of *Life* wanted to read. He and his stu-

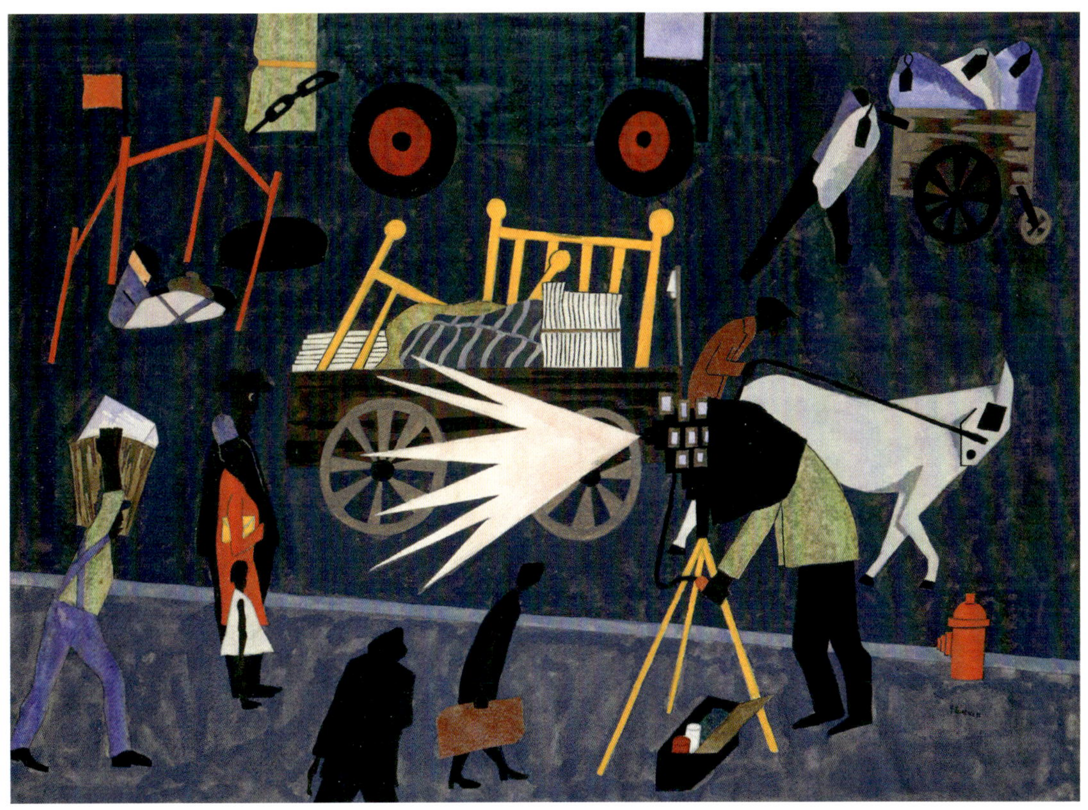

FIGURE 3.13 (opposite)

Russell Lee, *Street Photographer, New York*, 1935–1936.

Gelatin-silver print. Source: Briscoe Center for American History, University of Texas at Austin.

FIGURE 3.14 (above)

Jacob Lawrence, *The Photographer*, 1942. Lawrence's painting highlights an itinerant street photographer at work on the busy streets of Harlem.

Watercolor, gouache, and graphite on paper, 22⅛ × 30½ in. (56.2 × 77.5 cm). © The Jacob and Gwendolyn Knight Lawrence Foundation, Seattle, Washington / Artists Rights Society (ARS), New York. Source: The Metropolitan Museum of Art, New York.

dio ended up on the margins of this cultural movement, and scholars have looked elsewhere.

However, Van Der Zee and his services reflect a silent but present undercurrent or parallel existence to the documentary and journalistic photography that dominates accounts of the 1950s in histories of photography. For example, enlargement skills were sought after. The popularity of enlargements during this period can be gleaned from a 1955 advertisement by the New York Institute of Photography, a school located in mid-Manhattan at 10 West Thirty-Third Street, which trained a number of Van Der Zee's peers earlier in the twentieth century (figure 3.15). In the advertisement the school is celebrating its fortieth anniversary. The full-page ad contains four photographs, each representing an important aspect of photographic training. The largest shows a photographer taking a portrait of a well-dressed woman as an example of the genre of fashion photography taught at the school. The next image is a classroom scene of students working on photo-oil coloring, while another depicts a group discussion of students seated in front of a teacher at the head of the classroom. The most relevant is the photograph of a few men facing toward a large piece of equipment accompanied by the textual explanation "Expert Enlarging—You become proficient in this important phase of photography through our unique, learn-by-doing method using professional precision equipment." From fashion photography to coloring to enlargement, by 1950 potential photography students weren't just looking to set up a commercial photography studio and take portraits, which had been the focus during the 1920s. Instead, by the 1950s, enlargement services were valued enough to be highlighted as a teachable skill in this photography school advertisement. Although Van Der Zee's engagement with enlargement is regarded in scholarship as part of his demise, the practice was relevant and appropriate, seen as an asset and skill during this time in ways that aligned with the world of photography more generally in the 1950s. As Van Der Zee transitioned from one genre of photography to a different kind of engagement with the medium, underrecognized aspects of photography's history come into view.

Even aside from Van Der Zee's career, it is clear that within certain corners of the world of photography, the work of enhancing, enlarging, and copying photographs—a learned skill—was considered an arena in which any photographer worth their salt would be able to showcase their multiple talents. Professional publications on photography produced during the 1940s and 1950s draw attention to photography as a craft. In one catchy

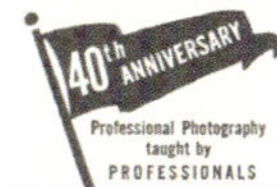
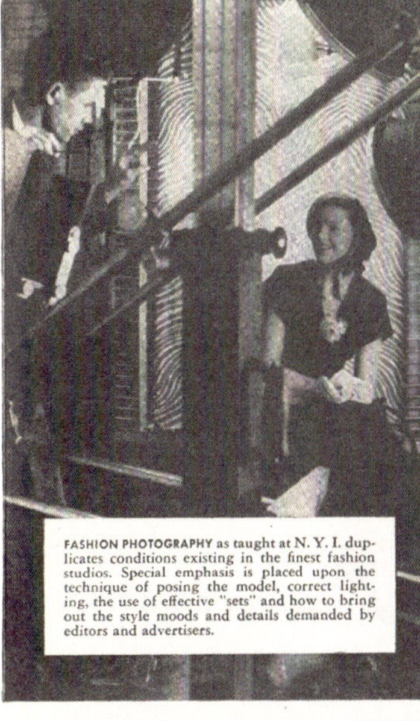
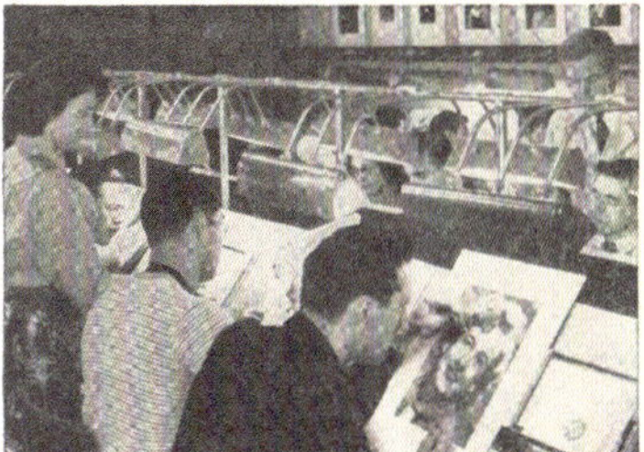
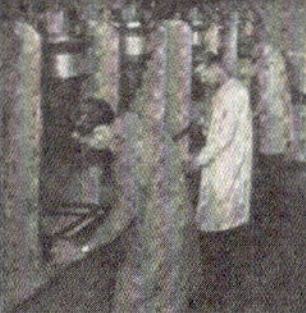
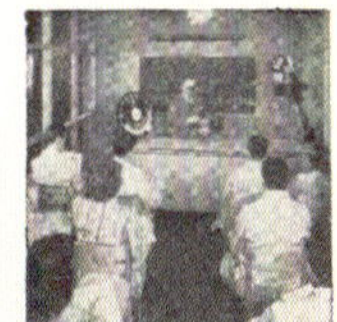
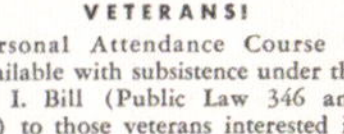
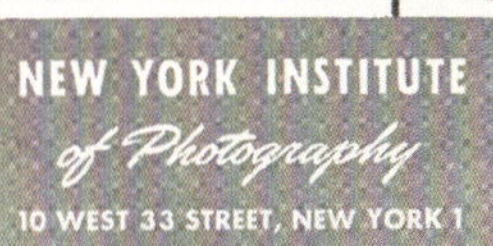

FIGURE 3.15

Advertisement for New York Institute of Photography, which ran in magazines including *Camera*, *American Photography*, and *Modern Photography*, 1955. Photography schools throughout New York City taught burgeoning photographers a range of important skills, including enlargement work.

Source: Center for Creative Photography, University of Arizona, Tucson.

example, readers are rhetorically asked to consider, "What skills must the photo-restorer have? He must wear three hats—that of the photographer, that of the retoucher, and that of the artist—because his craft requires the knowledge of photography, retouching, and artwork."[32] In another, more perspective is gained: "Success in copying old, faded and defaced photographs is based upon the recognition that each individual copy is a different problem. Former work in the field contributes to the solution only in so far as the experience gained may aid in formulating an attack upon the new problem."[33] Although both art history and Van Der Zee himself would insist on his status as an artist, the centrality of applying his skills to the task of reproduction meant that he was also a craftsman of photography. This dynamic work not only required hard-earned skill but was also a culmination of years of labor. Instead of viewing Van Der Zee's work during the 1940s and 1950s as a downturn, we should notice that his efforts drew out a photographic practice valued enough to be offered at photography school, framed as a developed skill, and maintained through active correspondence between Van Der Zee and his clients, both domestic and international.

Images Safeguarded through Multiplicity

Performance studies scholar Joseph Roach theorizes the copy through his writing on repetition. He insists, "No action or sequence of actions may be performed exactly the same way twice; they must be reinvented or re-created at each appearance." He continues, "In this improvisational behavioral space, memory reveals itself as imagination."[34] If we apply Roach's generative concept of repetition to Van Der Zee's modification services, this part of his photographic practice shifts from making a mere copy to engaging in imagination and other possibilities. Although Roach's reflections are grounded in the discourse of performance, other approaches to the copy effortlessly bring us back to the realm of African diasporic photography. For example, the writer Manthia Diawara discusses the copy in his scholarship on the studio photographer Malick Sidibé's portraits of youth during the era following Mali's independence from colonial rule in 1960. He insists that Sidibé attained mastery of his craft by copying copies. However, the copy is not a literal copy of a photograph but the poses of international rock stars mimicked by local youth in their reenactments captured in the photo studio. According to Diawara, "Sidibé, who never attended a photography school, had learned from the best in the field. By following the youth of Bamako, who were wearing flowered shirts made by famous designers because they saw their idols wearing them in magazine photos, Sidibé was training his eye by emulating great photographers. And by following the copy of the copy, he was internalizing the history of photography without knowing it."[35]

Similarly, Van Der Zee internalized a different history of photography through the work of the vernacular photographers who took the photographs that clients sent to his studio for modification. Even though, to Van Der Zee, the names of canonical photographers such as "Steichen, Stieglitz, Hine and Van Vechten rang no bells in his memory," the photographs by other photographers brought to him for restoration, recopying, and modification offered an alternate pedagogical archive.[36] They become the unrecognized canon to which his modifications contribute.

Not only did Van Der Zee indirectly engage with other photographers through the arrival of their images at his studio, but he also visually encountered the various individuals captured in these photographs. How might we create a new set of terms around Van Der Zee's engagement with reproduction, not through representation but through photographic practices linked to the kinds of hope, creativity, and persistence illustrated through his recopying, enlargement, and enhancement services? Van Der Zee offers a sense of stability, marked by change. As with his work posing subjects within the studio, through his modification services, he solidifies a person's wishes. However, this paradigm is set against a strikingly different context, one that brings the centrality of photography and the implications of its status as a copy to light.

The impact of multiple images, especially for African American subjects, has a long history. For example, recall the frequently cited examples of Sojourner Truth and Frederick Douglass, two nineteenth-century figures who strategically used the multiplicity and circulation of their own portraits to advance their activism.[37] The various *carte de visite* versions of Truth spoke volumes, specifically because the images reached viewers through their multiplicity. Similarly, Douglass—proclaimed as the most photographed American of the nineteenth century—used his portrait, produced over and over again, to stake a claim.[38] He did so by capturing his likeness but also through having his likeness seen through its constant circulation and repetition. Having control over an image through its reproduction—for well-known and less known people alike—allowed individuals to dictate the value and importance of their own images.

Although the extent of Van Der Zee's enhancement work is unclear, one quote offers insight into the kinds of promises of representation similar services offered. In describing the business of enlargement, one guide from the 1960s offers the following insight: "The orders for the copy enlargements were taken on by door-to-door salesmen who would send them on to the copy house. In their eagerness to get the order, they would promise almost anything the customer wanted. They accepted orders to change clothing, to make regroupings, to remove a person from a group for a portrait of that person by himself, to take off hats, etc."[39] While portraiture is praised for providing social capital and enhancing Black subjects' sense of self through adornment, composure, and imagining, it seems as though enlargement, recopying, and modification services could achieve a similarly august importance.[40] Those photographs sent to Van Der Zee for modification had a very specific end story: one that reflected the needs of clients and what they asked of photography and the photographs that already existed in their lives. However, unlike the photographs of Truth and Douglass, who went to specific studios for their sittings, in the case of the photographs sent to Van Der Zee, there was no origination story that started with posing in front of Van Der Zee's camera. Instead, these photographs speak to an occasion of propagation of what was previously created, most often by another photographer lost to history, and already existed. Therefore, the endurance of images is central here.

The scholar François Brunet argues, "Reproduction ... opens up a space of multiple reproduction. ... Reproduction has been, historically, born out of the urge not only to distribute but to safeguard copies of originals."[41] Thinking about Van Der Zee's services as an act of safeguarding his clients' photographs reframes the photographer's later career as generative, noble, and inspiring. This becomes especially important in the face of the loss and precarity often experienced by individuals of African descent.[42] In making a copy print for the restoration work, Van Der Zee was multiplying the number of images in circulation. As opposed to creating rarified objects with dashing representations, Van Der Zee was instead extending the reach of cherished items, regardless of their visual content, by giving individuals the opportunity to extend an image's quality and its possibility of creating an impact on its viewers through its size, its details, and its very existence in more than one copy. By extending the life of a photograph in this way, Van Der Zee expanded the possibilities of that image to impact the very positioning and subjectivity of its sitter or those who counted as viewers.

In addition to giving his clients the opportunity to safeguard images through multiplicity, Van Der Zee's services highlight how far and wide photographs traveled in order for this modification work to be carried out. For example, in discussing mortuary photographs, he explains, "I've gotten pictures from the West Indies, that they'd taken there, where they had them in the casket, kind of standing up. The pictures were sent here to me to recopy. I'd recopy them and probably put some of these biblical figures around them and make the picture look a little more like the ones that I had taken."[43] Beyond simply making copies, Van Der Zee added narrative enhancements to the photograph's surface. Through such a collaborative unfolding through place and time, each photograph becomes a layered image told through multiple photographers, presumably from distant locations. Van Der Zee takes over where the original photographer has left off in order to create a different version for clients far from his Harlem studio. These photographs, in a certain sense, become part of the chorus, a concept of transformation through a sense of shared experience among a group of people, as explained by scholar Saidiya Hartman. The chorus is "the vehicle for another kind of story. . . . [It] propels transformation. It is an incubator of possibility." The kind of redress that Van Der Zee's modified photographs provide illustrates one particular action within the possibilities of a chorus. A round in a musical composition connotes, as Hartman may suggest, someone else carrying on.[44] In contrast to a song sung in unison within a chorus, a round encourages each voice to begin and continue at different points in time within the song. Similarly, the originating photographer and Van Der Zee both harmonize through a kind of repetitive building, one following the other with slight differences, as is the case within a round.

These sorts of repetitions reached across the globe. An instance of the reach of Van Der Zee's clients' photographs can be found in an example currently in the possession of a family from Curaçao, now living in the Netherlands. As told by Sherman De Jesus, his grandfather arrived in Manhattan from Curaçao during the early 1920s and eventually made his way to Van Der Zee's studio. De Jesus surmises that his grandfather had a portrait photograph of himself that he brought to Harlem, where Van Der Zee then copied the image and stamped the verso with the studio's printed name and address (figure 3.16).[45] Examples such as these often slip past art historical inquiry, specifically because they exist in liminal places that defy easy definition within a traditional African American art paradigm. These modified photographs are not quite Van Der Zee's in the traditional sense

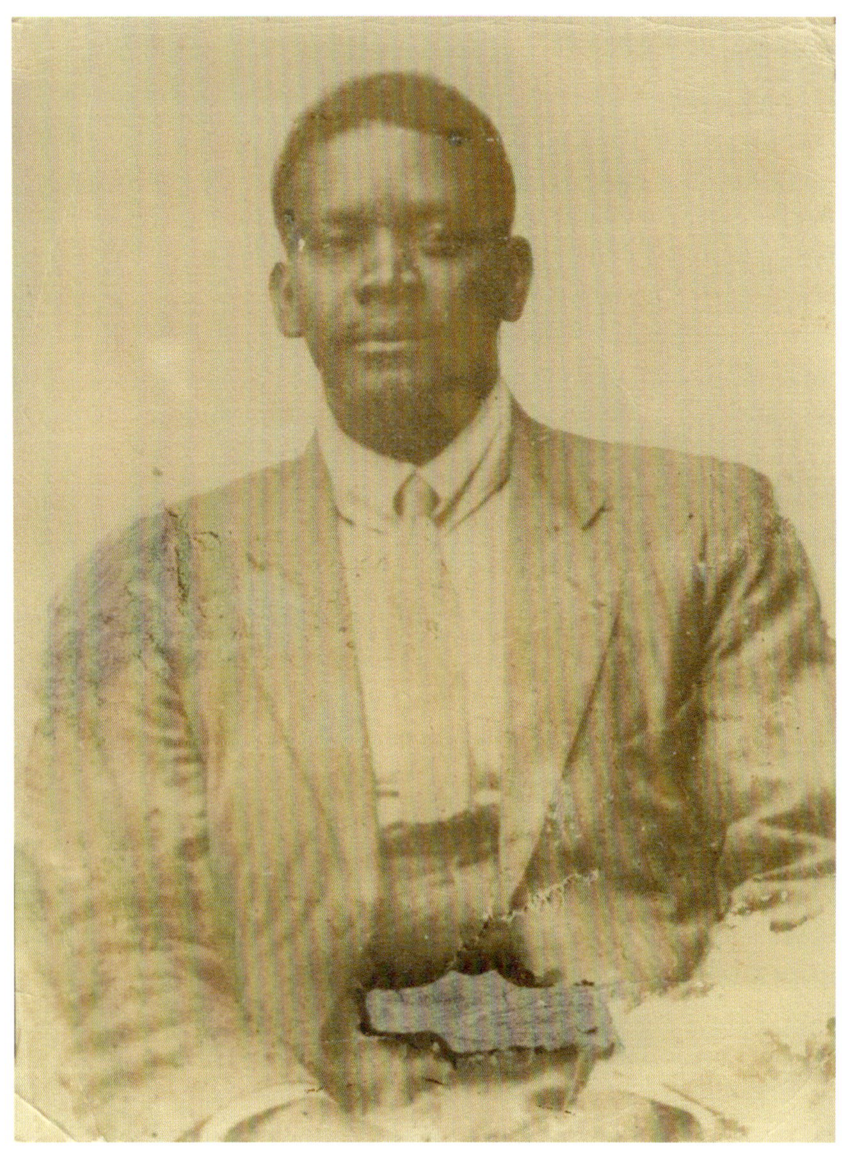

James Van Der Zee, copy photograph of Juan De Jesus (original photographer and date unknown), likely reproduced early 1920s. Juan De Jesus, grandfather of filmmaker Sherman De Jesus, visited Harlem from the Dutch Caribbean island of Curaçao.

Approx. 7 × 5 in. (17.78 × 12.7 cm). © James Van Der Zee Archive, The Metropolitan Museum of Art. Source: Collection of Sherman De Jesus.

but are nonetheless photographs impacted directly by his artistic services. Their ability to upend established narratives of an artist's oeuvre is one of the many reasons they are so compelling.

Such examples bring to light how vernacular photographs often move unseen or unnoticed through art history in uninhibited ways, precisely because they are deemed of little value by institutionalized standards. Of course, the owner values the image, but without what constitutes a photographic image or practice of note, these copied and modified photographs exist in the world differently from those that abide by established standards of importance. Instead, vernacular photographs usually exist in unorganized archives, in people's homes, in boxes under beds, on walls that are exposed to too much light and wind and heat. They are folded in half and placed in wallets, inadvertently altered with water stains, and willfully cropped when relationships shift. And when a photograph's owner hoped to enhance or rekindle their attachment to the photograph, Van Der Zee's services simultaneously answered the demand while activating the photograph through a change in appearance and—most intriguingly— through movement.

Such photographs traveled far—stewarded by crisp envelopes carried close to hearts in breast pockets, passed judiciously from one person to the next, and transported on someone else's timeline through the international and domestic mail—with few of the common hurdles that often shape everyday Black life. A photograph of a Black subject can skirt, or at least offer a space to avoid, the kinds of contexts that led Truth and Douglass to insist on their Black humanity through photography. In addition, traveling photographs recast the theme of the movement of Black people and populations: instead of Black bodies moving under conditions of force and duress, photographs—and therefore their subjects and their owners— are temporarily freed from corporeal constraints.

Migrating through the Mail

Within the context of Van Der Zee's services, the unknown details of the reasons behind each photograph's reproduction and the movement from one point to the next can make for a captivating narrative. The delayed sense of anticipation, the level of quality that would be evaluated, the act of sending something from afar without really leaving one's home to do so—all may have been valued aspects of this process for those clients who utilized Van Der Zee's services. Art historian Jennifer Roberts writes convincingly about lag time. Through her own engagement with Pierre Bourdieu's scholarship, she concludes, "Delay . . . is productive: deferral, uncertainty, and opacity help constitute the *form* and *meaning* of practices by compelling practitioners to make strategic use of them."[46] While Roberts's words speak to the art maker, envisioning the viewer's experience is especially useful here. The term *armchair traveler* has often been used to describe the viewer's experience of sitting and visually consuming the earlier photographic format of a stereograph.[47] Might we amend the phrase's meaning to include those longing for their photographs to return? It would include those brimming with anticipation—an experience intrinsic to the kind of travel one can imagine from the comfort of an armchair and one shared by so many African diasporic subjects familiar with migration and return.

This kind of travel became a possibility for vernacular photographs: not only through a stereoscope, used to view stereographs, but through the most mundane of institutions—the post office. Clues to the mail's integral role in everyday life illustrate the cultural logic through which, by the 1940s, the mail-order enlargement service actually made sense. From the popular practice of purchasing house plans and premade construction components from a catalog to the unusual occurrence of mail-order brides to a number of noted cases in which actual people were sent through the mail (such as the well-known case of Henry Box Brown using the mail as an escape from slavery), this mode of transportation initially was the stuff of august possibilities and spectacle before becoming such a commonplace service that the postal service's cultural impact is often obscured by its mundaneness.[48]

Postal advancements impacted the circulation of vernacular photography. As mail passed from the sender to the courier and then to the receiver with steps in between, the addition of air travel added a new dimension to the mail. For example, airmail started in 1918 and opened up even more opportunities for people to correspond throughout the world. But at the same time, the mundane facts that help us understand the mail as a trusted and important resource had important implications for Van Der Zee's mail-order services. Most notably, after World War II, the post office went through a major transition to modernize its equipment. What might sound like a minor case of improvement and development revolutionized the way the mail was sent, opening up a viable option for Van Der Zee to depend fully on the mail for the success of his business in his later years. There was an unprecedented growth in mail volume owing to the country's prosperity following the end of World War II. Therefore, the post office needed to figure out ways to move higher quantities of mail more efficiently. The shift from hand-sorted to mechanical mail processes did just that. The system became more efficient and therefore quickened the steps between a person dropping a photograph in the mail and its return by Van Der Zee, recopied, enhanced, or enlarged.

Clearly, photographs traveling through the mail became a mainstay in the early twentieth century. For example, one may recall photo postcards through which family members kept in touch. As scholars such as Erica Armstrong Dunbar and Jasmine Nichole Cobb illustrate, circulating correspondences such as friendship albums and scrapbooks were integral to maintaining distant familial and friend relationships.[49] Sending photographs in the mail for enlargement, recopying, and enhancement work can be regarded as an extension of this early social practice. However, questions come to mind. Keeping in touch with a distant relative through the mail is one thing, but why send one's photographs to distant places through the post office to have them enlarged when a local photographer might have been able to do the work? What kind of trust and hope needed to be instilled in the customer for an heirloom photograph to be sent through the mail? What culturally allowed for this not only to happen but to become so frequent that it dominated Van Der Zee's practice for years to come?

In terms of Van Der Zee's earlier portraits, there are some aspects of their initial making that are very likely. For example, the subjects walked into Van Der Zee's studio, he posed them to both parties' liking, and a camera captured their visage. This series of events was repeated over and over, with minor departures here and there. However, it becomes harder to recreate the act of exchange and even collaboration during Van Der Zee's later career, when mail orders were used. Yet the mail-order service often involved an extensive epistolary correspondence. As the photographer describes it, "I was getting letters from all over—Alaska, Gold Coast of Africa, Trinidad, Puerto Rico, Panama, even all the way from Russia. They'd send pictures to be enlarged and copied." Van Der Zee continues, "The business from the States was much better. Postage to the other countries was higher, and foreign customers would write a log of letters before they'd send any money. Sometimes, they'd want you to do a sample for nothing."[50] A log of letters, whether true or exaggerated, implies a cadre of very invested clients. Clients needed to feel confident about the service provided by Van Der Zee. What at first might seem like a very simple transaction for a minor manipulation of an image became an exchange with higher stakes.

Though Van Der Zee described his exasperation, his clients' care for these images, for their proper modification and safe return, becomes evident. Indeed, hefty doses of risk and trust are central to the kinds of exchange that took place between Van Der Zee and his clients from all around the world. He was no longer a lone artist working persistently to apply his skill and talent to the creation of signature portraits, as the modification services elicited a different paradigm. There is a sense of intimacy that needs to be developed for someone to send Van Der Zee an old photograph. Also intrinsic to this collaboration is a sense of chance, but not the kind of chance frequently discussed in relationship to photography. For example, photo historian Robin Kelsey is intrigued by how, when one presses the camera button, it's unclear if the resulting image has unintentionally captured a subject with their eyes closed or if something unwarranted entered the composition through unpredictable process-based factors. Just as easily, the photograph could be exactly what the photographer wished for and more.[51] In contrast, the chance at play with Van Der Zee's modified photographs warranted a kind of reassurance that the photographer could do the job as promised, as the photograph precariously traversed geographies for days upon days until it reached its intended destination.

One way to understand the desire and comfort that encouraged people to send their photographs through the mail for enlargement and recopying services is to turn to a revealing occurrence specific to the World War II era. Starting in 1942, to prioritize the transportation of war materials and supplies within air cargo space while simultaneously keeping up with the mail correspondence between families and those who served abroad, the US Postal Service initiated the Victory Mail system.[52] Special letter sheets were used to write letters. Then, once deposited at the postal facility, the letters were opened and censored and photographed on film in smaller proportions than the original. The technology meant that "the note to be sent V-mail was photographed on one hundred foot rolls of 16mm film, approximately five thousand messages to each roll."[53] Next, the microfilmed sheets were sent priority air express to their destination post office. From there, the filmed letters were enlarged and printed on photographic paper, and then each letter was sent to the person for whom it was originally intended.[54] The war and navy departments took on the responsibility of getting mail to the forces overseas. Officials suggested that V-mail built morale.[55] The *Annual Report of the Postmaster General* of the United States of that same year notes "that frequent and rapid communication with parents, associates, and other loved ones strengthens fortitude, enlivens patriotism, makes loneliness endurable, and inspires to even greater devotion the men and women who are carrying on our fight far from home and friends."[56] In addition, "by regulation, the [V-mail] microfilms were destroyed immediately after the paper prints were mailed."[57] Within such a context, the enlargement, recopying, and enhancement of photographs aligned with the logic that informed the popularity of V-mail. The reproduced version of the keepsake becomes the object of sentimental value while the original is discarded or filed away within a forgotten archive.

However, unlike photographs circulated through postcards or the V-mail film, mail-order services lacked any standardization. For example, the envelope size most likely varied, as did the actual size of the photographs enclosed within. Nowhere near the accepted dimensions and exposed message of a postcard or the uniform format of V-mail, the enlargement and recopying services operated via carefully sealed mail correspondences, with the photographs most likely tucked into letters or notes explaining the desires of the client. Thus, the photographs sent were very different from the outward-facing photographs that filled up every inch of Van Der Zee's window display for passersby to view, or from a postcard that might have piqued the mail carrier's interest as their eyes fell on the postcard during sorting or delivery. Presumably, the photographs sent in envelopes were more discreet, and the exchange personal.

Image manipulation is another level of imagining a modicum of freedom and choice over representation. Sending an image far away, so that it will come back improved, is a powerful act that illustrates a level of trust in the photographer's ability to transform a photograph into something better. This aligns with the very thing photography often did in documenting action, struggle, and freedom for African American communities.[58] In this case, photographs are things that can be modified to elicit different kinds of value or meaning than the original could.

Such truths relate to the cultural cachet of Van Der Zee's location. For clients abroad, Van Der Zee's status as a photographer in America proved appealing. As African art and photography scholar John Peffer writes in regard to painted and enlarged photographs of the late nineteenth century, "Aside from a few early studios, most enlargement work was sent overseas for processing, an aspect that likely enhanced their value in Africa. Portrait photographs, especially enlarged and retouched ones, were in a sense thought of as things from overseas and were used to enhance one's image and one's prestige in the African colonial setting."[59] And by the 1950s,

Peffer shares, "Clients were sometimes informed that their original photographs would be sent 'to America' for enlargement, painting and framing."[60] Van Der Zee's location may have served as a type of currency for eager audiences interested in experiencing the lure of the United States. In turn, Van Der Zee benefited from this trend by courting and establishing an international clientele.

In addition, the appeal of Van Der Zee's enlargement and retouching services to potential domestic clients outside of Harlem may have been intrinsically related not only to his status as an American photographer but more specifically to his location in the international cultural capital of New York City or more specifically the renowned Black mecca of Harlem. Might some of Van Der Zee's Black clients have re-created the movement of the Great Migration through sending their photographs to Van Der Zee with hopes of having their photograph return improved? Instead of individuals traveling from the South to the famous neighborhood of Harlem for better opportunities, could part of the desire for migration be mitigated and enacted by photographs traveling from the South to Van Der Zee's studio in the North in the hopes of some kind of enhancement? Consider one example of a photograph that most likely originated outside of Van Der Zee's Harlem. Within the portrait, a Black man stands while holding his coat, neatly folded over his arm (figure 3.17). The background depicts a front porch and windows more common in warmer climates, a decidedly un-Harlem scene that is more reminiscent of backdrops found in small towns, possibly down south. The photograph's backdrop suggests an outdoor setting, as does the man standing stiffly holding his coat, signaling his impending travels. Whether he was preparing to walk down the street or embarking on a migration is unknown. However, the inclusion of the coat hints at some form of upcoming movement. A significant departure from the domestic scenes that grace Van Der Zee's backdrops along with mindfully positioned figures who are comfortably settled before the camera, this photograph embodies a transient character.

Recopying, enhancing, or enlarging a photograph could have given Van Der Zee's clients access to a photographic value based on a kind of migration that is seldom considered. Such an act transforms the clients' relationship with the photograph through nuanced shifts, modifications, and travel in ways that illustrate the complexity of vernacular photographs as objects with multiple authors and interlocutors. This transformation offers insight into what happens when we look beyond valuations determined

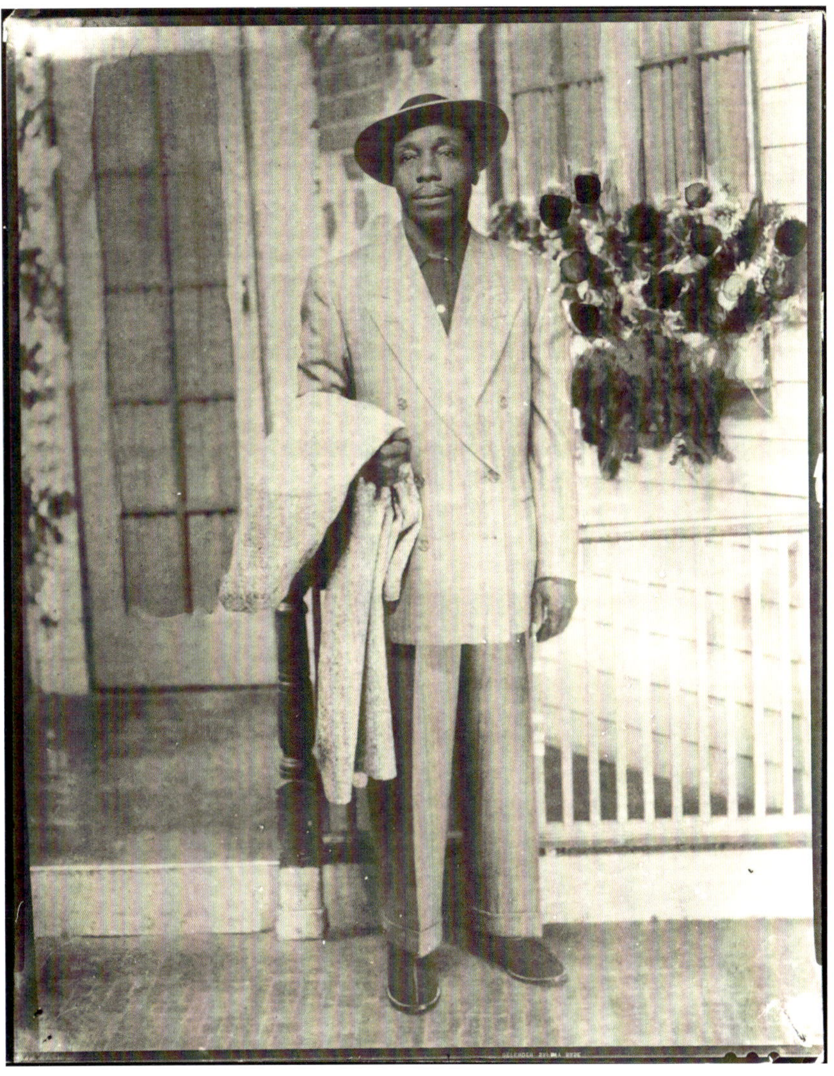

FIGURE 3.17

James Van Der Zee, copy photograph of a man standing in front of a porch backdrop (original photographer and date unknown), likely reproduced 1930s–1960s. The backdrop is a departure from the domestic interiors commonly featured in Van Der Zee's studio portraits.

9⅝ × 7⅝ in. (24.5 × 19.4 cm). © James Van Der Zee Archive, The Metropolitan Museum of Art. Source: James Van Der Zee Archive, The Metropolitan Museum of Art, New York.

by traditional art history alone and expand the implication of migration beyond the movement of individuals and families.

Gatekeepers of Vernacular Photography

If photography copies the world and invents the world at the same time, together and in the same act, then Van Der Zee's practice during this latter part of his career can be seen as radically generative and instructive for understanding how, as Van Der Zee reinvented his business, unrecognized aspects of his relationship to vernacular photographic practices come into view.[61] There was an endurance on Van Der Zee's part that allowed these kinds of images to persist in the world. Van Der Zee's tenacious engagement with the craft of photography can be noted in an article from 1976, years after the 1969 *Harlem on My Mind* exhibition discussed in the next chapter. Apparently, Van Der Zee invented a camera by using a pair of lenses to uniquely superimpose two images. Described as a special camera for three-dimensional photography that was set to be patented in the United States and Canada, Van Der Zee's invention illustrates just how central adaptability and innovation were to his continuously active and changing engagement with the camera and what it could provide in terms of modification and enhancement work. As biographer James Haskins insists, "Shooting the picture was the least important step in his creative process. He exercised his artistry in what he did before the photograph was taken, and in what he did as he processed the negative and the print."[62] Shifting the focus to Van Der Zee's artistry applied to photographs taken by other photographers reveals a different avenue of his creative process that takes shape throughout his career and really blossoms during his later years, given many of the shifts, changes, and client desires discussed in this chapter. It reflects a complex paradigm in which the copy and the reproduction of images are central to understanding vernacular photography as a constituent part of Van Der Zee.

In fact, it is through the copy that new visual configurations of meaning and purpose are created. For example, as opposed to prototypical Van Der Zee photographs like *Woman with Cat at Piano* (figure 3.2), the enlarged, recopied, and enhanced images arguably force us to consider the varied and circuitous paths through which vernacular photographic practices actually function in the world through their circulation, anonymity, and material transformations. They also allow for a contemplation of what these kinds of images reveal about the intersections of Van Der Zee and forgotten aspects of his photographic production. Overlooked by the art history of photography, the modification practice of Van Der Zee elicits many questions that cannot be answered. However, as we try to propose possible answers, new configurations of meaning come to light. Doing so time and time again encourages a return to Van Der Zee's archive for a different kind of inquiry. No longer the art historical approach of hand-picking singular photographs that epitomize Van Der Zee's style or capture a representative subject, the kind of looking this chapter encourages asks viewers to be attuned to the possibilities elicited by multiplicity, anonymity, and migration.

It is often forgotten that Van Der Zee's archive, in a certain sense, is an archive of copies. One of the things that makes this archive distinct is the number of prints, and specifically multiple prints, that Van Der Zee saved from his decades of work. The sheer number of such prints begs the question: Why are there so many multiples when Van Der Zee's business revolved around making photographs for other people that ideally ended up leaving the studio as important mementos? One possibility is that the photographs in Van Der Zee's archive are those that were not chosen or were not picked up by clients. Or he may have intentionally created multiples for the purpose of upselling.[63] Alternatively, they were working versions made by Van Der Zee that were filed away, while Van Der Zee showed the best photographs to his clients for their approval. Arguably, most of the preferred photographs—those selected by clients—are actually with their current owners. Those in Van Der Zee's archive, both those by him and those originally by other photographers, can all be regarded as images left behind. In many cases, the museums and scholars depending on Van Der Zee's archives are drawing from the pool of images that clients did not select.

In this understanding of the archive's status as a collection of copies, a few important points come to light. For one thing, the photographs of greatest value—those of first choice—are actually with clients or the descendants of clients. What exist in museums and the current archive are copy prints cherished by Van Der Zee and those photographs left over from the anonymous clients who traversed the streets of Harlem or who mailed sealed envelopes and waited for the return of remade and improved photographs. Such a shift in conceptualizing Van Der Zee's photographs reframes his most valuable photographs as not necessarily in the hands of those whose worlds are ordered by institutional understandings of what makes a photograph meaningful. The selection of photographs by anonymous clients becomes a provocative, personal, and intimate evocation of vernacular photography's value and an undoing of art's traditional hierarchy of value. Arguably, Van Der Zee knew that his clients were his photographs' true gatekeepers and entrusted them with his most valued creations. Therefore, it is often the clients, the Black individuals and families, who are the true tastemakers and value setters who decide what is the best of Van Der Zee's work.

The archive reflects Van Der Zee's dedication to multiples, to distinctions, to slight changes from one print to another. In other words, the archive is full of the possibilities of variance and reproduction afforded by the medium of photography, as opposed to a single object authored by a single photographer. This is evident through both the photographs for which he arranged the subjects and those he only copied and re-created. Through multiplicity and the photograph's status as a copy, viewers—on the outside of the complex economies of meaning and value that his clients constructed—get to peek into a quotidian world worthy of awe. That is, of course, if viewers know where to turn.

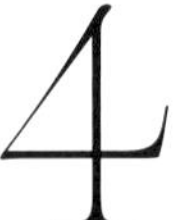

Black Quotidian Experiences

Revisiting the Met's *Harlem on My Mind*
Exhibition of 1969

Experiencing the Photographs

SHE VISITED MULTIPLE TIMES—five, to be exact. Photographer and photography historian Deborah Willis, at twenty-one years old, was among the many individuals who viewed the 1969 exhibit *"Harlem on My Mind": Cultural Capital of Black America 1900–1968*, the first in the Metropolitan Museum of Art's history to attract a significant number of Black visitors. The show was intended to present the culture of Harlem from 1900 to 1968 through an extensive selection of reproduced and enlarged photomurals, many of which were life-size and arranged to create an immersive experience deemed too ethnographic by the exhibition's many detractors. The museum's failure to engage Harlem's art community reinforced that community's sense of exclusion, setting off a fury of justified protests.[1] While uproar ensued at the time, so did an overlooked curiosity and interest in the photographs featured in the show. Years later, Willis, commenting on the images she remembered from 1969, writes, "I vividly recall walking through the exhibition wondering why protesters on the front steps were carrying placards. . . . I wanted to discuss my pride in the exhibition openly with the people I met on the picket line but was afraid to do so because of their obvious discontent."[2] Another account, this time a recollection from photographer Dawoud Bey, who was sixteen years old in 1969, further emphasizes the heightened experience of engaging with the exhibition's photographic images. In recalling that early encounter, Bey explains, "When I got to the Met to see the show my jaw must have dropped. I was mesmerized. Pictures. Black Folks. Room after Room. And other people walking around looking at these pictures. I couldn't believe it. I felt like I had stumbled into some world I knew nothing about. It gave me a sense of photography's documentary power, its potential to be a repository of collective memory, a doorway into another experience."[3] Both young, Black visitors describe the impact of looking at photographs of Black subjects in 1969 within an art museum in ways that depart from the more commonly addressed responses to the show. Another part of the then twenty-one-year-old visitor's recollection is worth lingering on, a statement that wholeheartedly illustrates the kinds of encounters this chapter aims to consider. She succinctly states, "I wanted to honor the picket line, but I also wanted to experience the photographs."[4]

Although a number of scholars have critically engaged the *Harlem on My Mind* show from the perspective of Black activists' responses to the museum's gross missteps, this chapter turns elsewhere.[5] It takes the recollections of Willis and Bey as a starting point for privileging photography and the multivalent perspectives and intersecting histories of the medium the exhibition brought into view. What if the exhibition's poor execution no longer serves as the entry point through which the photographs signify and instead other factors take the lead in reconsidering photography's role in *Harlem on My Mind*? And in the spirit of vernacular photography's separation from traditional art history, what might it mean to engage with photography untethered from the weight of prevailing art-world objectives and frameworks of interpretation?[6] What other photographic histories of the African diaspora become evident when we turn away from the logic that most frequently orders considerations of the show?

Photography within the context of *Harlem on My Mind* has most often been addressed as an opportunity to buoy arguments about the Met and its inadequacies. Indeed, a sharp critique of the museum is well founded.

This era was often defined by discriminatory practices being brought to light and challenged by activists working toward the universal recognition of Black humanity. Like the lunch counter, the bus, and the swimming pool, the museum—and the art world—served as a site of pervasive and debilitating discrimination. In describing his beginning tenure as the Met's director, Thomas Hoving recalls, "When I arrived at the museum I found that the Irish guards at the main entrance actually turned away African Americans and Hispanics saying that the [museum] was a private club."[7] Within such an environment, the *Harlem on My Mind* show went well beyond being a mere exhibition. In many ways, it served as a platform for protesters to make statements and advocate for change in light of the extent and depth of institutionalized discriminatory practices toward Black artists and audiences.

Simultaneously, the reflections by the burgeoning photographers offer some indication of what James Van Der Zee's photographs did for those who stood before them and contemplated them closely. Van Der Zee's commercial practice and archive had a formative role in the exhibition. These comments also demonstrate that the show's photographs were seen, engaged, and remembered by Black visitors whose accounts were voiced outside of the dominant proclamations of the museum, the media, or the activists whose priorities, opinions, and protests found a platform in picket signs, newspaper articles, and publications. The recollections illustrate another—less visible—perspective that must have been there all along: the perspective of a visitor who could experience the photographic images of *Harlem on My Mind* and value them for their compelling representation and for the ways they resonated with the viewer. By returning the role of the arbiter of value to the everyday visitor—and, by extension, recognizing what these viewers saw in the photographic images—this chapter begins to consider the possibilities of experiencing and contextualizing the *Harlem on My Mind* photographs in ways rarely validated by the mainstream art world or its reformers.

Photography's Rise as Fine Art

In the context of the *Harlem on My Mind* show, photography is often evaluated in opposition to the kinds of traditional artwork the Met displayed as an institution. For example, special exhibitions at the museum from 1969 alone unremarkably include *Greek Vases from the Collection of Walter Bareiss*; *American Painting, Drawings, and Watercolors from the Museum's Col-*

lection; and *Florentine Baroque Art from the Museum's Collection*.[8] Within such an exhibition context, the art historian Susan Cahan frames photography's place as relatively nonexistent within the Met around the time of *Harlem on My Mind*.[9] Art historian Bridget Cooks echoes this sentiment as it pertains to major art institutions, including the Met. She explains that "in the 1960s, the status of photography as an art was acceptable in some art circles, but not in an established receptacle of great 'masterpieces' of European painting, sculpture and decorative arts."[10] Nonetheless, just as the accounts of the young visitors offer a different perspective on the value of the photographic images featured in the show, so, too, were photographs seen and engaged within the museum sphere to an extent that has gone unrecognized within the context of *Harlem on My Mind*.[11]

Indeed, *Harlem on My Mind* overlapped with noteworthy shifts and developments within the history of photography, not yet considered a full-fledged art by some but no longer regarded solely as a technical tool for documentation. The perception of photography as inferior to or separate from the fine arts was slowly shifting, at least in some circles, as Cooks explains. In a 1976 *Washington Post* article that refers to Van Der Zee as a major figure in American photography, the journalist Jacqueline Trescott notes, "Van Der Zee's rise paralleled the skyrocketing recognition of photography as a fine art and the discipline's stamp of approval by collectors who bought vintage photographs."[12] Such a shift was also taking place within the very institution that organized *Harlem on My Mind*. As photography was slowly and intentionally being claimed as a fine art, additional examples within the museum can begin to illustrate its slow rise.

The Met first created a photography studio in 1906 to produce photographic records of objects. Even before that, photographs had made their way into the collection. For example, two albumen prints from 1878 depicting President Ulysses S. Grant in Egypt were donated to the Met in 1883. Nonetheless, aside from documentation purposes, the Met did not broach the subject of photography as worthy of collecting until 1928, when Alfred Stieglitz anonymously gave twenty-two prints of his own work to the Met that were accepted into the collection.[13]

As illustrated in curator Malcolm Daniel's scholarship, Stieglitz, and others, realized the great feat of this donation. For example, *Time* inaccurately reported, "Never before had Manhattan's greatest museum received photographs into its collections. Such a reception was thus a victory of great moment for photography and for Alfred Stieglitz."[14] This donation led to the first occasions on which photographs were hung as art in the Metropolitan Museum of Art. In 1933 the museum made its first purchase of a significant number of photographs, acquiring images attributed to Matthew Brady. Major advancements in support of photographs at the Met continued, including a show in 1939 to mark the centennial of the invention of the medium.[15] Other exhibitions at the Met planned under the tutelage of A. Hyatt Mayor, who headed the print department from 1946 to 1966, included mountings of the photographic careers of Eugène Atget (1952), David Octavius Hill (1958), and Adolphe Braun (1962).

The relationship between an organization called Photography in the Fine Arts (PFA) and the Met demonstrates photography's role within the museum around the time of *Harlem on My Mind* and decades before the creation of the Department of Photographs as an independent curatorial department in 1992. Established in 1959 by founder and director Ivan Dmitri, PFA intended to "further the acceptance of photography as a fine art, to advance the recognition of its practitioners as artists and to encourage the development of the talented photographer by opening outlets for his creative work."[16] The organization aimed to reach its goals by circulating exhibitions of photographs throughout the United States and, on a more limited basis, to Canada and Japan. The Met displayed a series of five PFA photography exhibits; equally important is that a significant number of Met staff members served in PFA leadership roles. The eleven-member PFA National Board of Selection for the exhibitions included three individuals affiliated with the Met: a former curator of prints, the associate curator in charge of prints, and the vice director for administration elect.[17]

Of particular interest is the PFA exhibit that opened—with its first showing held at the Met—on March 15, 1967, about two years before *Harlem on My Mind*. Described as a "comprehensive international survey," the exhibition included close to two hundred photographs. The Met curator John J. McKendry insisted, "The [photographers] seem ever more inventive, finding increasing interest in the difficult and unlikely subject, while avoiding the too obviously pretty and banal. Indeed, the entire range of photographic means at the disposal of the artist-photographer is so vast that his ability to say new things in new ways can be limited only by his own lack of vision. The promise of this exhibition is that the ceiling on vision is unlimited."[18] Photography (here a pursuit limited to those gendered as "he") was regarded by Met staff members and their colleagues in PFA as worthy of consideration. Flipping through any of the exhibition catalogs produced by PFA, viewers will come across the photographs selected for exhibition.

Even more telling are the candid photographs capturing the committee members engaged in what appears to be the laborious, highly intellectual task of selecting the winning photographs (figure 4.1). In a half-page black-and-white photograph included in the 1967 *Photography in the Fine Arts V* catalog, members of the PFA selection board review photographs for the exhibition.[19] The view-from-above perspective captures a group of men—and a single woman, whose back is to the camera—sitting in chairs arranged in a circle. Each person appears completely engrossed in the matted photograph they hold in their hand, while the stacks of untouched photographs found on tables dispersed throughout the room allude to what is to come. Some individuals hold pencils in their hand in anticipation of important notations, while two figures in particular capture the iconic stance of the intellectual at work. Two men concentrate on the same photograph while lifting their hands toward their chins as though in deep thought. Including these kinds of photographs in the exhibition catalog illustrates the rigorous environment in which the photographs were evaluated for inclusion in the exhibition. For nearly one-third of the committee to hail from the Met clearly signals that the museum itself had begun to value and seriously attend to photography.[20]

The museum's engagement with photography was not limited to examples like the PFA exhibitions, which were organized by an outside entity. Consider the museum's first *Bulletin* devoted entirely to photographs, notably published in March 1969, during *Harlem on My Mind*'s tenure at the museum. As a quarterly publication geared toward museum members, the *Bulletin* highlights works from the Met's collection along with news of exhibitions and programming. Before turning to the featured content in the March 1969 issue, readers would have seen an announcement on the first page for an exhibition opening on April 12, 1969, a few days after *Harlem on My Mind*'s April 6 closing. The exhibition, entitled *Thirty Photographers: A Selection from the Museum's Collection*, demonstrates the Met's continued interest in exhibiting photography as an art form deserving of attention and exhibition space. Culled from the museum's collection of photographs, the one hundred or so photographs in *Thirty Photographers* were on view in the museum's Prints and Drawings galleries. They reflected the collection's strengths in late nineteenth- and early twentieth-century photographs and drew from a range of aesthetic styles: portrait, pictorial, documentary, and reportage.[21]

Free from any rhetoric addressing photography as an exclusive art form, the press release for *Thirty Photographers* goes so far as to reference

Photography in the Fine Arts V

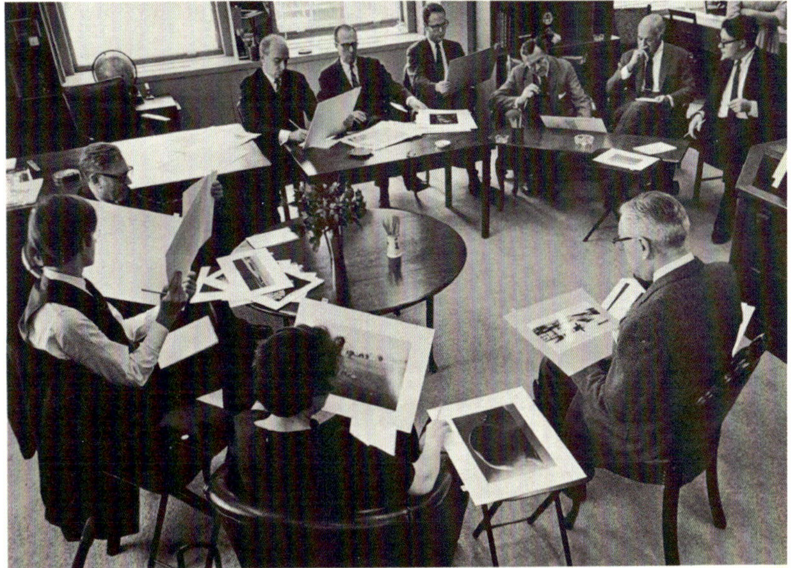

MEMBERS OF THE PFA NATIONAL BOARD OF SELECTION REVIEWING PHOTOGRAPHS FOR EXHIBITION V

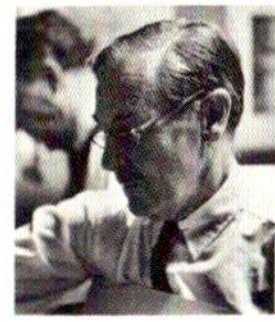

CLOCKWISE STARTING UPPER LEFT: JOSEPH V. NOBLE, *Vice-Director for Administration, The Metropolitan Museum of Art;* OTTO WITTMANN, *Director, The Toledo Museum of Art;* ALAN SHESTACK, *Assistant Curator, National Gallery of Art, Washington, D.C.;* PERRY T. RATHBONE, *Director, Museum of Fine Arts, Boston;* LESLIE CHEEK, Jr., *Director, Virginia Museum of Fine Arts;* EVAN H. TURNER, *Director, Philadelphia Museum of Art;* LAURENCE SICKMAN, *Director, William Rockhill Nelson Gallery of Art, Kansas City;* JEAN SUTHERLAND BOGGS, *Director, The National Gallery of Canada, Ottawa;* JOHN J. McKENDRY, *Associate Curator in Charge of Prints, The Metropolitan Museum of Art;* BARTLETT H. HAYES, Jr., *Director, Addison Gallery of American Art, Andover; and* (*at left*) A. HYATT MAYOR, *former Curator of Prints, The Metropolitan Museum of Art.*

3

FIGURE 4.1

Members of the PFA National Board of Selection reviewing photographs *for Photography in the Fine Arts V*, organized by Photography in the Fine Arts (PFA), Metropolitan Museum of Art, March 15–June 11, 1967.

Source: Museum Archives, Metropolitan Museum of Art, New York.

the world of the amateur in its discussion of the work of a featured photographer. Alfred Stieglitz's *Equivalents* (circa 1925–1930), a series of photographs of clouds that easily lends itself to an esoteric interpretation, is framed in the press release in the following way: "These photographs of cloud formations made mostly with a 4 × 5" Graflex camera and processed and printed by means well within the range of any amateur, were felt by Stieglitz to be equivalents of thoughts, hopes, aspirations, despairs, and fears. They are both photographic abstractions and straight photography, and demonstrate Stieglitz's unique mastery over photographic form."[22] Here the Met introduces photography as a medium uniquely mastered by exceptional talents like Stieglitz but nonetheless suggests that such a mastery is attainable through processes available to the amateur photographer. Evocative of a common argument that asserts the democratic nature of photography, this quote illustrates the flexibility with which photographs were discussed, a point reinforced by the range of types of images deserving of display, mentioned earlier in the press release.

Given that portraits and pictorial, documentary, and reportage photographs were included in the *Thirty Photographers* show, there were no grounds for similar types of work in *Harlem on My Mind* to be automatically discounted by some of the visitors to the Met. In the Museum of Modern Art (MoMA)'s successful 1955 *Family of Man* exhibit, the curator similarly departed from original vintage prints in favor of exhibition-made copies and still, unlike *Harlem on My Mind*, received a level of accolades and praise owing to the show's conceptually sound and compelling argument. Indeed, the practical simultaneity of *Thirty Photographers* and *Harlem on My Mind* suggests that visitors might have engaged with a range of photographs, even those that were not original vintage prints. Yet the overarching polemics of *Harlem on My Mind* overdetermined viewers' encounters with its images, discouraging any platform for generous ways of seeing. Instead, the exhibition staging took precedence, as opposed to the photographs, many of which were by Van Der Zee.

For *Thirty Photographers*, the Met chose to describe Alfred Stieglitz's work using language that prompted readers to contend with the endless possibilities available to the amateur photographer, which begs the question: Why was such an inviting and innovative stance not extended to the photographs selected for the *Harlem on My Mind* show? Within the existing record, *Harlem on My Mind*'s intended cultural and social significance dominates the discussion, thereby eliding any insightful reflections about the photographs and what they offered visitors through their visual attributes. Yet the materials on photography created by the Met within years of *Harlem on My Mind* demonstrate a surprising amount of leniency and flexibility, showing that staff generally approached photography as a worthwhile medium for display on the museum's walls.

In light of this openness, it is telling that Van Der Zee's work did not receive the same careful consideration the Met so graciously displayed in its exhibition and press releases for other shows focused on photography. Instead, the museum failed to consider the materials featured in *Harlem on My Mind* valuable beyond their capacity to ethnographically narrate Harlem and—by extension—Blackness. While the museum's March 1969 *Bulletin* focused on the institution's engagement with photography, with absolutely no mention of Van Der Zee, the preceding January 1969 issue focused on Black artists in America, a topic framed by the occasion of *Harlem on My Mind* and lacking any reference to the robust world of Black photography that was evident through, for example, the Kamoinge Workshop, founded in 1963. Although the *Bulletin* issues were produced within months of each other, the complete divide between the two topics illustrates the Met's failure to recognize Van Der Zee's work and the relevance—to both discussions—of Black photography more broadly.

Missed opportunities for the Met to acknowledge Van Der Zee's photography abounded. Still, Van Der Zee received the Honorary Fellow for Life Award from the museum in 1969 and was elected a Fellow for Life the following year—a year in which the museum acquired sixty-six of his original vintage photographs for its permanent collection as a gift from the artist's recently established institute. The same year the Met acquired these photographs, it included at least six of Van Der Zee's photographs in the exhibition titled *The Photograph: A Selection of Recent Acquisitions*.[23] Yet more could have been done to acknowledge Van Der Zee's work as deserving of a close look and attention, especially in light of photography's changing status. As the Met excluded Van Der Zee while simultaneously allowing photography to gain a small foothold of regard, responses to *Harlem on My Mind* from outside the Met similarly eclipsed the photographer.

The Overlooked Photographer

Harlem on My Mind—a multimedia exhibition featuring large photomurals—was distinct, as the Met's first show dedicated to the representation of African Americans. It also became what Cahan in her early scholarship calls one of the greatest public relations fiascoes in the history of American museums.[24] As opposed to a standardized wall hanging of paintings at the Metropolitan, the mounting, overblown size, and busy arrangement of the photographs produced an ethnography-like narrative of Harlem—aspects that enraged a number of constituents, who criticized the exhibition's design and its very premise, the overwhelming nature of the layout, and the lack of original work by Black fine artists on display.[25]

Those who commented on the show were, for the most part, people entrenched in art, whether on the art world's margins or in its central axis—people with a stake in making, displaying, and thinking about art. They brought these tools and perspectives to their critical consideration of the show. A significant number of responses—both from the mainstream art community and from the Black art community—leveraged photography's inferior status to articulate the exhibition's failures. In turning a blind eye to photography and its aesthetic value, this group often overlooked Van Der Zee and the wealth of his photographic images.

Some focused on insufficiencies considered intrinsic to the medium of photography. One quote illustrates the extent to which photography had yet to gain widespread legitimacy while revealing racialized assumptions. In *Art News*, the critic Amy Goldin explains:

> There are good reasons for not trying to do a Harlem show with photographs: 1. Photographs are static. Negro Dance, music and rhetoric are deeply linked to inventive and unexpected (to whites) patterns of movement. . . . Photographs are grey. 2. Their greyness needs dramatization or the lack of color reinforced emotional distance. 3. Cameras are near-sighted. They tend to focus on trivial detail and to depend on specifics of texture for formal interest. A dermatologist's view of relevance. The multiplication of the same visual details gives a false density to what is essentially a repetitive experience, limited to trivial and journalistic concerns.[26]

Not only is photography regarded as a completely deficient medium, but its ability to properly represent the critic's reductive version of Black life is challenged.

Others, such as art critic and essayist Hilton Kramer, had a problem with the Met's politicization of a space dedicated to preserving "high" art, a critique implying that the fine arts are intrinsically absolved from politics.[27] Kramer expressed this opinion in a *New York Times* review on January 26,

1969, one week after the show's opening. In the installation view accompanying his article, a young girl looks up at one of the enlarged, mural-sized photographs of a street scene (figure 4.2).[28] The unidentified image is described with text that introduces the biting tone of the article. It states, "An installation view of the 'Harlem on My Mind' exhibition at the Metropolitan. Making a social event out of a history of suffering."[29] The body of the article is consistently disparaging. It begins by describing the show as "lamentable in so many fundamental ways—in its conception, in its execution, and in its general ideological assumptions—that at times it hardly seems a proper subject for criticism at all."[30] Kramer then goes on to denounce the show for politicizing a space that is supposedly sanctioned only for matters relating to the preservation of an artistic heritage. He goes so far as to insist that "in mounting the 'Harlem on My Mind' exhibition Mr. Hoving has for the first time politicized the Metropolitan."[31] He proceeds to describe the exhibition as a "cheap form of photo-audio journalism."[32] For Kramer, the show did not belong in a place so revered and respected and therefore, somehow, implicitly nonpolitical. Its content, of questionable value, became a tool of "social evangelism." Kramer's comments are representative of the prevailing level of general skepticism directed at the show. Although his critique does not encompass every reproachful comment hurled at the Met, it does reflect a sense of widespread frustration.

Many Black artists had a different set of critiques. Following months of unproductive meetings with the Met during the museum's initial planning phases, a group of African American artists founded the Black Emergency Cultural Coalition (BECC) for the purpose of protesting *Harlem on My Mind*.[33] The BECC members, including African American artists Cliff Joseph, Romare Bearden, Norman Lewis, Benny Andrews, and Richard Mayhew, wanted to see a show about Harlem feature work by artists who, in their eyes, could best represent the neighborhood and its artistic treasures through the kinds of media traditionally valued by art history and art museums. As Joseph, the cochair of the BECC, explained in a 1972 interview, "One other omission was the fact that there were no Black painters or Black sculptors included in the exhibit. This was especially hard to understand since the show was supposedly set up for the purpose of showing to the public the cultural contributions that had been made by members of the Black community."[34]

They wanted a different curator and an alternate selection of paintings and sculptures instead of what a large range of commentators perceived as the rote and less sophisticated medium of photography. For example, at

Art: 'Harlem on My Mind'—Two Views

Politicalizing the Metropolitan Museum

By HILTON KRAMER

THE "Harlem on My Mind" exhibition at the Metropolitan Museum of Art is lamentable in so many fundamental ways—in its conception, in its execution, and in its general ideological assumptions—that at times it hardly seems a proper subject for criticism at all. This is, to borrow a phrase, an event that belongs to the history of publicity more than to the history of art—no matter how broad an interpretation we place on the word "art" in this context—and one would prefer to leave the matter in the hands of those who are well practiced in distinguishing the value of one form of publicity over another. But since the director of the Metropolitan—Thomas P. F. Hoving—insists that this exhibition be taken as a proper function of the venerable institution he presides over, and indeed promises that we may expect more such flamboyant responses to "social and political events" in the future, one has no choice but to come to terms with what is, in essence, not so much an exhibition as an amateur exercise in social evangelism.

I want, therefore, to address these remarks to a specific question: What is this exhibition doing at the Met—and to the Met? Or, to put it another way, what does it suggest about Mr. Hoving's belief, or lack of belief, in the function of art—and in the museological enterprise itself—if, in the face of an admittedly grave social crisis, he has felt compelled to abandon art for a cheap form of photo-audio journalism?

Mr. Hoving has himself declared that the exhibition "has nothing to do with art in the narrow sense—but everything to do with this Museum, its evolving role and purpose, what we hope is its emerging position as a positive, relevant, and regenerative force in modern society." One looks forward to the day when Mr. Hoving will favor us with an explanation of what he understands the value of "art in the narrow sense" to be, for his every utterance these days strongly suggests that he conceives it to be a negative, irrelevant, and unregenerative social force.

This is not an entirely indefensible position. There are undoubtedly many intelligent and socially concerned people in our midst who, in measuring the pressures of current social grievances against the often very private and specialized emotions of contemporary art, have decided to wash their hands of art altogether and devote their energies to a more immediately constructive task. What is odd, not to say alarming, is to discover this point of view harbored in the mind of the director of one of the greatest art museums in the world—a mind that shows itself increasingly impatient with the kind of slow and, in the short run anyway, often unmeasurable benefactions that a deep attachment to the art experience bestows on our spirit and on our emotions.

Mr. Hoving complains—I am quoting from the current issue of the Met's monthly Bulletin—that "For too long museums have drifted passively away from the center of things, out to the periphery where they play an often brilliant but usually tangential role in the multiple lives of the nation." This is not my reading of the recent history of museums. On the contrary, there has probably never been a time when the public, albeit only certain segments of the public, has been so responsive to what our museums have to offer. But I suppose the museum—and art itself—is always vulnerable to charges of passivity and irrelevance. Genuine works of art rarely pretend to offer us either solutions to social problems or—what the "Harlem on My Mind" exhibition provides in abundance—the illusion that we are experiencing such problems at first-hand. Art speaks to us in a language of feeling, and its generative effect on our lives is as slow and mysterious and socially incommensurable as the force of love, which art very much resembles in its delicate equations of the spiritual and the material.

To politicalize this subtle transaction of the mind and the emotions is, inevitably, to damage it, perhaps in the end to destroy it, and to declare that politics must have priority over every sphere of the human sensibility. Is it too much to suggest that this is, in embryo, a totalitarian attitude—an attitude that begrudges any avenue of human activity that cannot be effectively and immediately mobilized for some designated social purpose? However one answers this question, there can be no doubt that in mounting the "Harlem on My Mind" exhibition Mr. Hoving has for the first time politicalized the Metropolitan, and has thereby cast doubt on its future integrity as an institution consecrated above all to the task of preserving our artistic heritage from the fickle encroachments of history.

The particular form which this politicalization has taken is not itself the largest of the many issues raised by the "Harlem on My Mind" exhibition. No doubt in the future Mr. Hoving will learn to improve upon the kind of audio-visual entertainment he has currently mounted in the name of "relevance." Who knows? In the future he may even learn to refrain from seeking—in, of all places, a catalogue introduction—public absolution for his guilt over his privileged childhood, replete with black servants and chauffeured rides to school. In other words, he may become a little less of an amateur and a little more of a professional in his role as a social evangelist. But this will only intensify the question that he has now made paramount for anyone concerned with the politicalization of our museums and the eventual politicalization of our art. We have a right to know, I think, exactly how far Mr. Hoving intends to carry this process, and how large a part of the museum—and of our artistic heritage—he intends to sweep in the path of historical "relevance."

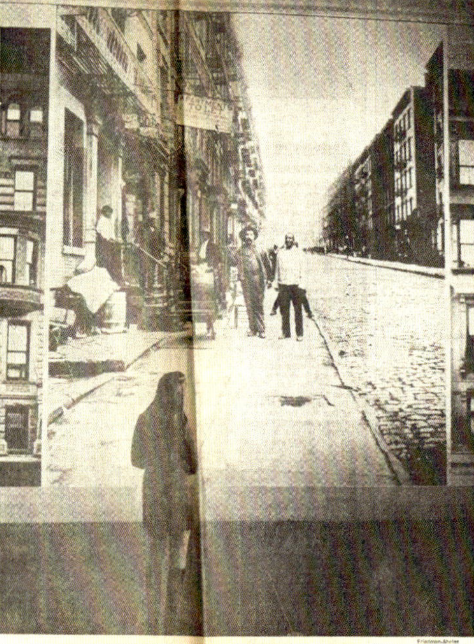

An installation view of the "Harlem on My Mind" exhibition at the Metropolitan
Making a social event out of a history of suffering

Friedman-Abeles

'On the Edge Of Hell'

By JERVIS ANDERSON

HARLEM on My Mind: It has an old, exotic, sentimental music to it; reeks of the 20's, the 30's, and even the 40's when more whites used to go uptown, especially at night, and when many black singers, musicians and writers fled to Europe from time to time either to make a living or to find out who, in addition to being black, they really were. All of which is not too surprising when one recalls that it is a phrase Irving Berlin put in Ethel Waters' mouth in 1933. Playing Josephine Baker in the revue "As Thousands Cheer," Miss Waters grieves from the exile of a Paris café: "I've a longing to be low down, and my parlez-vous will not ring true, with Harlem on my mind." They are, of course, more Mr. Berlin's thoughts than they are Miss Baker's; at best, they are the sentiments he imagines Miss Baker has, or ought to have. Since black and white Americans share some very intimate thoughts, he is not far wrong, but he is not quite right either.

Let's look at the chief moods that the term Harlem on My Mind seems to evoke. They are a kind of *yearning* (mixed with memory) and a kind of *uneasiness*—the two main tributes which post-1900 history has had to pay to that community. Up until today, in fact, approach is locked with avoidance in such a sweet and furtive embrace that nobody seems to remember that that's not the way it's supposed to be: that, like Huck, one should gamble everything on one's virtue and redemption and take a chance on going to hell. In any event, a yearning for or a sense of uneasiness about Harlem tends to take on quite different qualities when felt by blacks and by whites.

To the majority of blacks who are attracted by it, a yearning for Harlem is akin to the call of home: where struggling, hoping, speaking, loving, laughing, dancing, singing, and sharing in the rich fund of black American myth produce a sense of common experience, style, and cause; a place, too, where eyes and faces and gestures speak a language so familiar that it registers not so much in the brains as in the bones. Uneasiness is the rage they feel under the skin that all this communal warmth and psychological certainty should be enjoyed at the price of the appalling conditions in which the majority of Harlem families must live and bring up children.

To the majority of whites who are attracted by it, a yearning for Harlem seems quite often to be precisely what Mr. Berlin put in Miss Baker's (or Miss Waters') mouth—"a longing to be low down," a yearning for uninhibited pleasures, a desire to recapture an approximate sense of what it once was to be the pre-industrial natural man, and a wish to escape for a time from the rigors (and refined pleasures) of good judgment. Uneasiness is an underlying guilt that perhaps they are accessories with history in the survival of the appalling conditions in which all that spontaneity manages, miraculously, to flower.

But those whites who so romanticize Harlem ought not to forget one thing—that the place would not be quite what it is now if, starting in 1900, whites had not panicked and moved out when they saw blacks moving in. Thus plain guilt is really the only logical reason in our day why whites should continue to have Harlem on their minds. That is to say Harlem, whatever its native pleasures may be, is essentially a monument to the scorn and indifference that those who control this city and this country have always felt toward the quality of human existence in that community. "So we stand here," Langston Hughes wrote, "on the edge of hell in Harlem, and look out on the world, and wonder." The majority of those who survive Hughes are still wondering what they are going to do, or what is going to be done, to make the quality of their community can make the most of the pleasures of their community and not see them simply as an anodyne, and when the whites can see the appeals of Harlem as a valid and legitimate outgrowth of American culture rather than as an exotic and incredible flowering of frustration.

FIGURE 4.2

Page from the *New York Times*, January 26, 1969, with Hilton Kramer's article, "Politicalizing the Metropolitan Museum."

Source: Museum Archives, Metropolitan Museum of Art, New York.

one protest on the steps of the museum, a news media photograph captures Romare Bearden carrying a sign that reads "Harlem Shortchanged Again, Again, and Again," while Richard Mayhew supplements this statement with a sign reading "Visit the Metropolitan Museum of ~~Art~~ Photography."[35] Protesters pitted photography, as an all-encompassing term, against the fine arts, proclaiming it a lesser medium. Within this paradigm few critics addressed the distinction between a singular, vintage photographic print and an enlarged, reproduced photographic image, or, for that matter, any of the pluralities intrinsic to the medium. Such nuances disappeared within the umbrella term of *photography*. Along with this omission, reactions such as Willis's and Bey's recollections are commonly lost or overlooked within the charged discourse surrounding the show and its many failures. Instead, Black protest orders the visibility of Blackness in relationship to the show. So, too, were Black photographers routinely disregarded despite the existence of a very dynamic community of Black image makers for whom photography was the medium of choice.

Addressing the significance of the Kamoinge Workshop clarifies some of the larger issues at stake when it comes to Black photographers and the invisibility of their artistic efforts at the time of *Harlem on My Mind*.[36] Created in 1963, the New York–based Kamoinge Workshop served as an outlet for regular photography critique, show curation, group portfolio submission, and a sense of family-like fellowship for Black photographers committed to increasing the visibility of their work. Although the members engaged in a range of photographic styles, including work meant for both commercial and fine art purposes, the latter category received the most focus from the collective. Subjects including street photography, abstraction, and civil rights photography were up for discussion at regular meetings. The workshop represented a space created to generously, and generatively, support the ambitions of its members. Offering a high level of rigorous critique, meeting participants evaluated each other's work and its aesthetic successes and shortcomings, thereby contributing to each photographer's artistic development.

Such an environment exemplifies a sharp departure from the fine art photography scene at the time, in which every portfolio set, exhibition inclusion, networking opportunity, and slither of recognition was hard won and woefully limited for Black photographers. Within this cutthroat and often unwelcoming environment, the individuals of the collective both found spaces and made spaces for themselves and their work to be seen and appreciated as artistically relevant. In addition to two shows in the Kamoinge Gallery, founded in 1965, the works of individual photographers were featured in numerous gallery exhibitions outside of the group. For example, Adger Cowans exhibited at the Heliography Gallery at 859 Lexington Avenue, Louis Draper was included in Larry Seigel's Image Gallery in New York (1960), and Anthony Barboza had a solo exhibition at the storied LIGHT Gallery (1974).[37] Although access to exhibition opportunities varied from photographer to photographer, overall, the members' piecemeal inclusion within the world of fine art photography illustrates a paucity of acknowledgment for Black photographers during this moment of photography's nascent rise.

The Kamoinge members were interested in gaining visibility for their work, but not just any visibility. They were very mindful and strategic about how their photographs were conceptually framed. This is a departure from Van Der Zee and his photographs, many of which had social, material, and conceptual lives over which the artist exerted little control, as they signified as photographic images free from their creator's careful eye. This distinction between Van Der Zee and many of the Kamoinge photographers becomes especially apparent through a comparison of two publications.

In 1966 the magazine *Camera* featured a portfolio of Kamoinge members titled "Harlem," including Shawn Walker, Beauford Smith, Herbert Randall, Louis Draper, James M. Mannas, and Calvin Wilson. Subtitled "A Photographic Report on Harlem by a Group of Young Negro Photographers," the portfolio's essay, as art historian Erina Duganne highlights in her scholarship, exaggerated links between the photographs and racial identity, whereas the photographers' interests and intentions were more nuanced and diverse than the publication implied.[38] In addition, the magazine issue glosses over each photographer's individuality and makes generalized statements about the relationship between these photographers and Harlem, a place in which many of the photographers did not reside and which many of the photographs did not depict. As an addendum, the photographers penned a postscript that clarifies their intentions and signals the important differences in approach and style among the numerous members of Kamoinge. In a sense, they had a role in presenting themselves to the magazine's readership. Although they did not author the essay or script the subtitle, they were able to insert their own explanation of their own work, thereby exerting their reasonable wish to manage, shape, and give context to the very work they had created. Otherwise, well-intended editors or writers could end up getting the gist of the work all wrong, subsequently implying that Kamoinge's prints were mere documents of Harlem.

On at least one occasion, a reproduction of Van Der Zee's work received a similarly patronizing interpretation. A French version of Walter Benjamin's 1931 text "A Short History of Photography," republished with new illustrations and image captions decades later, in 1977, includes Van Der Zee's *Family Portrait* (1926). Titled "Les analphabetes de l'avenir" (The illiterates of the future) and published in the journal *Le Nouvel Observateur,* the essay features many of the same photographs that appear in

Roland Barthes's book *Camera Lucida: Reflections on Photography*, first published in French in 1980. Inserted under Van Der Zee's name in the 1977 version of Benjamin's essay, *Family Portrait* is accompanied by the following description:

> In his studio, Van Der Zee welcomes not only clients but brothers. He wants to show the beauty of being unmistakably American and, evidently, other things. . . . Here we see two women and one man. Their identities are forgotten as is their family connection. It is clear that they want to depict the prosperous American family way of life. Their faces serene and dignified. All disgrace is resisted in the hand of James Van Der Zee. Let us admire this reflection of Black Americans during a brave time when the slogan "Black is Beautiful" is proclaimed, but it is not the cry of challenge or despair, nor is it that Harlem is just a ghetto.[39]

With the help of this prompt, readers are encouraged to think about the formation of Black identity, just like in the *Camera* issue's treatment of Kamoinge. However, the Kamoinge's members intervened (albeit confined to the postscript) and offered a more nuanced narrative. In the case of Van Der Zee's photograph, there existed no corrective addendum written by the photographer. His images, on this and other occasions, led social lives for which interpretation and meaning could be either generously gifted or unsatisfactorily handed over—and everything in between—by entities other than Van Der Zee. To be unbound in this way is both his photographs' most generative characteristic and their most detrimental liability. While a consideration of Kamoinge offers insight into the ways in which one group of photographers navigated the challenges of visibility, it also clarifies compelling aspects of Van Der Zee's work and, by extension, the labor many of his photographs are asked to perform by individuals ranging from the young, Black visitors standing before a *Harlem on My Mind* photomural to the editors of *Le Nouvel Observateur*. Yet such interpretive malleability had no place within the polemics of *Harlem on My Mind*.

In a *Manhattan Tribune* article titled "Artists Say: 'No Soul,'" the stakes of the controversy surrounding the exhibit are captured in the image of a Black man standing in front of the museum's famous steps and facade, with the repeated word "Harlem" on the partial exhibition banner in the far background (figure 4.3). The ascending steps are filled with individuals wearing coats, and in the foreground stands the Black man. He

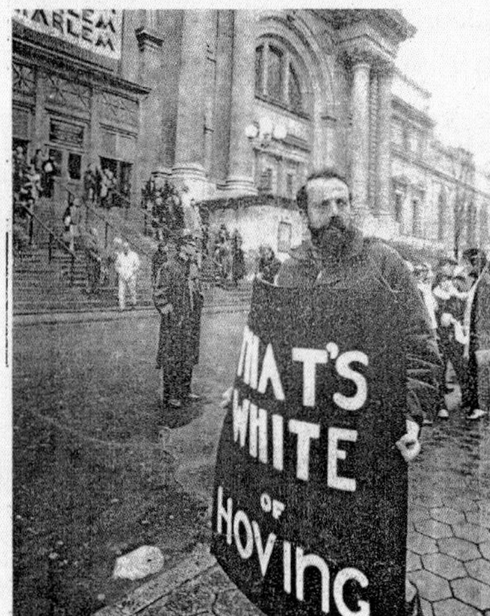
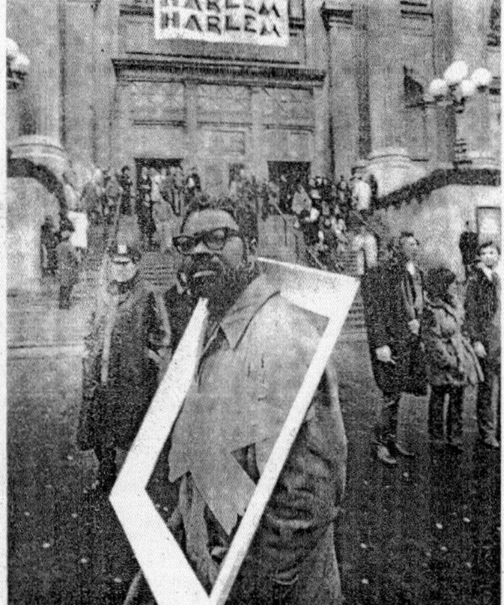

The following reproduces the front page of the *Manhattan Tribune*:

Manhattan Tribune

Serving the West Side and Harlem

VOLUME ONE, NUMBER 11 — JANUARY 25, 1969 — TEN CENTS

Score Met Exhibit

Artists Say: 'No Soul'

The controversial Harlem on My Mind exhibit opened last week amid conflicting charges that the show failed to adequately reflect the Harlem community it is supposed to depict. Opening night marred by the discovery that an H, presumably meant for Harlem, was scrawled on a Rembrandt and several other masterpieces at the Metropolitan Museum of Art, where the show is expected to run through April.

Outside pickets, led by Henri Ghent an artist and Edward Taylor, director of the Harlem Cultural Council, who resigned from the committee's advisory board because, he charged, the exhibit failed to reflect the Harlem community. "It's got no soul," said Taylor when asked about the exhibit. "It is an insult to the community. "They (black artists) should have been listened to and been more involved in the show."

The exhibit is largely a photo-journalistc essay of Harlem. No black painter or sculptors are represented. "Even the title 'Harlem on My Mind' was taken from an Irving Berlin tune which he wrote for a shuffle-along revue at the Cotton Club," said Charles Child, a writer. "The whole Harlem Renaissance is underplayed."

The demonstrators, some of them white vowed to picket the show until black artists are included. "We want to make it a better show," a stronger more valid show," said Benny Andrews, an artist of 31 Beekman Street. "It is such a superficial thing. It's a white man's Harlem once more," Andrews said.

The pickets attempted to discourage black persons from attending the exhibit, but with little success, despite jeers of "Aunt Thomasina, Uncle Tome and Aunt Jemima" hurled at them. Those who ran the gauntlet of the demonstrators' catcalls, smiled embarrassedly as the pickets yelled in mock dialect "Shuffle along on in there now."

Among those who visited the museum opening night was William C. Booth, chairman of the city's Human Rights Commission. Booth praised the show. Assemblyman Charles Rangel also attended the first night showing. Among those who came to the museum but did not attend the exhibit was James Hicks, former executive editor of the Amsterdam News and now a top aide to Robert Mangum, chairman of the State Division of Human Rights.

"In putting this show together," said Taylor, "they have done it in such a way as to insult the cultural expertise of the Harlem community." But despite the picketing, at week's end, a record number of persons had visited the Met to see the controversial showing.

DEMONSTRATORS. Black artists and their friends picket outside the Metropolitan Museum of Art to protest the 'Harlem on My Mind' exhibit. The artists, who say they are not represented in the show, charged that exhibit does not adequately reflect life in Harlem. Museum officials and producers of the show deny the charges.

Photos: Gil Vasquez

FIGURE 4.3

Front page of *Manhattan Tribune*, January 25, 1969, including images of *Harlem on My Mind* protests. The protests were motivated in large part by a lack of input into the show from Black artists as well as the exclusion of their artwork.

Source: Archives of American Art, Smithsonian Institution, Washington, DC.

is distantly framed on the left by a policeman, present to monitor the protesters, and on the right by a nondescript white man who could represent a range of roles—observer, fellow protester, or museum patron. The Black man wears glasses and sports a full beard and head of hair, a clear departure from the more conservative, clean-shaven appearance of the police officer. Most important in this composition is the empty frame hanging around the Black man's shoulders. He carries the frame around his body. Its angled position allows viewers to see the frame, not flush on his person to evoke a frame hung on a museum's wall, but an albatross balanced around his person. His hands are pushed into his pockets, conveying a sense of familiarity with the strange burden of his state of physical being—both physically and, as it becomes apparent, possibly quite literally. Across his chest is a huge X. Evocative of Malcolm X's renunciation of white patriarchal oppression, the huge X across the protester's chest captures the rejection of fine artwork by Black artists in the show and, by extension, the individuals themselves.

The frame is especially fitting as a prop since it represents traditional modes of displaying the fine art of painting. Like this man, many Black artists were highly critical of the exhibition's lack of what they considered the fine arts of sculpture, painting, and printmaking. Frames like the one around the protester's neck practically hold onto a work, while simultaneously announcing its importance as something deserving the attention and care of a display. Ensconced within this protest is the implication that photographs, especially as presented in the absence of any kind of noble framing device, are not sufficiently worthy of aesthetic consideration. Many of the Black artists protesting the show aligned with such a view and by extension overlooked the important artistic contributions of Van Der Zee's work. Such opinions came to light within a very active political moment, when protests and their visual manifestation were necessary and common occurrences. Within the intersecting realms of art and social protest, the years surrounding *Harlem on My Mind* were filled with demands for more inclusive practices.

Yet the issues went beyond the mere inclusion of Black artwork within mainstream museums. Frustrations surrounding the *Harlem on My Mind* show revolved in particular around the question, as Cahan aptly put it, of "Who is qualified to speak for whom?," or, as the signs held by BECC protesters stated, "Harlem on Whose Mind?" and "Whose Image of Whom?"[40] An example of how such stakes were addressed can be found in a letter to Hoving, one among numerous letters on the exhibition's repercussions. Written two weeks after the show's opening by the Columbia

University art history professor Meyer Schapiro, the letter (in part) reads, "I believe it was a mistake in the first place for the Museum to have sponsored the show—one could have found a space for it in Harlem or in an armory elsewhere under Negro Auspices, with the support of a committee of white friends, and given Harlem the satisfaction of producing its own great show."[41] Schapiro's letter highlights one of the issues central to the show's failure. According to its critics, both Black and white, the show on Harlem had excluded the people from Harlem from having a substantial voice in the exhibition's planning. In their eyes, the Met produced Harlem, as opposed to having Harlem's artists lead the charge.

A journalistic photograph from a January 27, 1969, *Newsweek* article titled "Stompin' at the Met" depicts two protesters, in the forefront of the image, standing behind a police barricade (figure 4.4). The barrier positions the figures away from the museum, distancing them from the exhibition. One protester carries a sign that states "Soul Has Been Sold Again" in all-capital letters; the last line of the sign is hidden from view. His fellow protester holds a sign that is even more obscured, with only the phrase "The Outsiders Tell It" visible. These incomplete messages on signs held by Black figures standing outside of the museum symbolically represent their partial, skewed, and incomplete vantage points. Again, the museum itself—as well as the protesters—failed to recognize many of the significant photographic images lining the Met's walls.

To point out the protesters' refusal to engage with the photographic images in the exhibition is not to displace the eminent importance of the protesters' approach. The paucity of Black artists within museum collections and exhibitions needed to be swiftly addressed, and the sense of urgency and the level of frustration captured by the protesting artists were well founded and necessary for changes to take place. As BECC's name suggests, this was, indeed, urgent. Yet, simultaneously, Van Der Zee embodied a displaced position among the many aspects that *Harlem on My Mind* came to represent at the time of its opening.

Whether it was the lack of Black artists, the omission of Harlemites from the planning, or the charge that *Harlem on My Mind* was an inappropriate kind of show to take place at the Met—all of these critiques share one thing: they fail to discuss the photographs (albeit reproduced images) and their makers. As a result, Van Der Zee's artwork and his inclusion as not only a longtime Harlem resident but also the largest contributor to the exhibition are consistently elided. So, too, were exhibition photographers whose work had told Harlem narratives of Black political and artistic sig-

January 27, 1969

Stompin' at the Met

In mid-1967, Thomas P.F. Hoving, director of New York's Metropolitan Museum gave Allon Schoener, of the New York State Council on the Arts, permission to mount a documentary show on New York's black community. "Harlem on My Mind," as the show is called, spelled trouble from the word go. Many white patrons of the arts protested that the august Met was a repository for high art only and no place for McLuhanesque sociology. Hoving retorted that "the Met was founded as a community museum and owned by the community for the community." Meanwhile, certain black members of the art world blasted the show when they learned that it would not include any paintings or sculptures by contemporary black artists, and some Harlem community leaders who were asked to work on the show felt they were being shunted aside by the non-Harlemite professionals.

The inevitable storm broke last week at the show's opening. For three nights, blacks and whites picketed before the Met's neo-classic façade, carrying signs like "That's White of Hoving," and "Soul Has Been Sold Again." Mayor John Lindsay, whom Hoving had loyally served as Parks Commissioner from 1965 to 1966 before moving to the Met, charged that the introduction to the show's catalogue, written two years ago by Candice van Ellison of Harlem, then 16 years old, was "racist." In her essay on Harlem life, she wrote that the "already badly exploited black" was allowed "to be further exploited by Jews" and that "behind every hurdle that the Afro-American has yet to jump stands the Jew who has already cleared it."

Lashed: Hoving at first bucked his close friend, the mayor, and defended Miss van Ellison's attitude as a "personal experience." But then former New York State Justice Bernard Botein, now of the city's Special Committee on Racial and Religious Prejudice, and filmmaker Dore Schary, national chairman of B'nai B'rith's Anti-Defamation League, lashed out at the essay. Miss van Ellison thereupon wrote a brief "disclaimer" reasserting that "the facts were organized according to the socio-economic realities in Harlem at that time," but also stating that "any racist overtones which were inferred from the passages quoted out of context are regrettable." The museum staff stayed up all night mimeographing the statement and inserted it in all catalogues on sale as the week ended.

Explaining the correction, Hoving admitted "we had to clamp the lid on this thing." But underneath the lid there was still a can of worms. Botein, who helped hammer out the disclaimer with Miss van Ellison, told Hoving he still felt "the introduction contained racial overtones, although unintentional."

While the fracas over anti-Semitism was building up, a vandal stole into the Met at high noon and, apparently as a protest gesture, carved the letter "H" (meaning perhaps Harlem or Hoving) very carefully with a knife into ten major canvases by Rembrandt, Guardi, Longhi, Boucher and others. "The act is morally disgusting," said Theodore Rousseau, vice director of the Met. "But I must insist that the damage was not very great and the paintings are now being restored. As a result of the desecration, Hoving immediately increased security forces and might even cover all the pictures in the collection with glass.

Jammed: Somehow "Harlem on My Mind" (the title comes from an Irving Berlin song) opened, offering an overview of the last 68 years of the New York black community in a thirteen-room multimedia environment of sight and sound jammed with photomurals, film projections, videotapes and recordings of Harlem's sounds and voices. Harlemites form a breadline during the Depression, Duke Ellington's band beats out jazz from the Cotton Club and Malcolm X

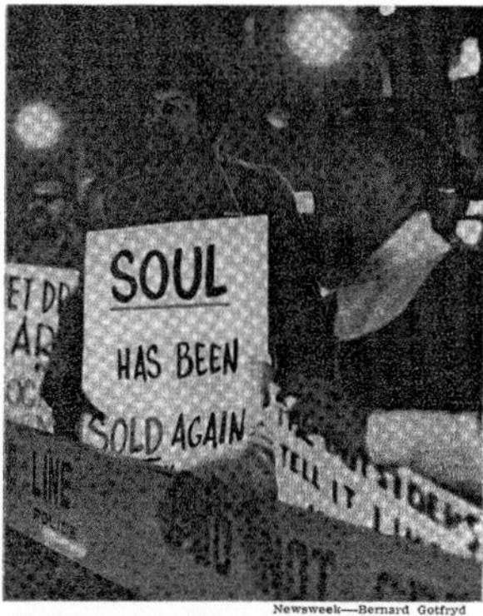

Newsweek—Bernard Gotfryd
Pickets outside Metropolitan: Facts of life

lies in state at a Harlem funeral. "Everybody else usually depicts only the grim side of Harlem but we've shown both sides," says Donald Harper, a black engineer who helped create the show. "We've shown there's a Harlem culture to be proud of."

Unfortunately, much of the show's information barrage is incomprehensible. There are too few captions to describe the sights and sounds. The voices of 115-year-old Mother Brown reminiscing about Harlem and Langston Hughes reading his poetry are badly muffled. And the slick installation, overwhelming and flashy, degrades Harlem into a black bazaar. By the end of the week, Harlem was on everyone's mind, even if no one felt very much like breaking into song. Whatever the museum's success in bringing Harlem inside its walls, it had inadvertently plunged itself into the facts of urban New York life.

—D. L. S.

FIGURE 4.4

A clipping from *Newsweek*, January 27, 1969, including an image from a *Harlem on My Mind* protest.

Source: Archives of American Art, Smithsonian Institution, Washington, DC.

nificance. For example, Jay Maisel's photographs of Harlem, reproduced in the show, had accompanied an essay on the 1964 civil unrest by the well-known African American essayist Richard Wright.[42] Although reproduced and enlarged into panels, the photographs included in the show had their own history and significance, which were overwhelmingly muted by extensive criticism of the show's many missteps. By failing to consider the significance of the actual photographs selected for display, many of the detractors of the show arguably missed out on the power of engaging with photographic images on their own terms and through attentive looking, as opposed to through a predetermined discourse of interpretation.

The Viewer's Undertaking

Illustrating an engagement with the physical photographs in *Harlem on My Mind* adds diversity to the many ways the show was experienced. There did exist some noteworthy examples of writers commenting directly on the exhibition's content and display. In one particular example, the exhibition photographs were praised (or at least engaged) to the extent that concrete criticisms of their display could be made. The photo critic Jacob Deschin wrote an article titled "Harlem's History in Visual Survey," published on January 19, 1969, the day after the exhibition's opening, in the *New York Times*. His article, featured in the photography section of the newspaper, is accompanied by a portrait photograph of two Black women with a caption crediting Van Der Zee as the photographer (figure 4.5). It states, "Bridesmaids in Old Harlem—this photograph by James Van Der Zee is one of hundreds in the exhibition, 'Harlem on My Mind.'"[43] Within the body of the article, Deschin describes the show as "a well-selected exhibition of photographs."[44] He continues to praise *Harlem on My Mind* with the statement that "gigantism vies with inventiveness and imagination in displays that involve the viewer emotionally." Readers also come across complimentary phrases such as "occasional surprises" and "unexpected visual rewards."[45] While generously describing the exhibition with positive commentary, Deschin also takes issue with its design and interprets the show's layout as a hindrance to the visitors' viewing experience. According to Deschin, "The designer's zeal in creating eye catching displays leads to some excess and a tendency to think in terms of clever design rather than communication. This occurs when pictures are hung so high that it is necessary to strain one's head unduly to look at them."[46] Such sentiments res-

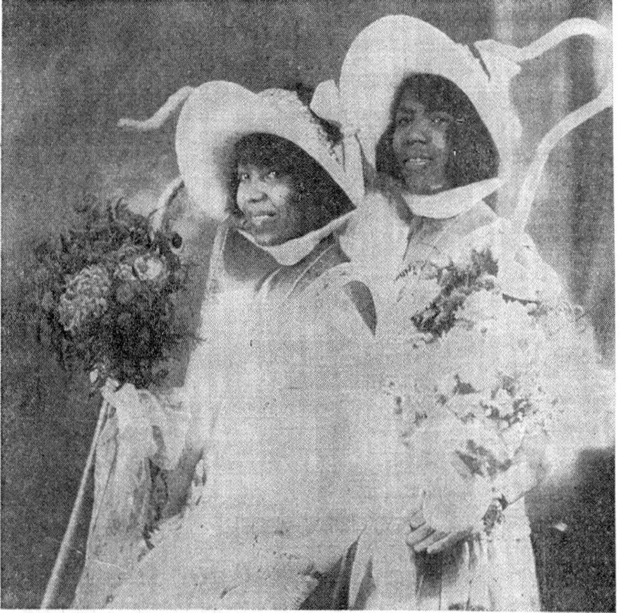

Photography

Harlem's History In Visual Survey

By JACOB DESCHIN

HARLEM'S development as a community over the course of seven decades to the present is described in visualized history with sound accompaniment and many innovative show techniques, in the huge exhibition, "Harlem On My Mind: The Cultural Capital of Black America, 1900-1968," which opened yesterday at The Metropolitan Museum of Art. It will run through April 6.

Occupying the entire second floor of the museum, the show is billed as a multimedia event designed to provide contemporary impressions of the various periods treated in the show. Thus, in addition to the several hundred photographs, from relatively normal size to enormous wall-size enlargements, displayed throughout the museum's 13 special exhibition galleries, the program offers continuous projection performances of slides, films, recordings from the past, taped interviews, music and street sounds.

Nevertheless, the show remains primarily a well-selected exhibition of photographs and projected images culled from many sources to illustrate the six historical periods into which the show is divided, from the pre-Black decade with which the show opens, to the current years of "militancy and identity."

Murals

Mere gigantism vies with inventiveness and imagination in displays that involve the viewer emotionally while providing a pictorial record of cultural development in Harlem's continuing history.

The show opens with floor-to-ceiling enlargements of apartment buildings occupied by the incoming Black residents toward the end of this century's first decade. Having been thus introduced to the notion of visual enormousness, the size of the 52-by-14-foot mural that fills an entire wall in the very next room is no more than merely startling. Technically, however, the mural, made in the Modernage laboratories, is a considerable achievement. The mural shows the Rev. Adam Clayton Powell, Sr. with his Sunday school class.

Beyond this lies a succession of galleries that one penetrates as in almost a maze to find some in which pictures are displayed on structural squares that vary in height to maximum elevations that often reach close to the ceiling. In one, depicting the Thirties, the display structures are so close together that one maneuvers about in an atmosphere seemingly tense and constrained.

All this simulates a kind of game, inspires curiosity as to what may lie just around a corner, and provides occasional surprises and unexpected visual rewards. The visitor has to work to take it all in and can miss individual pictures if he is not diligent enough in making the tour, but the effort is well worth while.

Perhaps inevitably, the designer's zeal in creating eye-catching displays leads to some excess and a tendency to think in terms of clever design rather than communication. This occurs when pictures are hung so high that it is necessary to strain one's head unduly to look at them. The most extreme example is the large room in which a number of portraits are suspended face down from near the very high ceiling.

Slide Projection

Thirty-two projectors distributed throughout the gallery add to the show's visual story. One room has nothing but projectors and screens, eight of each, all operating in continuous performance, allowing the visitor to watch a single screen or shift his gaze from one to another. Some of the slides date from the 1930's, most are in black and white, with some in color.

The show was created and organized by Allon Schoener, Visual Arts Director of the New York State Council on the Arts and Exhibition Coordinator, heading a special staff which included Robert Malone and Martin S. Moskof, who worked as a team on the installation.

The show was financed through a grant by The Henry Luce Foundation, Inc., and, according to the museum, "had the direct cooperation and participation of leaders of Harlem's cultural, religious, social and civic organizations."

Most of the big mural enlargements were done by Modernage, others by Compo, who also printed the smaller pictures.

Simultaneously with the exhibition, Random House has published and the museum is distributing a 256-page illustrated book of the same name. The book is similar in design and treatment to "Portal to America: The Lower East Side 1870-1925" (Holt, Rinehart, Winston), the book version of the trail-blazing exhibition Mr. Schoener did for The Jewish Museum several years ago.

The Harlem volume, which Mr. Schoener, its editor, describes as an extension of the exhibition, is divided like the show, into six text-and-picture sections. The book has a preface by Thomas P. F. Hoving, the museum's director, and an introduction by Candice Van Ellison, a 1967 Harlem high school graduate. A hard-cover edition is $12.95. A $1.95 soft-cover exhibition edition is available only at the museum.

BRIDESMAIDS IN OLD HARLEM—This photograph by James Van Der Zee is one of hundreds in the exhibition, "Harlem On My Mind," which will run through April 6 at The Metropolitan Museum of Art.

FIGURE 4.5

Page from the *New York Times*, January 19, 1969, featuring *Bridesmaids in Old Harlem*, a Van Der Zee work exhibited in *Harlem on My Mind*.

Source: Archives of American Art, Smithsonian Institution, Washington, DC.

onate with descriptions of the photographs serving as "design elements" or as part of an "audio-visual exposition."[47]

Roy DeCarava, a protester and one of the few prominent Black photographers within the larger world of the medium, also engaged the exhibition's physical content but came to different conclusions. Among five reviews of the show found in the May 1969 issue of *Popular Photography*, DeCarava's short text offers a revealing critique. His commentary is introduced by David Vestal, another reviewer and the individual who asked DeCarava (among others) to weigh in on the exhibition. Vestal explains that at first DeCarava refused, insisting, "I'm not objective."[48]

Later, according to Vestal, DeCarava changed his mind but "said he was confining himself to the physical aspects; I inferred that what he thought about its meaning might be unprintable."[49] The ensuing review responds solely to the exhibition's physical layout with no mention of the photographs themselves or the larger and assumedly far more critical position that the photographer kept to himself. However, DeCarava did express his utmost dislike of the show given the exhibition's arrangement of enlarged photographs: "The use of mural-size photographs is a waste because the aisles are so narrow that there is no room to step back and view the whole photo-mural."[50] DeCarava's disdain for the show's physical layout overshadows his opinion on the photographic images themselves. They become irrecoverable given their physically and contextually distasteful display.

Yet the photographs were present and seen by others—for example, by Van Der Zee himself. Pleased with how his work appeared in the show, Van Der Zee commented on how "everybody's life size in the pictures. I'd never seen such big pictures. But they were just as clear and sharp, all the details and brilliancy were still there."[51] Just as vernacular photographs operate outside of art history, many of the *Harlem on My Mind* images elicited meaningful readings despite the ill-conceived show.

A lack of proper recognition may also have counted among DeCarava's driving concerns with the show. DeCarava was initially asked to participate in *Harlem on My Mind*, but then the photographer's request to mount a room featuring his work alone was denied.[52] The photographer, who published *The Sweet Flypaper of Life* in 1955 with Langston Hughes, wanted his work to be included but, understandably, on his own terms. A need to be acknowledged and seen as an artist, through his own specifications, just like the Kamoinge members in the *Camera* feature, became imperative, as did presumably exhibiting original fine art prints that could properly capture the deep tonal ranges DeCarava's work embodies.

However, the terms of engagement for Van Der Zee's photographs have always been different. DeCarava was an artist in the traditional sense of the word, whereas Van Der Zee and his work navigated shifting states driven by art, commerce, precarity, and material adaptation—all aspects that afford vernacular photography its dynamic status. At times, this meant acknowledging Van Der Zee, producer of photographs, as an artist with valuable aesthetic skills. At other times, the impetus becomes lingering on the photographic image alone or, in contrast, the viewing experience offered through its material form. Still other contexts called forth little regard for Van Der Zee, the photographer, as other characteristics of a photograph took charge.

Traditionally, the intentionality an artist puts into their work is also channeled into how they develop and manage how their artworks exist in the world as physically distinct creative endeavors. As a studio photographer, Van Der Zee could do this but only on a limited basis. His engagement with photography encompassed both the treatment usually afforded to rarified artistic endeavors and the circumstance of not having his photographs viewed, reproduced, and circulated on his own terms. This very uncontainable and stretching range, this ambivalence, enabled his photographs' persistence as part of the Black quotidian in addition to being objects worthy of art historical study. Recognizing the vernacular aspects of Van Der Zee's work results in an expanded understanding of his images and the evolving role of photography's relationship to art history.

The photographs—as entities that existed before and after their placement in the show—could conjure insightful moments of encounter, recognition, and the very kinds of intimacy and thoughtfulness on which Van Der Zee built his studio practice. Just as his clients through mail order had to wait for photographs to arrive in the mail, so too did visitors of the show need to wait for, or make, a moment of reflection in order to attend to and behold each image for what it could represent. Such engaged attention reflects the refusal of some viewers to reduce Van Der Zee's photographs to less than they—or their subjects, for that matter—deserve.[53]

Accounts positioned outside of the worlds of art or journalism can offer insight into what it was like to see Van Der Zee's images in the exhibition. Perhaps the viewing experience of some visitors to *Harlem on My Mind* resonated with the experience of Van Der Zee's clients from decades earlier, who wanted a photograph by Van Der Zee through his enlargement services; or with the experience of those who were enamored with his photographs in the *Negro World*, despite not caring at all about the originating photographer; or with the experience of a Harlem Renaissance–era client deciding which studio to enter for their portrait. It can be assumed that such clients engaged Van Der Zee's photographs with perspectives different from those of the BECC members, or reporters at the *New York Times* or *Popular Photography*, or any individuals positioned in relation to a specific art world.

Other valid worlds of the visual always exist, some of which might come into view when a visitor engages with a photograph outside of the dominant system of value, in their own solitary imagination.[54] Instead of pivoting between a system ordered by art history and those activists who aimed to change it, additionally considering the voices of visitors—like those of the twenty-one-year-old and sixteen-year-old mentioned previously—enables an alternate direction for interpreting the exhibition, one that sits squarely within the everydayness of vernacular Black viewing practices. While Van Der Zee's photographs were not ideally displayed, they were present and there for each visitor to encounter. And Van Der Zee, surprisingly, had more of a hand in this visual engagement than has previously been addressed.

A Visit to the Exhibition

In one press photograph featuring visitors to the *Harlem on My Mind* show, a Black woman with a coiffed Afro appears in the crowd. She stands attentively looking at one of the enlarged, photographic images (figure 4.6). Can it be surmised that the photographs left her mesmerized? While this chapter aims to foreground the possibility of alternate viewing experiences, the lens through which the show is usually understood makes it difficult to take this kind of turn. However, a description of the exhibition's design may begin to offer insight into the experience of viewing the immersive photographs of Van Der Zee.

The director of the exhibition committee, Allon Schoener, organized the show with significant input from the museum's newly appointed director, Thomas Hoving, and a committee of diverse advisers. Hoving and Schoener, two white men, became the spokesmen and lead organizers. The remainder of the exhibition team included three African Americans—Reginald McGhee, Donald Harper, and A'Lelia Nelson—who played subsidiary roles that were comparatively behind the scenes and marginalized. McGhee, a photographer who had worked for magazines including *Jet* and *Ebony*, held the position of director of photographic research. Harper served as the audio curator, and Nelson as the administrator. To build his research committee, Schoener turned to African American professionals such as John Henrik Clarke, a Pan-African and Black nationalist historian and author; Jean Blackwell Hutson, a curator from the Schomburg Center; and Regina Andrews, whose early career as a librarian at the Schomburg Center overlapped with the Harlem Renaissance era.[55]

According to Hoving, the photographic exhibition served as a "study of Harlem's achievements and contributions to American life and New York City."[56] It covered the period from 1900 right up to 1968, just months preceding the show's January 1969 opening, with rooms dedicated to different decades within this time frame. The exhibition had a multimedia format uncommon to the Met. Having recently organized a successful multimedia exhibition called *The Lower East Side: Portal to American Life, 1870–1924* at the Jewish Museum, Schoener aimed for a show of similar design with an increased focus on enlarged photographs. He included hundreds of photomurals of varying sizes and mountings and audio components scattered throughout the exhibition's fifteen-room layout on the museum's second floor. He envisioned the multimedia aspects of the exhibition as capturing the actual experience of being in Harlem.

The enlargement and reproduction of more than fifty of Van Der Zee's images in the show made the photographer the leading contributor. Van Der Zee's works were represented in four of the fifteen exhibition rooms, those covering the years 1920–1929 and 1930–1939. The august size of Van Der Zee's reproduced photographs and their visual impact cannot be overstated. An installation photograph captures the experiential nature of viewing or displaying one of Van Der Zee's images (figure 4.7). In the center of the photograph is a large 4 × 8-foot photomural of Van Der Zee's widely circulated image of Marcus Garvey sitting in a convertible.[57] Much of the car and the background in the original photograph are omitted through the cropping of the image. Harlem as a backdrop is elided in this reproduction. Still, Garvey and his entourage are very much present and visible. In fact, the enlarged photograph approximates a life-size version of Garvey. Moreover, the positioning of the mural allowed those standing in front of it—like the man featured in the exhibition photograph—to look slightly up at the image, as if in reverence. This version of the image, within the context of the *Harlem on My Mind* exhibition, is a dramatic departure from its presence within the pages of the *Negro World*. Unlike the earlier iteration, which traveled through its multiplicity, in this case, Van

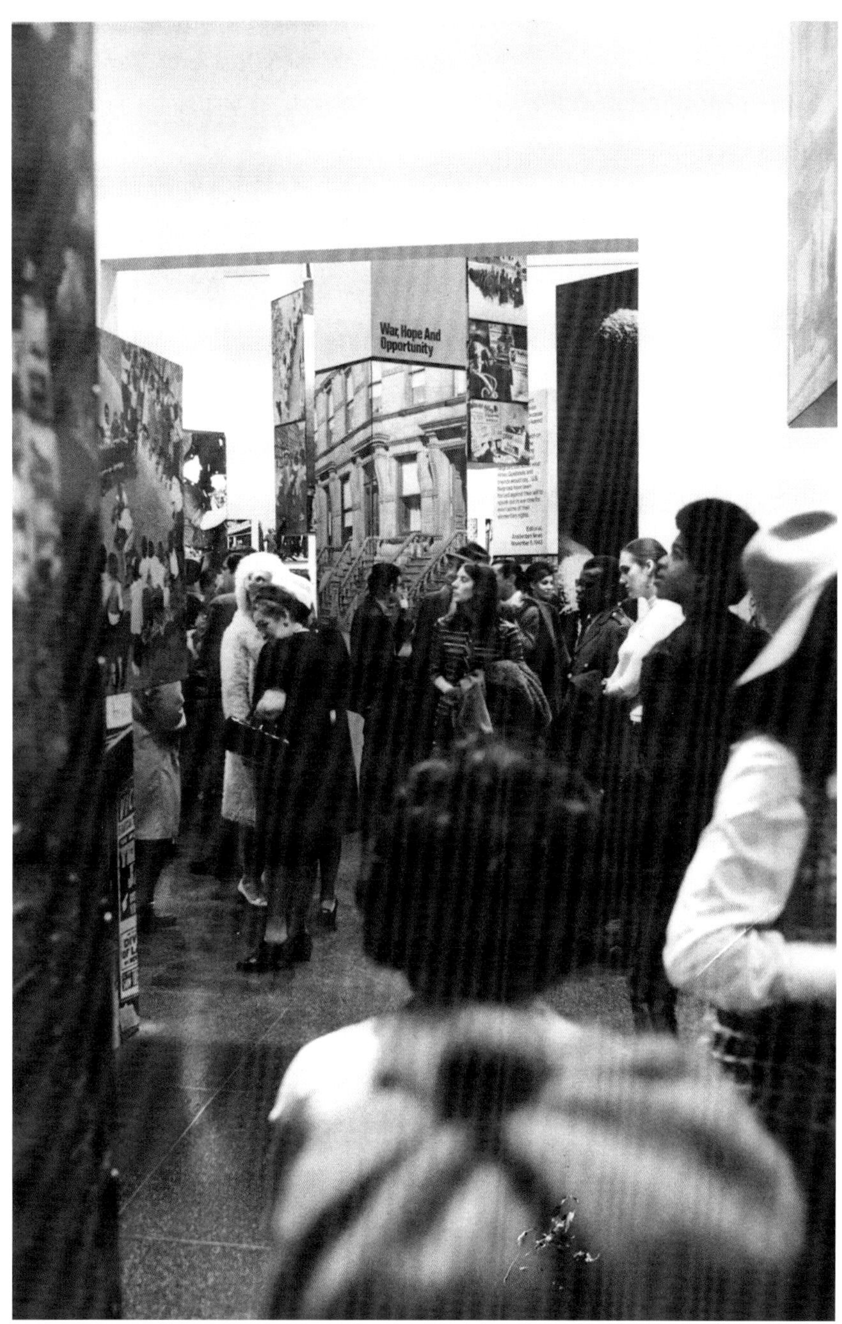

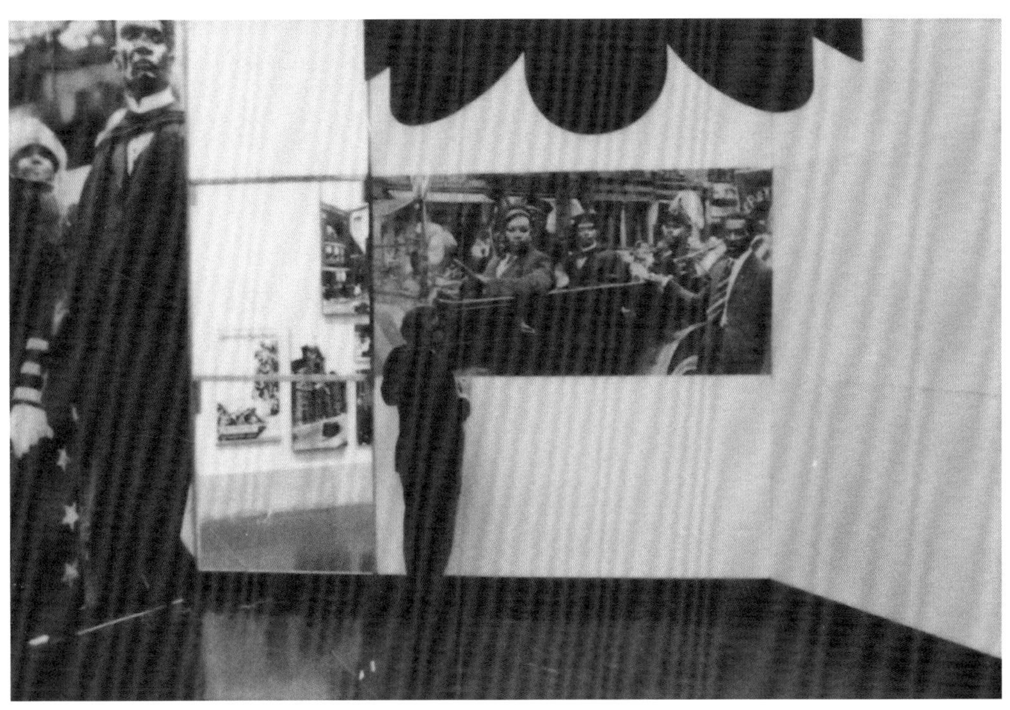

FIGURE 4.6 (opposite)

Gallery view of *"Harlem on My Mind": Cultural Capital of Black America 1900–1968*, Metropolitan Museum of Art, January 18–April 6, 1969.

Source: Collection of Allon Schoener.

FIGURE 4.7 (above)

Gallery view of James Van Der Zee's *Marcus Garvey in a UNIA Parade*, 1924, from *"Harlem on My Mind": Cultural Capital of Black America 1900–1968*, Metropolitan Museum of Art, January 18–April 6, 1969.

Source: Archives of American Art, Smithsonian Institution, Washington, DC.

Der Zee's image became effective as a life-size component of the curators' exhibition design. Even if the curators' ideas were poorly executed in numerous ways, Van Der Zee's images had a profound presence.

The chronologically organized exhibition of fifteen rooms, covering the decades between 1900 and 1968, was designed to create a one-hour viewing experience for visitors (figure 4.8).[58] With the exception of the handful of sound enhancements along with panels of poems, magazine covers, and other period memorabilia, the show chiefly comprised photographic images. The photographers of these images, whose names appeared as captions on wall labels, included Gordon Parks, Lee Friedlander, Helen Levitt, Jay Maisel, Aaron Siskind, Charles Stewart, Lloyd Yearwood, Leroy Lucas, Don Hogan Charles, and Van Der Zee. McGhee culled pictures from photo agencies and institutions such as Black Star, Brown Brothers, *Life* magazine, Magnum, the Museum of the City of New York, Underwood and Underwood, and United Press International.[59] Of the more than eighty Van Der Zee photographs borrowed for reproduction by the Met, approximately forty-nine were used in the *Harlem on My Mind* exhibition, while a smaller number appeared only in the accompanying catalog, *Harlem on My Mind: Cultural Capital of Black America, 1900–1968*.[60] Van Der Zee's works in the show included street scenes of parades and buildings, domestic interior scenes staged in Van Der Zee's studio and other business establishments, and group and individual portraits taken both outside and inside his studio.

The size of many of the photomurals made for an arresting viewing experience, one enabled through the quality of Van Der Zee's archive. For example, a photomural showing a Van Der Zee group portrait taken on the stairs of a Harlem brownstone is extremely large, radiating an august presence at 8 × 8 feet. The grandeur of such large photographs necessitated their being printed on two separate 8 × 4-foot panels that were exhibited side by side, making them appear as a singular entity (figure 4.9). However, a spectator facing the large photomurals could see the seams, which reinforced the material nature of the photographs, their reproduction, and their display. That Van Der Zee kept an archive enabled *Harlem on My Mind* to tell the story of Harlem more fully. Arguably, even though Van Der Zee didn't select the photographs that appeared in the show, the Met benefited from Van Der Zee's long-standing practice of archiving and from his meticulously maintained collection of photographs. For the exhibition to look the way it did, Van Der Zee needed the fortitude and foresight to create an archive in the first place.

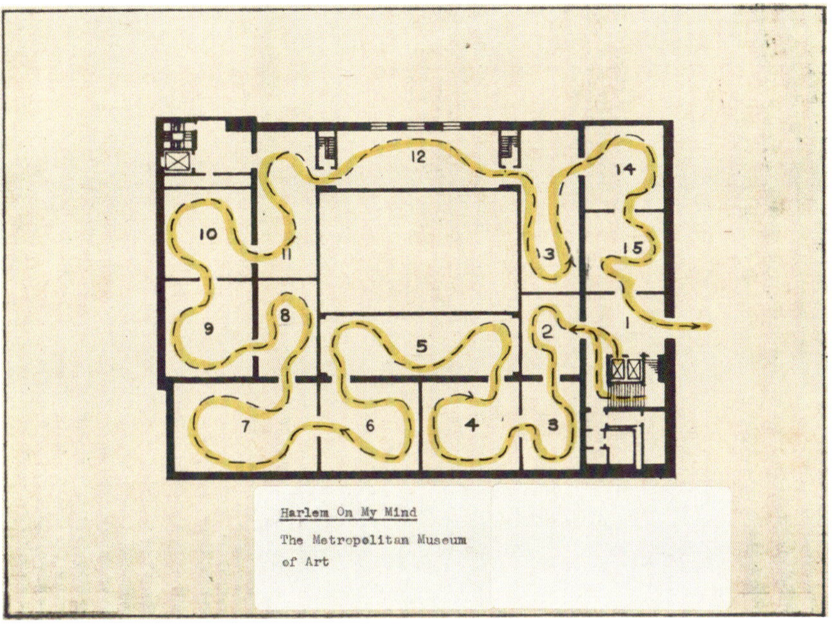

FIGURE 4.8

Floor plan of *"Harlem on My Mind": Cultural Capital of Black America 1900–1968*, Metropolitan Museum of Art, January 18–April 6, 1969.

Source: Archives of American Art, Smithsonian Institution, Washington, DC.

The impact of Van Der Zee's photographs becomes even more apparent when one considers their arrangement. The first room dedicated to 1920–1929 prominently featured Van Der Zee's gigantic 18 × 50-foot photomural of Reverend Adam Clayton Powell Sr., with his Abyssinian Baptist Church Sunday school class. This and other photographs by Van Der Zee visually defined the room through their size and number. The photomural of the Sunday school class shares a corner with the wall featuring Van Der Zee's 1925 photograph *Board of Trade and Commerce*. Suspended in the air in front of both wall murals is a third photograph by Van Der Zee. By looking toward the ceiling, perceptive viewers could see Van Der Zee's *Women at Manhattan Temple B.C. Lunch* (figure 4.10).

In at least one instance, Van Der Zee's archive directed the narrative of Harlem told through *Harlem on My Mind* toward an African diasporic

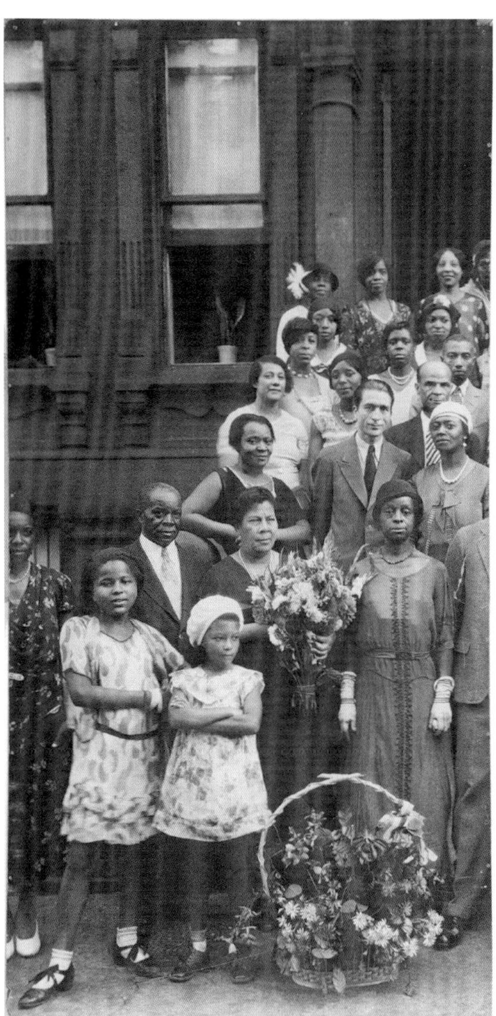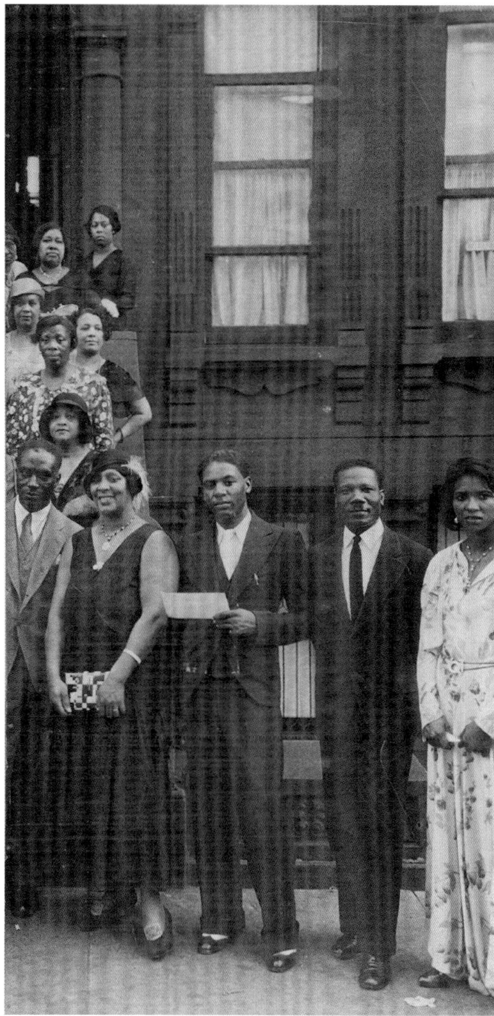

Two-panel enlargement of James Van Der Zee's *Family Group outside Brownstone*, 1920s, prepared for the 1969 Metropolitan Museum of Art exhibition *"Harlem on My Mind": Cultural Capital of Black America 1900–1968.*

Each panel 8 × 4 ft. (2.4 m × 1.2 m). Source: Harlem on My Mind Collection, I. P. Stanback Museum, South Carolina State University, Orangeburg.

bent. The presence of the Garvey section might be credited to John Henrik Clarke, who began working as a consultant for the show in the summer of 1967 and was crucial to the exhibition's thematic framework. In his own scholarship on Harlem, Clarke highlighted Garvey.[61] Especially noteworthy is that—in turning to Van Der Zee's collection to illustrate the narrative of the 1920s—the available visual material had an unusually high concentration and focus on Garvey. Either by chance or by the urging of Clarke, a self-proclaimed Pan-Africanist, this selection of photographs tilted this portion of the exhibition's narrative toward an organization whose reach went beyond Harlem to the larger African diaspora. The section represented a movement with a global purview, the Universal Negro Improvement Association (UNIA), as opposed to the US-focused National Association for the Advancement of Colored People (NAACP). Clarke's framework, combined with Van Der Zee's available archive, enabled a narrative of Harlem in the 1920s that gestured toward not only the national Black experience but also an international Black movement. Thus, Van Der Zee produces both a local and a diasporic photographic vision, just as he had persistently done throughout his career by leveraging the multiple ways photographs navigated the world through their vernacular qualities.

Such a narrative, which was constructed with and greatly enhanced by Van Der Zee's photographs, did not go unnoticed. The historian Eugene Genovese, in his February 1969 *Artforum* review of *Harlem on My Mind*, questions why W. E. B. Du Bois—the founding leader of the NAACP and one of the most prominent African American intellectuals of the time—is given little consideration within the show while the Pan-Africanist Garvey is prominently featured. Genovese calls this approach "a striking political judgment." It most likely demonstrates the extent to which Van Der Zee's photographs (and his work with Garvey and UNIA) shaped the exhibition's visual narrative. It also shows that Van Der Zee's photographic range included an important extension of the larger African diaspora while disrupting expectations of who should be highlighted.[62]

Most important, Van Der Zee did not keep just any archive of photographs but had one of excellent quality that he, at least in principle, intended for later use. Negatives were kept both for posterity, as a reflection of Van Der Zee's life's work, and for practical reasons, because of the possibility of future requests from clients. Although not featured in the exhibit, one example from Van Der Zee's archive illustrates this point. A 1915 Van Der Zee portrait taken of Blanche Powell, the daughter of the Reverend Adam Clayton Powell Sr., was reused as a superimposed feature within a 1926 fu-

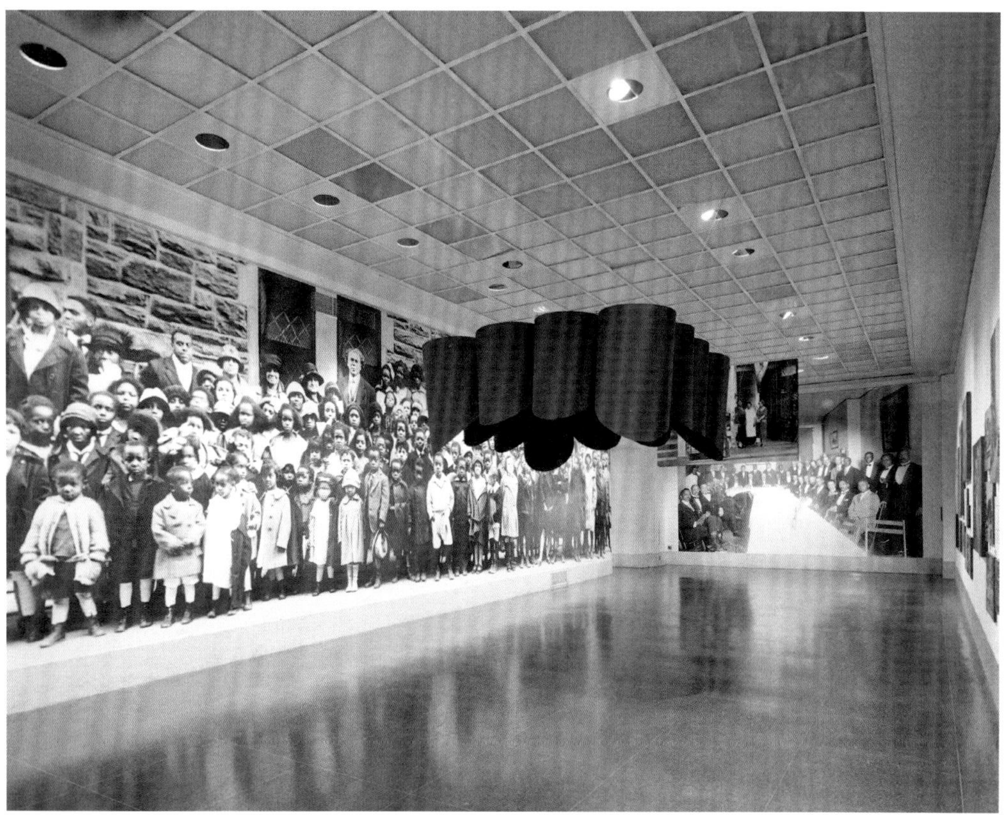

Gallery view of *"Harlem on My Mind": Cultural Capital of Black America 1900–1968*, Metropolitan Museum of Art, January 18–April 6, 1969. The exhibition featured enlarged photographs by James Van Der Zee, including *Reverend Adam Clayton Powell Sr. with Sunday School Class outside Abyssinian Baptist Church*, 1925.

Source: The Metropolitan Museum of Art, New York.

nerary photograph made by the photographer after her unexpectedly early death (figure 4.11). The foresight to keep negatives around was helpful for less morbid occasions as well. Wedding portraits and those capturing other life milestones were good candidates for reprinting. However, Van Der Zee probably never imagined that this belated reprinting would take the form of *Harlem on My Mind*. Nonetheless, the large number of Van Der Zee's photographs included in the exhibition is directly related to the massive quantity and high quality of images in the photographer's archive. After all, the life-size photomurals of Van Der Zee's images were distinct not only for the details such a size captured but for the fact that such compelling images could be produced using the materials pulled from Van Der Zee's collection. This is a point of practicality and technicality that has aesthetic repercussions.[63]

Translating Van Der Zee's image *Reverend Adam C. Powell Sr. with Children Outside* into a 50 × 18-foot mural, for instance, posed a particular set of challenges, given the unusually large size and the high resolution and crispness needed to make the photograph of museum quality (figure 4.12). According to Modernage, the company hired to print the photographs, there existed only a few options for photomurals in 1969. To produce gigantic prints, Modernage used an enlarger the size of a golf cart and projected portions of the image onto a wall across the room. A huge room needed to be employed that could allow for enough distance between the enlarger and the wall. Portions of the final image were printed and then seamed together to make a patched mural, a gigantic photograph comprising various pieces. However, before the printing and projection even took place, a large-format negative needed to be available to use within the enlarger. Although multiple options existed, the crispest photographs could be printed from an already existing negative as opposed to a paper print.

The kind of crisp photograph that visitors to the show witnessed in the *Reverend Adam C. Powell Sr. with Children Outside* photomural most likely was produced from a negative Van Der Zee released to the Met.[64] His archive not only supplied the negatives and prints but also provided a material format through which a photograph could come to life at such a size. In offering the Met the ability to reproduce photographs at the highest quality technically possible at the time, Van Der Zee indirectly influenced the extent to which his photographs persisted across time, space, and material. Van Der Zee had clients in mind when he carefully saved the negatives; he built his archive in anticipation of future viewing. Viewers like the one captured in profile with her Afro and the young visitors in awe of his images would be counted among these new "clients," gifted with the opportunity to linger and appreciate his photographic vision from decades past.

The show, albeit extremely problematic, allowed a small selection of Van Der Zee's photographic images to be fully seen. Audiences were treated to minimally cropped Van Der Zee photographs, which was not the case for the work of all photographers. Although Van Der Zee's sig-

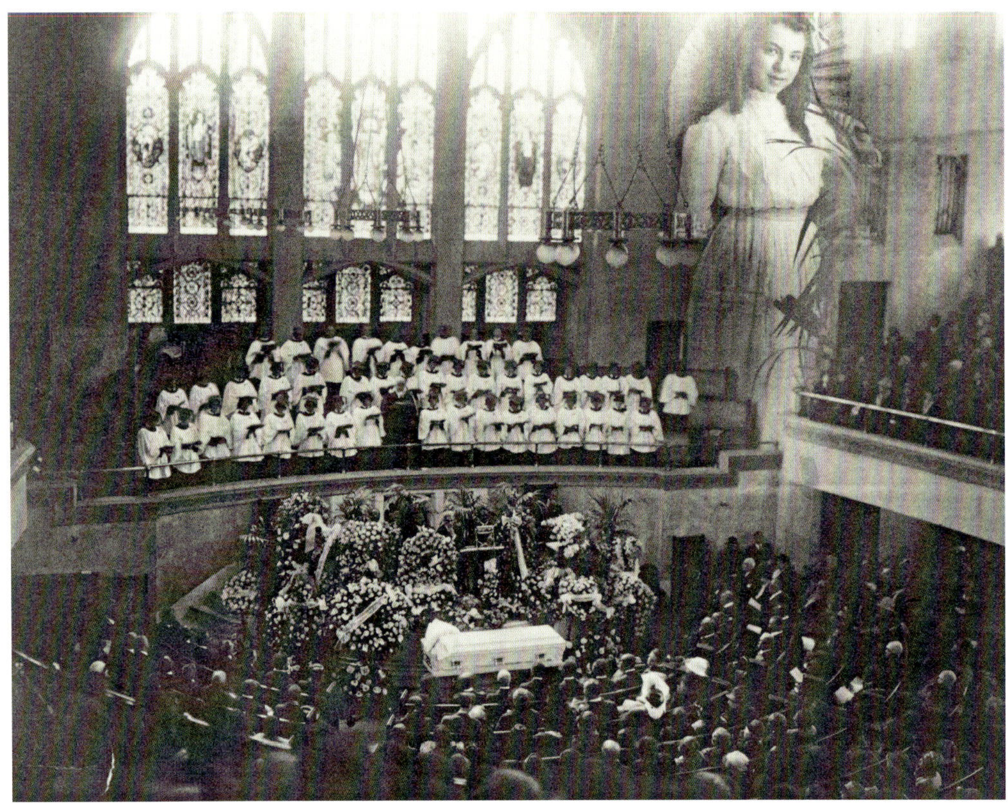

James Van Der Zee, *Funeral of Blanche Powell, Abyssinian Baptist Church* (with inset portrait, ca. 1915), 1926. The daughter of pastor and activist Adam Clayton Powell Sr. died unexpectedly while still in her twenties.

7⅝ × 10 in. (19.4 × 25.4 cm). © James Van Der Zee Archive, The Metropolitan Museum of Art, New York. Source: James Van Der Zee Archive, The Metropolitan Museum of Art, New York.

FIGURE 4.12 (opposite)

Staff at Modernage Photographic Labs preparing the photomural of James Van Der Zee's *Reverend Adam Clayton Powell Sr. with Sunday School Class outside Abyssinian Baptist Church*, 1925, for the Metropolitan Museum of Art's 1969 exhibition *"Harlem on My Mind": Cultural Capital of Black America 1900–1968*.

Source: Archives of American Art, Smithsonian Institution, Washington, DC.

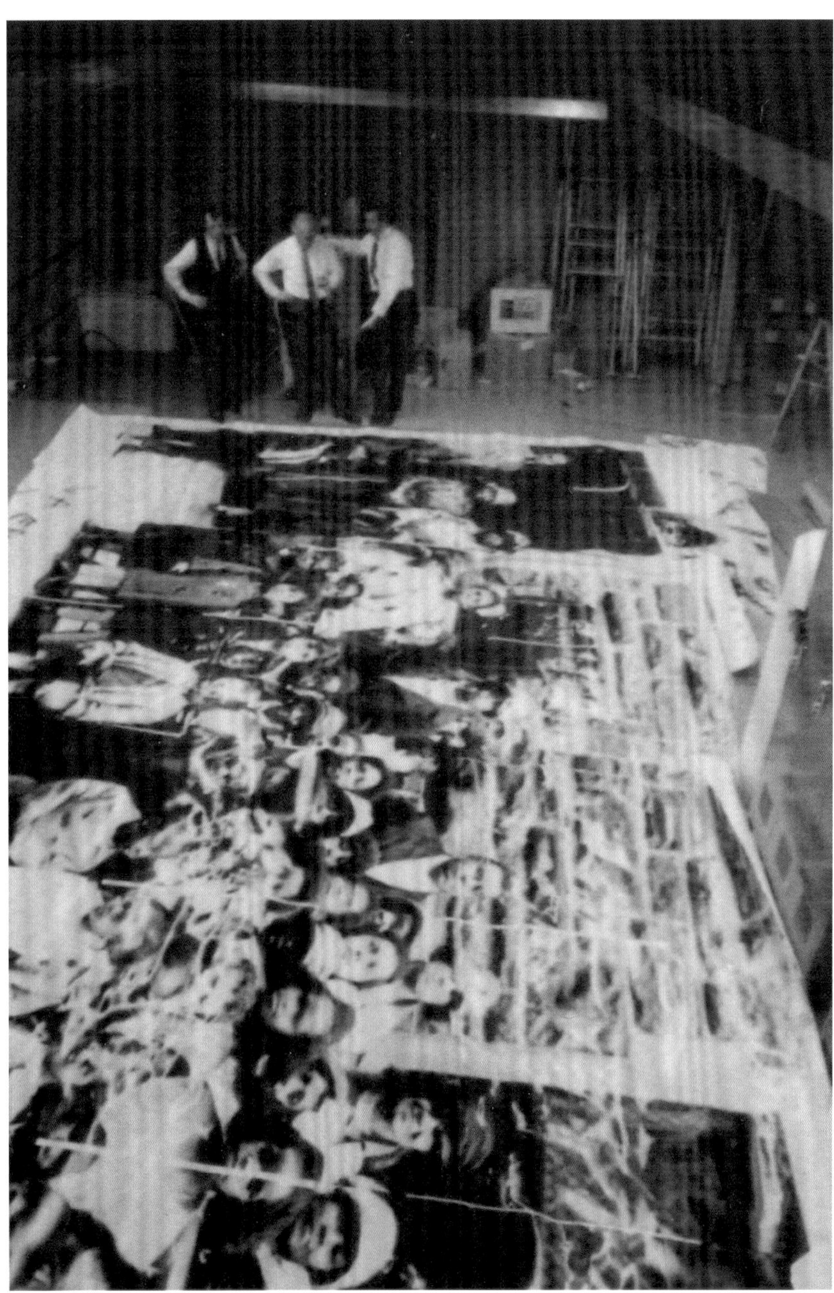

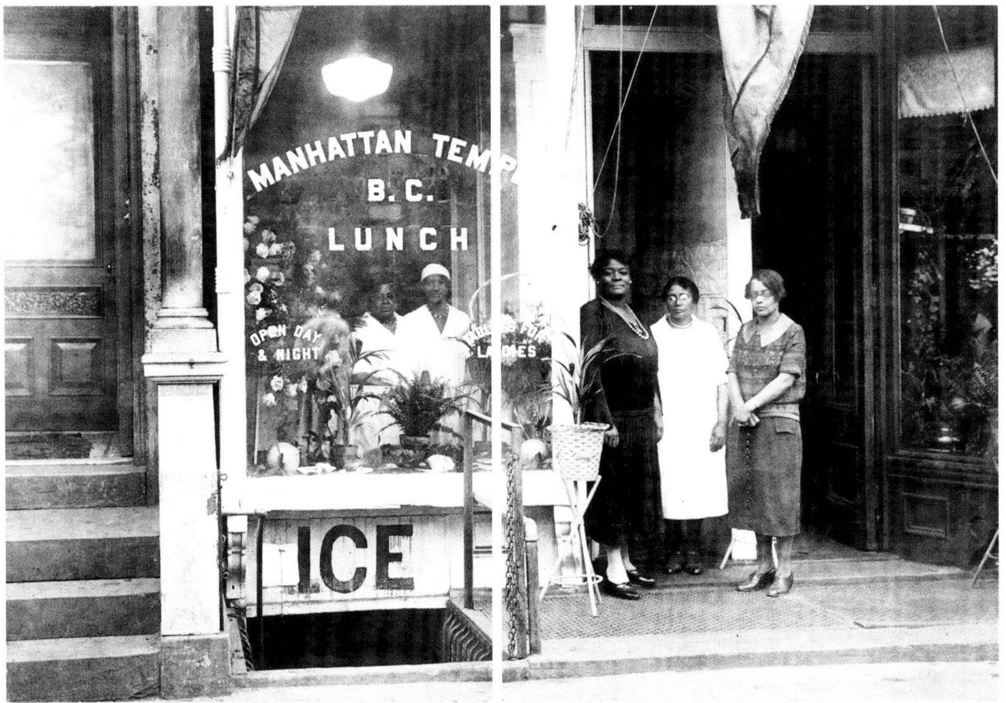

FIGURE 4.13 (A & B)

James Van Der Zee, two-panel enlargement of *Women
at Manhattan Temple B.C. Lunch*, 1926, prepared for the
Metropolitan Museum of Art's 1969 exhibition *"Harlem on
My Mind": Cultural Capital of Black America 1900–1968.*

© James Van Der Zee Archive, The Metropolitan Museum of Art.
Source: Harlem on My Mind Collection, I. P. Stanback Museum,
South Carolina State University, Orangeburg.

nature, commonly found in the lower corners of his photographs, is partially missing in the reproduced photomurals, which prevented the viewer from identifying the photograph's maker, the overall composition of his Harlem images remained mostly intact.[65] Consider the striking *Women at Manhattan Temple B.C. Lunch*, depicting five women separated into two groups (figure 4.13). The first two figures stand behind a glass window next to interior plants and decorations. They are positioned between lettering on the glass that announces the luncheon location. The women embrace as one puts her arm around the other. The other three women stand as a

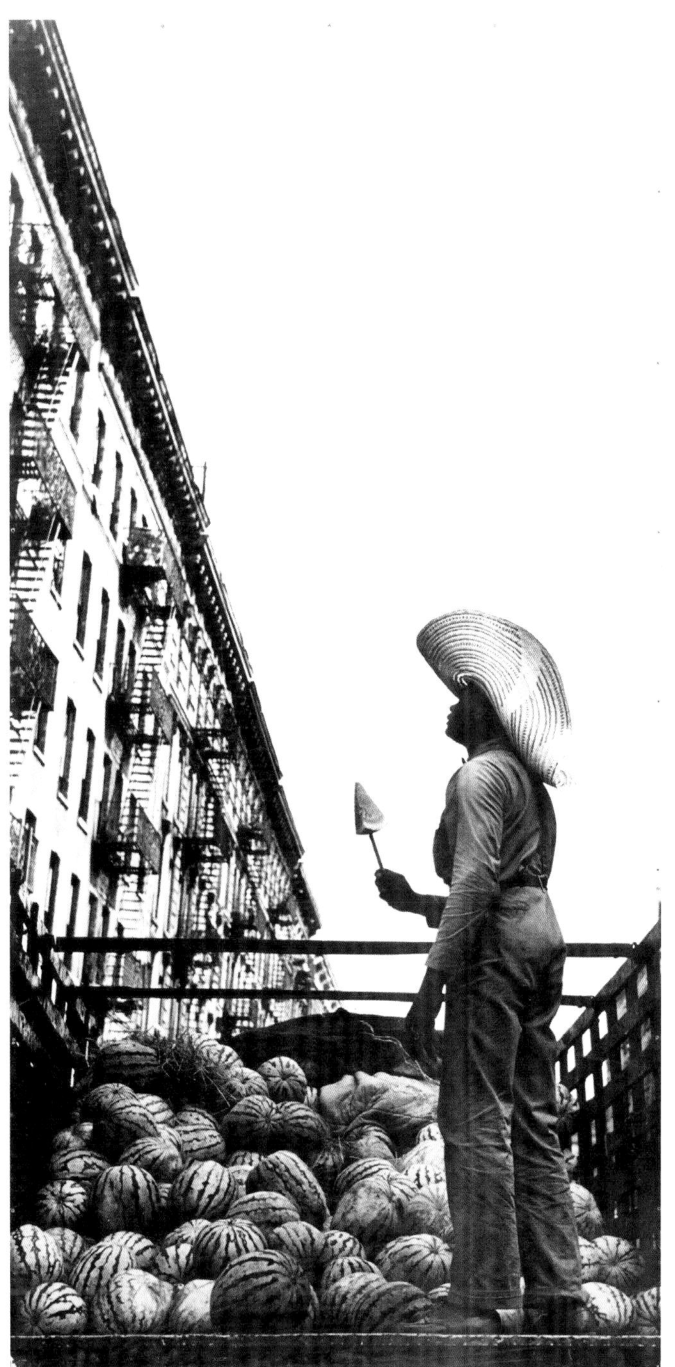

Aaron Siskind, *Watermelon Man*, 1940, cropped and enlarged for the Metropolitan Museum of Art's 1969 exhibition, *"Harlem on My Mind": Cultural Capital of Black America 1900–1968.*

© Virginia Museum of Fine Arts. Source: Harlem on My Mind Collection, I. P. Stanback Museum, South Carolina State University, Orangeburg.

collective right outside the building's door. All look straight toward Van Der Zee, mindfully aware of how they are represented in relation to their position either inside or outside the building. Given the size of the photomural, viewers from 1969 could stand, peering back at the highly choreographed women, strategically positioned and captured in 1926 by Van Der Zee's skillful practice.

In contrast, cropping decisions altered the composition of other reproductions in the show, such as Aaron Siskind's *Watermelon Man* (1940). The original nearly square Siskind photograph features a man with a wide-brimmed hat standing in the back of a truck filled with watermelons. He looks up toward the Harlem apartment building, just as the viewer looks up at the figure given the photograph's angled perspective. Within this original photograph, the man is framed on both sides by tall buildings that create a sharp perspectival V shape—the standing figure serving as the point at which all lines meet. In the version of *Watermelon Man* featured in the *Harlem on My Mind* exhibition, visitors are privy to a very different view (figure 4.14). The exhibition photograph is highly cropped, drastically omitting almost all of the building on the right side and removing a generous portion of the building on the left. What remains reinforces the open sky and its V shape, as it visually leads the viewer's gaze dramatically toward the man, who stands and gazes upward. The photograph is transformed to a vertical orientation, thereby changing the composition of the original photograph and altering the visual narrative conveyed in the exhibition.

In addition to the fidelity of their image translations, the arrangement of Van Der Zee's photographs impacted how audience members experienced them. Having spent three hours walking around and observing visitors at the exhibit on a Friday, a consultant named Meyer Braiterman offered insight in an extensive report into how these huge crowds may have experienced Van Der Zee's photographs.[66] Although his general purpose was to determine the number of audience members reading the object labels, if one considers his report with an eye toward the specific rooms in which Van Der Zee's work dominated, one version of how individuals engaged with Van Der Zee's version of Harlem can be pieced together. For example, his report explains that by the time visitors got to the rooms in which Van Der Zee's photographs were found, they rarely read the object labels. More specifically, only one in ten people even glanced at these captions (figure 4.15). Their attention was entirely on the photographic visual material, which they engaged with "great interest," as Braiterman describes.

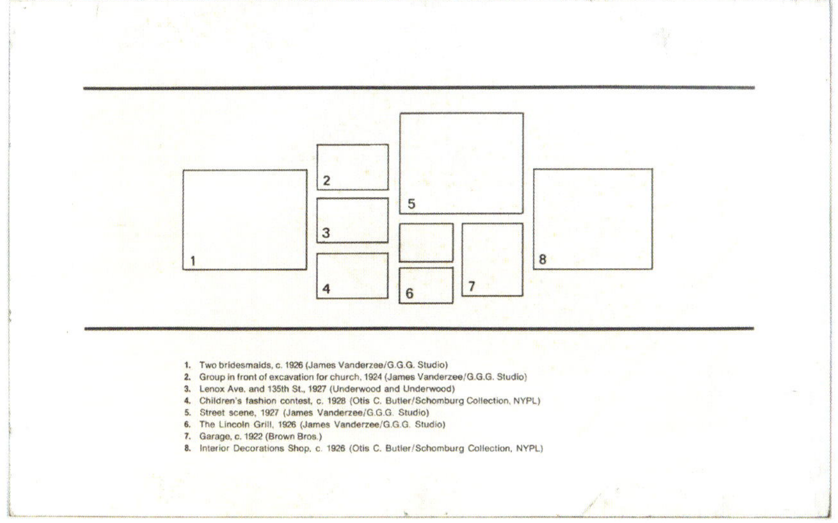

FIGURE 4.15

Object label, 1969, with captions for *"Harlem on My Mind": Cultural Capital of Black America 1900–1968.*

Source: Harlem on My Mind Collection, I. P. Stanback Museum, South Carolina State University, Orangeburg.

Much like the attention and interest described by the two young visitors to the show, many eyes lingered on Van Der Zee's work.

Similarly, when visitors arrived at Van Der Zee's gigantic *Board of Commerce* photomural, only seven in fifty people even looked for a caption, thereby minimizing the opportunity to identify Van Der Zee as the photographer.[67] However, viewers would have gained an impression of Harlem's residents as serious professionals participating in a formal business meeting. The perspectival angle captured by Van Der Zee highlights an elongated central board table, thereby reinforcing the decision-making power and influence of the dozens of black-suited gentlemen looking toward the camera with stern faces. This large-scale visual insight of Van Der Zee's enlarged photographs could not have been anything but absorbing to certain viewers, as the sixteen-year-old described in his encounter with many of the images at the exhibit. They offered an embodied experience of looking at photographs, one that parallels the physicality implicit in vernacular photographs as objects that are held, turned over, and passed from hand to hand as keepsakes.

Van Der Zee's photographs have always taken on a range of purposes. For example, his clients throughout the years turned to Van Der Zee to fulfill their ambitions for visibility. Both subtle requests, like recopying of an old photograph, and scheduled sittings, like a series of posed portraits within the studio space, allowed Van Der Zee's photographic images to make meaning in the world. Van Der Zee's archive came into being through the reproduction, modification, and selection of images over time. Understanding the full scope of Van Der Zee's photographs and their vernacular qualities allows us to recognize their role—beyond their belated display within a poorly executed exhibition—as useful entities that persistently disrupt art history's sight line. His photographs are able to transcend the very logic that ordered the show and its detractors. Like the works of a host of other image makers of African descent, not necessarily placed on the margins but invited into the center to never really be seen, Van Der Zee's work within the *Harlem on My Mind* show illustrates the pitfalls of Black representation within the museum space while also engendering a platform for Black viewers to see, to engage, and to be fascinated with whatever captured their imagination, while demoting the curatorial logic of *Harlem on My Mind*. Through this perspective Van Der Zee's photographs gained the kind of visibility that transcended their public presentation in the exhibition.

A Chance Encounter

A chance encounter in Harlem during December 1968 changed the course of Van Der Zee's photographs. In advance of the exhibition, McGhee unexpectedly came on Van Der Zee in his Harlem studio. After inquiring about photographs of the neighborhood between the wars, McGhee was led to a rear storage room housing hundreds of prints and negatives, stored in boxes and bags, that Van Der Zee had meticulously kept over his decades-long career. Van Der Zee was eighty-seven years old and in failing health; thus, his engagement with photography in 1968 lacked the level of activity defining the beginning decades of his career. Nonetheless, his G. G. G. Photo Studio still opened to the public every morning except Sunday.[68] At the time, his photographic output consisted almost entirely of mail-order photographic restoration work for clients near and far. Although such work served a purpose, the resulting income could not support the Van Der Zees to the extent needed to prevent their eventual eviction.[69] Many of the preceding years had been dire for the Van Der Zees. By the time of *Harlem on My Mind*, not only did they struggle to hold on to ownership of the house, but Harlem was not the same neighborhood as in its heyday decades earlier. The aging couple endured several home robberies, navigated unpleasant situations with boarders to whom they rented upstairs rooms, and witnessed assaults they were too vulnerable to intervene in. In addition, the mounting stress caused by their home being repossessed triggered a mental breakdown and a hospital stay for Gaynella Greenlee (Mrs. Van Der Zee). Their new housing arrangement required that all the photographs be put in storage, and the fourteen-room house that had once been their secure dwelling was replaced with a two-room apartment that Mrs. Van Der Zee never fully embraced in her remaining years. Van Der Zee recalled one day taking a photograph of her in a rocking chair during the last years of their sixty-years as a couple, unbeknownst to her. This tender and bittersweet gesture, captured through the medium that had shaped the course of their lives, illustrates the extent to which photography served as far more than a commercial enterprise for the pair.[70] While he recorded moments of interiority through his camera, another set of images taken by a photojournalist visualized a very public and celebrated depiction of Van Der Zee.

Consider an image featured in a *New York Times* story on the Van Der Zees' eviction, a misfortune that unfolded at the same time as reproduced and enlarged versions of Van Der Zee's work graced the walls of the Met. The newspaper photograph depicts Van Der Zee seated in the front room of his Harlem photography studio (figure 4.16).[71] Mrs. Van Der Zee is nowhere in sight, although in earlier decades her presence with clients coming in and out of the studio was most likely a given. However, within clear view are examples of many of the portrait photographs that had formed the core of their business over the decades. Arranged in an orderly grid, portraits of individual African American subjects create a display that has an equal if not predominant presence in the photograph. Other objects—such as two enlarged portraits displayed on their own and a set of regal wooden chairs—are grouped with the seated photographer on the left side of the image. The image portrays one kingly individual surrounded by his riches, a collection of works from which McGhee had selected more than eighty prints a mere few months earlier for consideration for the show.[72] Later, Louise Broecker, an exhibition staff member, selected several dozen additional negatives for possible inclusion.[73]

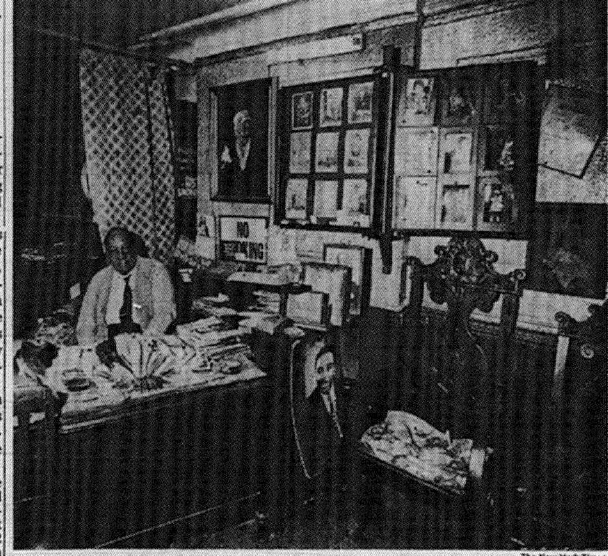

Evicted Photographer's Work Is in Demand

Publishers Seeking 50-Year Record of Life in Harlem

By ROBERT M. SMITH

The publishing industry yesterday sought out a little-known Negro photographer who has quietly been taking pictures of Harlem scenes and people for the last 50 years.

Eighty-seven-year-old James Van Der Zee did not come to the notice of Time-Life, Grove Press, McCall's book division and the Encyclopedia Britannica because of the prominent display of his works in the recent "Harlem on My Mind" exhibit at the Metropolitan Museum of Art.

What drew their attention was the appearance of a news account of his eviction Monday from his Lenox Avenue studio.

Yesterday afternoon the stocky Mr. Van Der Zee settled himself on an upended wastebasket amid the debris of what had been his studio at 272 Lenox Avenue, near 124th Street, and answered the telephone calls of publishers and

James Van Der Zee, earlier this year, in the studio in Harlem from which he was evicted

FIGURE 4.16

Robert M. Smith's article for the *New York Times*
(April 9, 1969) included an image of James Van Der Zee
in his studio.

Source: Serial and Government Publications Division,
Library of Congress.

This "gold mine," as McGhee called it, became a substantial part of *Harlem on My Mind*.[74] The large Van Der Zee archive from which the images were culled was later temporarily discarded on the sidewalk in "twenty card-board boxes and one wooden packing crate filled with negatives and photographs, some of them dating back to 1915 when Van Der Zee began his Harlem picture taking." Readers of the article on his eviction learned that the subject matter of his photographs covered "just about every event in Harlem" and featured well-known individuals such as Marcus Garvey, Adam Clayton Powell, and Father Divine.[75] The collection on the sidewalk was the same one from which McGhee had drawn his selection. That gold mine's preciousness apparently did not shield it from the denigration intrinsic to an eviction. So many photographs of Black sitters end up in unexpected places because of major life events that cause unwanted upheaval. As writer Teju Cole insists, behind many belatedly found photographs "lay invisible stories of evictions, dispossessions or separations."[76] Similarly, Van Der Zee's photographs took a bumpy route, albeit one that intersected with the *Harlem on My Mind* show. Ironically, his emergence in the art world did not lead to financial relief, whereas the consistent success of his commercial business, driven by his vernacular and quotidian importance, had kept him solvent throughout the earlier decades of his business's operation. Unlike the dynamic and generative ecosystem of Harlem during its heyday, his entry into the museum space provided little stabilizing support or opportunities for Van Der Zee to purposefully contribute his insight. Instead, the emphasis centered on carrying out the intentions of the show, per the Met's vision.

In choosing photographs from Van Der Zee's archive for *Harlem on My Mind*, McGhee's main objective was not to select favorites based on his or the photographer's individual preferences. Instead, McGhee aimed to find photographs that could represent Harlem. While Van Der Zee, if given the chance, might have based his selection on the photographs' aesthetic qualities and possibly the memorable narrative of that sitter, or that day in the studio, McGhee had a more streamlined goal of trying to represent a place through images. Unfortunately, the results of the exhibit were nowhere near ideal. Van Der Zee's photographs, once they left his studio, have often been used to build someone else's narrative without his oversight. The interpretive possibilities of studio photographs are routinely pushed beyond their original purpose. They enter new registers of meaning. They travel along a contextual arc that requires a reassessment of how and what they are signifying, sometimes as works of fine art and sometimes as vernacular images. To offer a nimble reading is to commit to genuinely engaging this arc, in light of or despite it all. Failing to recognize photography's malleability and its intersecting histories within the context of the *Harlem on My Mind* exhibition and beyond gives too much agency to museums—and, to a certain extent, art history—in defining how a photograph's value is determined. Yet Van Der Zee's photographs continue to serve as a generative site of meaning for the relationship between the Black quotidian and photography. Exploring his archive requires pivots in interpretation.

This sentiment resonates with what Willis saw in the *Harlem on My Mind* show when she visited it five times as her younger self. It may also find commonality with what the photographer Dawoud Bey experienced on that day when *Harlem on My Mind* struck him so profoundly as a sixteen-year-

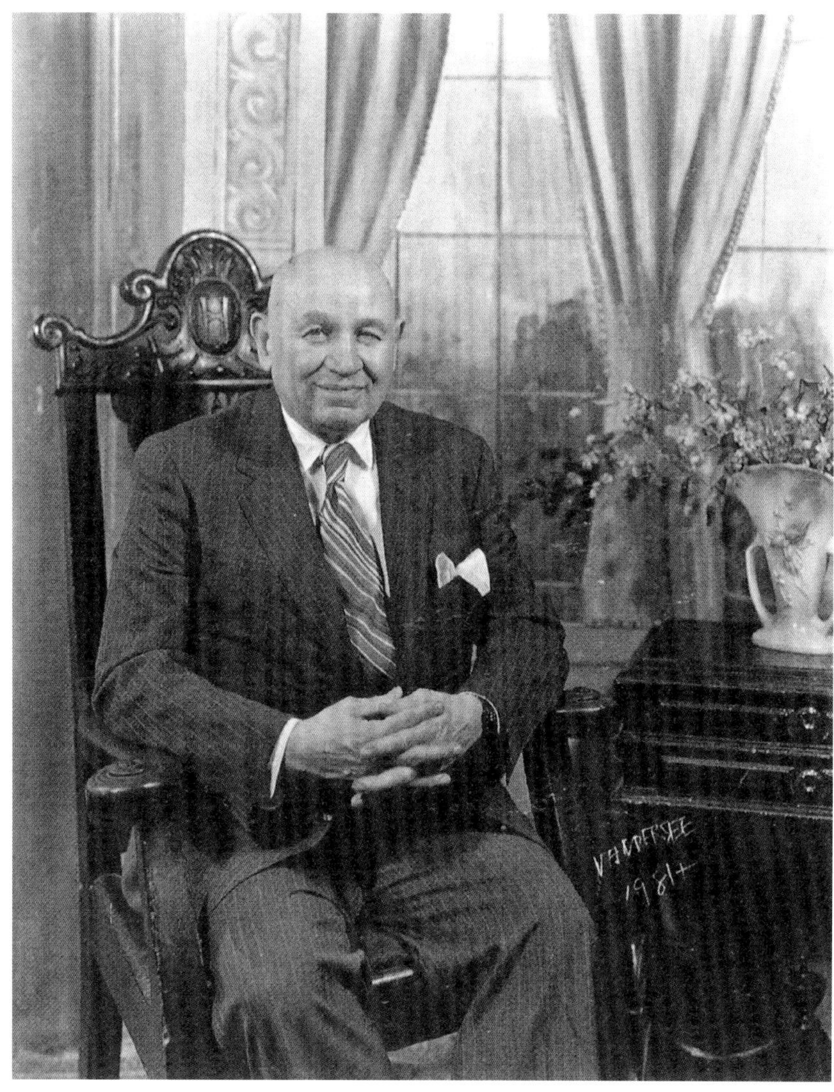

FIGURE 4.17

James Van Der Zee, *Romare Bearden*, 1981. Twelve years before this photograph was taken, Bearden was among the artists protesting the *Harlem on My Mind* exhibition.

10 × 8 in. (25.4 × 20.3 cm). © James Van Der Zee Archive, The Metropolitan Museum of Art, New York. Source: Willis-Braithwaite, *VanDerZee, Photographer, 1886–1983*, 185.

old youth. The *Harlem on My Mind* show was just one part of a sequence of impactful moments and revealing occurrences within the long life of one prolific and important studio photographer and his photographs. Van Der Zee's images—through their reproduction, enlargement, and reuse as vernacular photographs and fine art work—come into view for different audiences depending on how and where they look. In this 1969 iteration, his emergence reveals the very kinds of value systems and structures through which his photographs navigate. This moment for Van Der Zee also shows how the context of viewing his photographs can overdetermine an image's value, just as it can offer new possibilities of appreciation.

In 1981, following his activism with the BECC, the African American artist Romare Bearden sat for a portrait with Van Der Zee (figure 4.17). In the portrait Bearden appears against a backdrop that has much in common with Van Der Zee's photographs from the 1920s and 1930s. On the table stands a vase filled with flowers. Bearden sits wearing a formal suit, facing toward the camera's lens as he interlaces his fingers. He looks not only toward the camera but toward Van Der Zee, located behind his large 8 × 10-inch camera. This photograph—this moment of two artists having an exchange—has symbolic implications. During the *Harlem on My Mind* show, Bearden's energies were focused on protesting. But in this moment his gaze rests on Van Der Zee in recognition that the value of Van Der Zee's photographic production could finally be seen. In the case of other photographers, a cadre of Black image makers could now chart their own genealogy with Van Der Zee as an esteemed elder. For those committed to seeing commercial portraits and street scenes of Black life in Harlem, Van Der Zee's archive enables a whole generation of Black viewers to see anew. While *Harlem on My Mind* can be framed as a story of warranted protest, it can also be positioned as a chapter in a story of joy, the joy of seeing and celebrating Black photographs in an imperfect and woefully deficient context. It is the story of Black photographs that have sat waiting in numerous boxes, emerging for air decades later and receiving new relevance and meaning in the eyes of different beholders. This is the story of vernacular photographs, and in many ways this is a formative part of Van Der Zee's photographs too.

To Nimbly Rewind

Fixing a New Constellation of Ideas circa 1994

A NIMBLE ARC HAS FOCUSED on the relational and material dimensions of James Van Der Zee's photographs across the twentieth century, from his early years in Harlem to the moment of the *Harlem on my Mind* exhibit. The book attends to two poles of interpretation to argue that a synthesis of approaches is needed to fully capture the significance of this artist's photographs and his practice. On the one hand, an approach informed by an art history of photography upholds certain expectations about how and why photographs become relevant. On the other hand, this book gives credence and space to methods that wholeheartedly emphasize how everyday photographs are used by people in quotidian ways. By doing so, I insert Van Der Zee into a discursive place where he usually has not been considered but has always existed. Although the word *vernacular* has been uscd in publications to describe Van Der Zee's work, these occurrences are infrequent. I draw him into such discourse for the benefit of his legacy, as I aim to capture how Van Der Zee's work was commercial yet artistic, formally untrained yet highly masterful, artistically intentional yet uncontrollable in its afterlife.

Thus each of the chapters disrupts and complicates what we thought we knew about Van Der Zee and the significance of his practice by recognizing how art history has enabled Van Der Zee to be seen and celebrated while also offering frameworks of values and perspectives within the space of the Black quotidian. Doing so has yielded insight into the complexities, the range, the reach, and the importance of Van Der Zee's work as elite and popular forms of expression intersect. As Kobena Mercer writes, "Seemingly contradictory perspectives may yield new insight into the aesthetic complexities of black diaspora art."[1] Indeed, navigating both art history and the vernacular has brought into view the processes through which Van Der Zee's photographs became mediators of value within and beyond the art world.

My approach uses photographs to attend to context-based moments of encounter that the production or the afterlife of a photograph makes possible. It is also driven by the presumed and often overlooked interlocutors who help us understand how Van Der Zee's photographs generate occasions for interpretation from a range of different circumstances, for example, as people passed by and peered into his studio display or as anonymous viewers abroad engaged with Van Der Zee's images through easily crinkled newspaper pages. Photographs remade in the image of other photographs brought or sent to Van Der Zee's studio become an important site of meaning. Finally, the context of the world-renowned Metropolitan Museum of Art in 1969 illustrates how compelling interpretations often originate with not-yet-indoctrinated viewers as opposed to those entrenched in the center or on the margins of the art world. This book also troubles the long-held assumption of Van Der Zee's singularity. It departs from a focus on vintage prints to illustrate the power of his images' reproduction in newsprint, questions what qualifies as a Van Der Zee photograph, and reframes the *Harlem on My Mind* exhibition as an occasion for Black viewers to engage with powerful Black images. Taken together, these interventions reposition Van Der Zee's significance within art history.

This book remains indebted to art history, as it provides the framework to address Van Der Zee in the first place. It is this disciplinary structure that the book at times has aimed to challenge and at other times has very much appreciated. Without the more traditional treatment of Van Der Zee, in which his significance is tied to the Harlem Renaissance era, this book would not exist. Through this discourse his photographs are considered exceptional works of fine art, and the photographer himself is granted a place of regard and respect given to only a few other Black image makers in photography's history. At a time when there is a call to reform art history, in many ways, this book celebrates what art history has made possible for Van Der Zee while also critically addressing its myopia by taking a vernacular turn.

However, the book's applicability and uses for thinking about other photographers might not take shape in the ways that are most often taught and practiced in the discipline. There exists an expectation to explain how this book project can be relevant to thinking through the work of other photographers from the African diaspora. However, I have many reservations in making this kind of leap. When I ask, Who are in fact the other photographers that we can reframe by using this book as a model?, the names that come to mind do not quite fit. This is not because of a lack of Black photographers who deserve and could benefit greatly from a book-length critical and comprehensive consideration.

Instead, such attempts seem to amplify the distinctness of Van Der Zee's position as the revered African American studio photographer within art history. For example, while Van Der Zee's peers James Latimer Allen and Winifred Hall Allen deserve additional critical attention, neither has reached the celebrated status within art history that Van Der Zee has. In the case of the now-canonized Malian photographers Malick Sidibé and Seydou Keïta, pairing art history and the vernacular as frameworks of consideration makes sense.[2] However, African photographers' place within both discourses is drastically different from that of African American image makers. The specter of colonization and ethnography looms large for those from the African continent in ways that American photographers, to a certain extent, are less encumbered by. Then, of course, there is Gordon Parks (1912–2006), a renowned African American photographer in his own right. While scholarship on Parks continues to advance, a book that shifts gears and places Parks at the intersections of art history and the vernacular world would fall short. Even though both Parks and Van Der Zee navigated the commercial world of photography, the latter served a predominantly Black quotidian clientele through studio photography, in contrast to Parks's efforts to intentionally shape journalistic narratives for wider audiences as a photo-essayist. A vernacular turn and an art historical reconsideration are not as applicable to or productive for thinking through Parks's career or, really, those of any of the aforementioned photographers, at least not to the extent that it has proven advantageous to more comprehensively addressing Van Der Zee.

Therefore, in addition to emphasizing the polarized relationship between art history and the vernacular, I believe that one of this book's more expansive contributions, and its relevance to a larger field of study, can be found in its insistence on taking what is seemingly contradictory, or functional on separate planes of meaning, and putting these things together toward the end goal of rethinking the very structures that order what we thought we knew. To do so, we must also be attentive to the kinds of frameworks relevant to each artist, given their specific relationship with various contexts and structures of meaning. I have described my approach within these pages as nimble, moving comfortably back and forth among different ways of thinking about Van Der Zee in order to see him and his work as fully as possible.

This coda explores yet another kind of nimble movement, this time through a rewinding motion back in time to 1994 to witness an occasion of multivalence, a moment that exemplifies the multiplicity of the very kinds of thinking that can more broadly encourage other studies. It does so, not necessarily by always proposing new approaches, but by considering old ones in different arrangements of address.[3] Therefore, this coda also aims to illustrate that often what is needed to expand studies on African American photography is already in the historiography. To nimbly rewind is to explore and refine which groupings of ideas are worth reengaging in tandem. This coda offers but one example by turning back in time. Doing so highlights the kinds of diverse evidentiary materials that can create compelling constellations of ideas.

New Constellations

If creating new modes of thinking means, in Black feminist scholar Barbara Christian's words, fixing a new constellation of ideas for a time at least, then I propose the years circa 1994 as offering one important guide.[4] During these years Van Der Zee's photographs were set in motion through the tide of different kinds of narratives so that they could be reconsidered. Just as art historian Kobena Mercer has rhetorically asked, At what moment "does art history in the Black diaspora actually begin?," this coda reflects on the years circa 1994 when a concerted effort to analyze and critically respond to Black photographs and photographers first took shape.[5] In the pages that follow, I rewind through three interconnected events constituting this period: the essay collection *Picturing Us: African American Identity in Photography*; a major exhibition of Van Der Zee's work; and Lorna Simpson's tribute to Van Der Zee's practice and legacy, *9 Props*.

In 1994 Deborah Willis published *Picturing Us*, her seminal edited volume of scholarly and reflective essays, referred to as the "first of its kind within the realm of critical discourse in African American photography."[6] Also, in 1993–1994 a major Van Der Zee exhibition took place at the National Portrait Gallery, titled *VanDerZee, Photographer, 1886–1983*; its attending exhibition catalog offered the most in-depth scholarship on the photographer to date.[7] In addition, this coda positions Lorna Simpson as an interlocutor who engaged with the photographer's work during an artist residency in 1994 and in her ode to Van Der Zee, *9 Props* (1995). In tandem, when one considers this constellation of a conceptual contemporary art piece, an edited volume of autoethnographic essays on photography, and a conventional museum exhibition catalog, these instances set a new tone for thinking about Van Der Zee and, by extension, open the possibility of using various kinds of sources to rethink Black photography.

However, such intersecting perspectives were overlooked at the time. For example, in 1994 art historian James Smalls published "A Ghost of a Chance: Invisibility and Elision in African American Art Historical Practice," an article that considers the state of African American art history and the field's various shortcomings. While the medium of photography is nearly absent, one of the publications mentioned within his historiographical reflection offers a chronological, broad recognition of Black photographers. Published a few years before Smalls's article, Willis's *An Illustrated Bio-Bibliography of Black Photographers, 1940–1988* directly addresses the medium in what can be considered one of the earliest comprehensive considerations of Black photography. As Smalls makes clear, across all the artistic mediums, one of African American art history's major shortcomings is a lack of dynamic and critical examination of artists' work. Instead, a repetition of approaches and the valorization of the same set of artists marching toward canonization through their mere recognition become the norm. Writing in 1994, Smalls insists that this dearth serves as an Achilles' heel when existing scholarship does more in demonstrating legitimacy and competency rather than offering, as he writes, "critical probing into the substance and form of African American art."[8]

While Smalls sees the futurity of advancements in African American art, this coda takes the perspective that the building blocks of a more rigorous art history, especially when it comes to Van Der Zee, already existed circa 1994, specifically when looking beyond traditional art history.[9] As opposed to a too-narrow dependence on possibilities within the field for answers and directions, the best ideas can be found when significantly different interdisciplinary models collide. More explicitly, these didactic models can include a work of art, personal narratives, and an exhibition catalog—none of which traditionally take center stage in mapping one's methodology but which can and should if the goal is to push the limits of existing approaches.

Picturing Us and Centering Experience

A key aspect of this interwoven methodology can be found in the 1994 text *Picturing Us.* Renowned photo historian, curator, and photographer Deborah Willis's long engagement with thinking through photography yielded a life marked by many projects of note. One has served as a milestone, specifically because it takes a very personal and autoethnographic perspective.[10] The publication *Picturing Us* is a thematically organized collection of personal reflections on photographs of Black subjects, edited by Willis. Divided into four sections, the essays are written by a range of authors, many of whom are known in fields outside of photography. For example, Vertamae Smart-Grosvenor, the author of *Vibration Cooking, or The Travel Notes of a Geechee Girl*, a canonical book within Black food studies, is published alongside the Black feminist writer and professor bell hooks and E. Ethelbert Miller, the director of Howard University's African American Resource Center and the host of a weekly radio program at the time of the publication. In addition to Willis, authors Christian Walker, Clarissa Sligh, and Carla Williams identify as artists working in photography, while other contributors intersect with the museum world. Willis turns to this collection of authors, thinkers, policymakers, and creators to illustrate a critical engagement with photography—more specifically, the vernacular photography of quotidian Black living.

The essays attend to the contours of quotidian Black life and its entanglements with a praxis of image making and, most forcefully, image viewing: contemplating the absence of photographs owing to fire; turning to portraits to tell life stories about mothers; using the details of backdrops to locate a migration journey; sending photographs back south to family members waiting for news; imagining what it was like to reach out for the knob of the photo studio's door before entering; asking to make a copy of the only remaining photograph of one's father; considering photographs within photographs; reflecting on empty spaces on walls; encountering the likenesses of family members in unexpected places; exploring the intersections of photography and colorism; reflecting on when and where they first laid eyes on their selected photograph; and reiterating a photograph's role within different contexts.

The kinds of conversations found within the book, we can imagine, share much with those early encounters that Black viewers, image makers, and subjects experienced with photography from the time of its storied invention in 1839. But a collection of this kind of critical reflection, within the pages of one book, enacts a turning point in the publication of Black photographic history. Not long after the book's release, the artist and writer Bill Gaskins described the book as an "unprecedented act of art and scholarship" and reminded readers of its distinctness by insisting that "beyond their occasional place in obscure or marginalized journals, diverse writings on African American photographic identity by African Americans [have] been difficult to find in a single text."[11] More important, the book, as the lens-based artist Leslie Hewitt notes, "opened a world of criticality and emotion in [its] approach to photography, challenging [us] to see beyond the surface of things, to dare to uncover what lay unpictured, underexposed, or overexposed."[12] In *Picturing Us*, for the first time, an overarching view of various perspectives is gifted to the reader, along with an attending discourse to compare, contrast, and draw out the nuances of photography's role within Black life. The contributors make this kind of project possible by using their own personal encounters with images as a catalyst for serious reflection—a Black feminist approach that is now gaining more and more traction in studies engaged with African diasporic photography. Within this genre of writing, scholars Tina Campt, Nicole Fleetwood, Saidiya Hartman, Christina Sharpe, and others seem to lead the way by continuing where *Picturing Us* left off.[13] But proposed genealogies of thinking aside, let us return to the pivotal moment circa 1994.

The National Portrait Gallery and Its Touchstone Exhibition on Van Der Zee

Almost simultaneously with the publication of *Picturing Us*, another noteworthy development in the arc of approaches to Black photography took place on the walls of a national art institution. From October 22, 1993, to February 13, 1994, the National Portrait Gallery of the Smithsonian Institution in Washington, DC, presented *VanDerZee, Photographer, 1886–1983*, and published an exhibition catalog by the same title to accompany the show.[14] In addition to the Met, the institutional lenders of the 124 vintage and modern prints included the Studio Museum in Harlem; the Amon Carter Museum of American Art, Fort Worth, Texas; and the Museum of Modern Art (MoMA), while private lenders included Spike Lee, Donna Mussenden Van Der Zee, and Dr. Regenia A. Perry. The subject matter, including a mix of portraits of known and anonymous sitters, along with street scenes, reinforced and further cemented the iconic status of the photographs that are, to this day, familiar to audiences when Van Der Zee's work is considered. These include *Barefoot Prophet, Couple Wearing Raccoon Coats*, the *Black Elks*, portraits of Mamie Smith and Adam Clayton Powell Sr., photographs of the Universal Negro Improvement Association (UNIA) and Marcus Garvey, *Corsage* (which graced the catalog cover as well as a US postal stamp later in 2002), and the portraits of famous individuals taken in the 1980s when Van Der Zee resumed photography after a long hiatus. With this exhibition, Van Der Zee, a nationally recognized subject, took his place among other artists featured in solo exhibitions by the National Portrait Gallery, including Julia Margaret Cameron, Irving Penn, and Carl Van Vechten.

Whereas the exhibition featured 124 images, the exhibition catalog exceeded this number, with 187 photographs. Its two contributing writers, Deborah Willis (formerly Willis-Braithwaite) and photo historian Rodger Birt, authored in-depth essays on Van Der Zee's life and the significance of his work. While Birt penned a detailed biographical essay, Willis insisted on an important reframing of common approaches to Van Der Zee's work. In her scholarly essay, she critiques the limitations of viewing Van Der Zee as "a neutral observer of his times" and as a photographer who produces "a visual record of the emergence in America of the African American middle and upper classes."[15] Instead, she frames Van Der Zee as an innovative artist and one of the creators of Black visual culture during the Harlem

Renaissance era. She opens her essay by calling attention to the irony of a Black photographer with such a directorial style being cast as a mere neutral observer, as though his photographs simply reflected the times.

Willis's essay casts Van Der Zee as a significant figure within the history of photography, given his photographic skill and practice. As with *Picturing Us*, Willis accomplishes important space making through this publication. By offering a model of how one photographer could be recognized as aesthetically masterful, Willis makes space where few preceding publications of its quality, breadth, and depth on a single Black photographer existed.[16] She celebrates Van Der Zee's talent to an extent that led to her being reproached for overstating Van Der Zee's significance. One member of the editorial team insists that "the superlatives ('astonishing') need to be toned down."[17] The period around 1994 counted as a turning point indeed. The National Portrait Gallery catalog set the tone for the new terms of Van Der Zee's significance within the historiography at a moment in time when the talents of Black photographers were often overlooked and even challenged. No longer regarded only as a photographer documenting a community, Van Der Zee gained a heightened level of cultural cachet through the book's recognition of his artistic skills and vision. While autoethnographic approaches were drawing out the stakes of Black photography's address, ideas were also being stretched within the more traditional publishing outlet of the exhibition catalog.

Lorna Simpson's Homage

Referred to as a photo-text project, Lorna Simpson's *9 Props* (1995) is a portfolio of nine waterless lithographs on wool felt panels, attending to Van Der Zee's legacy (figure C.1).[18] Each panel contains a highly saturated black-and-white photographic print that depicts a piece of glassware, positioned on a table in front of a nondescript background. These objects are based on vases, goblets, martini glasses, and other props present in nine Van Der Zee photographs, the majority of which were taken in the early twentieth century.[19] Centered underneath each image is text detailing a title and date of the source photograph, followed by Van Der Zee's name and a description of the photograph to which the panel refers.

The glassware in *9 Props* was created during Simpson's artist residency at Pilchuck Glass School in Stanwood, Washington. Simpson had ini-

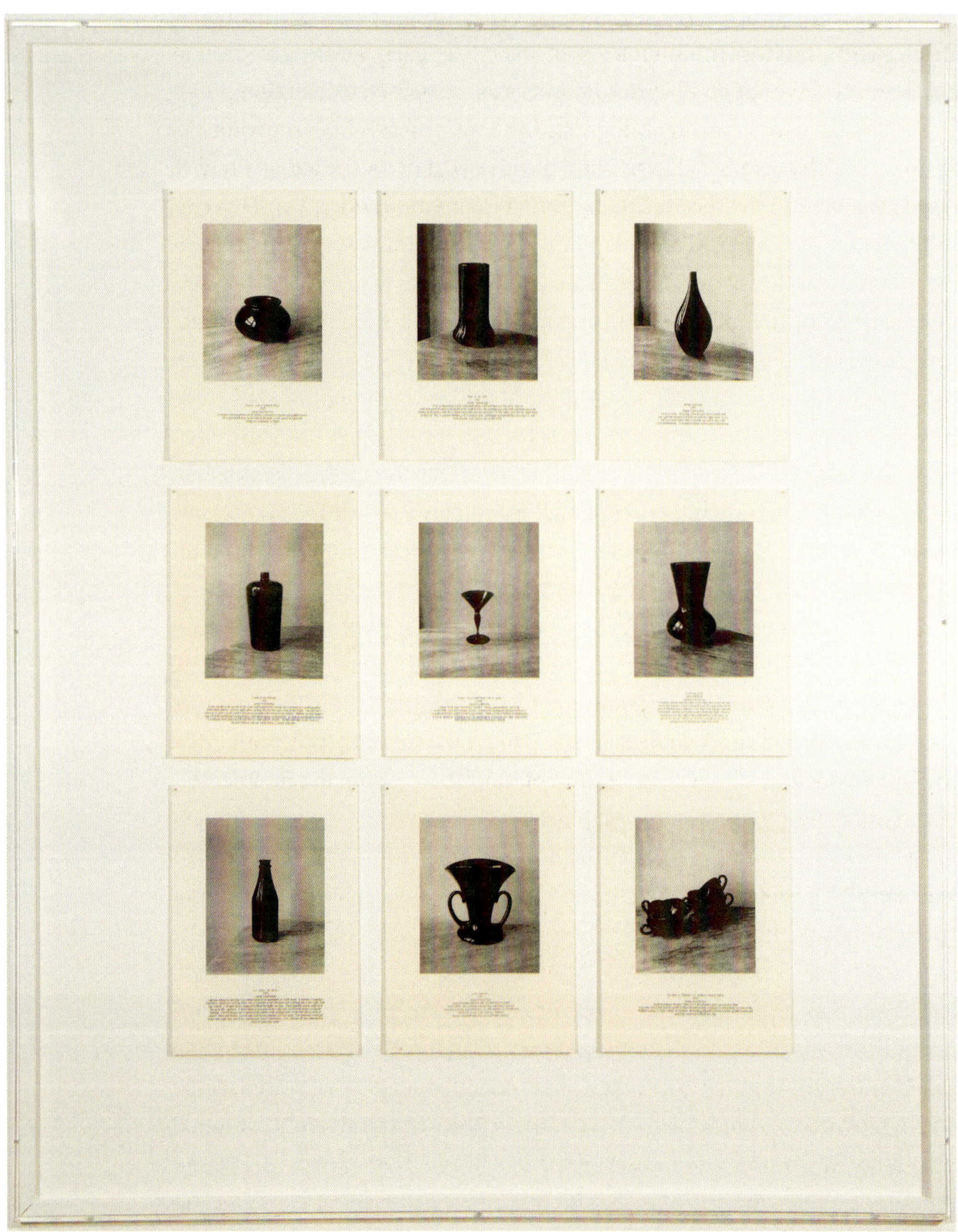

FIGURE C.1

Lorna Simpson, *9 Props*, 1995. Waterless lithograph
on wool felt panel.

15¾ × 11⅜ × 2¾ in. (40 × 28.9 × 7 cm). © Lorna Simpson.
Courtesy the artist and Hauser & Wirth, Zürich.
Source: The Metropolitan Museum of Art, New York.

tially intended to use her residency to construct an installation of vibrating glass objects, but that preliminary idea lost its appeal once she understood more about the culture of glass and became captivated by the theatricality of glassblowing.[20] While searching for a new direction, Simpson took a trip to Seattle, where she found and purchased a book she already had at home: the recently released catalog for the aforementioned Van Der Zee exhibition at the National Portrait Gallery. This text inspired aspects of the larger conceptualization of what would eventually become *9 Props*. Simpson requested that the gaffers assigned to assist her at Pilchuck blow replicas of Van Der Zee's props.[21] In the end, William Morris and Dante Marioni produced a number of large, smooth black-glass vessels.[22] After the residency concluded, Simpson shipped the pieces to her New York studio, where she photographed them. She later sent the images to 21 Steps in Portland, Oregon, where they were handprinted on wool felt, a material with distinct tactile properties resulting from its visibly compressed fibers.[23]

Simpson reflected on Van Der Zee through the art world context she knew best. As she explained in an interview in 1996, "To me, Nine Props has historical content. For instance, many people within the art world don't even know who James Van Der Zee is. Not that [*9 Props*] position[s] his work in a way that allows a lot of information to be gleaned, but on a certain level it's engaging a part of art history that does not seem of interest to the contemporary art world. The academy's canon has nothing to do with James Van Der Zee."[24] Simpson's piece *9 Props* enables a rethinking of Van Der Zee's impact across time and objects and therefore presents an amendment to the narratives that illuminate his work. If *9 Props*, as curator Jontyle Theresa Robinson posits, serves as a witness to Van Der Zee's sixty years of history, then this history is being imagined differently by Simpson.[25] Though Simpson notes that *9 Props* has "historical content," her project eschews a chronological presentation of Van Der Zee's oeuvre. In fact, the display of the nine identically sized panels in a neat rectangle visually reinforces a sense of timeless uniformity.[26] Furthermore, by omitting the language of respectability and upward mobility common to descriptions of Van Der Zee's photographs, Simpson allows his work to be seen as a generative site of meaning as opposed to a reinforcement or confirmation of an accepted historical narrative. Simpson's approach to Van Der Zee's work lingers on the visual elements of his photographs as opposed to being tethered to the preconceived understandings that Willis objected to in *VanDerZee, Photographer, 1886–1983*. Simpson offers a similar critique, not through the more traditional avenue of a published essay, but by using her artwork as a tool for theoretically reframing Van Der Zee's work. Through the very diverse outlets of a published collection of personal essays, an exhibition catalog, and a conceptual work of art, a proposition, or a road map for doing research on Black photography differently, emerges. To rewind back to 1994 offers an opportunity to highlight the multivalent ways in which images, like Van Der Zee's, have elicited a transformation in how we talk about photography.

Along the Arc

A reimagining of what future studies of Black photographers can look like depends on letting the complexity of African diasporic photographic practices—their diverse subjects, creators, viewers, and networks of interpretation and, too, the causes for their reconsideration—come into view with fullness and integrity. The forms can be works of art, different genres of writing, and a broader sphere of creative endeavors. Which constellations will others choose to highlight next? Might there be a return to the Van Der Zee archive for the purpose of placing one photograph alongside books, essays, objects, or personal memories that activate new correlations of histories, narratives, and approaches?

The archive, as I type, is moving from the boxes that it inhabited for decades to a new home within the same city, metaphorically being transported across land and sea to a completely different world. Married to the photographer in 1978, Donna Van Der Zee has singlehandedly continued to oversee the preservation of, access to, and legacy of a significant portion of Van Der Zee's work since his passing in 1983. Another portion of the collection has remained, almost untouched owing to legal limitations, at the Studio Museum in Harlem. The impetus behind this move represents several intersecting factors, which include the personal wishes of Donna Van Der Zee, who is now in her seventies. These materials are no longer cared for by one dedicated person but by a team of museum professionals; responsibility for this project and its range of possibility is now placed where wide-ranging public audiences can engage with the materials. The transfer of the Van Der Zee archive to the Department of Photographs in the Metropolitan Museum of Art has the potential to create another whirlwind of shifts and tidal changes in how Van Der Zee is understood. More im-

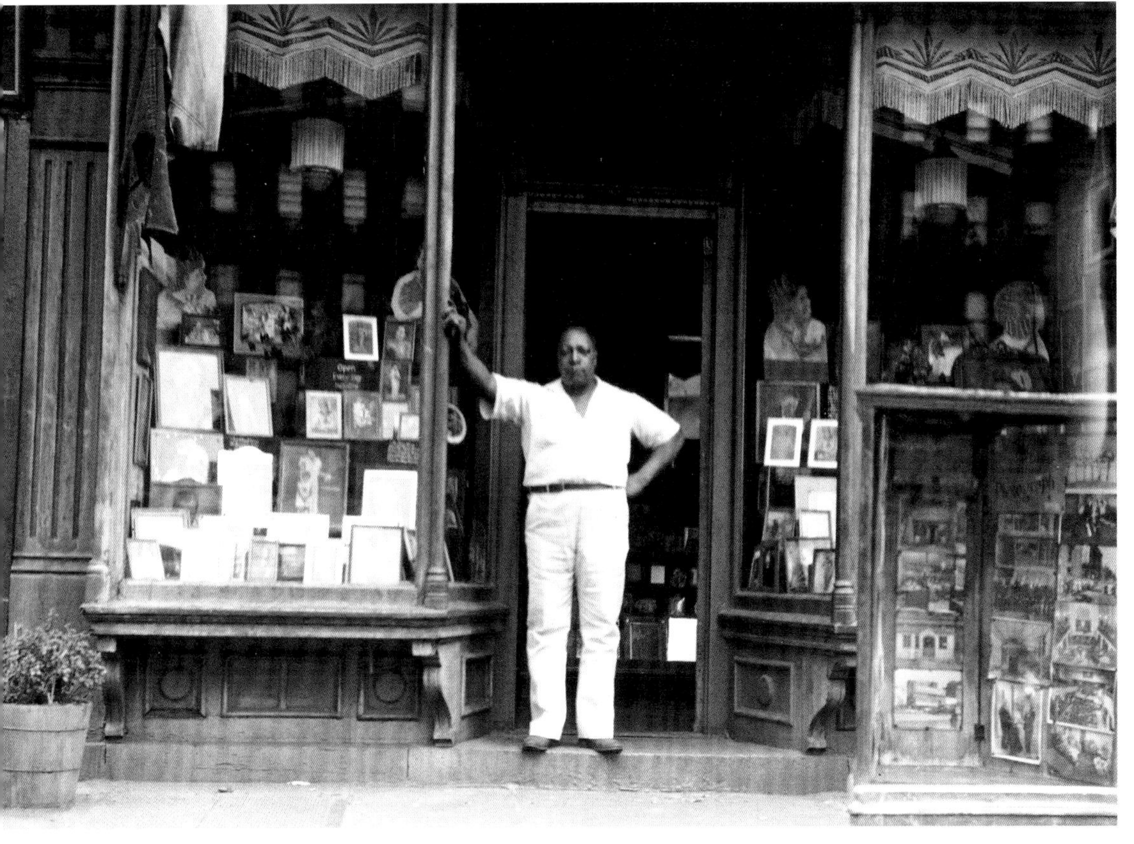

FIGURE C.2

James Van Der Zee, *Self Portrait, G. G. G. Photo Studio, 2077 Seventh Avenue*, 1937–1943.

4 15/16 × 7 1/4 in. (12.5 × 18.4 cm). © James Van Der Zee Archive, The Metropolitan Museum of Art, New York. Source: James Van Der Zee Archive, The Metropolitan Museum of Art, New York.

portant than the institutional placement of this archive, however, are the questions of those seeking out the works—and the insights articulated in their viewing of the collection over time. A cyclical relationship can come into view for all to see and for various constituents to participate in during this next occasion of constellation building. Each site of redress brings forth the multivalent meanings of and uses for Van Der Zee's body of work as the nimble arc continues (figure C.2).

Introduction

1   See Barthes, *Camera Lucida*, 43. An earlier reproduction of *Family Portrait* is included in the 1974 publication *Harlem, 1900–1929: Spiritual Home of Black America*, an exhibit portfolio edited by Louise Broecker on behalf of the New York Public Library's Schomburg Center for Research in Black Culture. The 1977 French version of Walter Benjamin's 1931 "A Short History of Photography" provides a second example. Titled "Les analphabetes de l'avenir" (The illiterates of the future) and published in the journal *Le Nouvel Observateur: Special Photo*, the essay included many of the photographs that appeared later in Barthes's *Camera Lucida: Reflections on Photography*.

2   Powell, "Linguists, Poets, and 'Others,'" 17; S. Smith, *At the Edge of Sight*; and Olin, "Touching Photographs." Also see the questions about scholarship's constant return to Barthes's idea of the punctum that are posed by Patricia Hayes in her conference paper "Photography and African History: Rethinking 20th Century Categories." Hayes, "Photography and African History," quoted in Gupta and Adams, "(Vernacular) Photography from Africa," 2.

3   Rodger Birt writes on the photographs of the period between 1900 and 1904 as exhibiting Van Der Zee's early mastery of exposure, development, and printmaking. Birt, "Life in American Photography," 30. Van Der Zee passed

away on May 15, 1983, while in Washington, DC, to receive an honorary degree at Howard University. His final photographic sitting, on February 5, 1983, captured the art historian and close friend Regenia Perry as his subject. Van Der Zee, Lawrence, and Perry, *Roots in Harlem*, 40.

4   The description of portraits as "something socially curative and familiar" is from Powell, *Cutting a Figure*, 177.

5   Willis, *Reflections in Black*, 42.

6   In December 2021, the Metropolitan Museum of Art established the James Van Der Zee Archive in collaboration with the Studio Museum in Harlem.

7   *Pop photographica* is a term coined by Daile Kaplan. Among her many publications on the topic, see Kaplan, *Pop Photographica*.

8   See advertisement for "Negro Art Photo Calendars, Fans, Blotters, Thermometers. Negro Subjects artfully posed, home scenes, beautiful women and children for advertising your business in a modern way." Negro Art Advertising Company, Cathedral 8–4070, 2077 Seventh Avenue, New York City, *Crisis*, May 1935, 130.

9   Batchen, *Each Wild Idea*, 57. Also see Cutshaw and Barrett, *In the Vernacular*; Campt, *Listening to Images*; and Campt et al., *Imagining Everyday Life*.

10   This statement parallels ideas addressed in Collins, *Black Feminist Thought*, 274–75.

11   Thompson, "Sidelong Glance," 23–24.

12   Crawford, "James Van Der Zee," 50.

13   For a compelling consideration of Black interior life, see Alexander, *Black Interior*. I use *Black quotidian* in ways that resonate with historian Matthew Delmont's use of the term in his book and digital humanities project *Black Quotidian: Everyday History in African-American Newspapers*. See https:// blackquotidian.supdigital.org/bq/overview, accessed December 15, 2022. The Black quotidian for Delmont illuminates instances that go beyond the iconic figures and key moments that commonly represent the definitive importance of African American history. Although Delmont uses the Black press as his entry, I turn to Van Der Zee and his practice in order to attend to photography's role in the complexities of everyday, mundane Black life. Also see scholar Nicole Fleetwood's scholarship on noniconicity and artist Derrick Adams's exhibition catalog for his show *Buoyant*. Fleetwood, *Troubling Vision*; and Adams, *Buoyant*.

14   Alternately, Campt uses the phrase "nimble and strategic practices" to describe the quotidian practices of refusal on the part of a photograph's subject in order to undermine the categories of the dominant. Campt, *Listening to Images*, 32.

15 I use the term *social life* here as Christopher Pinney does in his publication *Camera Indica: The Social Life of Indian Photographs*, to mean the social practices in which photography is embedded as though each photograph has a life on its own.

16 E. Edwards, "Material Beings," 67.

17 Hall, "Cultural Identity and Diaspora," 235.

18 See Arabindan-Kesson, "Caribbean Absences," 64.

19 Lee, "American Histories of Photography," 4.

20 Hayes and Minkley, "Introduction," 3–4.

21 Wofford, "Whose Diaspora?," 79.

22 Enwezor, "Postcolonial Constellation," 58; and Glissant, *Poetics of Relation*, 62.

23 McKittrick, "Dear April," 4.

24 Zuromskis, "Vernacular Photography," 1610.

25 Als, "First Step," 28.

26 See Thompson, "Sidelong Glance."

27 Raiford and Raphael-Hernandez, *Migrating the Black Body*, 5.

28 For a less extensive precursor to this argument, see Smalls, "Ghost of a Chance," 7.

29 See Quashie, "Trouble with Publicness."

30 See, among others, VanDiver, *Designing a New Tradition*; and Monahan, *Horace Pippin*.

31 Haskins, *James Van DerZee*, 10.

32 Thanks to curator Jeff Rosenheim at the Metropolitan Museum of Art for bringing this point to my attention.

33 Sassoon, "Photographic Materiality," 192.

34 Willis-Braithwaite, *VanDerZee, Photographer*, 128.

35 Sancho, "Respect and Representation," 56.

36 Muñoz, "Photographies of Mourning," 347.

37 Campbell, "Foreword"; D. Johnson, "Black Photography," 18.

38 Thaggert, *Images of Black Modernism*, 159.

39 The general acceptance of Van Der Zee as exceptional was hard-won within the early historiography by scholars including Regenia Perry and Deborah Willis. For example, for an account of how an editor in the early 1990s criticized Willis's description of Van Der Zee as inflating his artistic achievements and innovation, see Willis, "Why Deborah Willis Thinks the Photobook Can Be Transformative."

40 Examples, among others, include Powell, *African American Art*; and Hagen, "Black and White."

41 Cheroux, "Introducing Werner Kuhler," 23.

42 For another photograph of the Liggett's drugstore window display, this time by the photographer G. W. King, see Cutshaw and Barrett, *In the Vernacular*, 80.

43 Crawford, "James Van Der Zee," 51.

44 Cheroux, "Introducing Werner Kuhler," 25.

45 Writers used the phrase *vernacular photography* well before 2000. However, Geoffrey Batchen's canonical essay marks the start of a deep consideration of the phrase's implications and meaning. Batchen, "Vernacular Photographies."

46 Campt et al., *Imagining Everyday Life*.

47 Brian Wallis writes, "Vernacular photographs comprise the core of the visual culture of the modern era." Wallis, "Why Vernacular Photography?," 17.

48 This point builds on the following statement by Willis: "Van Der Zee's photograph of Marcus Moziah Garvey (1887–1940) at a 1924 UNIA parade depicts a popular, confident, self-assured black leader, a radical depiction for the time." Willis, "Photography (1900–1970s)," 113.

49 See Mooney, "Photos of Style and Dignity"; and Gates, "Frederick Douglass's Camera Obscura," 50, 51.

50 Tousignant, "Relocating the Vernacular," 69.

51 Quashie, "Trouble with Publicness," 329.

52 Quashie, "Trouble with Publicness," 336.

53 As art critic Antwaun Sargent writes, "The Black body . . . so routinely has his or her value tied to distress, labor or a moral, higher good such as liberty or equality." Sargent, "Derrick Adams," 10.

54 The full quote is "Vernacular photographs refuse to be organized or analyzed according to the paradigms that have guided traditional historical studies of photography." Cutshaw and Barrett, "In the Vernacular," 11.

55 "Monograph," *Oxford Reference*, accessed February 3, 2023, https://www .oxfordreference.com/view/10.1093/oi/authority.20110803100206229. For information on how the College Art Association, the major US-based association for professional art historians, has approached monographs within their focus and roster of publication initiatives, see Houser, "Changing Face of Scholarly Publishing."

56 Of course, it is also through his clients that Van Der Zee has gained his visibility as a photographer of exceptional aesthetic facility.

57 The term *hypervisible* has also been used to great effect and for different purposes by several scholars, including in Fleetwood, *Troubling Vision*.

58   Chong, "Photograph as a Receptacle of Memory," 130.

59   Kelsey, *Photography and the Art of Chance*, 4.

60   It should be noted, as Rodger Birt has, that Van Der Zee is included in H. W. Janson's *History of Art*, "what some would consider the 'official' history of art albeit as a source of 'great documentary value.'" Birt, "Life in American Photography," 191n89; Janson, *History of Art*, 801.

61   As Anna Arabindan-Kesson writes regarding African American art, "Our field need no longer be focused solely on gestures of space-making, but it seems, now, must consider what its position within academia entails. We have reached a point in which it is possible to make space to review the field, take its measure, probe its limits." Arabindan-Kesson, "Caribbean Absences," 68.

62   Sheehan, "On Display," 101.

63   This interpretation of decolonizing art history reflects the model offered by curator and photographer David A. Bailey: "When I was working on the Harlem Renaissance exhibition *Rhapsodies in Black* in the 1990s (with Richard Powell and Roger Malbert for the Hayward Gallery) our main concern was not to write and curate a counter black art-historical narrative but to produce one that was cohabited by multiple and diverse artists—black and white." Bailey, in Catherine Grant and Price, "Decolonizing Art History," 10. For other decolonizing art/history models, see Sifford and Cohen-Aponte, "Call to Action"; Holton, "Decolonizing History"; and Copeland et al., "Questionnaire on Decolonization."

64   For a full explanation of the mail fraud, see chapter 2.

65   Hayes and Minkley, "Introduction," 2.

66   See discourse on the importance of naming artists (and subjects within the art and visual culture) of the African diaspora, including text/projects by art historian Charmaine Nelson, artist Theaster Gates, author and activist Randall Robinson, and curator Denise Murrell. Nelson, "Introduction"; Theaster Gates, "To Speculate Darkly: Theaster Gates and Dave the Potter," Milwaukee Art Museum, Milwaukee, Wisconsin, April 16–August 1, 2010; R. Robinson, "Introduction"; Denise Murrell, *Posing Modernity: The Black Model from Manet and Matisse to Today*, Wallach Art Gallery, Columbia University, New York, October 2018–February 2019.

67   See Cozier and Flores, *Wrestling with the Image*.

Chapter 1. "More, Many More"

1   Davis, "Photography and Afro-American History," 27. Davis's statement resonates with Kellie Jones's assertion, written years later in 1990, "It is baffling to consider that in most art historical texts, a handful of practitioners rep-

resents the industry and ideas of 50 years, while hundreds go unaccounted for—until such time, of course, as they serve the purposes of the commercial or cultural power structure." Jones, "In Their Own Image," 133.

2   Mercer, "Art History and the Dialogics," 220.

3   DeCock-Morgan, McGhee, and Perry, *James Van Der Zee*, 9; Mercer, *James Vanderzee*, 4; and Willis-Braithwaite, *VanDerZee, Photographer*, 8.

4   For example, see Farrington, *African American Art*, 139; and the exhibition *James Van Der Zee: Collecting History*, Williams College Museum of Art, January 31–June 2, 2019, Williamstown, Massachusetts, https://artmuseum .williams.edu/james-van-der-zee-collecting-history/, accessed December 21, 2022.

5   Sheehan, "On Display," 97.

6   Campt, *Image Matters*, 17.

7   Arabindan-Kesson, "Caribbean Absences," 64.

8   DeCock-Morgan, McGhee, and Perry, *James Van Der Zee*, 12. Also see Van Der Zee's recollection of Eddie Elcha: "I watched Eddie Elker [*sic*] retouch in the early days. He was a pretty good photographer, and I got quite a few ideas from him about retouching. Then I expanded the technique." J. Van Der Zee, "Interview," 157.

9   Smalls, "Ghost of a Chance," 7.

10   Van Der Zee, *World of James Van Der Zee*, n.p.

11   Haskins, *James Van DerZee*, 49.

12   Birt, "Life in American Photography," 39.

13   "Toussaint" is an alternate spelling.

14   Birt, "Life in American Photography," 42; Haskins, *James Van DerZee*, 61; Pollard, "Harlem As Is," 197.

15   Haskins, *James Van DerZee*, 194.

16   The dates for Van Der Zee's studios are supported by existing scholarship and advertisements. For example, for the earliest advertisement of Van Der Zee's studio at 272 Lenox Avenue, see "Old Photographs Are Priceless," *New York Age*, November 8, 1941. Many thanks to Karan Rinaldo for this information.

17   Haskins, *James Van DerZee*, 205.

18   Beaton, *Cecil Beaton's New York*, 180.

19   Powell, *Black Art*, 53–54.

20   VanDiver, "Breaking Ground," 443.

21   Since Regenia Perry wrote the introductory essay to the calendar, it can be assumed that she also authored the descriptive text for each month. Perry's

caption for this photograph reads: "Couple in Raccoon Coats, 1932: January 1984." Perry, *Van Der Zee 1984 Calendar*, n.p.

22   W. E. B. Du Bois, "Opinion of W.E.B. Du Bois," *Crisis*, October 1923, 250.

23   Davis, "Photography and Afro-American History," 27.

24   Pollard, "Harlem As Is," 197. Pollard draws the boundaries of Harlem as being at Saint Nicholas Avenue on the west, 155th Street on the north, Madison Avenue on the east, and 125th Street on the south. Although I base my boundaries of Harlem on Pollard's statement, other scholars look elsewhere. According to scholars Shane White and Stephen Robertson, Harlem "boundary lines are based on maps in Gilbert Osofsky, *Harlem: The Making of a Ghetto* (1971) & James Weldon Johnson, *Black Manhattan* (1930), and are derived from the Federal censuses of 1920 and 1930, and the New York State census of 1925." See Robertson, "Putting Harlem on the Map," 188.

25   In a complete review of the available issues of Kodak's *Studio Light* from 1914 to 1945, I did not come across any evidence of Blacks as part of the photography studio world as portraitists, studio owners, employees, or clientele. The only individual photograph reprinted in *Studio Light* featuring a Black person is not a portrait but part of an image for a product. The photograph's intimate composition features a man's dress hat in the forefront held by a smiling Black man whose eyes concentrate on his task of grooming the hat with the help of a handheld brush. See advertisement, *Studio Light*, August 1928, 18. Per Deborah Willis-Thomas's *Black Photographers* (16), Van Der Zee appears in Kodak's *Studio Light* in 1982.

26   See advertisement for Sol. Young, *Evening World*, June 18, 1920, final edition, 14.

27   "Hundreds Routed Out of Homes by Blaze," *Evening World*, January 26, 1922, 9.

28   These other Black photographers include James Latimer Allen, Eddie Elcha, Austin Hansen, Robert McNeill, R. E. Mercer, Edgar Eugene Phipps, and Marvin Smith, and Morgan Smith. Willis-Thomas, *Black Photographers*, 13–22.

29   Birt, "For the Record," 39.

30   According to Camara Dia Holloway, "In part because his wife later threw out the boxes in which he stored the remnants of his New York studio, fewer than two hundred identified photographs by James Allen survive today." Holloway, *Portraiture and the Harlem Renaissance*, 11.

31   J. Van Der Zee, *World of James Van DerZee*, n.p.

32   Haskins, *James Van DerZee*, 190.

33   James Van Der Zee, audio interview by Benny Andrews, March 1, 1977, 30 mins., 47 secs., Camille Billops and James V. Hatch Archives, Stuart A. Rose Manuscript, Archives, and Rare Book Library, Emory University, Atlanta, GA.

34   Deborah Willis-Braithwaite, draft of an article later published in Willis-Braithwaite, *VanDerZee, Photographer, 1886–1983*. Deb Willis Professional Files, box 11, SC MG 452.

35   See "Enlarges Studio," *New York Amsterdam News*, December 3, 1930, 10.

36   Corbould, "Race, Photography, Labor, and Entrepreneurship," 144–45.

37   See Corbould, "Race, Photography, Labor, and Entrepreneurship."

38   1925 is the year etched in the lower left corner of the photograph, along with Van Der Zee's signature. Limited provenance information exists for Maurice Hunter's scrapbook from the Photographs and Prints Division, Schomburg Center for Research in Black Culture, New York Public Library.

For a history of American scrapbooks, see E. Garvey, *Writing with Scissors*. For more focused considerations on select African American albums, see Willis, "Speaking in Pictures"; and Raiford, "Soldiers and Black Beauty Queens."

39   For a comparison of Allen's and Van Der Zee's work, see, among others, Valdés, *Diasporic Blackness*, 122.

40   Holloway, *Portraiture and the Harlem Renaissance*, 7.

41   Corbould, "Race, Photography, Labor, and Entrepreneurship," 147.

42   Photography studios with Harlem addresses can be found under the lengthy listing for "photographers," as opposed to comparatively shorter sections for "photographic materials" or "photographers, commercial," whose services included work with drawings, maps, blueprints, and legal papers. Interestingly, a comparison between the Harlem-based studios listed in the 1919–1920 directory and those listed years later in the 1929–1932 directory, for example, illustrates the persistent presence of photography studios in Harlem but the lack of continuity and longevity among these businesses. I have chosen to compare these two periods to gain a better understanding of the photographic landscape in Harlem at a time that overlaps with Van Der Zee's most prolific years.

While my research is based on the *Phillips' Business Directory of New York City*, scholars Shane White and Stephen Robertson have compared Black business sources among a 1916 *New York Age* newspaper Black business survey, a 1921 *New York Age* newspaper Black business survey, George Haynes's 1921 survey of Black businesses, and James N. Simms's *Simms' Blue Book and National Negro Business and Professional Directory*'s 1923 survey of Harlem Black businesses. In terms of Black photographers, the 1921 *New York Age* survey lists five, and the George Haynes 1921 survey lists fourteen. See Robertson, "Putting Harlem on the Map."

43   *Phillips' Business Directory* (1919–1920). All but two businesses are individual entities with different addresses. Overall, the studio locations on busy Harlem streets—125th Street, Lenox Avenue, and Amsterdam Avenue—

situate the businesses as spatially central to the Harlem neighborhood. Every Harlem studio is listed here, at length, to convey the abundance of studios found within walking distance of Van Der Zee's locations: Alhambra Photo Studio, 2102 Seventh Avenue; E. W. Bailey, 112 West 125th Street; Berlin Studio, 250 West 125th Street; Diekmann and Co., 2423 Seventh Avenue; Julius Feinberg, 743 Lenox Avenue; Fordon Studio, 2138 Seventh Avenue; Sam Gardner, 68 West 116th Street; Gibson Studios, 262 West 125th Street; N. Giller, 184 East 124th Street; Harlem Photo Studio, 272 West 125th Street; I. Issoff, 42 West 125th Street; A. Konrad, 42 West 125th Street; Kron and Kollatz, 227 Lenox Avenue; La Marseillaise, 743 Lenox Avenue; Lopez Studios, 108 East 125th Street; A. P. Mitchell, 55 East 125th Street; Moss Photo Laboratory, 170 East 125th Street; C. E. Patino and Co., 110 East 125th Street; Philip's Art Studio, 137th and Broadway; Wm. S. Rich, 229 Lenox Avenue; L. Rosetti, 110 East 125th Street; Al L. Simpson, 113 West 132nd Street; Steinberg Studio, 1807 Amsterdam Avenue; S. Tarr, 164 West 125th Street; and Victor Photo Studio, 250 West 125th Street.

44   *Phillips' Business Directory* (1929–1932). The Harlem-based studios are J. H. Boozer, 673 Lenox Avenue; Claire Studio, 70 West 125th Street; Fordon Studio, 2138 Seventh Avenue; Gibson Studio, 264 West 125th Street; Selma Leeman, 23 East 125th Street; J. Levin, 115 East 125th Street; J. F. Lloyd and Co., 116 Lenox Avenue; A. P. Mitchell, 55 East 125th Street; L. Moss, 172 East 125th Street; Plaza Photo Studio, 42 West 125th Street; J. Randel, 1836 Amsterdam Avenue; S. Redfield, 112 East 125th Street; Rockwood Photograph Studio, 1836 Amsterdam Avenue; Rothman's Photo Studio, 187 East 116th Street; Victor Photo Studio, 250 West 125th Street; Clarence H. White, 460 West 144th Street; and Allen S. Winter, 116 Lenox Avenue.

45   The businesses listed in both directories were Fordon, Gibson, Mitchell, Moss, and Victor Studios.

46   In describing his move to his second studio, Van Der Zee says, "After 1930, I moved to Seventh Avenue, at 123rd Street. It was still white then, but changing." Quoted in George W. S. Trow, "Photographer," *New Yorker*, January 29, 1972, 30.

47   Quoted in Thaggert, *Images of Black Modernism*, 157. Also, for example, Stephen Perloff writes, "Van Der Zee is a totally naïve artist, a studio photographer who knew nothing of the work of other photographers, nothing of art movements." Perloff, *James Van Der Zee*, n.p.

48   Haskins, *James Van DerZee*, 150.

49   Azoulay, *Civil Imagination*, 70.

50   Trachtenberg, *Reading American Photographs*, 40. Also see Jones, "Dawoud Bey."

51   Audrey Peterson, "Eddie Elcha's Harlem Stage," *American Legacy*, Summer 2007, 39.

52   Peterson, "Eddie Elcha's Harlem Stage," 39.

53   David S. Shields, "Edward Elcha," Broadway Photographs, accessed May 2,
        2022, https://broadway.library.sc.edu/content/edward-elcha.html. Thanks
        to Eric Colleary, Cline Curator of Theater and Performing Arts at the Harry
        Ransom Center, University of Texas at Austin, for sharing his knowledge and
        the center's collection of theater portraits by Elcha.

54   Holloway, *Portraiture and the Harlem Renaissance*, 37.

55   Holloway, *Portraiture and the Harlem Renaissance*, 10.

56   Van Der Zee's studio, at this time, was practically across the street from Al-
        len's location.

57   In a letter between Alain Locke and James Latimer Allen, the prices of por-
        traits discussed were on par with Van Der Zee's fees as listed in figure 3.4, an
        advertisement titled "Old Photographs Are Priceless!" James Latimer Allen,
        letter to Alain Locke, June 4, 1927, Alain Locke Files, Moorland-Spingarn Re-
        search Center, Howard University, Washington, DC.

58   Holloway, *Portraiture and the Harlem Renaissance*, 12.

59   An additional example can be found on page 2 of the Saturday, April 9, 1921,
        New York Age of a decade earlier. The text of a short ad titled "Making Post
        Card Pictures" states, "There are several photographic studios in this block,
        of which the best known is the Guarantee Photo Studio at 109 West 135th
        street. This business was formerly located at 451 Lenox avenue, and moved
        to its present location two years ago. Besides having a large patronage, this
        company is making postal card pictures of the business places of interest in
        Harlem, and is also making a collection of pictures to include the Negroes
        of note in his country. G. G. Greenlee is the proprietor of the business.
        J. A. Vanderzee, the chief photographer, has had ten years' experience as a
        photographer here and in other cities."

60   The rest of the article states, "Modern journalistic trends give daily abundant
        proof of the wisdom that inspired the ancient Chinese proverb about one pic-
        ture being of more descriptive value than a thousand words. And nowhere is
        the value of the photographic art over the written word better realized per-
        haps, than in Harlem, where the public has the advantage of the facilities af-
        forded by the GGG Photo Studio at 2065–7th Avenue at 123rd street."
        "GGG Photo Studio Offers a Superior Photo Service," *New York News*, Octo-
        ber 8, 1932.

61   Willis, *Reflections in Black*, 44.

62   For example, Peter O'Tesky, the man Van Der Zee worked for at the photog-
        raphy studio in Gertz Department Store (listed in other sources as Hahne
        & Co. Department Store) in Newark, New Jersey, exposed Van Der Zee to
        a practice that sounds like the photographic silhouette. As Van Der Zee ex-
        plains, "I'd never seen the type of work he was doing before, 2½ × 2½[-inch]

glass plates. He had a projection machine and he would project them on the screen, cut them out, and paste them onto a card." J. Van Der Zee, "Interview," 154. In other sources, photographer Charles Gertz is the person who operated the photo concession and with whom Van Der Zee worked at Hahne & Co. Department Store. Birt, "A Life in American Photography," 39.

63   Willis, *Reflections in Black*, 44.

64   "James L. Allen Has a New Studio," *New York Amsterdam News*, October 19, 1932, 3; and Willis-Thomas, *Black Photographers*, 17.

65   "James L. Allen Has a New Studio."

66   C. Gerald Fraser, "Noted Harlem Photographer Is Dead," *New York Times*, May 16, 1983, https://www.nytimes.com/1983/05/16/obituaries/noted -harlem-photographer-is-dead.html.

67   "A View of the Photographic Studio of Thos. H. Green, Photographer of New York," *Crusader*, February 1921, 1012/12.

68   "Single Men Victorious," *New York Amsterdam News*, March 28, 1923, 4.

69   Advertisement for Cyrus School of Photography, *Crisis*, August 1931, 258.

70   Advertisement for Walter Baker's School of Photography, *Crusader*, October 1920, 883/21.

71   See Piper, "Cameras at Work."

72   Advertisement for Walter Baker's School of Photography, 883/21.

73   Advertisement for Walter Baker's School of Photography, 883/21.

74   Advertisement for Walter Baker's School of Photography, 883/21.

75   "Four Students of the Walter Baker's School of Photography," *Crusader*, February 1921, 1105/7. Also see Wallace, *Constructing the Black Masculine*.

76   Advertisement for Walter Baker's School of Photography, 883/21.

77   James Van Der Zee, interview by James Haskins, James Haskins Collection, Howard Gotlieb Archival Research Center, Boston University, 1976, 60.

78   I completed an unsuccessful word search in the *Jamaican Gleaner Newspaper* online database, and although other photography studio advertisements list "Jamaica, Long Island," I did not come across any with the name Walter Morace. For example, see advertisement for "Lucky Baby Contest," *New York Amsterdam News*, January 28, 1950, 6.

79   Hall, "Cultural Identity and Diaspora," 227.

80   Advertisement for William E. Woodard, *New York Amsterdam News*, May 2, 1936, 17. For more information on Woodard, see Mooney, "Photos of Style and Dignity."

81   Pollard, "Harlem As Is," 259.

82   For more information on Allen, see Moutoussamy-Ashe, *Viewfinders*, 60–71.

83   Nancy Kandoian, New York Public Library Map Division, email to author regarding the Lido Recreation Center address, April 16, 2014.

84   Finding aid for Manet Harrison Fowler Papers, 1913–1960, Stuart A. Rose Manuscript, Archives, and Rare Book Library, accessed December 8, 2015, http://findingaids.library.emory.edu/documents/fowler978/printable/.

85   Anna Hedgeman, interview by Katherine Shannon, July 25, 1967; interview by Robert E. Martin, August 27, 1968. Oral History Collection, Moorland-Spingarn Research Center, Howard University, Washington, DC.

86   Willis-Thomas, *Black Photographers*, 21; and Douglas Martin, "Marvin Smith, 93, Whose Photographs Defined Harlem Life," *New York Times*, November 12, 2003, https://www.nytimes.com/2003/11/12/business/marvin-smith-93-whose-photographs-defined-harlem-life.html, accessed December 21, 2022.

87   Morgan Smith and Marvin Smith, *Harlem*, 10.

88   Rozhon, "At Home with: Marvin Smith; The Heartbeat of a Photogenic Life," *New York Times*, December 25, 1987, https://www.nytimes.com/1997/12/25/garden/at-home-with-marvin-smith-the-heartbeat-of-a-photogenic-life.html, accessed December 21, 2022.

89   Wajda, "Commercial Photographic Parlor," 218.

90   See McMillan, *Front Room*.

91   "Enlarges Studio," *New York Amsterdam News*, December 3, 1930, 10.

92   "Enlarges Studio," *New York Amsterdam News*, December 3, 1930, 10.

93   James Van Der Zee, audio interview by Benny Andrews, July 1, 1975, 47 mins 19 secs, Camille Billops and James V. Hatch Archives, Stuart A. Rose Manuscript, Archives, and Rare Book Library, Emory University, Atlanta, GA. For more information on the unacknowledged/acknowledged role of Black women working with their husbands at photo studios, see Coar, *Century of Black Photographers*, 12. Also see Brady, "'Boss Lady.'"

94   "View of the Photographic Studio of Thos. H. Green," *Crusader*, February 1921.

95   Pollard, "Harlem As Is," 260.

96   Pollard, "Harlem As Is," 260.

97   A'Lelia Bundles, "Berenice Abbott's 1930 Photographs of A'Lelia Walker," Madam Walker/A'Lelia Walker Family Archives, May 23, 2011, http://madamwalkerfamilyarchives.wordpress.com/2011/05/23/alelia-walker-and-berenice-abbott/.

98   Willis-Thomas, *Black Photographers*, 20.

99   Raiford, "Marcus Garvey in Stereograph," 275.

100   Fanon, *Black Skin, White Masks*, 2.

101   Thaggert, *Images of Black Modernism*, 155.

102   Thaggert, *Images of Black Modernism*, 155.

103   Berger, "Man in the Mirror," 31.

104   For example, see Moten, "Case of Blackness," and Quashie, *Black Aliveness*.

105   Sekula, "Body and the Archive," 10.

106   hooks, "In Our Glory," 50.

Chapter 2. The Newspaper and Ubiquity

1   The concept of the photograph as a moving object has been engaged by a range of scholars, including Ariella Azoulay and Pamila Gupta and Tamsyn Adams. See Azoulay, *Civil Contract of Photography*; and Gupta and Adams, "(Vernacular) Photography from Africa."

2   Van Der Zee mentions sending a mortuary photograph to a family in California. See J. Van Der Zee, Dodson, and Billops, *Harlem Book of the Dead*, 85. A photograph from Van Der Zee's studio mounted on a wall in Sherman De Jesus's grandfather's home in Curaçao became the inspiration behind the documentary *The Photograph*, by Sherman De Jesus.

3   Van Der Zee states the following: "I became the official photographer for Marcus Garvey.... All the jobs I got, I always got paid before I went out.... I had an assignment to make the job, I'd make the job and I'd be done." J. Van Der Zee, interview by James Haskins, 18. Although Van Der Zee does not use the word *commission* but, rather, *assignment*, I will use the former term to describe their arrangement—as do other scholars.

4   Gilroy, *Black Atlantic*, 4.

5   Gilroy, *Black Atlantic*, 16–17.

6   In the transcribed interview, Van Der Zee states, "I became the official photographer for Marcus Garvey, Father Devine, Daddy Grace." J. Van Der Zee, interview by James Haskins, 18. Also see Birt, "Life in American Photography," 46–48. I use the term *official photographer*, as do Haskins and Birt.

7   This is the Reverend R. Van Richards, chaplain to the Senate of Liberia, mentioned in the *Negro World* spread featuring this photograph.

8   When this newsprint image of Marcus Garvey in a UNIA Parade is magnified, it becomes unclear who signed this version of the image reproduced in the *Negro World*, introducing the possibility that more than one photographer captured the same scene.

9   Many thanks to scholar Leigh Raiford for sharing her *Negro World* research materials following our 2013 meeting at the Smithsonian.

10   Willis-Braithwaite, *VanDerZee, Photographer*, 94; and Willis, "Photography (1900–1970s)," 112.

11   Gilroy, "Modern Tones," 105.

12   Raiford, "Marcus Garvey in Stereograph," 265.

13   Raiford, "Notes toward a Photographic Practice of Diaspora," 212.

14   B. Edwards, *Practice of Diaspora*, 6–7. This description of *diaspora* borrows from Anna Arabindan-Kesson's succinct articulation of the term. Arabindan-Kesson, "Caribbean Absences," 64.

15   Mercer, "Stuart Hall and the Visual Arts," 84.

16   Hall, "Reconstruction Work," 152.

17   At the time of his organization's founding, Garvey originally called it The Universal Negro Improvement and Conservation Association and African Communities (Imperial) League; he later dropped the word *Conservation*. T. Martin, *Race First*, 6. Although some accounts do not include Amy Ashwood as one of the organization's founders, Ashwood's central role in the creation of UNIA is considered an important part of the organization's history, thanks to scholars including Natanya Duncan.

18   T. Martin, *Marcus Garvey, Hero*, 36.

19   T. Martin, *Race First*, 9.

20   The exact dates of this temporary base for UNIA are unknown; it was most likely sometime between 1916 and 1918. For more details regarding this moment in Garvey's life, see T. Martin, *Race First*, 10.

21   T. Martin, *Race First*, 10.

22   T. Martin, *Pan African Connection*, 134. New Orleans, Mobile, and Charleston count as some of the cities in the United States that had a significant UNIA presence. For more information on UNIA's presence in the southern United States, see Rolinson, *Grassroots Garveyism*, 86.

23   New Orleans, Mobile, and Charleston are cities in the United States that had a significant UNIA presence. For more information on its presence in the southern United States, see Rolinson, *Grassroots Garveyism*, 86.

24   "Biggest Negro Convention in the History of the World," *Negro World*, June 14, 1924, 10.

25   Hill, *Marcus Garvey and Universal Negro Improvement Association Papers* (henceforth cited as *Marcus Garvey and UNIA Papers*), 5:xxxi.

26   Hill, *Marcus Garvey and UNIA Papers*, 5:xxxiii.

27   Crowder, *John Edward Bruce*, 156–57.

28   Colin Grant, *Negro with a Hat*, 2.

29   Hubert Harrison, quoted in Streeby, *Radical Sensations*, 198–99.

30   T. Martin, *Race First*, 14.

31   Hill, *Marcus Garvey and UNIA Papers*, 5:xxxvii.

32   Hayes and Minkley, *Ambivalent*, 3.

33   Wallis, "Dream Life of a People," 9–10; and Cutshaw and Barrett, "In the Vernacular," 16.

34   Birt, "For the Record," 48.

35   Birt, "For the Record," 46, 48.

36   J. Van Der Zee, interview by James Haskins. For more information on Prince Kojo Tovalou-Houénou, see Zinsou and Zouménou, *Kojo Tovalou Houénou*; M'Baye, "Marcus Garvey and African Francophone Political Leaders"; and Claude McKay, "What Is and What Isn't," *Crisis*, April 1924.

37   J. Van Der Zee, *World of James Van Der Zee*; Poupeye-Rammelaere, "Garveyism and Garvey Iconography," 14. The Van Der Zee portraits of the prince that are currently housed in a private family archive in France are most likely from this original batch of reproduced portraits, according to Olympe Bhely-Quenum. Bhely-Quenum, email message to author, February 3, 2014.

38   Vincent, *Voices of a Black Nation*, 20.

39   Reiss, facsimile of *Crisis* Christmas card, Carl Van Vechten Papers (1925), Manuscripts and Archives Division, New York Public Library.

40   Burns and Cleary-Burns, *News Art*, 11.

41   For example, in 1921 Van Der Zee advertised in the *Negro World*, and his studio was profiled in a short article published in the *New York Age*. "Guarantee Photo Studio" advertisement, *Negro World*, February 12, 1921; "Making Post Card Pictures," *New York Age*, April 9, 1921, 2.

42   Vincent, *Voices of a Black Nation*, 29.

43   For more information on Du Bois and the talented tenth, see S. Smith, *Photography on the Color Line*, 1–24.

44   "Thriving Business Enterprises of the Universal Negro Improvement Association Operated by the Parent Body, New York," *Negro World*, July 8, 1922.

45   "Thriving Business Enterprises," *Negro World*.

46   See B. Edwards, *Practice of Diaspora*; Leininger-Miller, *New Negro Artists in Paris*; Thompson, "Preoccupied with Haiti"; Vendryes, *Barthé*; and Baldwin and Makalani, *Escape from New York*.

47   B. Edwards, *Practice of Diaspora*, 2–3.

48   Locke, "Enter the New Negro," 633–34.

49   Harrison, "Our Larger Duty," 101.

50   An exception is a profile of the studio in a short article published in the *New York Age*, "Making Post Card Pictures," April 9, 1921, 2.

See Beaton, *Cecil Beaton's New York*, 162–74. Likewise, scholars rarely have opportunities to study how Van Der Zee's photographs were arranged and organized among his other photographs for early twentieth-century viewers. Rare instances of this include images highlighting sample photographs displayed in his Harlem studio, the arrangement of prints for sale in a Liggett's drugstore window case, and pages from a family album of his earlier years in Lenox, Massachusetts, the last of which was found in 2013 in the Derrick Beard Collection, temporarily held at the Kavi Gupta Gallery, Chicago.

51 Bieze, *Booker T. Washington*, 85–86.

52 The description of vernacular photography as comprising the bulk of photographic production can be found in various publications, including Tousignant, "Relocating the Vernacular," 62.

53 It is known that Van Der Zee advertised in the *Negro World* as early as 1921. For example, see "Guarantee Photo Studio" ad, *Negro World*, February 12, 1921.

54 Dahlgren, *Travelling Images*, 1.

55 *New York Age*, August 2, 1924.

56 The same issue contains a photograph of Garvey and Prince Kojo. *Negro World*, August 30, 1924, 3.

57 Colin Grant, *Negro with a Hat*, 185.

58 This essay considers only three of the four full pages of Van Der Zee photographs found within the *Negro World*. The convention-hall scenes captured on the fourth page modestly depart from this chapter's street-scene focus.

59 "Big Gathering of Negroes Will Be History-Making," *Negro World*, July 12, 1924.

60 "Huge Crowds at Liberty Hall Reveal New Spirit of Unity and Mass Movement Created by U.N.I.A.," *Negro World*, August 2, 1924.

61 "Fourth Convention of Negro Peoples Opens in New York amid Great Splendor," *Negro World*, August 9, 1924, 2.

62 See Gates, "Frederick Douglass's Camera Obscura," 31–33.

63 "One of Four," *Pittsburgh Courier*, May 21, 1929.

64 M. Garvey and A. Garvey, *Philosophy and Opinions*, 79.

65 Pascoe, *What Comes Naturally*, 183; and M. Garvey, "Essays on Race Purity."

66 For an extensive discussion of the significance of poor images, see Steyerl, "In Defense of the Poor Image."

67 Mercer, "Stuart Hall and the Visual Arts," 86.

68 Perry, "James Van DerZee."

69 Campbell, "Introduction," 36.

70 Perry, "James Van DerZee."

71 Esner, Kisters, and Lehmann, *Hiding Making, Showing Creation*, 11.

72 Pickens, *New Negro*, 231.

73 It is unclear whether or not Van Der Zee's original intention was to separate the two scenes before distribution.

74 William L. Sherrill, quoted in *Negro World*, "Huge Crowds at Liberty Hall."

75 G. E. Chamberlin, Consul, to American Consulate, Georgetown, Guiana, May 9, 1919, Subject: "Requesting inf[or]mation for the British Guiana Government concerning certain publications issued in the United States," republished in Hill, *Marcus Garvey and UNIA Papers*, 1:426.

76 See Postal Censorship Report [New Orleans, Louisiana, February 24, 1919]; Colville Barclay, Charge d'Affaires Ad Interim, British Embassy, to William Phillips, Asst. Secretary of State, Washington, DC, February 24, 1919; L. Lanier Winslow, Counselor, Department of State, to W. E. Allen, Washington, DC, February 26, 1919, republished in Hill, *Marcus Garvey and UNIA Papers*, 1:370–72.

77 Hill, *Marcus Garvey and UNIA Papers*, 10:lxxvi.

78 Hill, *Marcus Garvey and UNIA Papers*, 10:lxxvi; Postal Censorship Report, 371.

79 For an example, see the advertisement "U.N.I.A. Photo Sheet," *Negro World*, January 26, 1924. Also see Poupeye-Rammelaere, "Garveyism and Garvey Iconography," 14.

80 J. Edgar Hoover to Special Agent Ridgely, memorandum, Washington, DC, October 11, 1919, reprinted in *Garvey and UNIA Papers*, 2:72.

81 Smith quoted in Pisano, *Airplane in American Culture*, 119.

82 For more information on representations of the slave ship, see Finley, *Committed to Memory*.

83 Finley, *Committed to Memory*, 110.

84 Finley, *Committed to Memory*, 110.

85 Hill, *Marcus Garvey and UNIA Papers*, 1:407.

86 Hill, *Marcus Garvey and UNIA Papers*, 1:545.

87 For more information on image modification in newsprint, see Lester, "Picture Manipulation."

88 DJ-FBI, file 61, TD, Mortimer J. Davis, reprinted in Hill, *Marcus Garvey and UNIA Papers*, 4:546.

89 The 1869 trial of William Mumler, which revealed that two negatives were used to create a spirit photograph, illustrates the first famous episode of photographs manipulated to fool the public. Burns and Cleary-Burns, *News Art*, 7.

90 Hill, *Marcus Garvey and UNIA Papers*, 1:556.

91   *Mail Fraud Charges against Marcus Garvey: Hearing before the Subcommittee on Criminal Justice of the Committee on the Judiciary, July 28, 1987*, 2.

92   Hill, "Case of Marcus Garvey," 76–77.

93   Hill, "Case of Marcus Garvey," 66.

94   Hill, "Case of Marcus Garvey," 65.

95   Dancy was "a Pennsylvania railroad station cleaner who had purchased 53 shares of Black Star Line Stock." Hill, "Case of Marcus Garvey," 80.

96   Dancy's address was 34 West 131rd Street, New York City. Hill, "Case of Marcus Garvey," 83.

97   Hill, "Case of Marcus Garvey," 84.

98   T. Martin, *Race First*, 102; and M. Garvey, *United States of America vs. Marcus Garvey*, 3.

99   Marcus Garvey to Amy Jacques Garvey, April 25, 1926, letter text reproduced in Hill, *Marcus Garvey and UNIA Papers*, 6:423.

100   A few of Van Der Zee's mortuary photographs feature a deceased figure in a casket along with a superimposed image of the figure taken during his or her lifetime. Such examples suggest Van Der Zee's long-term relationship with some of his clients, in addition to his having had access to old negatives within his archive. For multiple examples, see J. Van Der Zee, Dodson, and Billops, *Harlem Book of the Dead*.

101   Hill, "Making Noise," 187.

102   Raiford, "Marcus Garvey in Stereograph," 272.

103   Hill, *Marcus Garvey and UNIA Papers*, 4:273.

104   Stein, *World of Marcus Garvey*, 37.

105   Stein, *World of Marcus Garvey*, 37.

106   This is a slight departure from Raiford's view of Garvey and Van Der Zee as having New Negro sentiments in common. For Raiford, "each was committed in his chosen vocation to renovating black self-perceptions. . . . Van Der Zee's portraits image exactly the self-possession and stability that Garvey hoped the photographer would bring to his summer-long commission with UNIA. These two men, placed side by side, would seem to form a stereograph, making tangible New Negro consciousness." Raiford, "Marcus Garvey in Stereograph," 273.

107   Kaplan, *Pop Photographica*.

108   Swann Auction Galleries, "Group Photograph of the Black Cross Nurses of the U.N.I.A.," lot 170, Printed and Manuscript African Americana, New York, February 25, 2010, https://catalogue.swanngalleries.com/Lots/auction-lot /(BLACK-RADICALISM—GARVEY-MARCUS)-Group-photograph-of-the -Bl?saleno=2204&lotNo=170&refNo=627967, accessed December 27, 2022.

109   T. Martin, *Race First*, 44.

110   Poupeye-Rammelaere, "Garveyism and Garvey Iconography," 15.

111   "Fourth Convention of Negro Peoples Opens in New York amid Great Splendor," *Negro World*, August 9, 1924, 2.

112   "Huge Crowds at Liberty Hall Reveal New Spirit of Unity."

Chapter 3. A Reframing of Value

1   *Recopy* and *copy*, terms Van Der Zee used in his ads and interviews, will be included throughout this chapter to refer technically to his practice of rephotographing old photographs and then making new copy negatives from which he could then make multiple copy prints. Many thanks to photography specialist Karan Rinaldo for her insight on this topic.

2   Shafran, *Restoration and Photographic Copying*, 5. Other guidebooks consulted for this chapter include *Kodak Data Books* on enlarging and copying from the 1940s to 1960s from the Laura Volkerding Study Center, Center for Creative Photography Archives, University of Arizona, Tucson.

3   Shafran, *Restoration and Photographic Copying*, 13. Also see Woodbury and Fraprie, *Photographic Amusements*, 71. While they offer instructions for "A Simple Method of Enlarging," their method assumes a glass plate negative, not the photographic prints actually sent to Van Der Zee for enlargements.

4   Here I use *orphaned image* as Tina Campt applies the term, borrowed from film studies, to amplify the social lives of these photographs as copied images. See Campt, *Image Matters*, 88–89.

5   See Thompson, "Sidelong Glance."

6   Cho, "Darkroom Material," 122.

7   Haskins, *James Van DerZee*, 205.

8   For example, see Sawyer, "James Van Der Zee," 177.

9   Powell, *Cutting a Figure*, 14.

10   Finley, *James Vanderzee*, 14.

11   Olin, *Touching Photographs*, 105.

12   Perloff, *James Van Der Zee*, n.p.

13   Haskins, *James Van DerZee*, 206. For example, see the ad for G. G. G. Photo Studio, *Sacred Heart Messenger*, January 1946, 79.

14   Birt, "Life in American Photography," 55. Also see Perry, "James Van Der Zee."

15   Birt, "Life in American Photography," 51.

16   J. Van Der Zee, interview by James Haskins.

17   Jennie Touissant Welcome continued to strategically use the pages of Black publications to advance her entrepreneurial project. See her advertisement trying to appeal to Black soldiers ("Attention! Wounded Soldiers Back from France") in *The Favorite Magazine*, December 14, 1918. Thanks to scholar Amy Mooney for bringing this advertisement to my attention.

18   "Crayon Portraiture," *Art Amateur* 12, no. 5 (April 1885): 107.

19   D. Van Der Zee, "Van Der Zee," 28.

20   Perry, "Introduction," n.p.

21   Perry, "Introduction," n.p.

22   However, Van Der Zee's camera appears in Anthony Barboza's photographs of Van Der Zee taken in the 1980s. Personal collection, Anthony Barboza.

23   D. M. VanDerZee, "Meet Mrs. VanDerZee," 24.

24   Also see Perry, "James Van Der Zee," n.p.

25   J. Van Der Zee, interview by James Haskins, 69.

26   Cho, "Darkroom Material," 122.

27   Augustus Wolfman, "Photographic Business in the U.S.A., 1950–1953," *Modern Photography*, September 1956, 295–96.

28   Blair, *Harlem Crossroads*, 8.

29   See Berger, "Man in the Mirror."

30   Fineman, *Faking It*, 31–32.

31   See Gordon Parks, "Harlem Gang Leader: Red Jackson's Life Is One of Fear, Frustration and Violence," *Life*, November 1, 1948, 97–104, 106.

32   Shafran, *Restoration and Photographic Copying*, 22.

33   Herbert C. McKay, "Notes from a Laboratory: Restoration Copying," *American Photography*, July 1948, 452.

34   Roach, "Culture and Performance," 125.

35   Diawara, "1960s in Bamako," 262.

36   Coar, *Century of Black Photographers*, 27.

37   See, for example, Stauffer et al., *Picturing Frederick Douglass*; and Grigsby, *Enduring Truths*.

38   Stauffer et al., *Picturing Frederick Douglass*, ix.

39   Shafran, *Restoration and Photographic Copying*, 6.

40   On portraiture, see Powell, *Cutting a Figure*, xv.

41   Brunet, "Introduction," 23.

42   See Sharpe, *In the Wake*.

43   J. Van Der Zee, Dodson, and Billops, *Harlem Book of the Dead*, 3.

44   Hartman, *Wayward Lives, Beautiful Experiments*, 348.

45   Sherman De Jesus, in conversation with author during taping for the documentary film *The Photograph*, summer 2018; and email exchange with Sherman De Jesus, May 23, 2022. Please note that there are multiple opinions on how this photograph came to be. See, for example, De Jesus's 2021 documentary *The Photograph*, which is based on the presumption that Van Der Zee took the photograph.

46   Roberts, *Transporting Visions*, 8.

47   For an explanation of stereographs and the armchair traveler, see Levine, "Introduction," 9.

48   See Zug, *Buying a Bride*; Stevenson and Jandl, *Houses by Mail*; and Robbins, "Fugitive Mail."

49   For example, see Dunbar, *Fragile Freedom*; and Cobb, *Picture Freedom*.

50   J. Van Der Zee, interview by James Haskins.

51   See Kelsey, *Photography and the Art of Chance*.

52   Scheele, *Short History of the Mail Service*, 173.

53   Holmes, "Wartime Photographic Activities," 288.

54   Scheele, *Short History of the Mail Service*, 173.

55   Holmes, "Wartime Photographic Activities," 289.

56   Quoted in Litoff and Smith, "'I Wish That I Could Hide,'" 103.

57   Scheele, *Short History of the Mail Service*, 293.

58   For example, see Willis and Krauthamer, *Envisioning Emancipation*.

59   Peffer, "Vernacular Recollections," 123.

60   Peffer, "Vernacular Recollections," 124.

61   Derrida, Richter, and Fort, *Copy, Archive, Signature*, 37.

62   Haskins, *James Van DerZee*, 147.

63   Thanks to Jeff Rosenheim, curator, Metropolitan Museum of Art, for bringing this possibility to my attention.

Chapter 4. Black Quotidian Experiences

1   Cooks, *Exhibiting Blackness*, 53.

2   Willis, "Introduction," 7−8.

3   Jones, *Dawoud Bey*, 66.

4   Willis, "Introduction," 8.

5   In addition, see the Metropolitan Museum of Art Archives *Harlem on My Mind* folders for extensive reportage on the activism and fallout that took

place over the exhibition catalog's anti-Semitic comments within an essay by Harlem resident and recent high school graduate Candice Van Ellison. Thomas Hoving records, 1935–1977, "'Harlem on My Mind': Cultural Capital of Black America 1900–1968," box 37, folders 1, 2, and 3, Metropolitan Museum of Art Archives, New York.

6   Batchen, "Vernacular Photographies," 269.

7   Hoving, quoted in Cahan, *Mounting Frustration*, 16.

8   "The Metropolitan Museum of Art Special Exhibitions, 1870–2017," Metropolitan Museum of Art Archives, 2018, https://www.metmuseum.org/-/media/files/art/watson-library/museum_exhibitions_1870-2017.pdf?la=en, accessed January 3, 2023.

9   Cahan, *Mounting Frustration*, 33.

10   Cooks, *Exhibiting Blackness*, 76.

11   For example, the exhibition *Thirty Photographers: A Selection from the Museum's Collection*, discussed later in this chapter, opened days after *Harlem on My Mind*'s closing, and the shows *Victorian Photography* and *Photography in the Fine Arts V* (a show of more contemporary images) a few years earlier, in 1967, speak to photography's changing status within the Met.

12   Jacqueline Trescott, "Unfaded Portraits of the Artist as an Old Man: James Van Der Zee," *Washington Post*, March 7, 1976, K1.

13   Daniel, "Photography at the Metropolitan," 110–11.

14   "Stieglitz into Metropolitan," *Time*, February 25, 1929, quoted in Daniel, "Photography at the Metropolitan," 112.

15   Daniel, "Photography at the Metropolitan," 113–14.

16   Photography in the Fine Arts: Exhibit V, miscellaneous ephemeral material, Mar. 15–June 11, 1967, MMA Vertical File, Thomas J. Watson Library, Metropolitan Museum of Art Archives, New York.

17   *Photography in the Fine Arts Exhibition V* (exhibition catalog), photo caption, 3, Photography in the Fine Arts: Exhibit V.

18   Press release, "Metropolitan Museum of Art Opens Exhibition of Outstanding Contemporary Photographs," 2, Photography in the Fine Arts: Exhibit V.

19   *Photography in the Fine Arts Exhibition V* (exhibition catalog), photo caption, 3, Photography in the Fine Arts: Exhibit V.

20   *Photography in the Fine Arts Exhibition V* (exhibition catalog), photo caption, 3, Photography in the Fine Arts: Exhibit V.

21   Press release, "Metropolitan Museum Exhibit Selected Works of Thirty Photographs Chosen From the Museum's Own Extensive Collection," 1, Photography in the Fine Arts: Exhibit V.

22 Press release, "Metropolitan Museum Exhibit Selected Works of Thirty Pho-
    tographs," p. 2, Photography in the Fine Arts: Exhibit V.

23 Meredith Friedman (now Reiss), formerly of the Department of Photographs,
    Metropolitan Museum of Art, email to author, September 22, 2014.

24 Cahan, "Inventing the Multicultural Museum," 92.

25 For example, see Hilton Kramer, "Politicalizing the Metropolitan Museum,"
    New York Times, January 26, 1969; and Jacob Deschin, "Harlem's History
    in Visual Survey," *New York Times*, January 19, 1969.

26 Goldin, "Harlem out of Mind," 65.

27 Kramer, "Politicalizing the Metropolitan Museum," D31.

28 In the article the photograph of the girl and the photomural is credited to
    Friedman-Abeles, as in Friedman-Abeles Studio, created by Joseph Abeles,
    Leo Friedman, and Sy Friedman. Kramer, "Politicalizing the Metropolitan
    Museum."

29 Kramer, "Politicalizing the Metropolitan Museum."

30 Kramer, "Politicalizing the Metropolitan Museum."

31 Kramer, "Politicalizing the Metropolitan Museum."

32 Kramer, "Politicalizing the Metropolitan Museum."

33 Cliff Joseph, oral history interview by Doloris Holmes, 1972, Archives of
    American Art, Smithsonian Institution, Washington, DC.

34 Joseph, Holmes interview. In another example, William T. William shared
    his thoughts on the *Harlem on My Mind* show at a symposium at the Met
    in 1969 called "The Black Artist in America," stating that the show was an
    "example of total rejection on the part of the establishment, of saying 'well,
    you're really not doing art.'" William, quoted in "The Black Artist in America:
    A Symposium," *Metropolitan Museum of Art Bulletin* XXVII, January 1969,
    246. Cooks echoes this reasoning in her own analysis of the show, writing
    that "painting would have testified to the artistic abilities of Black people and
    included their point of view" but that "Schoener chose instead to construct
    an exhibition that would re-create the way that he experienced Harlem on his
    mind from his position of privilege." Cooks, *Exhibiting Blackness*, 66.

35 Although I am unable to credit the photographer, the image is reproduced as
    figure 5 in Cahan, "Performing Identity," 433.

36 For an excellent overview of Kamoinge, of which Van Der Zee was not a
    member, see Eckhardt, *Working Together*.

37 For these and other exhibition examples, see Cochran, "Chronology of Louis
    Draper."

38 "Harlem," *Camera*, July 1966, 4, 25; Duganne, "Transcending the Fixity
    of Race," 190–99.

39   Benjamin, "Les analphabetes del'avenir," 19.

40   Cahan, "Inventing the Multicultural Museum," 63; Cooks, *Exhibiting Blackness*, 65.

41   Allon Schoener reproduced the letter in a PowerPoint presentation in 2006. The quote begins with the following text: "To have installed such a show at the Museum is more than an artistic or educational venture. It is, whether knowingly or blindly, a political act, and all the more vulnerable since it is clearly a break with ordinary museum policy. . . . Such a show was bound to be a political problem. There are too many violently conflicting interests in any large-scale statement about Negro history . . . for such an exhibition to escape the passions of militant groups." Allon Schoener, email message to author, December 22, 2014. Unfortunately, I was unable to track down the original letter. However, see Hoving's letter of response to Schapiro. Thomas Hoving, Metropolitan Museum of Art, to Meyer Schapiro, February 28, 1969, box 149, folder 5, Meyer Schapiro Collection, Columbia Rare Book and Manuscript Library, Columbia University, New York.

42   Blair, *Harlem Crossroads*, 245.

43   Deschin, "Harlem's History in Visual Survey."

44   Deschin, "Harlem's History in Visual Survey."

45   Deschin, "Harlem's History in Visual Survey."

46   Deschin, "Harlem's History in Visual Survey."

47   Kelly Baum, Maricelle Robles, and Sylvia Yount. "'Harlem on Whose Mind?': The Met and Civil Rights," Now at the Met (blog), February 17, 2021, https://www.metmuseum.org/blogs/now-at-the-met/2021/harlem-on-my-mind.

48   Roy DeCarava, in David Vestal et al., "Can Whitey Do a Beautiful Black Picture Show?," *Popular Photography*, May 1969, 79.

49   DeCarava, in Vestal et al., "Can Whitey Do," 80.

50   DeCarava, quoted in Vestal et al., "Can Whitey Do," 80.

51   Van Der Zee, quoted in Haskins, *James Van DerZee*, 230.

52   Margery Mann, in Vestal et al., "Can Whitey Do," 122.

53   To further consider the connection between refusal and photography, see Azoulay, *Civil Imagination*; and Campt, *Listening to Images*.

54   See Morrison, *Source of Self-Regard*, 265.

55   Cahan, "Inventing the Multicultural Museum," 54.

56   Thomas Hoving, quoted in "The Art World," *Negro Digest*, January 1968, 50.

57   Image found in installation photographs, box 1, folder 23, *Harlem on My Mind* exhibition records, 1966–2007, Archives of American Art, Smithsonian Institution, Washington, DC.

58   Cooks, *Exhibiting Blackness*, 62.

59 *Harlem on My Mind* exhibition records, 1966–2007. Although not all scholarly accounts recognize the existence of wall text in the exhibit, my statement
is based on viewing some of the original text panels that are held in South
Carolina State University's I. P. Stanback Museum Collections, Orangeburg,
South Carolina.

60 From the archived records, it seems as though—of the fifty-eight photographs in total used by the Met—forty-nine appeared in the exhibition as
photomurals, while the remaining photographs were only in the catalog.

61 Cahan, "Inventing the Multicultural Museum," 52. See also Clarke, *Harlem,
U.S.A.*; and Clarke, *Harlem*.

62 Genovese, "Harlem on His Back," 34.

63 Modernage Photo Labs did the printing, along with a company called
Compo. See Deschin, "Harlem's History in Visual Survey."

64 Peter Gravine of Modernage Photolabs, interview by the author, November
21, 2014.

65 Judging by the extant installation photographs showing Van Der Zee's photos,
we can conclude that only the aforementioned *Marcus Garvey in a UNIA Parade* was significantly cropped.

66 Although it is unclear what caused Braiterman to complete this report,
given the formal nature of its description and presentation, it can be surmised that the Met requested and paid for his services. See Meyer Braiterman's letter to Allon Schoener, January 25, 1969, regarding audience
response to literary items and related movement, *Harlem on My Mind* exhibition records, 1966–2007, Archives of American Art, Smithsonian Institution, Washington, DC.

67 *Harlem on My Mind* exhibition records, 1966–2007.

68 Willis-Braithwaite, *VanDerZee, Photographer*, 57.

69 See Perry, "Declining Years, Belated Recognition."

70 Haskins, *James Van DerZee*, 222–27.

71 Robert M. Smith, "Evicted Photographer's Work Is in Demand," *New York
Times*, April 9, 1969.

72 Willis-Braithwaite, *VanDerZee, Photographer*, 58.

73 Willis-Braithwaite, *VanDerZee, Photographer*, 58–59. For more information
about Broecker's role, see Deborah Willis Professional Files, SC MG 452, box 11.

74 McGhee, quoted in Birt, "A Life in American Photography," 57. Although
McGhee's encounter led to what has been referred to as a "discovery" or "rediscovery" of Van Der Zee, the sentiment captured in an August 6, 1975, letter by Ruth Sherman, a friend of Van Der Zee's, to Mr. Mel Tapley of the
Amsterdam News offers an important reframing. She writes, "There are those
who say that our 89-year-old Master Photographer, James Van Der Zee who

has been developing his art since age 14, was recently 'discovered.' I would assume that this means he was given the white seal of approval with its consequent exposure. However, the lists and lists of Black people who have been beautifully photographed by him attest to the fact that Black people discovered James Van Der Zee long before the 'Harlem on My Mind' show at the Metropolitan." Deborah Willis Professional Files, SC MG 452, box 12.

75 R. Smith, "Evicted Photographer's Work."

76 Teju Cole, "The Digital Afterlife of Lost Family Photos," *New York Times*, April 26, 2016, https://www.nytimes.com/2016/05/01/magazine/the-digital-afterlife-of-lost-family-photos.html.

Coda

1 Mercer, "Art History and the Dialogics of Diaspora," 214.

2 For an example of Van Der Zee considered in parallel relationship to African photographers, see Okeke, "Evidencing Selfhood."

3 For a parallel alternative to "rushing to the new," see Copeland, "Tending-toward-Blackness," 144.

4 Barbara Christian, quoted in Tinsley, *Ezili's Mirrors*, 1. Tinsley writes that Barbara Christian told her years ago that creating theory means "fixing a new constellation of ideas for a time at least." Also see Christian, "Race for Theory," 68.

5 Mercer, "Erase and Rewind."

6 Deborah Willis, essay draft, Deborah Willis Professional Files, SC MG 452, box 15.

7 Willis-Braithwaite, VanDerZee, Photographer, 1886–1983.

8 Smalls, "Ghost of a Chance," 4.

9 Smalls, "Ghost of a Chance," 5.

10 For reflections on the methods and challenges of autoethnography, see Ferdinand, "(Un)comfortable Truths."

11 Bill Gaskins, review of *Picturing Us: African American Identity in Photography*, *New Art Examiner*, November 1995, 49. For a 1990 bibliography of books and articles on Black photographers, see Willis, "Selected Bibliography." This bibliography does not include larger scholarly efforts within the African diaspora in the early 1990s to address photographers of African descent.

12 Hewitt, "List of Favorite Anythings," 28.

13 For example, see Campt, *Black Gaze*; Fleetwood, "Posing in Prison"; Hartman, *Wayward Lives, Beautiful Experiments*; and Sharpe, *In the Wake*.

14   Willis-Braithwaite, *VanDerZee, Photographer.* Willis also published her first monograph treatment of a Black photographer, James Presley Ball, in 1993. See Willis, *J. P. Ball.*

15   Willis-Braithwaite, *VanDerZee, Photographer, 1886–1983*, 8.

16   In addition to preceding books on Van Der Zee, other examples of monographs on Black photographers included Alinder, *Roy DeCarava, Photographs*; Dawson, *Sound I Saw*; Colombo and Beard, *John W. Mosely*; T. Johnson and Dunn, *True Likeness*; Livingston, *P. H. Polk*; Lomax, *P. H. Polk, Photographer*; H. Lewis, *Photographs of Harvey James Lewis*; Van Haaften and Willis, *Moneta Sleet, Jr.*; and Willis-Thomas and Dawson, *Introspect.*

17   Willis, "Why Deborah Willis Thinks the Photobook Can Be Transformative," 3.

18   Blair, *Harlem Crossroads*, 253.

19   The nine Van Der Zee photographs referenced in *9 Props* are (from top left) *Woman with a Goldfish Bowl*, 1923; *Beau of the Ball*, 1926; *Benny Andrews*, 1976; *A Man in His Bedroom*, 1931; *Dinner Party with Boxer Harry Wills*, 1926; *Reclining Nude*, 1920s–1940s; *Just before the Battle*, 1920s; *Max Robinson*, 1981; and *Tea Time at Madame C. J. Walker's Beauty Salon*, 1929. The Metropolitan Museum of Art has prints of *Dinner Party with Boxer Harry Wills, Reclining Nude*, and *Tea Time at Madame C. J. Walker's Beauty Salon.*

20   Simpson, "Artist Talk."

21   Simpson, "Artist Talk."

22   See the 1996 program catalog of the Pilchuck Glass School, Pilchuck Glass School records, Stanwood, Washington. Both Morris and Marioni are established glass artists.

23   S. Smith, *Photographic Returns*, 94. According to Majorie Devon, 21 Steps was known as "a workshop that specializes in waterless printing methods." Devon, *Tamarind*, 92.

24   In Simpson, "Lorna Simpson," 75.

25   J. Robinson, "Passages," 35.

26   Simpson, "Lorna Simpson," 75. For Simpson's intended ordering and display of the nine panels, see guidelines within the Lorna Simpson artist file, Modern and Contemporary Art department, Metropolitan Museum of Art, 2019.

Archives and Public Record

Andrews, Benny. Audio interview of James Van Der Zee, March 1, 1977. 30 mins., 47 secs. Camille Billops and James V. Hatch Archives. Emory University Special Collections.

Barboza, Anthony. Personal collection.

Beard, Derrick. Collection. Temporarily held at the Kavi Gupta Gallery, Chicago.

Finding aid for Manet Harrison Fowler Papers, 1913–1960. Stuart A. Rose Manuscript, Archives, and Rare Book Library, Emory University, Atlanta, GA. Accessed December 8, 2015. http://findingaids.library.emory.edu/documents/fowler978/printable/.

Harlem on My Mind exhibition records, 1966–2007. Archives of American Art, Smithsonian Institution, Washington, DC.

Hedgeman, Anna Arnold. Interview by Robert E. Martin. Transcribed oral interview, August 27, 1968. Ralph Bunche Oral History Collection, Moorland-Spingarn Research Center, Howard University, Washington, DC.

Hedgeman, Anna Arnold. Interview by Katherine Shannon. Transcribed oral interview, July 25, 1967. Ralph Bunche Oral History Collection, Moorland-Spingarn Research Center, Howard University, Washington, DC.

Hill, Robert. "The Case of Marcus Garvey." Testimony presented before US House of Representatives, 100th Congress, 1st Session, House Judiciary Committee, Subcommittee on Criminal Justice, Hearing, H. Con. Res. 84, Tuesday, July 28, 1987.

Hoving, Thomas. Letter to Meyer Schapiro. February 28, 1969. Box 149, folder 5, Meyer Schapiro Collection, Columbia Rare Book and Manuscript Library, Columbia University, New York.

Hoving, Thomas. Records, 1935–1977. Metropolitan Museum of Art Archives, New York.

Joseph, Cliff. Oral history interview by Doloris Holmes. 1972. Archives of American Art, Smithsonian Institution, Washington, DC.

Kodak Data Books. Laura Volkerding Study Center, Center for Creative Photography Archives, University of Arizona, Tucson.

Locke, Alain. Files. Moorland-Spingarn Research Center, Howard University, Washington, DC.

Lorna Simpson artist file. Modern and Contemporary Art department, Metropolitan Museum of Art, New York.

Mail Fraud Charges against Marcus Garvey: Hearing before the Subcommittee on Criminal Justice of the Committee on the Judiciary, July 28, 1987. Washington, DC: US Government Publishing Office, 1988.

Photography in the Fine Arts: Exhibit V. Thomas J. Watson Library, Metropolitan Museum of Art Archives, New York.

Van Der Zee, James. Audio interview by Benny Andrews, March 1, 1977. Camille Billops and James V. Hatch Archives, Stuart A. Rose Manuscript, Archives, and Rare Book Library, Emory University, Atlanta.

Van Der Zee, James. Audio interview by Benny Andrews, July 1, 1975. Camille Billops and James V. Hatch Archives, Stuart A. Rose Manuscript, Archives, and Rare Book Library, Emory University, Atlanta.

Van Der Zee, James. Transcribed interview by James Haskins, 1976. James Haskins Collection, Box 4. Howard Gotlieb Archival Research Center, Boston University.

Van Vechten, Carl. Papers. Series X: Scrapbooks (1906–1955). Mss Col 3142. Manuscripts and Archives Division, New York Public Library.

Willis, Deborah. Professional Files. SC MG 452. Manuscripts, Archives, and Rare Books Division, Schomburg Center for Research in Black Culture, New York Public Library.

Newspapers, Magazines, and Blogs

Art Amateur. "Crayon Portraiture." April 1885.

B., D. L. *Newsweek.* "Stompin' at the Met." January 27, 1969.

Baum, Kelly, Maricelle Robles, and Sylvia Yount. "'Harlem on Whose Mind?': The Met and Civil Rights." Now at the Met (blog), February 17, 2021. https://www.metmuseum.org/blogs/now-at-the-met/2021/harlem-on-my-mind.

Camera. "Harlem." July 1966.

Cole, Teju. "The Digital Afterlife of Lost Family Photos." *New York Times*, April 26, 2016. https://www.nytimes.com/2016/05/01/magazine/the-digital-afterlife-of-lost-family-photos.html.

Crisis. Advertisement for Cyrus School of Photography. August 1931.

Crisis. Advertisement for G. G. G. Photo Studio. February 1934.

Crisis. Advertisement for Negro Art Advertising Company, 2077–75 Seventh Avenue, New York City. May 1935.

Crisis. Advertisement for Touissant Conservatory of Art and Music. November 1910.

Crusader. Advertisement for Walter Baker's School of Photography. October 1920.

Crusader. "Four Students of the Walter Baker's School of Photography." February 1921.

Crusader. "New York at School." Advertisement for the Walter Baker School of Photography. May 1920.

Crusader. "A View of the Photographic Studio of Thos. H. Green, Photographer of New York." February 1921.

Deschin, Jacob. "Harlem's History in Visual Survey." *New York Times*, January 19, 1969.

Du Bois, W. E. B. "Opinion of W.E.B. Du Bois." *Crisis*, October 1923.

Evening World. "Hundreds Routed Out of Homes by Blaze." January 26, 1922.

Evening World. Sol. Young advertisement. June 18, 1920, final edition.

Favorite Magazine. "Attention! Wounded Soldiers Back from France." Advertisement for J. L. Van Der Zee. December 14, 1918.

Favorite Magazine. Jennie Touissant Welcome advertisement. December 14, 1918.

Fraser, C. Gerald. "Noted Harlem Photographer Is Dead." *New York Times*, May 16, 1983. https://www.nytimes.com/1983/05/16/obituaries/noted-harlem-photographer-is-dead.html.

Kaplan, Daile. "Pop Photographica: An Interview with Daile Kaplan." Interview by Michelle Hauser. *Design Observer*, February 8, 2012. https://designobserver.com/feature/pop-photographica-an-interview-with-daile-kaplan/31948.

Kramer, Hilton. "Politicalizing the Metropolitan Museum." *New York Times*, January 26, 1969. https://www.nytimes.com/1969/01/26/archives/politicalizing-the-metropolitan-museum.html.

Manhattan Tribune. "Artists Say: 'No Soul.'" January 25, 1969.

Martin, Douglas. "Marvin Smith, 93, Whose Photographs Defined Harlem Life." *New York Times*, November 12, 2003. https://www.nytimes.com/2003/11/12/business/marvin-smith-93-whose-photographs-defined-harlem-life.html.

McKay, Claude. "What Is and What Isn't." *Crisis*, April 1924, 257–62.

McKay, Herbert C. "Notes from a Laboratory: Restoration Copying." *American Photography*, July 1948, 452.

Metropolitan Museum of Art Bulletin XXVII. "The Black Artist in America: A Symposium." January 1969.

Negro Digest. "The Art World." January 1968.

Negro World. "Big Gathering of Negroes Will Be History-Making." July 12, 1924.

Negro World. "Biggest Negro Convention in the History of the World." June 14, 1924.

Negro World. "Fourth Convention of Negro Peoples Opens in New York amid Great Splendor." August 9, 1924.

Negro World. "Guarantee Photo Studio." Advertisement. February 12, 1921.

Negro World. "Huge Crowds at Liberty Hall Reveal New Spirit of Unity and Mass Movement Created by U.N.I.A." August 2, 1924.

Negro World. "Thriving Business Enterprises of the Universal Negro Improvement Association Operated by the Parent Body, New York." July 8, 1922.

Negro World. "U.N.I.A. Photo Sheet." January 26, 1924.

New York Age. "Legion Head Repudiates Garvey." August 2, 1924.

New York Age. "Making Post Card Pictures." April 9, 1921.

New York Age. "Old Photographs Are Priceless." November 8, 1941.

New York Amsterdam News. Advertisement of William E. Woodard photography studio. May 2, 1936.

New York Amsterdam News. "Enlarges Studio." December 3, 1930

New York Amsterdam News. "James L. Allen Has a New Studio." October 19, 1932.

New York Amsterdam News. "Lucky Baby Contest." January 28, 1950.

New York Amsterdam News. "Single Men Victorious." March 28, 1923.

New York Amsterdam News. "Van Der Zee Invents 3-D Camera." September 18, 1976.

New York News. "GGG Photo Studio Offers a Superior Photo Service." October 8, 1932.

Parks, Gordon. "Harlem Gang Leader: Red Jackson's Life Is One of Fear, Frustration and Violence." *Life,* November 1, 1948.

Peterson, Audrey. "Eddie Elcha's Harlem Stage." *American Legacy,* Summer 2007.

Pittsburgh Courier. "One of Four." May 21, 1929.

Rozhon, Tracie. "At Home with: Marvin Smith; The Heartbeat of a Photogenic Life." *New York Times,* December 25, 1987. https://www.nytimes.com/1997/12/25/garden/at-home-with-marvin-smith-the-heartbeat-of-a-photogenic-life.html.

Sacred Heart Messenger. Untitled advertisement for G. G. G. Photo Studio. January 1946.

Smith, Robert M. "Evicted Photographer's Work Is in Demand." *New York Times,* April 9, 1969. https://www.nytimes.com/1969/04/09/archives/evicted-photographers-work-is-in-demand-publishers-seeking-50year.html.

Studio Light. Advertisement. August 1928.

Time. "Stieglitz into Metropolitan." February 25, 1929.

Trescott, Jacqueline. "Unfaded Portraits of the Artist as an Old Man: James Van Der Zee." *Washington Post,* March 7, 1976.

Trow, George W. S. "Photographer." *New Yorker,* January 29, 1972.

Vestal, David, Roy DeCarava, Ray Francis, and Margery Mann. "Can Whitey Do a Beautiful Black Picture Show?" *Popular Photography,* May 1969.

Wolfman, Augustus. "Photographic Business in the U.S.A., 1950–1953." *Modern Photography,* September 1956.

Media

De Jesus, Sherman, dir. *The Photograph*. Utrecht, Netherlands: Memphis Film and
     Television, 2021.
Simpson, Lorna. "Artist Talk: Lorna Simpson." Video, May 14, 2010. Walker Art
     Center, Minneapolis, MN. http://walkerart.org/channel/2010/artist-talk
     -lorna-simpson.

Books and Journals

Adams, Derrick. *Buoyant*. Yonkers, NY: Hudson River Museum, 2020. Exhibition
     catalog.
Alexander, Elizabeth. *The Black Interior: Essays*. Saint Paul, MN: Graywolf, 2004.
Alinder, James. *Roy DeCarava, Photographs*. Carmel, CA: Friends of Photography,
     1981.
Als, Hilton. "The First Step of Becoming an Art Historian." *Black American Litera-
     ture Forum* 19, no. 1 (Spring 1985): 28–30.
Arabindan-Kesson, Anna. "Caribbean Absences in African American Art History."
     In *The Routledge Companion to African American Art History*, edited by Ed-
     die Chambers, 62–71. New York: Routledge, 2019.
Azoulay, Ariella. *The Civil Contract of Photography*. New York: Zone Books, 2008.
Azoulay, Ariella. *Civil Imagination: A Political Ontology of Photography*. Lon-
     don: Verso, 2015.
Baldwin, Davarian L., and Minkah Makalani. *Escape from New York: The New Negro Re-
     naissance beyond Harlem*. Minneapolis: University of Minnesota Press, 2013.
Barthes, Roland. *Camera Lucida: Reflections on Photography*. New York: Hill
     and Wang, 1981.
Batchen, Geoffrey. *Each Wild Idea: Writing, Photography, History*. Cambridge, MA:
     MIT Press, 2002.
Batchen, Geoffrey. "Vernacular Photographies." *History of Photography* 24, no. 3
     (September 2000): 262–72.
Beaton, Cecil. *Cecil Beaton's New York*. Philadelphia: J. B. Lippincott, 1938.
Benjamin, Walter. "Les analphabetes del'avenir." *Le Nouvel Observateur: Special
     Photo*, no. 2 (November 1977): 7–20.
Berger, Maurice. "Man in the Mirror: Harlem Document, Race, and the Photo
     League." In *The Radical Camera: New York's Photo League, 1936–1951*, edited
     by Mason Klein and Catherine Evans, 30–45. New Haven, CT: Yale Univer-
     sity Press, 2011.
Bieze, Michael. *Booker T. Washington and the Art of Self-Representation*. New York:
     Peter Lang, 2008.
Birt, Rodger. "For the Record: James Van Der Zee, Marcus Garvey, and the UNIA
     Photographs." *International Review of African American Art* 8, no. 4 (Sum-
     mer 1989): 39–48.

Birt, Rodger C. "A Life in American Photography." In Willis-Braithwaite, *VanDerZee, Photographer, 1886–1983*, 26–74.

Blair, Sara. *Harlem Crossroads: Black Writers and the Photograph in the Twentieth Century*. Princeton, NJ: Princeton University Press, 2007.

Brady, Emily. "'Boss Lady': The Diagonal Networks of African American Women Photographers from Reconstruction to the Harlem Renaissance." Master's thesis, University of Nottingham, 2018.

Broecker, Louise. *Harlem, 1900–1929: Spiritual Home of Black America*. Introduction by James Haskins. New York: Schomburg Center for Research in Black Culture, 1974. Exhibition portfolio.

Brunet, François. "Introduction: No Representation without Circulation." In *Circulation*, edited by François Brunet, 10–39. Paris: Terra Foundation for American Art, 2017.

Burns, Stanley B., and Sara Cleary-Burns. *News Art: Manipulated Photographs from the Burns Archive*. Brooklyn, NY: powerHouse Books, 2009.

Cahan, Susan. "Inventing the Multicultural Museum: A Critical Study of 'Harlem on My Mind.'" PhD diss., City University of New York, 2003.

Cahan, Susan. *Mounting Frustration: The Art Museum in the Age of Black Power*. Durham, NC: Duke University Press, 2016.

Cahan, Susan E. "Performing Identity and Persuading a Public: The *Harlem on My Mind* Controversy." *Social Identities* 13, no. 4 (July 2007): 423–40.

Campbell, Mary Schmidt. "Foreword." In *Harlem Heyday: The Photography of James Vanderzee; Portraits of the Harlem Community during the 1920s and 1930s*, n.p. New York: Studio Museum in Harlem, 1982. Exhibition catalog.

Campbell, Mary Schmidt. "Introduction." In *Harlem Renaissance: Art of Black America*, 11–56. New York: Studio Museum in Harlem/Abradale Press, 1987.

Campt, Tina. *A Black Gaze: Artists Changing How We See*. Cambridge, MA: MIT Press, 2021.

Campt, Tina. *Image Matters: Archive, Photography, and the African Diaspora in Europe*. Durham, NC: Duke University Press, 2012.

Campt, Tina. *Listening to Images*. Durham, NC: Duke University Press, 2017.

Campt, Tina, Marianne Hirsch, Gil Hochberg, and Brian Wallis. *Imagining Everyday Life: Engagements with Vernacular Photography*. Göttingen, Germany: Steidl/Walther Collection, 2020.

Cheroux, Clement. "Introducing Werner Kuhler." In Tina Campt et al., *Imagining Everyday Life*, 22–32.

Cho, Lily. "Darkroom Material: Race and the Chromogenic Print Process." *Postmodern Culture* 28, no. 2 (2018): 1–16. http://doi.org/10.1353/pmc.2018.0010.

Chong, Albert. "The Photograph as a Receptacle of Memory." *Small Axe: A Caribbean Journal of Criticism* 13, no. 2 (July 2009): 128–34.

Christian, Barbara. "The Race for Theory." *Feminist Studies* 14, no. 1 (Spring 1988): 67–79.

Clarke, John Henrik, ed. *Harlem: A Community in Transition*. New York: Citadel, 1964.

Clarke, John Henrik, ed. *Harlem, U.S.A.* Berlin: Seven Seas, 1964.

Coar, Valencia Hollins. *A Century of Black Photographers, 1840–1960*. Providence: Museum of Art, Rhode Island School of Design, 1983. Exhibition catalog.

Cobb, Jasmine Nichole. *Picture Freedom: Remaking Black Visuality in the Early Nineteenth Century*. New York: New York University Press, 2015.

Cochran, Sharayah. "A Chronology of Louis Draper, the Kamoinge Workshop and Significant Events of Their Time." In *Working Together: Louis Draper and the Kamoinge Workshop*, edited by Sarah L. Eckhardt, 284–94. Richmond: Virginia Museum of Art; Durham, NC: Duke University Press, 2020. Exhibition catalog.

Collins, Patricia Hill. *Black Feminist Thought: Knowledge, Consciousness, and the Politics of Empowerment*. New York: Routledge, 1990.

Colombo, Paolo, and Richard Beard. *John W. Mosely: Photographs, 1937–67*. Philadelphia: Temple University, Tyler School of Art, 1987.

Cooks, Bridget R. *Exhibiting Blackness: African Americans and the American Art Museum*. Amherst: University of Massachusetts Press, 2011.

Copeland, Huey. "Tending-toward-Blackness." *October*, no. 156 (Spring 2016): 141–44.

Copeland, Huey, Hal Foster, David Joselit, and Pamela M. Lee. "A Questionnaire on Decolonization." *October*, no. 174 (Fall 2020): 3–125.

Corbould, Clare. "Race, Photography, Labor, and Entrepreneurship in the Life of Maurice Hunter, Harlem's 'Man of 1,000 Faces.'" *Radical History Review* 2018, no. 132 (October 2018): 144–71.

Cozier, Christopher, and Tatiana Flores. *Wrestling with the Image: Caribbean Interventions*. Port of Spain, Trinidad and Tobago: Artzpub/Draconian Switch. Exhibition catalog.

Crawford, Joe. "James Van Der Zee: A Lot of Gratifying Things Have Happened." *Black Photographers Annual*, no. 4 (1980): 48–60.

Crowder, Ralph. *John Edward Bruce: Politician, Journalist, and Self-Trained Historian of the African Diaspora*. New York: New York University Press, 2004.

Cutshaw, Stacey McCarroll, and Ross Barrett, eds. *In the Vernacular: Photography of the Everyday*. Boston: Boston University Art Gallery, 2008. Exhibition catalog.

Cutshaw, Stacey McCarroll, and Ross Barrett. "In the Vernacular: Photography of the Everyday." In Cutshaw and Barrett, *In the Vernacular: Photography of the Everyday*, 11–28.

Dahlgren, Anna. *Travelling Images: Looking across the Borderlands of Art, Media, and Photography*. Manchester, UK: Manchester University Press, 2018.

Daniel, Malcolm. "Photography at the Metropolitan: William M. Ivins and A. Hyatt Mayor." *History of Photography* 21, no. 2 (Summer 1997): 110–16.

Davis, Angela. "Photography and Afro-American History." In Coar, *A Century of Black Photography, 1840–1960*, 25–28.

Dawson, C. Daniel. *The Sound I Saw: Jazz Photographs of Roy DeCarava*. New York: Studio Museum of Harlem, 1983.

DeCarava, Roy, and Langston Hughes. *The Sweet Flypaper of Life*. New York: Simon and Schuster, 1955.

DeCock-Morgan, Liliane, Reginald McGhee, and Regenia Perry. *James Van Der Zee.* Dobbs Ferry, NY: Morgan and Morgan, 1973.

Delmont, Matthew F. *Black Quotidian: Everyday History in African-American Newspapers.* Stanford, CA: Stanford University Press, 2019.

Derrida, Jacques, Gerhard Richter, and Jeff Fort. *Copy, Archive, Signature: A Conversation on Photography.* Stanford, CA: Stanford University Press, 2010.

Devon, Marjorie. *Tamarind: Forty Years.* Albuquerque: University of New Mexico Press, 2000.

Diawara, Manthia. "The 1960s in Bamako: Malick Sidibé and James Brown." In *Black Cultural Traffic: Crossroads in Global Performance and Popular Culture*, edited by Harry Justin Elam Jr. and Kennell Jackson, 242–65. Ann Arbor: University of Michigan Press, 2005.

Du Bois, W. E. B. *The Souls of Black Folk.* New York: Dodd, Mead, 1903.

Duganne, Erina. "Transcending the Fixity of Race: The Kamoinge Workshop and the Question of a 'Black Aesthetic' in Photography." In *New Thoughts on the Black Arts Movement*, edited by Lisa Gail Collins and Margo Natalie Crawford, 187–209. New Brunswick, NJ: Rutgers University Press, 2006.

Dunbar, Erica Armstrong. *A Fragile Freedom: African American Women and Emancipation in the Antebellum City.* New Haven, CT: Yale University Press, 2008.

Eckhardt, Sarah. *Working Together: Louis Draper and the Kamoinge Workshop.* Richmond: Virginia Museum of Fine Arts, 2020.

Edwards, Brent Hayes. *The Practice of Diaspora: Literature, Translation and the Rise of Black Nationalism.* Cambridge, MA: Harvard University Press, 2003.

Edwards, Elizabeth. "Material Beings: Objecthood and Ethnographic Photographs." *Visual Studies* 17, no. 1 (April 2002): 67–75.

Effinger-Crichlow, Marta. "Photos by Guarantee." *African American Heritage* 7, no. 5 (Nov.–Dec. 2005): 6–9.

English, Darby. *How to See a Work of Art in Total Darkness.* Cambridge, MA: MIT Press, 2007.

Enwezor, Okwui. "The Postcolonial Constellation: Contemporary Art in a State of Permanent Transition." *Research in African Literatures* 34, no. 4 (Winter 2003): 57–82.

Esner, Rachel, Sandra Kisters, and Ann-Sophie Lehmann. *Hiding Making, Showing Creation: The Studio from Turner to Tacita Dean.* Amsterdam: Amsterdam University Press, 2014.

Fanon, Frantz. *Black Skin, White Masks.* Translated by Richard Philcox. New York: Grove, 2007.

Farrington, Lisa. *African American Art: A Visual and Cultural History.* New York: Oxford University Press, 2017.

Ferdinand, Renata. "(Un)comfortable Truths about Voice, Authorial Intent, and Audience Response in Autoethnography." In *International Perspectives on Autoethnographic Research and Practice*, edited by Lydia Turner, Nigel P. Short, Alec Grant, and Tony E. Adams, 148–56. New York: Routledge, 2018.

Fineman, Mia. *Faking It: Manipulated Photography before Photoshop*. New Haven, CT: Yale University Press, 2012.

Finley, Cheryl. *Committed to Memory: The Art of the Slave Ship Icon*. Princeton, NJ: Princeton University Press, 2018.

Finley, Cheryl. *James Vanderzee: Harlem Guaranteed; September 12–November 2, 2002*. New York: Michael Rosenfeld Gallery, 2002. Exhibition catalog.

Fleetwood, Nicole R. "Posing in Prison: Family Photographs, Emotional Labor, and Carceral Intimacy." *Public Culture* 27, no. 3 (Fall 2015): 487–511.

Fleetwood, Nicole R. *Troubling Vision: Performance, Visuality, and Blackness*. Chicago: University of Chicago Press, 2010.

Garvey, Ellen G. *Writing with Scissors: American Scrapbooks from the Civil War to the Harlem Renaissance*. New York: Oxford University Press, 2013.

Garvey, Marcus. "Essays on Race Purity by Marcus Garvey." In *The Marcus Garvey and Universal Negro Improvement Association Papers. Vol. 4: September 1921–September 1922*, edited by Robert A. Hill, 217–20. Berkeley: University of California Press, 1989.

Garvey, Marcus. *United States of America vs. Marcus Garvey: Was Justice Defeated?* New York: n.p., 1925.

Garvey, Marcus, and Amy J. Garvey. *The Philosophy and Opinions of Marcus Garvey, or, Africa for the Africans*. Dover, MA: Majority Press, 1986.

Gates, Henry Louis, Jr. "Frederick Douglass's Camera Obscura: Representing the Antislave 'Clothed and in Their Own Form.'" *Critical Inquiry* 42, no. 1 (Autumn 2015): 31–60.

Genovese, Eugene D. "Harlem on His Back: An Historian Looks at Hoving's Harlem." *Artforum* 7, no. 6 (February 1969): 34–37.

Gilroy, Paul. *The Black Atlantic: Modernity and Double Consciousness*. Cambridge, MA: Harvard University Press, 1993.

Gilroy, Paul. "Modern Tones." In *Rhapsodies in Black: Art of the Harlem Renaissance*, edited by Joanna Skipwith, 102–53. London: Hayward Gallery, 1997.

Glissant, Édouard. *Poetics of Relation*. Ann Arbor: University of Michigan Press, 1997.

Goldin, Amy. "Harlem out of Mind." *Art News* 68, no. 1 (1969): 52–65.

Grant, Catherine, and Dorothy Price. "Decolonizing Art History." *Art History* 43, no. 1 (February 2020): 8–66.

Grant, Colin. *Negro with a Hat: The Rise and Fall of Marcus Garvey and His Dream of Mother Africa*. New York: Oxford University Press, 2008.

Grigsby, Darcy G. *Enduring Truths: Sojourner's Shadows and Substance*. Chicago: University of Chicago Press, 2015.

Gupta, Pamila, and Tamsyn Adams. "(Vernacular) Photography from Africa: Collections, Preservation, Dialogue." *Critical Arts* 32, no. 1 (2018): 1–12.

Hagen, Charles. "Black and White." *Art and Antiques* 17, no. 6 (Summer 1994): 68–75.

Hall, Stuart. "Cultural Identity and Diaspora." In *Identity, Community, Culture, Difference*, edited by Jonathan Rutherford, 222–37. London: Lawrence and Wishart, 1990.

Hall, Stuart. "Reconstruction Work: Images of Post-war Black Settlement." In *Family Snaps: The Meaning of Domestic Photography*, edited by Patricia Holland and Jo Spence, 152–64. London: Virago, 1991.

Harrison, Hubert. "Our Larger Duty." In *A Hubert Harrison Reader*, edited by Jeffrey B. Perry, 99–101. Middletown, CT: Wesleyan University Press, 2001.

Hartman, Saidiya. *Wayward Lives, Beautiful Experiments: Intimate Histories of Social Upheaval*. New York: W. W. Norton, 2019.

Haskins, James. *James Van DerZee, the Picture-Takin' Man*. Trenton, NJ: Africa World Press, 1991.

Hayes, Patricia. "Photography and African History: Rethinking 20th Century Categories." Paper presented at University of Johannesburg, Visual Identities in Art and Design (VIAD) Research Centre, October 2017.

Hayes, Patricia, and Gary Minkley, eds. *Ambivalent: Photography and Visibility in African History*. Athens: Ohio University Press, 2019.

Hayes, Patricia, and Gary Minkley. "Introduction: Africa and the Ambivalence of Seeing." In Hayes and Minkley, *Ambivalent: Photography and Visibility in African History*, 1–34.

Hewitt, Leslie. "A List of Favorite Anythings." In *It's All Dreaming: Essential Writings about Photography from Aperture*, edited by the editors at *Aperture*, 26–30. New York: Aperture, 2018. https://www.photopedagogy.com/uploads/5/0/0/9/50097419/aperture_guide_2018_final.pdf.

Hill, Robert. "Making Noise: Marcus Garvey Dada, August 1922." In Willis, *Picturing Us: African American Identity in Photography*, 181–205.

Hill, Robert, ed. *The Marcus Garvey and Universal Negro Improvement Association Papers*. Vols. 1–10. Berkeley: University of California Press, 1983–2006.

Holloway, Camara Dia. *Portraiture and the Harlem Renaissance: The Photographs of James L. Allen*. New Haven, CT: Yale University Art Gallery, 1999.

Holmes, Donald. "Wartime Photographic Activities and Records Resulting Therefrom." *American Archivist* 10, no. 3 (July 1947): 287–93.

Holton, Adalaine. "Decolonizing History: Arthur Schomburg's Afrodiasporic Archive." *Journal of African American History* 92, no. 2 (Spring 2007): 218–38.

hooks, bell. "In Our Glory: Photography and Black Life." In Willis, *Picturing Us: African American Identity in Photography*, 43–54.

Houser, Craig. "The Changing Face of Scholarly Publishing: CAA's Publications Program." In *The Eye, the Hand, the Mind: 100 Years of the College Art Association*, edited by Susan Ball, 47–88. New Brunswick, NJ: Rutgers University Press, 2011.

Janson, H. W. *History of Art*. New York: Abrams, 1991.

Johnson, Deborah J. "Black Photography: Contexts for Evolution." In Coar, *A Century of Black Photographers, 1840–1960*, 15–20.

Johnson, Thomas L., and Phillip C. Dunn. *A True Likeness: The Black South of Richard Samuel Roberts, 1920–1936*. Columbia, SC: Bruccoli and Clark, 1986.

Jones, Kellie. "Dawoud Bey: Portraits in the Theater of Desire." In *EyeMinded: Living and Writing Contemporary Art*, 187–206. Durham, NC: Duke University Press, 2011.

Jones, Kellie. *Dawoud Bey: Portraits, 1975–1995*. Minneapolis: Walker Art Center, 1995. Exhibition catalog.

Jones, Kellie. "In Their Own Image." *Artforum* 29, no. 3 (Nov. 1990): 133–38.

Kaplan, Daile. *Pop Photographica: Image Objects*. New York: Poppy Press, 2014. Exhibition catalog.

Kelsey, Robin E. *Photography and the Art of Chance*. Cambridge, MA: Belknap Press, 2015.

Lee, Anthony W. "American Histories of Photography." *American Art* 21, no. 3 (Fall 2007): 2–9.

Leininger-Miller, Theresa A. *New Negro Artists in Paris: African American Painters and Sculptors in the City of Light, 1922–1934*. New Brunswick, NJ: Rutgers University Press, 2001.

Lester, Paul Martin. "Picture Manipulation." In *Photojournalism: An Ethical Approach*, 90–132. London: Routledge, 2016.

Levine, Barbara. "Introduction: Confessions of an Armchair Traveler." In *Around the World: The Grand Tour in Photo Albums*, edited by Barbara Levine and Kirsten Jensen, 8–15. Princeton, NJ: Princeton Architectural Press, 2007.

Lewis, Harvey James. *The Photographs of Harvey James Lewis (1878–1968)*. Chicago: Black Woman Collaborative, 1981.

Litoff, Judy Barrett, and David C. Smith. "'I Wish That I Could Hide Inside This Letter': World War II Correspondence." *Prologue: The Journal of the National Archives*, no. 24 (Summer 1992): 103–114.

Livingston, Jane. *P. H. Polk*. Washington, DC: Corcoran Gallery of Art, 1981. Exhibition catalog.

Locke, Alain. "Enter the New Negro." *Survey Graphic* 6 (March 1925): 631–35.

Lomax, Pearl Cleage. *P. H. Polk, Photographer*. Atlanta: Nexus, 1980.

Martin, Tony. *Marcus Garvey, Hero: A First Biography*. Dover, MA: Majority Press, 1983.

Martin, Tony. *The Pan African Connection: From Slavery to Garvey and Beyond*. Dover, MA: Majority Press, 1984.

Martin, Tony. *Race First: The Ideological and Organizational Struggles of Marcus Garvey and the Universal Negro Improvement Association*. Dover, MA: Majority Press, 1986.

M'Baye, Babacar. "Marcus Garvey and African Francophone Political Leaders of the Early Twentieth Century: Prince Kojo Tovalou Houenou Reconsidered." *Journal of Pan African Studies* 1, no. 5 (September 2006): 1–10.

McKittrick, Katherine. "Dear April: The Aesthetics of Black Miscellanea." *Antipode* 54, no. 1 (January 2022): 3–18.

McMillan, Michael. *The Front Room: Migrant Aesthetics in the Home*. London: Black Dog, 2009.

Mercer, Kobena. "Art History and the Dialogics of Diaspora." *Small Axe: A Caribbean Journal of Criticism* 16, no. 2 (July 2012): 213–27.

Mercer, Kobena. "Erase and Rewind: When Does Art History in the Black Diaspora Actually Begin?" In *The Migrant's Time: Rethinking Art History and Diaspora*, edited by Saloni Mathur, 17–31. Williamstown, MA: Sterling and Francine Clark Art Institute, 2011.

Mercer, Kobena. *James Vanderzee*. London: Phaidon, 2003.

Mercer, Kobena. "Stuart Hall and the Visual Arts." *Small Axe: A Caribbean Journal of Criticism* 19, no. 1 (March 2015): 78–87.

Monahan, Anne. *Horace Pippin: American Modern*. New Haven, CT: Yale University Press, 2020.

Mooney, Amy. "Photos of Style and Dignity: Woodard's Studio and the Delivery of Black Modern Subjectivity." In *Beyond the Face: New Perspectives on Portraiture*, edited by Wendy W. Reaves, 212–31. Washington, DC: National Portrait Gallery, Smithsonian Institution, 2018.

Morrison, Toni. *The Source of Self-Regard: Selected Essays, Speeches, and Meditations*. New York: Alfred A. Knopf, 2019.

Moten, Fred. "The Case of Blackness." *Criticism* 50, no. 2 (2008): 177–218.

Moutoussamy-Ashe, Jeanne. *Viewfinders: Black Women Photographers*. New York: Dodd, Mead, 1986.

Muñoz, José E. "Photographies of Mourning: Melancholia and Ambivalence in Van Der Zee, Mapplethorpe, and *Looking for Langston*." In *Race and the Subject of Masculinities*, edited by Harry Stecopoulos and Michael Uebel, 337–58. Durham, NC: Duke University Press, 1997.

Murrell, Denise. *Posing Modernity: The Black Model from Manet and Matisse to Today*. New Haven, CT: Yale University Press, 2018. Exhibition catalog.

Nelson, Charmaine A. "Introduction: Toward a Black Feminist Art History." In *The Color of Stone: Sculpting the Black Female Subject in Nineteenth-Century America*. Minneapolis: University of Minnesota Press, 2007.

Newhall, Beaumont. *The History of Photography from 1839 to the Present Day*. New York: Museum of Modern Art, 1949.

Okeke, Chika. "Evidencing Selfhood." *Nka: Journal of Contemporary African Art*, no. 4 (Spring 1996): 58–59.

Olin, Margaret. *Touching Photographs*. Chicago: University of Chicago Press, 2012.

Olin, Margaret. "Touching Photographs: Roland Barthes's Mistaken Identification." *Representations*, no. 80 (Fall 2002): 99–118.

Pascoe, Peggy. *What Comes Naturally: Miscegenation Law and the Making of Race in America*. Oxford: Oxford University Press, 2011.

Peffer, John. "Vernacular Recollections and Popular Photography in South Africa." In *The African Photographic Archive: Research and Curatorial Strategies*, edited by Christopher A. Morton and Darren Newbury, 115–34. London: Bloomsbury Academic, 2016.

Perloff, Stephen. *James Van Der Zee: Photographs; An Exhibition at the Delaware Art Museum and the Downtown Gallery, June 8–July 8, 1979*. Wilmington: Delaware Art Museum, 1979. Exhibition catalog.

Perry, Regenia. "Couple in Raccoon Coats, 1932: January 1984." In *Van Der Zee 1984 Calendar*, New York: n.p., 1984.

Perry, Regenia. "The Declining Years, Belated Recognition and Retirement 1950–1980." In J. Van Der Zee, *Roots in Harlem*, 16–18.

Perry, Regenia. "James Van DerZee: Introduction." In James Van Der Zee, *James Van DerZee: Eighteen Photographs, 1905–1938*, n.p. Washington, DC: Graphics International, 1974. Portfolio.

Phillips' Business Directory of New York City. New York: W. Phillips, 1919–1920.

Phillips' Business Directory of New York City. New York: W. Phillips, 1929–1932.

Pickens, William. *The New Negro: His Political, Civil and Mental Status, and Related Essays*. New York: Neale, 1916.

Pinney, Christopher. *Camera Indica: The Social Life of Indian Photographs*. Chicago: University of Chicago Press, 1997.

Pinney, Christopher. *Photography's Other Histories*. Durham, NC: Duke University Press, 2003.

Piper, William B. "Cameras at Work: African American Studio Photographers and the Business of Everyday Life, 1900–1970." PhD diss., College of William and Mary, 2016.

Pisano, Dominick A. *The Airplane in American Culture*. Ann Arbor: University of Michigan Press, 2004.

Pollard, Myrtle Evangeline. "Harlem As Is." Master's thesis, College of the City of New York, 1936.

Poupeye-Rammelaere, Veerle. "Garveyism and Garvey Iconography in the Visual Arts of Jamaica." *Jamaica Journal* 24, no. 1 (June 1991): 9–21.

Powell, Richard J. *African American Art in the 20th Century*. New York: Skira Rizzoli, 2012.

Powell, Richard J. *Black Art: A Cultural History*. New York: Thames and Hudson, 2003.

Powell, Richard J. *Cutting a Figure: Fashioning Black Portraiture*. Chicago: University of Chicago Press, 2008.

Powell, Richard J. "Linguists, Poets, and 'Others' on African American Art." *American Art* 17, no. 1 (Spring 2003): 16–19.

Quashie, Kevin Everod. *Black Aliveness, or a Poetics of Being*. Durham: Duke University Press, 2021.

Quashie, Kevin Everod. "The Trouble with Publicness: Toward a Theory of Black Quiet." *African American Review* 42, nos. 2–3 (Summer/Fall 2009): 329–43.

Raiford, Leigh. "Marcus Garvey in Stereograph." *Small Axe: A Caribbean Journal of Criticism* 17, no. 1 (March 2013): 263–80.

Raiford, Leigh. "Notes toward a Photographic Practice of Diaspora." *English Language Notes* 44, no. 2 (2006): 209–16.

Raiford, Leigh. "Soldiers and Black Beauty Queens: Making Home Abroad in the Miss Black America Album." In Tina Campt et al., *Imagining Everyday Life*, 223–27.

Raiford, Leigh, and Heike Raphael-Hernandez. *Migrating the Black Body: The African Diaspora and Visual Culture*. Seattle: University of Washington Press, 2017.

Roach, Joseph. "Culture and Performance in the Circum-Atlantic World." In *Performance Studies*, edited by Erin Striff, 124–36. New York: Palgrave Macmillan, 2003.

Robbins, Hollis. "Fugitive Mail: The Deliverance of Henry 'Box' Brown and Antebellum Postal Politics." *American Studies* 50, nos. 1–2 (Spring–Summer 2009): 5–25.

Roberts, Jennifer L. *Transporting Visions: The Movement of Images in Early America*. Berkeley: University of California Press, 2014.

Robertson, Stephen. "Putting Harlem on the Map." In *Writing History in the Digital Age*, edited by Jack Dougherty and Kristen Nawrotzki, 186–97. Ann Arbor: University of Michigan Press, 2013.

Robinson, Jontyle Theresa. "Passages." In *Bearing Witness: Contemporary Works by African American Women Artists*, edited by Jontyle Theresa Robinson, 13–37. New York: Spelman College and Rizzoli International, 1996. Exhibition catalog.

Robinson, Randall. "Introduction." In *The Debt: What America Owes to Blacks*, 1–10. New York: Plume, 2001.

Rolinson, Mary G. *Grassroots Garveyism: The Universal Negro Improvement Association in the Rural South, 1920–1927*. Chapel Hill: University of North Carolina Press, 2007.

Sancho, Victoria A. T. "Respect and Representation: Dawoud Bey's Portraits of Individual Identity." *Third Text: Third World Perspectives on Contemporary Art and Culture* 12, no. 44 (Autumn 1998): 55–68.

Sargent, Antwaun. "Derrick Adams: Black Leisure." In *Buoyant*, by Derrick Adams, 10–13. Yonkers, NY: Hudson River Museum, 2020. Exhibition catalog.

Sassoon, Joanna. "Photographic Materiality in the Age of Digital Reproduction." In *Photographs Objects Histories: On the Materiality of Images*, edited by Elizabeth Edwards and Janice Hart, 186–202. London: Routledge, 2005.

Sawyer, Drew. "James Van Der Zee." In *I Too Sing America: The Harlem Renaissance at 100*, edited by Wil Haygood, 176–77. New York: Rizzoli Electa, 2018. Exhibition catalog.

Scheele, Carl. *A Short History of the Mail Service*. Washington, DC: Smithsonian Institute Press, 1970.

Schoener, Allon, ed. *Harlem on My Mind: Cultural Capital of Black America, 1900–1968*. 1979. New York: New Press, 1995. Republished.

Sekula, Allan. "The Body and the Archive." *October*, no. 39 (Winter 1986): 3–64.

Shafran, Alexander. *Restoration and Photographic Copying*, Philadelphia: Chilton, 1967.

Sharpe, Christina. *In the Wake: On Blackness and Being*. Durham, NC: Duke University Press, 2016.

Sheehan, Tanya. "On Display: The Art of African American Photography." In *The Routledge Companion to African American Art History*, edited by Eddie Chambers, 92–103. New York: Routledge, 2019.

Sifford, Elena FitzPatrick, and Ananda Cohen-Aponte. "A Call to Action." *Art Journal* 78, no. 4 (Winter 2019): 118–22.

Simpson, Lorna. "Lorna Simpson: *9 Props*: An Interview and Art Portfolio." By Maria Christina Villaseñor. *Paris Review* 138 (Spring 1996): 72–76, 78–87.

Smalls, James. "A Ghost of a Chance: Invisibility and Elision in African American Art Historical Practice." *Art Documentation: Journal of the Art Libraries Society of North America* 13, no. 1 (Spring 1994): 3–8.

Smart-Grosvenor, Vertamae. *Vibration Cooking: Or, the Travel Notes of a Geechee Girl*. Garden City, NY: Doubleday, 1970.

Smith, Morgan, and Marvin Smith. *Harlem: The Vision of Morgan and Marvin Smith*. Lexington: University Press of Kentucky, 1998.

Smith, Shawn Michelle. *At the Edge of Sight: Photography and the Unseen*. Durham, NC: Duke University Press, 2013.

Smith, Shawn Michelle. *Photographic Returns: Racial Justice and the Time of Photography*. Durham, NC: Duke University Press, 2020.

Smith, Shawn Michelle. *Photography on the Color Line: Du Bois, Race, and Visual Culture*. Durham, NC: Duke University Press, 2004.

Stauffer, John. "Creating an Image in Black: The Power of Abolition Pictures." In *Beyond Black Face: African Americans and the Creation of American Popular Culture, 1890–1930*, edited by W. Fitzhugh Brundage, 66–94. Chapel Hill: University of North Carolina Press, 2011.

Stauffer, John, Zoe Trodd, Celeste-Marie Bernier, Henry L. Gates Jr., and Kenneth B. Morris. *Picturing Frederick Douglass: An Illustrated Biography of the Nineteenth Century's Most Photographed American*. New York: Liveright, 2015.

Stein, Judith. *The World of Marcus Garvey: Race and Class in Modern Society*. Baton Rouge: Louisiana State University Press, 1991.

Stevenson, Katherine H., and H. W. Jandl. *Houses by Mail: A Guide to Houses from Sears, Roebuck and Company*. Washington, DC: Preservation Press, 1996.

Steyerl, Hito. "In Defense of the Poor Image." *e-flux Journal* 10 (November 2009). https://www.e-flux.com/journal/10/61362/in-defense-of-the-poor-image/.

Streeby, Shelley. *Radical Sensations: World Movements, Violence, and Visual Culture*. Durham, NC: Duke University Press, 2013.

Thaggert, Miriam. *Images of Black Modernism: Verbal and Visual Strategies of the Harlem Renaissance*. Amherst: University of Massachusetts Press, 2010.

Thompson, Krista. "Preoccupied with Haiti: The Dream of Diaspora in African American Art, 1915–1942." *American Art* 21, no. 3 (Fall 2007): 74–97.

Thompson, Krista. "A Sidelong Glance: The Practice of African Diaspora Art History in the United States." *Art Journal* 70, no. 3 (Fall 2011): 6–31.

Tinsley, Natasha Omise'eke. *Ezili's Mirrors: Imagining Black Queer Genders.* Durham, NC: Duke University Press, 2018.

Tousignant, Zoë. "Relocating the Vernacular: The Yves Beauregard Collection at the Musée National des Beaux-Arts du Québec." *Archivaria* 65 (Spring 2008): 61–74.

Trachtenberg, Alan. *Reading American Photographs: Images as History, Mathew Brady to Walker Evans.* New York: Hill and Wang, 1989.

Valdés, Vanessa K. *Diasporic Blackness: The Life and Times of Arturo Alfonso Schomburg.* Albany, NY: State University of New York Press, 2017.

VanDerZee, Donna Mussenden. "Meet Mrs. VanDerZee." Interview by Lowery Stokes Sims. *African American Heritage* 7, no. 5 (Nov.–Dec. 2005): 24–26.

Van Der Zee, Donna Mussenden. "Van Der Zee." *International Review of African American Art* 8, no. 4 (Summer 1989): 23–35.

Van Der Zee, James. "Interview." In *Portrait: Theory*, edited by Kelly Wise, 151–75. New York: Lustrum, 1981.

Van Der Zee, James. *The World of James Van DerZee: A Visual Record of Black Americans.* Compiled by Reginald McGhee. New York: Grove, 1969.

Van Der Zee, James, Owen Dodson, and Camille Billops. *The Harlem Book of the Dead.* Dobbs Ferry, NY: Morgan and Morgan, 1978.

Van Der Zee, James, Patricia Bladon Lawrence, and Regenia Perry. *Roots in Harlem: Photographs by James Van Der Zee from the Collection of Regenia A. Perry: January 8–February 19, 1989,* Memphis Brooks Museum of Art. Memphis, TN: Memphis Brooks Museum of Art, 1988. Exhibition catalog.

VanDiver, Rebecca. "Breaking Ground: Constructions of Identity in African American Art." In *The Routledge Companion to African American Art History*, edited by Eddie Chambers, 440–49. New York: Routledge, 2020.

VanDiver, Rebecca. *Designing a New Tradition: Loïs Mailou Jones and the Aesthetics of Blackness.* University Park: Pennsylvania State University Press, 2020.

Van Haaften, Julia, and Deborah Willis. *Moneta Sleet, Jr., Pulitzer Prize Photojournalist.* New York: New York Public Library, 1986.

Vendryes, Margaret R. *Barthé: A Life in Sculpture.* Jackson: University Press of Mississippi, 2008.

Vincent, Theodore G. *Voices of a Black Nation: Political Journalism in the Harlem Renaissance.* San Francisco: Ramparts, 1973.

Wajda, Shirley Teresa. "The Commercial Photographic Parlor, 1839–1889." *Perspectives in Vernacular Architecture* 6 (1997): 216–30.

Wallace, Maurice O. *Constructing the Black Masculine: Identity and Ideality in African American Men's Literature and Culture, 1775–1995.* Durham, NC: Duke University Press, 2002.

Wallis, Brian. "The Dream Life of a People: African American Vernacular Photography." In *African American Vernacular Photography*, 9–14. New York: International Center for Photography, 2005.

Wallis, Brian. "Why Vernacular Photography? The Limits and Possibilities of a Field." In Campt et al., *Imagining Everyday Life*, 17–21.

Willis, Deborah. "Introduction: Picturing Us." In *Picturing Us: African American Identity in Photography*, edited by Deborah Willis, 3–28. New York: New Press, 1994.

Willis, Deborah. *J. P. Ball: Daguerrean and Studio Photographer*. New York: Garland, 1993.

Willis, Deborah. "Photography (1900–1970s)." In *The Image of the Black in Western Art: Part V*, edited by David Bindman and Henry Louis Gates Jr., 74–128. Cambridge, MA: Belknap Press in collaboration with the W. E. B. Du Bois Institute for African and African American Research and the Menil Collection, 2014.

Willis, Deborah, ed. *Picturing Us: African American Identity in Photography*. New York: New Press, 1994.

Willis, Deborah. *Reflections in Black: A History of Black Photographers, 1840 to the Present*. New York: Norton, 2000.

Willis, Deborah. "Selected Bibliography on African-American Photographers." *SPE Exposure* 27, no. 4 (Fall 1990): 47–50.

Willis, Deborah. "Speaking in Pictures: Shaping and Creating Narratives in the African American Family Album." In Campt et al., *Imagining Everyday Life*, 297–303.

Willis, Deborah. "Why Deborah Willis Thinks the Photobook Can Be Transformative." Interview by Brendan Embser. *PhotoBook Review*, no. 018 (Fall 2020): 2–3.

Willis, Deborah, and Barbara Krauthamer. *Envisioning Emancipation: Black Americans and the End of Slavery*. Philadelphia: Temple University Press, 2017.

Willis-Braithwaite, Deborah. *VanDerZee, Photographer, 1886–1983*. New York: Harry N. Abrams, 1993. Exhibition catalog.

Willis-Thomas, Deborah. *Black Photographers, 1840–1940: An Illustrated Bio-Bibliography*. New York: Garland, 1985.

Willis-Thomas, Deborah. *An Illustrated Bio-Bibliography of Black Photographers, 1940–1988*. New York: Garland, 1989.

Willis-Thomas, Deborah, and C. Daniel Dawson. *Introspect: The Photography of Anthony Barboza*. New York: Studio in Harlem, 1982.

Wofford, Tobias. "Whose Diaspora?" *Art Journal* 75, no. 1 (Spring 2016): 74–79.

Woodbury, Walter E., and Frank R. Fraprie. *Photographic Amusements: Including Tricks and Unusual or Novel Effects Obtainable with the Camera*. 9th ed. Boston: American Photographic Publishing, 1922.

Zinsou, Emile D., and Luc Zouménou. *Kojo Tovalou Houénou: Précurseur, 1887–1936—Pannégrisme et modernité*. Paris: Maisonneuve et Larose, 2004.

Zug, Marcia A. *Buying a Bride: An Engaging History of Mail-Order Matches*. New York: New York University Press, 2016.

Zuromskis, Catherine. "Vernacular Photography." In *Encyclopedia of Twentieth Century Photography*, edited by Lynne Warren, 1610–16. New York: Routledge, 2006.

Page numbers in *italics* refer to figures. The name Van Der Zee refers to James Augustus Joseph Van Der Zee.